THE RISE OF RESPECTABLE SOCIETY
1830–1900

F.M.L. Thompson was born into a Quaker family of north-country origin, and educated at Bootham School, York, The Queen's College, Oxford, and, as a postgraduate, Merton College, Oxford, with an interval of service with the Indian Artillery between 1943 and 1947. He taught history at University College London from 1951 until 1968 when he was appointed Professor of Modern History at Bedford College, London. He was editor of the *Economic History Review* from 1968 until 1980, and was elected a Fellow of the British Academy in 1979.

Since 1977 Michael Thompson has been Director of the Institute of Historical Research. He also conducts the British National Committee of Historians, and is the British member of the Standing Committee for the Humanities of the European Science Foundation, and Chairman of the ESF steering committee on 'Governments and Ethnic Minority Groups in Europe, 1850–1940', which involves one hundred historians from sixteen countries.

Professor Thompson's books include *English Landed Society in the Nineteenth Century*; *Chartered Surveyors: the Growth of a Profession*; *Hampstead: Building a Borough, 1650–1964*; and *Victorian England: the Horse-drawn Society*.

THE RISE OF RESPECTABLE SOCIETY

A Social History of
Victorian Britain

1830–1900

F.M.L. Thompson

FONTANA PRESS

First published in 1988 by Fontana Paperbacks
8 Grafton Street, London W1X 3LA

Copyright © F.M.L. Thompson 1988

Set in Linotron Imprint

Printed and bound in Great Britain
by William Collins Sons & Co. Ltd, Glasgow

Contents

Editor's Preface

It has sometimes been remarked that all forms of history are becoming social history, and, less frequently, it has been claimed that social history is total history, alone capable of comprehending and articulating all facets of past human experience. This series, which aims to present in three volumes a view of the social history of Britain from the early eighteenth century to the mid-twentieth century, is not particularly attached to either proposition; it has no designs on the autonomy of other branches of history, though conscious of its close relations with economic history, and no pretensions to be all-embracing. It has the more modest and pragmatic aim of tackling the great outpouring of research and publication in British social history which has taken place in the last twenty years, and of attempting to integrate the fruits of these detailed and original studies into works which will be more accessible to students coming fresh to the subject and readers who have no time or inclination to scan a hundred books and articles in order to get the feel of a century. The aim, however, is also more ambitious than this may sound: the purpose is not to provide a survey and summary of what other scholars have said, but to construct an interpretation of continuity and change in society, in its structure, its institutions, its customs and habits, and its class and gender relationships. The three volumes cover the 'long' eighteenth century, extending to 1830; the Victorian period; and the twentieth century. The editorial brief leaves each author to make sense of the material on his century in his own way: there is uniformity of structure in the thematic organization of each volume, but no uniformity of views, no party line. This is not a way of avoiding brickbats or shirking editorial responsibilities, it is just the way history works as a humane and liberal profession. If the result is a series which provokes discussion and stimulates further research and re-interpretation, that will be more than sufficient justification for the enterprise.

January 1988   F.M.L. THOMPSON

Author's Preface

It is fitting that an Editor who announces that the time is ripe to take stock of the effects of the explosion of interest in the social history of Britain should be the first to respond to his own call, if only to demonstrate that it is possible to offer a synthesis whatever the hazards of being tripped up on this or that point by the specialists. The expansion of social history, moreover, has not been a simple matter of the unearthing of new facts, new information, and new material by researchers digging in previously unknown or untapped sources, although there has been plenty of that. It has been above all a redefinition and enlargement of the territory of social history using instruments and concepts adapted from social anthropology and sociology, as well as quantitative methods, alongside the older guides derived from political economy whether of liberal or Marxist varieties. Where matters of faith, doctrine, or ideology are involved the synthesizer is necessarily stepping through a minefield. Nevertheless, the very fact that social history is about ideas and ways of viewing the behaviour and relationships of groups, genders, communities, generations, and classes, and not simply about the 'facts' of life – although sex is an important and often central activity which earlier generations of historians preferred to sweep under the carpet – means that no single overview can ever claim to be either comprehensive or definitive. Hence the present volume is offered as no more than one out of several possible ways of depicting and attempting to understand what made Victorian society tick, and how it developed.

An overview such as this, which attempts to be more than a plain survey, which tries to look at all levels of society and not simply at the working classes, and which seeks to present a seriously argued revision of Victorian social history, has to be selective. Rather than attempting to squeeze everything in, certain topics and themes have been sliced up, spread over several chapters, or set aside: some will think they have been ignored. Rural society, religion, social policy, the social dimension of politics, whether parliamentary or popular, the professions, and even aristocratic society, for example, may – rightly – appear to have been dealt with in a perfunctory fashion, or not at all. This is not because of any dearth of recent literature on these subjects; on the contrary, plenty of excellent work exists which would have been grist to another kind of synoptic mill. It is because the organizing principle for a dynamic anatomy of Victorian society dictated a different way of arranging material thematically, so that some familiar categories have either vanished altogether, or play relatively minor supporting roles. Readers should be warned, however, that this is not a textbook which claims to contain all they want to know, or need to know, about the social history of Victorian Britain. It is only fair to warn them that although it is a book about Britain, it is definitely Anglocentric. In a mechanical way Scotland and Wales may receive proportionately as much space as their populations contributed to total British population, about 12 per cent and 5 per cent respectively; but that is not offered as a justification for the neglect of the specifically Scottish or Welsh characteristics of social structure and social institutions, a neglect normally excused on grounds of limitations of space or knowledge, but in fact evidence of the persistence of national divisions within Britain which limit the possibilities of framing generalizations about British society.

A book of this kind does not rest upon original personal research, but upon research conducted, analysed, and published by other scholars. Rightly or wrongly the chosen format precludes the use of footnotes or detailed references, in order to sustain the flow of argument and avoid a parade of attribution, exegesis, and qualification which some readers might find irritating or superfluous. My complete reliance on the flood of monographs and articles is, I hope, sufficiently indicated by the short bibliographies linked to each chapter (but for convenience collected together at the end of the text), which list the works on which I have drawn. My sense of indebtedness to friends and colleagues, the authors of these works, is most inadequately expressed by the formality of these listings; it goes without saying that it is entirely due to their collective efforts that the opportunity of writing such a book as this exists at all. In one or two cases I have also listed unpublished doctoral theses, where they have been important sources of ideas and material. Only the exceptional reader is likely to have access to them; but the theses apart, the chapter bibliographies may perhaps serve as guides to further reading as well as acknowledgements of my debts.

June 1987   F.M.L. THOMPSON

CHAPTER ONE

Economy and Society

In the autumn of 1830 the Liverpool and Manchester Railway opened, in an atmosphere of triumphant excitement turned to tragedy by the fatal accident to Huskisson, and the Reform Parliament met in a buzz of expectant speculation at Westminster. The two events were not unconnected. The railway, the first locomotive-operated public line in the world, was the culmination of the application of the new technological skills, enterprise, and capital which had been transforming the British economy for the previous half century or more. The first Reform Act was an attempt to adapt political institutions to the alteration in the balance of social forces brought about by this transformation. While they shared these common roots and may both be viewed as at once instruments and symbols of the start of a new age, Reform essentially glanced backward with an approving eye on the traditional order which it sought to buttress, and the railway pointed forward into the unknown territory of urbanized and industrialized society. Therein lies the kernel of their message: not that 1830 was some decisive turning-point and outstanding landmark in social history, but that it stood in a particularly prominent way at the crossroads between the traditional and the new, neatly demonstrating the twin forces of continuity and change that are always at work in society.

Nowhere was this tension between old and new more obvious than in the political structure, which was widely believed to have become dangerously out of touch with social realities. Power and influence were concentrated in the hands of a privileged few, mainly the landed classes aided and abetted by allies and hangers-on from the wealthier reaches of commerce and the professions, operating through a system whose agglomeration of curious franchises, pocket and rotten boroughs, was so bizarre as to defy rational justification. The unreformed system was tolerable only so long as it worked, through manipulation of its ramshackle machinery by networks of influence, patronage, and deference, to produce reasonably acceptable and enforceable exercise of authority. That this ceased to hold true for some sections of the ruling class itself, which were alienated from the governments of the 1820s by their handling of the issues of agricultural distress, deflation, and Catholic Emancipation, may indeed have triggered Reform by producing a critical shift within the charmed circle of the political nation that enabled an unreformed Parliament to reform itself without resort to unconstitutional means. Politically this was extremely important. More significant socially, however, was the resentment at their exclusion from the political nation expressed by many groups in society in the rumblings and eruptions of parliamentary reform agitation from the later eighteenth century onwards, since this defined the points at which political and social structure were felt to be seriously out of mesh.

The salient characteristic of those who spoke for the excluded was that they came from every rank in society, save for the poorest and most illiterate, and framed their attacks on the old order in the language of justice and equality rather than in appeals to the interests of class. The leaders of popular radicalism were predominantly artisans, whose skills as printers, compositors, tailors, or cobblers stretched even further back than the ancestry of their ideas, which may be traced to the sturdy independence and self-respect of the Civil War Levellers. These were no more representatives or products of a recently created industrial order clamouring to be admitted to their rightful place in the body politic than were the gallery of orators from middle-class backgrounds – the farmers Cobbett and Hunt, and the army officer Cartwright were the most prominent – which played such a large role in the popular cause. They thought of themselves as the champions of the rights of downtrodden and neglected ordinary people, who counted increasing numbers of industrial workers, particularly factory workers, in their ranks; these undoubtedly formed an important element in the great reform meetings and demonstrations of 1816–19 or 1830–2, but there is no evidence that they were the backbone of popular protest. Information about the rank and file of such movements is invariably patchy, but such as there is suggests a different conclusion. A list of 'the leading reformers of Lancashire' at the end of 1816, for example, names two cotton manufacturers, two letterpress printers, a draper, a tailor, a hatter, a shoemaker, a stone cutter, and a clogger, who were all small masters or artisans; three cotton weavers, three silk weavers, and one wool weaver, who would all have been handloom weavers; and not a single cotton spinner, the sole type of factory worker to be found in the region in any numbers at that time. At the other end of the scale the great Reform riots of 1831 took place in Derby and Nottingham, manufacturing towns but not factory towns; Bristol, a commercial more than a manufacturing town; and Bath and Worcester, well removed from the centres of industrialization. The factory towns of Lancashire and the West Riding were absent from this list not because they enjoyed a superior form of social discipline and unanimity in support of reform which rendered rioting against the traditional authorities that had rejected the second Reform Bill superfluous, but because the class antagonism between millowners and operatives was so strong that there was no popular support for what was seen as an employer's measure. Disciplined leadership of the struggle for parliamentary reform was taken by precisely those towns, Birmingham above all others but also Newcastle, which had seen considerable growth and industrial expansion but had retained the structure of small workshops that blurred the divisions between masters and men and supported sufficient social harmony and cohesion to nourish an interclass radical alliance.

There was, then, massive working-class involvement in reform, and it centred in the traditional, preindustrial, groups rather than in those spawned by factory and machine. This is not to say that these groups had been unaffected by the course of economic change; but it is to say that viewed from this angle the perceived conflict between the established political structure and social reality was not a simple, direct consequence of the emergence of a factory proletariat. Viewed through the ruling-class end of the telescope, all workers, irrespective of their precise status or relationship to the means of production, being propertyless were either potentially dangerous as liable to subvert property and the social order, or at best not worthy of political recognition as being incapable of taking a balanced and responsible view of the public interest. The vital thing in the situation of 1830–2, so it seemed to Whig ministers, was to break the radical alliance by driving a wedge between the middle and the working classes, buying off the one with votes and representation and leaving the other, isolated and weak, outside the pale. The tactic, in Grey's words, was 'to associate the middle with the higher orders of society in the love and support of the institutions and government of the country'. Accordingly, the middle classes were accommodated with the £10 householder franchise, the hallmark of the 1832 Reform Act in the boroughs. It has often been remarked that this action defined, even created, the working class by lumping together all those unable to afford to occupy a house of at least £10 annual value as unfit to exercise the franchise, thus forging a common bond of resentment and frustration between otherwise diverse social groups. The other side of this coin is that the franchise also defined the middle class as all those who came above the £10 line regardless of differences in social position.

The middle classes who asserted their claims to be included in the political nation were a very mixed bag, and it would be as difficult to claim for them as for the working classes that their alienation from the old order stemmed wholly or even principally from the new social forces generated by industrialization. To be sure, by 1830 many industrialists had come round to the view that the protection of their interests and recognition of their status required direct representation in Parliament, whereas a generation or so earlier they had been largely indifferent to notions of parliamentary reform and direct involvement in politics, being content to accept the arguments of virtual representation and leave the conduct of public affairs to those accustomed to handling such matters. Northern manufacturers, in Lancashire and the West Riding, were active in the cause of reform in 1830–2; and a Wolverhampton manufacturer neatly expressed the sharpening of political awareness in his class: 'Fifty years ago we were not in that need of Representatives, which we are at present, as we then manufactured nearly exclusively for home consumption, and the commercial and manufacturing districts were then identified with each other; where one flourished, both flourished. But the face of affairs is now changed – we now manufacture for the whole world, and if we have not members to promote and extend our commerce, the era of our commercial greatness is at an end.' Manufacturers were key recruits to the cause of limited reform, and their demands for representation for themselves and the chief industrial centres were clear expressions of the failure of the political structure to reflect new social and economic developments. Nevertheless, manufacturers were recruits to a band of bankers, lawyers, writers, traders, editors, and other professional men, who continued to provide most of the drive and organization of middle-class political action: men of property, conscious of their position and probity no doubt, but not unmistakably men of the Industrial Revolution.

The towns which were given representation for the first time in 1832 were indeed in the main the chief centres of 'manufacturing capital and skill' in the Midlands and the north, whose fair representation Lord John Russell picked out as a major purpose of the Reform Bill when introducing it. It is worth remarking, however, that Brighton, the fastest growing town of the 1820s and in its fashionable seaside frivolity the very antithesis of an industrious town, and Stroud, a small pocket of the traditional woollen industry set in rural Gloucestershire, were included in the same company as the familiar industrial giants, Manchester, Birmingham, Leeds, and Sheffield, and were placed on a par with Bolton, Bradford, Blackburn, or Oldham. Similarly, Cheltenham, Frome, and Kendal were equated with the second-ranking industrial towns like Dudley and Walsall in the Black Country, Rochdale, Salford, and Warrington in Lancashire, or Gateshead, South Shields, and Tynemouth on Tyneside, in being elevated to single-member boroughs. These are reminders that the new constituencies did not all fall into a single category, and that scope was deliberately found for some increase in the weight given to traditional and non-industrial urban interests, quite apart from the five new parliamentary boroughs created in metropolitan London, itself a kaleidoscope of aristocratic, financial, commercial, administrative, and professional, as well as manufacturing, interests. In addition the boroughs which were preserved from extinction, although shorn of one of their former two members, and those which were continued unaltered from pre-reform days, were predominantly county towns, small market towns, long-established ports, and the like, albeit they did include some places – Liverpool, Preston, Hull, Newcastle, or Sunderland, for example – that were in the mainstream of industrial growth. In sum, however, the collection of new and surviving boroughs that made up the total of 187 post-1832 parliamentary boroughs in England was dominated by small towns, hangovers from the preindustrial past.

The fact that something like two thirds of the post-1832 boroughs might be thus classed could indicate no more than the limited, cautious, imperfect, and muddled nature of the Reform Act itself, removing only the most glaring defects of the un-reformed system, perpetuating many anomalies and inequalities of representation, and never intending to supply an accurate political mirror of the actual distribution of economic and social weight and consequence in the nation. Even so, it is significant that among the top third of boroughs, measured by the size of their electorates, less than half would figure on any list, however widely drawn, of thrusting, expanding places at the forefront of economic change. Thus Chester, Exeter, Bath, Worcester, or York were in the same league as Manchester, Birmingham, or Leeds in numbers of voters, although not, of course, in total population; while Bedford, Reading, Colchester, Canterbury, and Maidstone could out-vote but not out-number Stockport, Salford, Bolton, Oldham, and Wolverhampton. This was an effect of the franchise and the fact that the distribution of £10 householders differed, often quite sharply, from the distribution of population. In part this was due to marked regional differences in house values, themselves produced by complex interactions of custom and market forces, with the great majority of houses in London having rents of over £10 a year so that many working-class householders obtained the vote, while essentially similar houses in Leeds or Manchester were rented at £5 to £8 a year. In part, however, it was due to regional variations in the numbers and proportions of men with high enough incomes to command a £10 house and the standing of respectability and modest substance that went with it; in relation to total population the older established towns tended to have a higher proportion of such householders than those of most recent rapid growth.

While it is clear that the £10 householders did not constitute a single social class, since there were wide social differences within towns between those who just qualified and those whose houses could be worth £50 or £100 a year, as well as between towns, it is also clear that this property qualification embraced virtually the entire population of middle-class family men, even if in some localities it also had the effect of bringing some artisans and skilled workers within the net. The middle class thus attached, in expectation, to the support of the constitution contained large numbers of small shopkeepers, traders, and dealers, small masters and lesser professional men, men of some consequence and influence in their communities but far removed in wealth and status from the great overseas merchants, the bankers and financiers, and the industrial capitalists. Whether they were precisely the sort of men Earl Grey had had in mind when he had spoken of 'the middle classes who form the real and efficient mass of public opinion, and without whom the power of the gentry is nothing', may perhaps be doubted, since at the time he was more concerned with the intelligent, educated and articulate men who shaped informed opinion in the press, the journals, the literary and philosophical societies, and the counting houses. Nevertheless, they formed the core of the middle classes, the most numerous and most widely spread groups with a solid stake in the country, however small their individual properties. This core had been growing in size and wealth as a result of the general influences of population growth and economic expansion, but only in some parts, depending on location, had it become integrated into industrial society in direct economic and cultural dependence on the great capitalist employers. In bringing the urban middle classes within the political nation the new franchise brought in something at once more varied, and more traditional, than simply an industrial-based middle class. This was as much a matter of reflecting the nature of the existing social structure as it was one of political calculation, although it did not escape notice that the lesser bourgeoisie of the smaller towns were amenable to patronage and influence.

Political calculation entered strongly into the Reform Act's treatment of the countryside, and it is arguable that the entire business of reaching some kind of accommodation with the towns and the urban middle classes was of secondary importance to the political managers, whose prime concern was to revitalize and strengthen the power of the landed interest. In this view an inescapable minimum of concessions to the aspirations of the towns was a small price to pay for securing the power base of the landed classes in the counties. The trouble with the unreformed regime had not been its failure to reflect adequately the importance of new social forces in the community, but its increasingly corrupted and attenuated representation of the opinions and interests of the country landowners. Those opinions, it was argued, could only be properly expressed by county members chosen because of the trust placed in them by county constituencies which were too large to be dominated by one or two individuals, and too independent to be bribed. Instead, too many of the landed MPs sat for rotten or pocket boroughs, represented nothing except their patrons' or their own personal wealth, were prone to be ensnared by the Administration of the day, and failed to voice the feelings of their order. The answer was to increase the county representation, and to purify the county electorates of urban and non-agricultural foreign bodies. This was done in 1832. The number of county members was increased from 188 to 253; and the parliamentary distinction between county and borough was made to correspond much more closely than before to the economic and social distinction between country and town. On the one hand, the invasion of county electorates by extraneous elements who qualified for the 40-shilling freehold county vote by the ownership of urban property was rolled back by the creation of boroughs in which such property conferred the vote; on the other hand, the agricultural character of county electorates was boosted by the enfranchisement, on a Tory amendment it should be noted, of the £50 a year tenants-at-will, that is the middling and larger tenant farmers.

As with so much else about the Reform Act, the line between town and country was not so clearly drawn in practice as this picture implies. To begin with, there were still many lesser towns, particularly in the manufacturing districts, that had not been made into parliamentary boroughs; those who owned freehold property in them worth over 40 shillings a year, whether in the form of warehouses, workshops, offices, factories, mills, or houses did not matter, qualified for votes in the county in which the town lay. Then, while anyone owning property in a borough worth at least £10 a year was expressly restricted to acquiring only a vote in that borough, those who owned smaller parcels of property within a borough worth between 40 shillings and £10 a year remained eligible for votes in the surrounding county. Some dilution of county electorates with urban blood therefore remained, and in the industrial counties it was of considerable political moment. The Whigs in fact had hedged their bets over the wisdom of securing the preponderance of the landed interest in the counties, doubtless calculating that the increase in landlord influence stemming from tenant farmers' votes would chiefly benefit the Tories, and had therefore retained the urban propertied counter-weight in the counties which they or their liberal allies might hope to turn to advantage. Nonetheless, although it was thus fudged in its execution partly at least for party reasons, one important strand in the Reform design was to pen up the middle classes in the boroughs the better to secure the power base of the aristocracy and gentry in the counties, and thus preserve landed and agricultural interests from being undermined.

In retrospect it might seem that this was a purely defensive and protective measure, the use of entrenched aristocratic power while there was yet just time to fashion a barricade of franchises and constituencies which would keep the mounting urban and indus-trial forces at bay, thus delaying or preventing altogether their capture of the commanding heights of society and the economy. The barrier was severely tested during the Corn Law debates of the 1840s, when the most radical wing of the Anti-Corn Law League hoped to use repeal as a lever for toppling the entire 'aristocratic monopoly'; but it survived, thanks to the opportunism and realism of the ruling class, and lived on to shelter the anachronism of a predominantly landed control of an essentially industrial society. Such a view, however, begs many questions: in what sense the landed dominance of government, Parliament, and much of local administration was artificially contrived rather than an expression of the essence of the social order; in what sense Britain was, or became, an industrial society; and in what sense urban and industrial interests and values were in conflict with the rural and agricultural world.

In the 1830s, at any rate, it made perfectly good sense to accord the preponderant place in the political nation to the landed and rural elements. This was not just a matter of privilege, property, and tradition, but one of economic and social reality. It is true that fundamental and far-reaching changes in the scale and methods of production had been under way for the past seventy years: an older generation of historians regarded the Industrial Revolution, in its headlong pioneering phase, as complete by 1830; a younger generation, intrigued by models of economic growth, placed the take-off into self-sustained growth as long since accomplished and viewed the economy of 1830 as being at least half-way through its drive to maturity, the maturity of a modern, fully industrialized economy. All would agree that structural, technical, and organizational changes had gone so far that a wholly new kind of society was bound to develop; and all would accept G. R. Porter's statement that 'it is to the spinning-jenny and the steam-engine that we must look as having been the true moving powers of our fleets and armies, and the chief support also of a long-continued agricultural prosperity.' The revolutionary character of technological innovations and their potential for producing social transformation are one thing, however; the extent and pace of their impact on the social fabric are another matter, and the key to understanding the state of society.

It was a pardonable exaggeration to claim that the spinning jenny and the steam engine had been carrying the economy on their backs since the turn of the century. Cotton goods had replaced woollens as Britain's principal export, and the meteoric rise of the cotton industry, if not literally attributable to the jenny alone, could be justifiably ascribed to the new breed of spinning machinery, particularly the mule, and its harnessing to water and steam power. The spinning mills, the advance guard of the factory system, had momentous effects on work habits, living conditions, and social relationships, possibly more momentous and revolutionary than their effects in increasing production and creating wealth, since they were the birthplace of the industrial proletariat. Much attention was concentrated on the mills, their marvels and their miseries, their awesome grandeur and awfulness, as contemporaries commented on the apparently limitless power of machinery and speculated on the chances of society handling, or indeed surviving, the arrival of a factory population.

The curiosity and anxiety were most understandable, in face of the novelty of the development and uncertainty about what it might portend for the future. For, in 1830, the day when typical English men or women would be town dwellers, or factory workers, still lay emphatically in the future. The cotton industry was very important, it was far and away the largest factory industry, and it was growing rapidly; but its factory element was not yet all that imposing. There had been around 100,000 factory operatives in the mills towards the end of the Napoleonic Wars, and by 1830 there were about double that number; they were still outnumbered by the quarter million or so non-factory workers who made up the rest of the labour force in the cotton industry, chiefly handloom weavers but also many ancillary workers, some working in quite large weaving sheds but many working in the home. Moreover, when factory inspectors began to count millworkers more accurately, from the mid-1830s, it was revealed that half the cotton factory operatives were women, a proportion that was to creep up in the course of the century to over 60 per cent. Child labour in the mills created an immense stir, and excited deep feelings of indignation, pity, and outrage; indeed, it is responsible for the enduring popular image of the Industrial Revolution as a shameful and regrettable episode fatally flawed by the 'evils of the factory system' heartlessly inflicted on innocent children. There is plenty of evidence, to be sure, of incidents of maltreatment and cruelty to children in the mills, although whether it is sufficient to indict a whole generation of millowners is another question. For the moment the point to notice is that children under fourteen were about 13 per cent of the factory labour force, perhaps slightly more in 1830; 26,000 or so is certainly not a negligible number of children, but it was but a minute fraction of the age group, and the factory children were far from representative of the general body of child workers, let alone of children at large.

In a comparatively poor society with low productivity and limited resources, children had always had to earn their keep, since it was impossible to support large numbers of non-workers. Traditionally most children had probably been at work by the age of seven or nine, frequently helping at their parents' occupations but not uncommonly working for other masters. There was nothing remarkable about child labour in the mills, apart from the novelty of the factories themselves and the publicity they attracted. More remarkable was the minor role of men in the cotton mills, only a little more than a quarter of the factory workers, perhaps 50,000 or so in 1830, being adult males. Being men in a man's world, they had collared the plum jobs, as mulespinners; but by the same token, in a world which defined workers as essentially male, their minority position tended to emphasize the peculiarity and untypicality of factory workers among the working population as a whole. The early recruitment and continued dominance of the mill girls has frequently been remarked and explained, in terms of the resistance of established, male, workers to employment in unfamiliar and possibly degrading conditions, and of the greater docility, submissiveness, and adaptability of the women. Since in the eyes of generations of commentators from Engels onwards virtue, in the promise of democratic and socialist achievements, has been seen to reside in the factory proletariat, it is more surprising that little emphasis has ever been placed on the influence of women as the major element in the first factory proletariat in the world. It could be that they contributed a decisively non-violent and non-revolutionary tone to the nascent proletariat at the one moment, in the late 1830s and 1840s, when for a variety of reasons social tensions were so acute that a determined move from the mills might have tipped the scales towards disintegration of the social order.

Powered machinery and factory organization of course existed in other industries besides cotton by 1830, notably in parts of the woollen and worsted industries of the West Riding, in flax spinning, in some branches of engineering, and in the large works engaged in the manufacture of iron. But, all told, there were probably still fewer than 100,000 male factory workers in 1830, outnumbered by the women although they were concentrated in fewer industries and were scarcely to be found outside Lancashire, Lanark, and the West Riding. There were more cobblers and shoemakers, craftsmen working on their own or in small workshops, than there were male factory workers; and there were between three and four times as many working in the completely unmechanized building trades. Tailors outnumbered coalminers, and there were three blacksmiths for every man employed in making iron. The message is plain. Industry had been growing rapidly since the late eighteenth century, and employment in manufacturing, mining, and building, inside and outside the factory, had grown from about 30 per cent of the total working population in 1811 to over 40 per cent by 1831, or from 1.7 million men and women to 3 million. Yet most of this expansion took the form of multiplying the number of people working with traditional tools in traditional occupations: much less than 10 per cent of industrial workers had any experience of factories, or about 3 per cent of the occupied population.

Agriculture had long been in relative decline, certainly since the early seventeenth century if not before, since it is the essence of commercial and industrial growth that the non-agricultural proportion of the population should increase, fed and supplied either by the increasing efficiency of those who worked on the land, or by growing advantages and opportunities for importing agricultural produce. Both had been happening in Britain, although since in the early 1830s, given normal to good harvests, the country was virtually feeding itself, the emphasis had been on improvements in agricultural productivity, bolstered by growing imports of grain and livestock from Ireland. Agriculture had probably ceased to provide the livelihood of a majority of the population before the middle of the eighteenth century, and the agricultural sector had declined from over a third of the working population at the beginning of the nineteenth century to a quarter by 1831. Nevertheless, the actual numbers engaged in farming were still increasing, growing from about 1¾ million then to the historical peak of over 2 million in 1851; it was only from the plateau of the 1850s that the long and practically uninterrupted decline in the number of farmworkers began. These numbers included nearly 300,000 farmers, about half of whom employed some hired labour while the other half used only the labour of themselves and members of their families. That left something like a million agricultural labourers, landless and propertyless, owning neither their homes nor their tools, and entirely reliant on wage labour. This was far and away the largest single occupation of male workers, about twice the size of the next largest group, those working in textiles of all sorts, and not far short of three times larger than the body of workers in the building trades. Many women also worked in agriculture, some full-time like the dairymaids, the members of the new and growing labour gangs in East Anglia, or the Northumbrian bondagers who were regular field workers as brawny as any men; many more were drawn in at the seasonal work peaks of turnip hoeing and singling, or harvest. Ambiguities of self-perception and of definition make the number of women who described themselves as agricultural workers (in the 1841 census) somewhat suspect; they appear to have been the fourth largest group of women workers, after those employed in domestic service, textiles, and the clothing trades, but they may have been more numerous than the 80,000 enumerated in 1841 or 230,000 in 1851.

Insofar as it makes any sense at all to look for the average British workingman, he was to be found in 1830 working in the broadly defined industrial sector, but not in a factory; the most representative workingman, however, was the agricultural labourer. The typical working woman, there is no doubt, was a domestic servant. The nature of work is a major influence on a person's sense of identity, but its place is scarcely less important, and most people lived and worked in the countryside, whether directly involved in farming or not. It was not until 1851 that a majority of the British population was classified as being urban, on the unexacting definition of living in a place with 2000 or more inhabitants. Population size is a convenient, but rough and ready, measure of urbanity; while the judgement of contemporaries in the Registrar-General's office should be respected, that this size represented the dividing line between country and town, it is clear that many of the smallest notional 'towns' would have been overgrown villages, their inhabitants as close to the land in their way of life as their cottages were to the surrounding open country. It should be acknowledged that small country towns like Aberystwyth (Cardiganshire), Burford (Oxfordshire), Midhurst (Sussex), Sedbergh (West Riding), or Spilsby (Lincolnshire), all of which had populations in the 1500–2000 range in the 1830s, were unmistakably town-like in the sense that they were something more than collections of agricultural workers and agricultural trades. They performed marketing, administrative, and professional functions for their rural hinterlands; and in their small way they looked like towns in layout and contiguity of buildings. Nevertheless, diminutive towns like these, and the great majority of the places which clearly had the look and feel of towns, were essentially traditional country towns. In 1831 about 90 per cent of the places which physically and often administratively were towns had populations of under 20,000, and in most of them the inhabitants were accustomed to country sights, sounds, and smells in the streets, and had strong links of kinship or friendship in the surrounding countryside. This considerable slice of the 'urban' population remained, therefore, well integrated into a traditional economic and social order, and by and large had not recently experienced upheavals in jobs or living conditions, or changes in the texture and scale of their environment, of a kind likely to produce disruptive social effects or to alienate them from established authorities in church, corporation, and neighbouring country house.

To be sure, the 20,000 threshold, like any other, is no more than an approximate and imperfect guide to a town's character, and there were places like Bury, Wigan, Bradford, or Huddersfield which had only just crossed it or were poised to do so, that were unmistakably parts of the new industrial order. All the same, it was in the really large towns that a new kind of urban society was taking shape; it was there that the sheer scale of concentration of numbers produced something like a quantity–quality change and threw up those features of segregation, social distancing, overcrowding, pollution, public order, and health hazards most commonly associated with nineteenth-century urban living. In 1831 about one quarter of the total British population lived in towns with more than 20,000 inhabitants, but the essentially urban element of society may be usefully visualized as smaller than that. By 1951, it should be noted, over half the population lived in urban clusters with more than 100,000 people, and that has become the normal setting of the typical British citizen. By contrast, in 1801 there had been no towns in Britain, outside London, with as many as 100,000 inhabitants. By 1831 there were seven – Manchester, Glasgow, Liverpool, Edinburgh, Birmingham, Leeds, and Bristol – and together with London they contained one sixth of the total population. This fraction, it can be argued, was both the central core and the advanced guard of modern urban society. It was here and in the next layer of the urban hierarchy that the most rapid and dramatic social changes took place, here that the most pressing problems and acute tensions and contrasts developed, here that new habits and lifestyles were evolved which ultimately percolated through to the rest of the country, and here that familiar and accustomed patterns of behaviour were most strongly challenged.

This was also the most rapidly expanding face of society in the nineteenth century, for by 1901 there were nearly forty towns over the 100,000 mark and between them they accounted for well over one third of the total population. To put it another way, 10 million out of the net increase in British population between 1831 and 1901 of 11 million lived in these very large towns, which can thus be said to have monopolized expansion. The most significant point, however, was that the large-town urban base of early Victorian Britain, although not inconsiderable, was comparatively small. Moreover, at least two thirds of that base was occupied by London, and whatever the metropolitan scene offered in lavish wealth or abject poverty, magnificent buildings or filthy courts, happiness or misery, social harmony or social conflict, it was not exactly a new phenomenon. Already for several centuries government and society had been obliged to come to terms with the existence of a huge concentration of people in London, and to adjust to the consequences of the fact that a tenth or more of the entire population lived there. This is not to say that London was necessarily a static or particularly stable and unproblematic element in society, nor that it exercised a constant and predictable influence on the rest of the country. Far from it. The internal dynamics of changes within London in its size and structure, and the external dynamics of its changing relationships with Britain and the rest of the world, were and continued to be of fundamental importance in determining the main lines of British social, just as much as economic, development. It does imply, however, that the experience of urban life on the metropolitan scale, and of London's impact on the lives of provincials and countrymen, had been absorbed and familiarized over the preceding generations into a normal and accepted feature of the early Victorian social fabric.

Viewed in this light the quintessentially novel feature of Victorian urbanization was the growth of the large-town population outside London from just over one million in 1831 to nearly nine million in 1901, from less than one tenth to about a quarter of the British people. It would be wrong to infer from this that London was outpaced or displaced by the large provincial cities, for if the continuous built-up area of Greater London is taken as the appropriate demographic and social unit for measurement, it increased its share of total population from 11.5 to 17.8 per cent in this period, thus decisively resuming its relative growth which had virtually halted in the eighteenth century. Equally it would be simplistic and misleading to leap from the unprecedented growth of extra-metropolitan large towns to the conclusion that all the exciting action of Victorian social history took place in that arena. Nevertheless that growth, and its timing, are crucial in placing the time-scale of the emergence of a modern urban and industrial society in Britain: however far the British economy may have travelled by 1830 beyond the point of no return on the path towards industrialization, Britain was still far from possessing that kind of society.

Its emergence was a Victorian affair. It was not a question of the Victorians improving, reforming, institutionalizing, and more or less cleaning up a rough and raw society which they took over from the preceding half century of headlong economic change; it was rather a matter of their fashioning the elements of a new society in step with the appearance of its material and human components. This is not to deny that there were raw, indigestible, and unassimilated new elements already present in society as a consequence of previous urban and industrial growth. Manchester was already acquiring its reputation as the shock city of the Industrial Revolution, and Leeds was not far behind; but this was precisely because such places were so unusual and unfamiliar.

More traditional environments and communities remained so much more typical, even if jobs and workplaces might have altered radically, that society as a whole had tolerated such exceptions without being transformed. Transformation was a long-drawn-out process, longer drawn out than the coming of machines and power and the transformation of the means of production. The making of the working class, once thought to have been accomplished by 1830, is now placed firmly in the 1890s; and many of the features of modern society, trivial and profound, from smaller families to bacon and eggs, from production-line working to fish and chips, or from class politics to branded foods, only made a strong appearance in the closing years of the nineteenth century. Family and neighbourhood ties, upbringing, inherited cultures, and group loyalties proved more persistent and resilient than technologies, which might change almost overnight. These social forces were sufficiently powerful to smooth the impact of new working and living conditions, and to ease the passage towards large-town society without disastrous dislocation. A fruitful tension, and accommodation, between social continuity and conservatism, and economic innovation and discontinuity, was an underlying theme of the Victorian period.

The economy and society of the early 1830s, then, was not grossly distorted by the political mirror of the first Reform Act. Factory industry and urban concentrations were present, but not in sufficient proportion to eclipse the familiar world of farm and workshop, labourer, craftsman, and trader, village and small town, and it made reasonable sense to leave authority substantially in the hands which had held it for generations, those of landowners, clergy, lawyers, and greater merchants. The economic foundations of this social and political order were changing rapidly. The most momentous end-product of those changes was the growth of large towns, and it used to be assumed that industrialization and urbanization were synonymous. The distinction between the two processes, however, is critical to understanding the way in which people at all levels of society contrived to weather the shocks and stresses of revolutionary changes in working conditions or living arrangements without society itself experiencing the catastrophic disintegration or outright social revolution which were widely thought, especially in the 1840s, and not only by alarmists, to be inescapable and imminent.

Much more is involved than the observation that not all industry was urban and that not all the fastest growing, or largest, towns were industrial. Although this was a most important point about the early 1830s, when Brighton, emphatically a pleasure rather than a business let alone an industrial town, had been the fastest growing town of the previous decade, and when an important group of water-powered cotton mills were in semi-rural locations, it was of diminishing relevance over the rest of the century. The general tendency was for the mechanization of a broadening range of industrial activities, the adoption of steam power, and a gravitation towards coalfield sites; while all the larger towns supported some manufacturing industries, even if these might in some cases be geared only to their own internal markets. What continued to be important in the shaping of social structures was the diversity of developments within and between industries, in timing, technologies, and organization, and the variety of different occupations and activities forming the economic base of towns.

Industrialization, even considered in the restrictive and potentially misleading sense as something that happened simply to manufacturing industry rather than to all sectors of the economy, was far from being a one-way procession into the factory. Mechanization of one sector or process in an industry, and its move into the factory, could well generate increased demand for handwork and outwork in other sectors. The classic example was in the cotton industry, where from the later eighteenth century the rise of the spinning mills had led to an enormous expansion in the number of handloom weavers, most of them outworkers (a minority were pseudo-factory workers, working in large weaving sheds for a single employer), and many of them rural workers with dual employments in farming. In cotton that expansion was over by the mid-1820s, and the decline in the number of handloom weavers as weaving moved swiftly into the mills in the 1830s and 1840s was little short of catastrophic in material hardship and social dislocation. In spite of the evident triumph of the powerloom, however, there were still nearly 50,000 cotton handloom weavers left in 1850, many of them in extreme destitution at the lowest paid and coarsest end of the industry, but some of them working upmarket on fancy designs in short runs which were still beyond the technical capacity, or economics, of power weaving. A few lingered into the 1860s, but by then the surviving handloom weaver in cottons was no more than a curiosity. The worsted industry followed much the same pattern as cotton, although barely one fifth as large in terms of total employment, and by the early 1830s worsted spinning was almost entirely a factory occupation; the key preparatory process of combing, however, remained a manual operation, and the woolcombers were among the cream of skilled workers until combing machinery undermined their scarcity and status extremely rapidly from the mid-1840s. Worsted weaving, indeed, became a factory industry even more rapidly and conclusively than cotton: until the mid-1830s there were virtually no powerlooms in worsteds, and by the mid-1850s handloom weavers had all but vanished. In the process the industry, spinning and weaving branches alike, achieved a far more complete geographical concentration than the cotton industry which had an important secondary base in Lanarkshire centred on Paisley as well as its Lancashire–Cheshire heartland. Worsted workers, by the 1850s, were almost all to be found in the West Riding, strongly localized in the Bradford area, and this sharp focus of a particular kind of factory experience was not without social significance.

The woollen industry, by contrast, took to the mills later, much more slowly, and in a pattern which permitted factory work and outwork – at least in the handweaving of tweeds in the Highlands and Hebrides – to continue to coexist until the end of the century. The preponderance of the West Riding was firmly established long before 1830; it continued to become more pronounced over the century but did not achieve complete concentration to the exclusion of locally significant branches of the industry in Stroud, the West Country, Cumbria, or the Scottish Borders region. It was in the West Riding that factory methods and organization made most rapid progress, and even there half those engaged in the manufacture of woollens were still in 1850 non-factory manual and

domestic outworkers. Spinning itself was not completely mechanized, although leading firms had adapted the mule to woollen yarns
by the 1820s; and the intermediate process of preparing rovings
from the carded wool, before mule-spinning them, was firmly in the
hands of the billy slubbers working their little wooden machines
called billies, within the mill precincts but not properly factory
workers. These handworkers were, in their turn, displaced by
machinery, the condenser; but it was a very gradual matter. The
condenser was known, and in use, from the mid-1830s, but it was
not until the end of the 1870s that the billy slubbers vanished and
woollen spinners became entirely factory workers. Woollen fabrics
came in such a profusion of types and qualities that it is not
surprising that in the early decades of their adoption powerlooms
were as much complementary to as competitive with handlooms.
Until mid-century it is probable that the numbers of handloom
weavers, at roughly 100,000, had scarcely declined at all, at which
point there were no more than 9439 powerlooms in woollens, giving
work to 5–6000 factory weavers; there being at the same period over
32,000 powerlooms in worsteds, and 250,000 in cotton. Plenty of
handloom weavers remained in the West Riding in the third quarter
of the century, their numbers only gradually falling, and on the
whole there was a reasonable amount of work for them at the fancy
end of the trade. It was not until the 1880s that weaving was fully
consolidated in the mills and virtually all the quarter million men
and women employed in the woollen and worsted industries, taken
together, could be classed as factory workers.

In the lesser but traditional textile industries, linen and silk,
outwork remained at least as important in relation to factory work
as in woollens. Jute, practically speaking a new industry of the
1850s and strongly localized in Dundee, was by contrast a mill
industry from the start; the few handloom weavers still there in the
late 1860s were a sad leftover from Dundee's earlier linen-working
phase. For a while the linen industry operated with something of a
national division of labour, machine-spun yarn from English mills,
epitomized by Marshall's great flax mill in Leeds of the 1820s,
being woven by the cheaper domestic labour of Scotland and
Ulster. By mid-century there may have been about 70,000
handloom weavers of linens in Scotland, clustered mainly around

Aberdeen and Dundee, and in Dunfermline where much fine table-linen was woven. Thereafter the English section of the industry went into decline, but the Scottish held its own until the 1870s by switching into power weaving; in the late nineteenth century growth was Ulster's province. The silk industry grew rather rapidly from the 1830s, practically doubling its workforce between then and the early 1860s; at that time nearly two thirds, or about 100,000 people, were domestic outworkers, chiefly weavers. Silk weaving was expanding fast enough in the 1840s, indeed, to be able to absorb many of the displaced handloom weavers from cotton, so that by 1851 there were about 25,000 silk workers in Lancashire, a county where they had been almost unknown twenty years before. From the 1860s the silk industry declined continuously, so that by the end of the century its labour force, at around 40,000, was back to half the size of the mid-1830s; from the 1880s this shrinking industry was predominantly a factory industry.

The general impression from this survey of the textile industries is that there was a succession of bursts of demand for outworkers, mainly handloom weavers, at different dates in different sectors, triggered either by the mechanization of spinning or by general expansion in the industry; and that these bursts were followed by periods of contraction of very variable duration, leading to the ultimate disappearance of non-factory workers. The conclusion that it was not until the 1880s that textiles in general were firmly settled in factories is less important than the lack of synchronization or uniformity in the process of shedding outworkers or in the speed at which factory work expanded; those were the factors which affected the work experience of the people involved, and hence their lives and those of their families.

The textile industries as a whole were the leading edge of the transformation of manufacturing from home and hand to power and mill, and it is therefore especially significant that outside cotton the decisive phases of this transformation took place after the overall expansion of textiles, as a provider of jobs, was over. Total employment grew rapidly in the decade after 1841, when the census occupation returns first make it possible to measure numbers, and the proportion of all manufacturing workers who were involved in textiles rose from one third to two fifths. After

1851, however, the numbers of textile workers ceased to expand and remained more or less constant at around 1.3 million for the rest of the century, while in relation to total employment in manufacturing they entered a period of continuous decline, their share falling back to one third by 1881 and one quarter by 1901. The overall stability of numbers in the textiles group in the second half of the century was clearly the statistical end-product of shifts between the different branches and of movements between outwork and factory work, and certainly does not imply stability in the circumstances of individuals or families. The declining share of textiles in total manufacturing employment in turn reflects the expansion of other sectors of manufacturing, particularly in the metalworking and engineering group, and has no necessary implications for the continued prosperity or otherwise of those actually working in textiles. Nevertheless the growing diversity in the structure of manufacturing industry in the second half of the century and the ending of the lopsided dominance of textiles were both evidence of increasing maturity and balance in the industrial economy, and signals that the general social impact of any single industrial occupation was being progressively blunted and diluted.

Factory work itself was very far from being a single homogeneous category of experience, but varied widely with size of establishment, date, industry, location, and employer, as will be seen in a later chapter. But it was, in the age of almost universal adoption of steam power after mid-century, pretty well exclusively urban work. The handworkers and outworkers who survived for so long in the textile industries, on the other hand, might live and work either in towns or in the countryside. The Spitalfields' silk weavers, for example, still 16,000 strong in 1851, were decidedly town dwellers, as were most of their fellow weavers in Macclesfield; the majority of Lancashire's sore-pressed cotton handloom weavers in the 1840s were probably in the weaving towns, and maybe not actually working in their own homes, but a sizeable element of domestic outworkers in outlying villages undoubtedly persisted; this pattern was repeated with the Yorkshire woollen weavers, with an opposite balance between town and village, while weaving in the Stroud district was almost entirely a cottage industry. In the lace and hosiery trades, usually classified with the textile industries although they were engaged in processing materials – cotton, wool, or silk – produced by the primary industries, country and small-town locations remained character-istic until the 1880s. Hosiery, strongly localized in Leicestershire, Nottinghamshire, and Derbyshire, was a domestic industry on the classic model, the framework knitters in their cottages and their villages being organized, dominated, and exploited by layers of merchant-middlemen from petty bag-hosiers to master hosiers, who threw in extortionate frame-renting practices for good measure. It remained that way, in large part, until the 1890s; for although factories were known in the industry by the 1870s many of them were only large frame-shops full of hand frames, and it was not until the very end of the century that factories with power-driven machinery had taken over all the business. Lace, centred on Nottingham, had perhaps completed a slow move into the factory several decades earlier, since the machinery required to satisfy the great Victorian appetite for lace curtains was complicated and costly, and perforce had to run in factory fashion.

The socks and stockings produced by the framework knitters were ready to wear, but for the rest the fabrics issuing from the textile industries had to be made up into final products before they could be used by the consumers. Much of this work, with furnishing fabrics as well as in clothesmaking, was done in the home and forms part of that domestic household production which is unmeasured in employment or national income accounting. But a great deal of clothing was made for the market, and the clothing trades (among which boot- and shoemaking are normally classi-fied) were second in importance only to the textile industries themselves. Until 1861 just over one quarter of all the men and women engaged in manufacturing were working in this varied group of trades; thereafter the proportion gradually declined until it was down to one fifth by the end of the century. Total numbers in the group continued to rise, however, from a million in 1861 to 1.2 million in 1901, and by 1911 were on a par with those in the textile industries. No simple generalizations can cover such a diversity of occupations and industries, which ranged from independent village craftsmen-tailors to the sweated labour of seamstresses in city garrets, and from making fashionable gloves to making clogs.

An important social feature, indeed, was the ubiquity of country craftsmen in tailoring and shoemaking, and the extent to which local demands were met by local production. There were, however, concentrations of workers producing for more than local markets, the glovemakers of Worcestershire being a case in point. Some of these, like the straw plaiters and straw-hat makers of Bedfordshire and Hertfordshire, constituted an important rural industry, a cottage and village industry of outworkers, mainly women and children, its commercial and finishing organization imparted from the centre at Luton. Others, particularly in clothing proper, came to have a distinctly urban character. The initial effect of mechanization here was to increase the scope for outwork and its commercial organization, for the hand-operated sewing machines which were being introduced from the 1850s onwards were well suited to domestic working and to management by putting-out employers. Clothing factories, in which Leeds led the way from the 1860s, similarly served to increase the numbers of outworkers while pulling more of them into the urban environment; for the very speed and efficiency with which machinery performed some processes in these factories, such as cutting out or buttonholing, generated a massive demand for outworkers for other stages of production which still had to be done by hand, individuals or small workshops specializing in repetitive work on maybe collars, or sleeves, or linings for the large factories.

Clothing factories grew steadily in number and size, and in the quality of their product, in the last two decades of the century, in Manchester and London as well as in Leeds; and they branched out from ready-to-wear men's clothing into blouses, skirts, and dresses. But at the end of the century even the making of mass-produced clothing, let alone the higher quality and fashion end of the business, was far from having become a pure factory industry. The factory workers needed the cooperation of perhaps hundreds of thousands of outworkers and other manual workers in the small workshops of subcontractors; the distinctive effect of mechanization was to draw more and more of the outworkers into a few large towns, rather than to eliminate or even sharply curtail their occupations. Boot- and shoemaking had a broadly similar history, with different concentrations of large-scale commercial production in Northamptonshire and lesser centres in Somerset and Westmorland. Machines for some parts of the manufacturing process began to be introduced from the mid-1850s, for some of the stitching and cutting-out work. The sequel was a half century of division of labour, albeit not a static division, between what was done by machine and in a factory, and what was done by hand and mainly by outworkers. So late as the early 1890s nearly half the work of bootmaking in Leeds was still done by outworkers in their homes, and the shoemaking villages of Northamptonshire around Kettering, Wellingborough, and Northampton itself were full of outworkers. Complete conquest by machine and factory – outside the high-quality bespoke trade – came late and in a rush in the ten years after 1895, with the adoption of perfected machinery for closing uppers on to soles, and under the spur of competition from imported factory-made American shoes. By this time the image and reality of factory work had come full circle: factory conditions and factory wages were a boon to many of the workers, and boot and shoe operatives pressed for an acceleration of the move into factories as an escape route from penury.

Although textiles and clothing continued to employ more than half the manufacturing population until after 1881, the metal-working and engineering sector had clearly moved into the van of industrial change by mid-century. The Great Exhibition of 1851 was a shrine to machinery of immense variety, ingenuity, and complexity, as well as a festival of manufactured consumer goods; its temple, the Crystal Palace, was itself an engineering product. This symbolized and foreshadowed the fields of innovation and expansion which were to dominate industrialization in the second half of the century. The growth of this sector from one seventh to one quarter of the manufacturing workforce is less important than the diversity of callings and of work situations which sheltered under the broad umbrella of this industrial classification. In economic terms, of technology, capital intensity, or business organization, there was precious little in common between the components of an industrial sector which included traditional crafts and trades like nailmaking, cutlery, or blacksmithing; long-established but totally revolutionized processes like iron- or steelmaking; and completely new occupations like the building of locomotives, and the making of textile machinery, bicycles, or electrical apparatus.

This heterogeneous sector was at the heart of Britain's position as the workshop of the world, and it was in important respects indeed more of a workshop than a factory. Many traditional occupations of the Sheffield cutlery trades variety, or the manufacture of Birmingham wares, long retained their workshop structure, hundreds of small units perhaps coexisting with a few large establishments in the same general line of business, while small-scale use of power and specialized machinery, displacing former hand tools, could be incorporated into production methods without displacing the skilled workers. In some branches outworkers continued to survive, if not flourish, into the early twentieth century, either because their products could not be made by machines in factories, as with Black Country chainmaking, or because factory-made articles were inferior substitutes, as in nailmaking where the best horseshoe nails remained hand forged even though a factory trade in machine-cut nails and wire nails had been growing since the 1830s. Some categories, like vehicle-making, were no more than convenient labels artificially uniting such disparate trades as coach and carriage building, a handicraft business with a highly articulated hierarchy of specialized skills, and the manufacture of railway carriages and wagons, a new industry which lent itself to large works and assembly methods. Above all, the making of machines generated a whole series of new industrial activities and occupations, multiplying and bifurcating from roots in the work of smiths, millwrights, and toolmakers. It is not too much to say that the development of machine tools, stemming from pioneering work on lathes, planing machines, slotting machines, steam hammers and the like in the 1820s and 1830s, lay at the heart of all subsequent mechanization in manufacturing and growth in the range and variety of consumer goods as well as capital goods. Yet not only was this development of more sophisticated and specialized machinery – turret lathes, milling machines, grinding machines – a long-drawn-out and continuing affair, of American rather more than British origin, but also it had scarcely begun to produce automatic machinery before the beginning of the twentieth century. In effect workers acquired power tools in place of hand tools, files, saws, drills, or hammers, and they had vastly greater speed, capacity, and accuracy. But the operation of these power tools continued to depend on the skill and experience of the operator, while the actual construction of the machine tools themselves continued to rely on the craftsmanship of individual workers and a great deal of skilled handwork in fitting together the components. This situation began to change from the 1890s, but the processes of minute subdivision of labour, production-line working, and deskilling had not reached very far before 1914. Until that time one highly important effect of the advance of mechanization was to generate new and rapidly increasing battalions of skilled workers, highly conscious of their scarcity value. Boilermakers, steam-engine makers, and engineers – makers or operators of machine tools in the main – were craft-minded even if they were not exactly handicraftsmen; they liked to think of themselves as working in engineering shops, not factories, thus conveying the workshop atmosphere of the individual's control of his tools and his product, even if the scale of operations was likely to be a world away from the traditional workshop.

The engineering shops and the works producing or fabricating metals were in the vanguard also of the urbanization of industry. But whereas the heavy end of the industry, particularly the making of iron and steel, was tightly bound to the coalfields by its high fuel consumption, much engineering work with its high skilled-labour content was not equally constrained. The result was that iron and steel works tended to generate towns around themselves, while engineering and metalworking tended to grow where there were existing supplies of skilled labour, external economies in the form of supporting trades and services, and easy access to final markets, thus reinforcing and diversifying already large towns. Manchester and Leeds, Clydeside and Tyneside, became important centres for machine tools and other kinds of engineering, building outwards from core interests in textile machinery, shipbuilding, colliery equipment, and locomotives. London, far from any coalfield, was however the pioneer of mechanical engineering in the 1820s, and although technical leadership may have passed to the northern towns after mid-century it continued to have a larger mechanical engineering industry than any other region except Lancashire until after 1871, an industry which went on growing to the end of the century and beyond. In the much smaller industry of instrument-making, with its large handicraft element, London held a pre-eminent position throughout the century, while in the new occupation of the 1880s, electrical engineering, it at once established dominance: such were the advantages of a large pool of highly skilled workers and an enormous market on the doorstep. The pulling power of the large towns should not be exaggerated. In such a specialized business as the making of agricultural machinery, proximity to the customers and direct knowledge of their requirements helped manufacturers to flourish in country towns like Lincoln, Grantham, Peterborough, Ipswich, Bedford, or Banbury, and to live with their competitors in Leeds or Manchester; but by the last quarter of the century firms with such country locations were supplying national and international markets, showing ability to outgrow any narrowly local initial locational factors and to ignore any apparent disadvantages of distance from their supplies of raw materials and fuel. It has been in the twentieth century that the spread of electric power has severed the umbilical cord tying engineering – and industry generally – to coalfield sites; but the link was not universally binding even in the full flush of steam power.

Large towns also had a strong but not overpowering attraction for other sectors of manufacturing industry. Some of these, although not large employers of labour in national terms, were well established as factory-type industries by the 1830s because of their large and costly plant, and were concentrated in a few areas with favourable access to resources, where they could be of great importance in the local economy. The pottery, glass, and chemical industries are cases in point, with their concentrations in the five towns of the Potteries, Merseyside, Tyneside, and Clydeside. The woodworking industry, by contrast, employing roughly as many people as these other three throughout the period, was widely diffused. It was in effect a bundle of trades and crafts, from cabinet-makers and french polishers to willow-strippers and hurdle-makers, and like these last some remained parts of rural woodland economies. The chief effect of the growth of urban population and markets, however, was to stimulate the wood-working trades in towns generally, through a proliferation of workshops, small businesses, and outworkers, rather than through any rise of furniture factories.

The basic consumer industries, those concerned with processing food, drink, and tobacco, presented a mixed pattern of development of the growth of large enterprises using factory methods alongside both the survival of slowly declining traditional producers, and the multiplication of new small businesses. This group consistently held fourth place as an employer of workers in manufacturing, after textiles, clothing, and metals and engineering; and its steady rise in relative size after 1871, to reach over 15 per cent of the manufacturing workforce by the end of the century, was a reflection of the commercialization of much food preparation and preserving which had previously been part of the household economy, as well as of a general increase in consumption. The Kellogg effect, or cornflakes revolution, was by this time under way, and in sweets and biscuits, cigarettes or margarine, it was in the late Victorian years that Cadbury and Rowntree, Huntley and Palmer, Wills and Player, and Lever were establishing themselves as household names. Much of the expansion of demand, however, perhaps particularly before the 1880s, was met by a simple increase in the numbers of small bakeries, confectioners' shops, and the like; indeed many processes long continued to be performed behind the shop counter, and it was not until the early twentieth century that a clear-cut distinction between manufacture on the one hand, and distribution and retailing on the other, became normal in the food trades. In corn-milling also the dramatic changes came in the 1880s. Steam mills were established in the larger towns earlier in the century, using traditional millstones, but they did not make serious inroads into the trade of windmills and watermills. The perfection of roller-grinding, coupled with the rise in wheat imports, led to rapid growth of giant flour mills in the major wheat-importing ports, London, Liverpool, and Hull, in the decade or so after 1881. Even so, although country milling came under pressure, its decline was not precipitous, and as late as 1907 not far short of a quarter of all the power used in flour-milling was still provided by water.

*

Manufacturing occupied the centre of the stage in the industrial economy which was consolidated during the Victorian period. Machines, factories, and power were the key elements in innovation and productivity growth, and catch the eye of the historian as they did of contemporaries on account of their novelty, modernity, and success. The phasing of the introduction of factory methods over a long period, with steady diffusion in the third quarter of the century and a decided burst from the 1880s, coupled with the survival of pre-factory methods of production and the creation of new non-factory trades, means however that the overall social impact of manufacturing industry was much more diverse and complex than the straightforward creation of a factory proletariat. In any event one of the apparent paradoxes of industrialization is that the share of manufacturing industry as a whole in the national workforce did not increase over the century; it may possibly have been rising in the early decades of the nineteenth century, but from the 1840s onwards its share remained remarkably constant at around one third of the occupied population, although there were the considerable shifts between different sectors within manufacturing that have been noted. The relative decline of agriculture was inexorable, although the actual numbers employed in farming went on rising slowly until 1851; thereafter absolute numbers fell by 100,000 or more every decade, with the result that agriculture's share of the labour force declined from a quarter to a fifth between 1831 and 1851, and had dropped to under 9 per cent by 1901. This was the shrinking sector of the economy. Since the manufacturing sector did not expand, relatively, it can be argued that the net effect of the restructuring of the Victorian economy was the redistribution of some 16 per cent of the labour force away from agriculture and into non-manufacturing, expanding, sectors.

Most of this expansion took place in the service sectors of the economy, commerce, transport, the professions, central and local government service, and domestic and personal service; some of it was in mining and quarrying, and building and construction, usually classified as non-manufacturing industries. In terms of economic analysis part of this expansion can be viewed as a necessary condition of the course of industrialization, and part as a consequence of generally rising incomes. Manufacturing clearly depended on increasing inputs from mining and building, and on more elaborate and sophisticated transport and commercial services; and, towards the end of the century, on more specialized services, in accountancy or advertising maybe, which industrialists had once supplied for themselves. The capacity of manufacturing to produce an enormous increase in industrial output from an unchanging share of the labour force depended – apart from its own internal rise in labour productivity through mechanization – upon the relative expansion of those sectors where labour productivity actually fell, as in mining, scarcely altered, as in building, or rose much less rapidly, as in the provision of services. If it were possible to quantify these elements of expansion, they could be accounted transfers out of agriculture for the necessary support of manufacturing. On the other hand, some part of the expansion in building went to providing better housing, in transport to increasing and widening the opportunities for personal travel, and in other services to providing more education and health and more employment in entertainment, leisure, and holiday occupations. This part of the restructuring was an expression of the ways in which increasing wealth and incomes were enjoyed. In terms of social analysis, however, the prime interest of these expanding sectors lies more in their individual characteristics than in the identification of the different economic forces at work: a railwayman was a railwayman, up to a point, whether shunting coal wagons or driving an excursion train.

Mining had long been a strategically important activity for the industrial economy but in the 1830s it was still a comparatively small occupation, probably numbering less than 200,000 workers, among whom coalminers were scarcely more numerous than miners of copper, lead, tin, and iron; while a third of the coal output was destined for burning in domestic grates. The broad lines of nineteenth-century developments were for non-ferrous metal mining to decline to insignificance, either dwindling away as did lead from the 1870s, or collapsing swiftly as did copper also in the 1870s and tin in the 1890s, in the face of imports from vastly richer and more cheaply worked overseas mines; for coal output and coalminers to increase roughly tenfold between 1830 and the end of the century, so that the 800,000 coalminers of 1901 and million of 1911 constituted virtually the whole of the mining industry; and for coal to become first the fuel of manufacturing, ironmaking, transport, and gas, a position reached by 1870, and then to become in addition a major export, so that by the early twentieth century one third of output was being exported. The continued relative expansion of the mining sector after 1881 can, indeed, be attributed as much to the rise of coal exports as to the decline in labour productivity.

There were many changes in the organization of this expanding industry, which may be crudely summarized as a tendency towards deeper workings and larger colliery undertakings, the mechanization of ventilation and vertical haulage – leaving advance in underground haulage to the pit ponies – and the retention of hewing as skilled manual labour. These changes were accompanied by shifts in the relative importance of different coalfields, principally the rise of the South Wales, Scottish, and South Yorkshire fields, the decline of Staffordshire, and the ending of the traditional predominance of the north-east. They did not, however, do a lot to modify or dilute the separateness, internal cohesion, and cultural independence of mining communities, with their strong tendencies to be places apart whose folk did not mingle much with others. Some mining communities became large settlements, and there were indeed pure, or almost pure, coal towns like Barnsley, Wigan, the linear towns of the Rhondda, or new towns like Ashington, Northumberland, which mushroomed with the development of mining under the bed of the North Sea in the 1890s. These, also, were somewhat outside the mainstream of urban life, rather more than mining villages writ large but still retaining strong affinities with those typical, self-reliant, vigorous, and aloof communities.

Miners shared some of the conditions of factory workers, in being employed in large units, but scarcely shared in the life of ordinary towns at all. Builders, by contrast, were to be found in every town but had little from their work experience in common with factory workers. Building was an industry scarcely touched by technological change until the present century, and although some machinery was introduced in joinery shops it remained essentially a matter of assembling building materials, and fabricating some of them, by manual labour on the site. Many different skills were involved, those of masons, bricklayers, carpenters, plasterers, glaziers, plumbers, slaters, and the like, traditional skills which were joined by the new ones of gas-fitters early in the period, and electricians towards its end, as new equipment entered offices, shops, and homes. By no means all of these were, or managed to remain, crafts which were highly skilled and could be entered only by serving apprenticeships; but they were skilled trades with strongly persistent customary work practices. The formal structure of the industry changed hardly at all in the nineteenth century – or indeed before the 1960s – with a great preponderance of small firms employing ten men or less, and large employers a rarity. This continuity of structure, however, concealed a change in organization, the rise of the entrepreneur-builder who contracted for all the different work required for a complete building, which had far-reaching effects on the status and customs of the trades. Here, then, was a major industry growing, with its mass of unskilled labourers underpinning the trades, from 400,000 workers in 1841 to 1.3 million by 1901, which was far from being a simple preindustrial remnant. Its producers were fundamental to both urban and industrial growth, and it played a key role in the cycles of expansion and depression in the economy at large. Yet with its lack of mechanization, its manual labour and skilled trades, its small firms, and its continually moving workplaces, it was an industry whose workers remained a distinctively idiosyncratic element of late Victorian industrial society.

Symbolically and literally the railway lay somewhere near the centre of that society. Whether the railways did in fact impel the whole economy 'down the ringing grooves of change' is debatable. The extent and nature of the contribution to economic growth of both railway construction, as an investment, and railway operation, as a transport service, have been extensively studied; in general terms the conclusion is that the contribution was considerable but some way short of decisive. There is less doubt that railways were a major influence in stimulating and consolidating regional concentrations of industry, and in encouraging the move to town; and no doubt at all that railway speed, railway convenience, and railway timetables produced wholly new perceptions of individual horizons and profound changes in social habits, of work and leisure, in the pace as well as the place of living. Railways paraded the power of the machine across the whole country, they eroded localism and removed barriers to mobility, and they created new jobs and new towns. Their very modernity and success in generating new traffic, however, also generated expansion in older forms of transport, for all the feeder services bringing freight and passengers to the railway stations were horse-drawn. This, coupled with the needs of road transport within the larger towns, produced a three- or fourfold increase in horse-drawn traffic on Victorian roads. The result, in employment terms, was that there were consistently more than twice as many road transport workers as there were railwaymen until after 1891, and that in the early twentieth century the road transport men, by now including some handling electric trams and soon to include others on motor vehicles, remained easily the largest group of transport workers. Railway companies, the first organizations outside the army and navy to have the control of thousands of men, and with the problem of managing and coordinating a workforce dispersed over tens or hundreds of miles, ran their labour with a discipline and hierarchical structure that no factory could rival. Railwaymen indeed could have been the leading example of the new type of labour created by industrialization and subordinated to machine and employer, were it not that the very paramilitary nature of their regime instilled habits of obedience and sentiments of loyalty to the company which separated them from other workers. Those who worked with horse transport, on the other hand, remained in a highly traditional environment, modified here and there by the rise of large-scale commercial organizations for horse bus companies or some carriers' businesses, but technically conservative with work patterns which did not alter a lot.

The transport industry, with its merchant seamen and dockers as well as its railwaymen and carters, rather more than doubled its share of the total occupied population in the Victorian period. So, too, did the group formed by the professions and public service, which also chanced to be the same in absolute size, providing occupations for 1.3 million people in 1901. The postmen and policemen in this group had uniforms, discipline, and the attraction of job security in common with railwaymen; but most of the group were the salaried middle class of public servants, and the middle-class professions which expanded and multiplied as the economy grew more complicated and as society demanded more education and more health care. Much of the employing middle class was to be found counted in with the industrial sector in which each firm lay, since the occupational tables of the census did not distinguish between employers and employed. But most of the trading middle class were in the group providing commercial and trading services, which included merchants, traders, dealers, brokers, bankers, and insurers, as well as the lower-middle-class ranks of clerks, office workers, and small shopkeepers and shop assistants. The group was not exclusively middle-class, since it included coal heavers, rag-and-bone men, and street traders, any more than was the group of public service and the professions; but taken together their growth from 14 per cent of the occupied population in 1841 to 22 per cent in 1901 may not be too badly misleading as an indicator of the growth of the middle classes. Domestic service has often been seen as the mirror reflecting middle- and upper-class status; this is definitely misleading, since while virtually all middle- and upper-class households had servants, all domestic servants were not to be found in such households. At one level domestic service was an outlet for otherwise unemployable and destitute girls from the workhouse, who for a pittance became drudges for other working-class families. At other levels it was a career of disciplined respectability in which something of the status and manners of wealthy employers might rub off on the servants, whose loyalty to employers and sense of superiority tended to keep them apart from other workers who regarded domestic service as degrading and inferior. Here was a very large, if varied, group of workers, swelling steadily along with others in personal service such as waiters, waitresses, charwomen, and laundresses, to over 15 per cent of the labour force by 1891 before beginning to subside slightly. Numerically four times as large as the transport sector at the start of the period and still twice the size at the close, domestic service was clearly not part of the dynamic of economic growth and industrialization; domestics can indeed be seen as underemployed human resources, although they were not so entirely unproductive as is sometimes supposed. Their very large numbers, however, were evidence that an increasingly wealthy society preferred to use a considerable part of its wealth on consuming services rather than on consuming more goods; and they furnished another facet of the way in which an industrializing society spawned old-fashioned, menial jobs alongside the new.

The major shifts in the structure of the Victorian economy are only partially revealed by an approach through the occupations of the people, since that largely hides from view questions of international trade and investment, and assumes without discussion the different movements in productivity between sectors which were the essence of economic growth. The occupational results of economic changes, however, were the ones of most direct relevance to social structures and to individual lives. They suggest the complexity, diversity, and unevenness of the impact of the maturing industrial economy upon society, and indicate that continuity of the familiar was as important as change and disruption of work habits. They do not in themselves show how some uniformity and coordination was conjured out of occupational diversity, not only by the articulation of the different sectors into an effective economy, but also by common experience of expansion and depression, and these will be brought out later. Nor do they provide more than a partial explanation, or illustration, of the move to the towns, that other great social fact of the century. It is perfectly true that a restructuring of the kind observed, between agriculture and non-agriculture to put it at its most basic, had it been conceivable within a static population would have occasioned an increase in urbanization. The actual course of urbanization, however, the emergence of the large towns and the living conditions in them, were determined more by the pressure of increasing population than by industrialization. Increasing numbers migrated to the towns to escape from rural poverty and overpopulation; they went in greater numbers to the industrializing towns than to other towns, because job opportunities were better there, but they went to other towns as well. Increasing numbers, in turn, were only to a limited extent a response to industrialization; they were the result of fertility and mortality experiences within the basic population unit and social unit, the family.

CHAPTER TWO

—•—

The Family

The population of Britain entered on its prolonged and still continuing period of sustained growth from the middle of the eighteenth century. It built up to its fastest rate of increase between 1811 and 1821, after which the pace slackened somewhat although remaining at historically high levels, before it turned decisively downwards from 1881. This deceleration had little effect in the short run on the economy, because the age structure of the population and slight variations in the proportion that the active labour force formed of the total population, or activity rate, were sufficient to ensure that the size of the labour force continued to increase at much the same rate throughout the seventy years after 1831, and indeed until the 1920s. Similarly, the braking effects upon the growth of total population of the demographic changes plainly discernible from 1881 did not bite hard for a further generation; it was only after 1911 that population increase slowed to its typical twentieth-century level of 5 per cent or less per decade, having previously been at or above 10 per cent per decade ever since the first census. Nevertheless, although they might be ripples which barely affected the surface of population aggregates for another thirty years or more, the changes which surfaced in the vital statistics of the 1880s were of profound social significance. These concerned birth rates and fertility, and the prolonged decline in both, which began at this time and continued without interruption until after the Second World War, signalled the appearance of what were to become characteristic features of modern industrial societies: family limitation and small families.

Ever since Arthur Young observed that 'the increase of employment will be found to raise men like mushrooms' and that 'it is employment that creates population: marriages are early and

51

numerous in proportion to the amount of employment', it has often been supposed that British population growth was a response to the expansion of manufacturing in the later eighteenth century and a perception that large families could become an economic asset through widening openings for child labour. This is to take an unjustifiably insular view, since the transition from the centuries-old demographic regime of very little long-term growth punctuated by sudden and violent fluctuations, to sustained increase, occurred at much the same time in most of north-western Europe and most notably in Ireland, rural areas with little or no increase in industrial activity, just as it did in Britain. The contrary and much more widely held view is that population growth was the result of a very general reduction in mortality brought about by increased agricultural productivity, improvements in nutrition, and a decline in plague and smallpox. While allowing that such factors may have had some influence, it now seems, however, that the key change was a decline in the age at marriage, with earlier marriages resulting in more children and larger families. The earlier marriages were a response to general improvements in material conditions and prospects, particularly in the price and availability of food, rather than to any increase of opportunities specifically in industry; and probably to the increasing irrelevance, outside peasant circles, of inheritance expectations as incentives to delayed marriage. With these qualifications, Arthur Young may not have been so far wrong.

The age of women at marriage continued to fall until the middle of the nineteenth century, but the decline was small and with the mean age remaining around twenty-five marriage could still be considered late, both in relation to puberty and to late twentieth-century habits, where twenty-two has become the average age at which women marry. Of more importance for trends in fertility and in total population, marriage was becoming more frequent and popular until the 1870s. Significant numbers never married, so that in 1881 12 per cent of the women aged forty-five to fifty-four, in England, and 19 per cent in Scotland, had never married; but the proportion remaining unmarried had declined, in every age group over the age of fifteen, since the first available figures, for 1851 (teenage marriages, however, were extremely uncommon, at only 2 or 3 per cent of the age group). It was primarily these marriage patterns which sustained the crude birth rate at around 35 per thousand of total population throughout the forty years after 1840, when the figures for births under the civil registration instituted in 1837 become reliable, and raised the fertility rate of births per thousand women in the childbearing age group of fifteen to forty-four, from 135 in the early 1840s to its peak of 156 in the mid-1870s. This increase in fertility was almost entirely due to increased nuptiality, rather than to any rise in the number of children per marriage.

From 1878 both the crude birth rate and the fertility rate entered upon their prolonged decline, and by 1901 were down to 28.5 and 114 in England (remaining slightly higher in Scotland), a drop of about 25 per cent from the peak rates. The start of the twentieth century did not, of course, mark any particular milestone in these trends, which continued on their downward course until more or less stabilized at new low levels reflecting the reproductive behaviour of late industrial or post-industrial society in the second half of the twentieth century. The social mechanisms producing these trends did, however, undergo a radical reversal, if not immediately after 1901 then after 1914, and this subsequent change was sufficiently radical to mark off the years between 1878 and 1914 (or, as these were the nearest census dates, between 1881 and 1911) as a highly distinctive phase in the marital behaviour of a fully industrialized society.

It is frequently thought that the fall in fertility from the 1880s was the result of a general and growing adoption of birth-control practices amongst most classes in the community, and there is indeed plenty of evidence that contraception became more openly talked about and knowledge of methods became more widespread from this time. More traditional mechanisms were at work, however, although in non-traditional directions. The age of women at marriage began to rise from its low point in 1871 and by 1901 was over twenty-six years, the increase of a full year in the average age signifying a major shift comparable in magnitude to any pre-nineteenth-century changes within a similar period of time. At the same time marriage became less frequent, the proportion of women who never married rising to nearly 14 per cent by 1901 and 16 per cent by 1911 in England, and 20 per cent in Scotland. Such tendencies were perverse, in the sense that real incomes were rising fast for most of this period, and that the overall sex ratio in the population was moving in women's favour with the numbers of males per thousand females rising, circumstances which in earlier times would have led to earlier and more frequent marriages. They were, moreover, peculiar to the late Victorian and Edwardian world, for since 1914 there has been a striking increase in the amount of marriage, as marriage rates have risen and marriages have become more and more youthful. The marital posture of the country at large in this late Victorian period was, therefore, decidedly odd in the light of the normal habits and preferences of earlier and later times. Granted that Britain only gradually matured into an industrial society, a process scarcely completed before the 1880s, and granted that it generally took a generation for patterns of individual behaviour to adjust to broad shifts in economic circumstances, it may well be that this apparent peculiarity of later marriages and increasing celibacy was society's collective response to industrialization.

This is distinctly paradoxical, when it is considered that Irish society responded with more emphatic versions of the same marital trends to the precisely opposite situation, the absence of industrialization. When Famine signalled that the population had gravely outrun the resources available to sustain it, a balance was restored in predominantly agricultural Ireland, first by the grim check of starvation, and subsequently in part by mass emigration, and in part by a steep fall in the marriage rate and rise in the age at marriage, with the numbers of children within families restrained only by this last factor. Emigration plus the swelling ranks of unmarried Irish abruptly halved the total population of Ireland in the second half of the nineteenth century, and stabilized it at a new, low, level more suited to the capacities of its non-industrial economy. The Irish logic was the traditional logic of making marriages and families fit the available means of subsistence. The British logic was a new logic of rising material expectations and of a society in which only a small minority was directly dependent on producing food; delayed marriage or no marriage at all were the end results of individual pursuit of better conditions and larger shares of goods and services, a strategy well suited to a time when the technical means of controlling births, and thus enlarging personal freedom and choice in making families, were still extremely limited.

This interpretation of the great tidal waves in family history which are expressed in the ups and downs of marriage will acquire many qualifications as the analysis develops. But insofar as decisions whether and when to marry were rational, and matters of calculation, it made sense to pursue the maintenance and improvement of standards of living by postponing marriage, reducing the number of children to be supported, and reducing the rate at which new families and households were formed. The development and widespread dissemination of reliable contraceptive techniques in the twentieth century, it can be argued, liberated people from dependence on these preventive checks and enabled them to pursue the same ends of improving their lot while indulging in as much marriage at as early stages as individuals happened to prefer. Confirmation of the technologically intermediate basis of the late Victorian behaviour is provided by the observation that delayed marriages and rising celibacy were sufficient to account for approximately half of the decline in fertility between 1871 and 1911; the other half was the result of birth control. More and earlier marriages in the half century after 1911, by contrast, would have raised fertility by at least 50 per cent if even the already shrunken family sizes of the early 1900s had remained normal; instead, fertility actually declined by half, a decline entirely attributable to the increasing efficiency and popularity of family limitation.

The late Victorians were, therefore, practising family limitation on a scale that made a marked, although not an exclusive, impression on the figures of births. They were not doing it, however, through a wholesale donning of rubber sheaths. The condom, generally made from animal intestines on the sausage-skin principle, had indeed been known since at least the early eighteenth century, the 'English overcoat' or 'armour' being used by upper-class men as a prophylactic against venereal disease rather than as a contraceptive. The successful substitution of rubber for skin was accomplished in the 1870s, by the 1890s there were several firms supplying the market, with the makers of Durex already well established, and barbers' shops had emerged as the main retail outlets. Nevertheless, it is abundantly clear from contemporary accounts that the limitation of conceptions within working-class marriages, whatever may have been the case among the upper classes, was not achieved by sheathing, although the slight fall in illegitimacy at this period may have owed something to this. Still less were the variety of sponges, douches, syringes, and pessaries responsible for the result, although they were fairly widely, if surreptitiously, advertised and were certainly available commercially. It was the First World War which familiarized almost an entire generation of young men with rubber sheaths, as they were used, or at least distributed, on a massive scale by the army in an effort to check venereal disease; hence perhaps the entry of French letters into common usage. Before this the great majority of married couples, even if they had information about contraceptives, found them either too expensive or too complicated. They relied on withdrawal, abstinence, or possibly prolonged breastfeeding which was thought to inhibit conception. The concept of the safe period was also current in rather restricted circles, but since the medical men were disastrously mistaken in the advice which they gave, pinpointing quite the wrong time in the menstrual cycle, it made no difference if this information was not widely disseminated.

The trouble with natural methods, apart from that of protracted suckling, was that they depended on male decisions and male self-discipline and control at the moment of maximum sexual excitement, and were inherently accident-prone. Despite the well-attested prevalence of coitus interruptus as the most widely practised form of birth control it is, therefore, a shade unlikely that it was sufficient to account for the extent of family limitation which was actually attained, with family size declining from about six for couples married in the decade of the 1860s to about four for the 1900 cohort. It seems highly likely that abstinence as well as withdrawal had been at work, and although the bedroom is a largely unrecorded area, the inference is that there was less sexual activity within late Victorian marriages than within earlier ones, which is odd if prudery and inhibition are thought of as essentially mid-Victorian attitudes. The trouble with coitus interruptus, for the social historian, is that it was not some newly discovered technique of the late nineteenth century but was a highly traditional method of attempting to limit pregnancies or control birth intervals, which had been used by some couples at all levels of society virtually from time immemorial. The problem then is to explain why a tried – but not necessarily completely proven – technique which had always been available should have been adopted on an apparently very general scale at this particular time rather than any sooner. Clearly what happened was not so much the enlargement of the range of personal choices, as a change in the direction of the social choices of large groups of people.

A social diffusion model has found much favour, in which smaller family sizes were pioneered by the upper class, were subsequently adopted by the middle classes, and eventually percolated down to the working classes, a model which fits snugly into more general concepts of social change as a process in which changes spread downwards from the top to the bottom of society by imitation and emulation. There is indeed good evidence that the British aristocracy, from the sixteenth century at least, consistently went in for smaller family sizes than did the generality of the population, and that these began to contract from about the 1830s, a good generation in advance of the rest. Thus the average aristocratic family was down to four children in the third quarter of the nineteenth century from its high mark of five children fifty years earlier, at a time when six children was the national average; a steep fall in aristocratic family size, however, did not set in until after 1875, at much the same time as the general decline. The persistently lower levels at which aristocratic families operated were the outcome of later and less frequent marriages, which can be explained by the importance of property questions in marriage arrangements and by the reluctance of many to marry beneath themselves in the social scale. Eldest sons almost invariably did marry, in order to continue the line and because they could readily attract women who were both their social equals and were backed by satisfactory marriage portions. Younger sons, however, might find it difficult or impossible to make such good matches, or to live at the standards to which they had been brought up in childhood, and might thus tend to stay single, thereby depriving a similar number of aristocratic daughters of eligible marriage partners and obliging them, on the social parity principle, to remain spinsters. The smaller family sizes were also, in part, the result of family limitation, and this appears to have been more practised with increasing effect from about the mid-1820s onwards. This could well have been a lagged response to the decline in child mortality which had set in some thirty to fifty years before, since it would have become obvious that the chances of children surviving to maturity had risen markedly and that it had become necessary to have fewer babies in order to achieve a target number of grown-up children, and prudent to do so to avoid the mounting costs and responsibilities of supporting larger families of survivors. The decline in child mortality may well have included a fall in infant mortality, although that cannot be separately measured; the growing unfashionability of putting aristocratic babies out to wet nurses would certainly have produced such a fall. Most of the decline, however, was probably due to better child care, improving nutrition, and better home conditions, all matters in which aristocratic resources were clearly likely to put them comfortably ahead of the masses. Further, such material improvements could well have been accompanied by, and indeed have helped to foster, a change in parental sentiments leading to growing attachment to each individual child and hence to a more caring, and careful, kind of parenthood.

There are clear suggestions, although no hard statistical proof, that the urban middle classes were beginning to follow suit in the 1850s and 1860s. It could even be that the middle classes had for long had families that were small in relation to the national average, and conceivably smaller than those of the aristocracy. One strand in middle-class opinion which was already well established by the 1830s, after all, was a puritanical disapproval of aristocratic extravagance, indulgence, frivolity, and excess. This was openly expressed by criticism of luxurious and improvident styles of living, and of moral laxity in sexual behaviour; but it is not impossible that this contained an unspoken criticism of improvidence in the begetting of children, with the implication that the middle-class critics behaved differently. The improvident marriages which were loudly condemned, however, were those of the labouring classes. The thrust of the Malthusian case on the pressure of increasing numbers of mouths upon the means of subsistence, leading inexorably to growing impoverishment, was directed at imprudent and youthful marriages of the poor which produced insupportably and undesirably large families. Criticism of the system of poor relief, which was held to encourage such imprudent marriages by subsidizing them at the ratepayers' expense, was a well-publicized special application of this view in the run-up to the reform of the Poor Law in 1834. The validity of the case is one thing, and it has been demolished by historical research; but those who held these views were presumably satisfied that they themselves were not guilty of imprudence in their own family affairs. The middle classes had, indeed, every reason to exercise moral restraint in delaying their own marriages until the bridegroom was sufficiently established in his career to be able to afford to keep a wife and family in the style considered suitable to his station in society. That this was the ideal to aim at was taken for granted in guidance literature and fiction alike, and was presumably largely observed in practice.

The postponement of marriage by middle-class men to their late twenties or early thirties did not necessarily affect the ultimate size of their families, although the delay is commonly held responsible for the Victorian's 'double standard' which connived at or even stimulated the sexual activities of bachelors while insisting on chastity for unmarried women. Other things being equal, the number of children born in a marriage depended on the age of the wife at marriage; the husband's age, provided let us say he was under fifty when he started, made little difference. Given that middle-class daughters were brought up to regard marriage and motherhood as their main purpose in life – although generally kept in ignorance of the mechanics of procreation – there was nothing in their upbringing to suggest that they, or their parents, had a duty to exercise restraint by delaying marriage, unless sexual ignorance and fears of childbirth may have nourished anxiety to postpone the start of the long haul of childbearing. Middle-class standards, in other words, may simply have led to an unusually large difference between the ages of husbands and wives, with women starting married life at much the same age as in any other section of society. There are, unfortunately, no studies and no statistics of any of the particular social groups – apart from the peerage – which go to make up the national averages. On the other hand, the prudence which made middle-class men feel they were too poor or insecure to marry until they had reached some target level of income and independence, must also have made them feel too poor to support in acceptable style the indefinite, or very large, number of children with which God was all too likely to bless a very young wife.

It is, therefore, entirely possible that normal middle-class patterns were for above average ages at marriage for both sexes, which would have given them below average sized families. Another possibility is that middle-class intercourse was infrequent: male abstinence or weakness of sex drives, or female adroitness in rebuffing or avoiding encounters, would not have been inconsistent with prevalent evangelical attitudes to carnal pleasures, indeed pretences that sex was not pleasurable at all, however hard it may be to believe that intimate private practice did not render such attitudes mere public hypocrisy. A third possibility is deliciously ironic. Middle-class couples may have been practising family limitation within marriage, by coitus interruptus or otherwise, at the very time in the 1820s and 1830s that middle-class, and clerical, opinion was vehemently denouncing radical campaigns for birth control among the working classes, in the name of public decency and morals.

It is thus plausible to speculate that middle-class fertility and family sizes were already functioning on a comparatively low level, for a variety of social and economic reasons, before demographic evidence begins to surface that shows they were on a declining trend from the 1860s. This evidence, mainly from the first census of fertility taken in 1911, which recorded information by social and occupational classes from all women then living, supplemented by a few studies using mid-Victorian census enumerators' books, indicates that middle-class family size had fallen to about 2.8 children by 1911 and had virtually closed any earlier gap there may have been between them and the upper class, since aristocratic families were only slightly smaller, at 2.5 children. Beatrice Webb has been cited as a dramatic illustration of the experience of the late

Victorian generation of the wealthy middle classes: born in 1862 as one of the ten children of an industrialist and railway director, her marriage to Sidney in 1892, though it lasted over fifty years, was childless – whether by design or from infertility is not known. A less ambiguous illustration of upper-middle-class habits, if Oswald Mosley's account is to be trusted, is provided by Margot Asquith, who married in 1894 and had two children (and three stillborn): when she visited Mosley's wife Cynthia after she had had her first baby, Margot is said to have advised, 'Dear child, you look very pale and must not have another baby for a long time. Henry always withdrew in time, such a noble man.' More expertly in bed than in politics, perhaps.

In restricting their families the middle classes were responding to their generally growing prosperity, punctuated by short periods such as in the 1880s when they may have felt retrenchment necessary to cope with economic pressures, and to a fall in child mortality starting in the mid-Victorian years. In brief, middle-class lifestyles were becoming more costly and ambitious, and it seemed more and more desirable to shift family expenditure away from numerous children and towards other things. The central place of domesticity and the family home in middle-class culture in itself implied a larger call on incomes than had previously been devoted to residential needs, and although this central place had already been marked out by the 1830s, the growing availability of creature comforts and domestic conveniences from mid-century – from more elaborate and differentiated furniture and furnishings to bathrooms, from gas lights to family photographs – and the growing attachment to them for reasons of personal comfort or social status, undoubtedly generated insistent pressures for more expenditure on housing and the home. Servant-keeping, a universal middle-class aspiration if not a universally accomplished fact, became more expensive, until by the end of the century domestic servants were probably among the highest paid female workers in the country. Above all, perhaps, the cost of educating middle-class children was increasing, particularly as competitive parental ambition for their children pushed them towards more expensive schools and longer schooling.

The costs of respectability were rising, and one obvious way of affording them was through smaller families. Multiplication of the methods available for achieving smaller families, and wider dissemination of knowledge about them, were occurring at much the same time as the decline in middle-class family sizes; but this coincidence in timing should not be taken as establishing cause and effect. Religious teaching, which consistently held that procreation was the purpose and justification of sexual intercourse and the chief purpose of marriage itself, and that efforts to avoid conception were immoral and sinful, was indeed being weakened at this time both by the self-doubts within the Church over Darwin and by the challenge of the agnosticism or atheism of secularists. The specific birth-control propaganda of the neo-Malthusian secularists, kept alive by George Drysdale in the 1850s with his advocacy of 'preventive sexual intercourse' in which 'precautions are used to prevent impregnation [so that] love would be obtained, without entailing upon us the want of food and leisure, by overcrowding the population', and by the *National Reformer* journal in the 1860s, blossomed after the publicity of the Annie Besant–Charles Bradlaugh trial for indecency – for distributing birth-control tracts – and the foundation of the Malthusian Society, in 1877. The championing of women's rights which had previously been the preserve of a tiny minority easily portrayed as extremist, eccentric, or subversive adherents of Mary Wollstonecraft or Robert Owen, became several shades more respectable when John Stuart Mill cautiously argued in his *Principles of Political Economy* (1848), and more decidedly in *The Subjection of Women* (1869), that women should have the same rights as men, and should be relieved of the physical suffering and intolerable privation and drudgery of excessive childbearing. A more direct impact on the ruling class was made by Josephine Butler and her campaign against the Contagious Diseases Acts of 1864 and 1866, which empowered the police to arrest, examine, and regulate suspected prostitutes in specified garrison towns. Her fight, carried on in the name of rights of women to freedom from capricious arrest and to control of their own persons, rather than in the cause of purity and against state-licensed vice, was constantly before the public from 1870 until the suspension of the Acts in 1883; although it was not a campaign about birth control, it was one with obvious connections with the emancipation of women, sex, and women's control of their own sexual lives.

None of these activists, however, whether secularists, family planners, or feminists, were in the least likely to have made any impression on the country's birth statistics or on those middle-class circles and middle-class wives among whom family limitation was first practised. The activists were educated men and women in reasonably comfortable circumstances, but they were consciously uttering extremely unconventional and heretical views out of a strong sense of intellectual and moral conviction, views which effectively excluded them from membership of conventional society or acceptance by the majority of their social class. The pioneers of family limitation, on the other hand, were families at the very heart of upper-middle-class Victorian society, guardians of respectability who by no stretch of the imagination could have been the first to succumb to avant-garde influences. They were the families of army and naval officers, accountants, doctors, civil engineers, solicitors, and the non-Anglican ministers. Only the authors and journalists, artists and sculptors, and tobacconists, could be considered outside the pale of unimpeachable respectability – on the ground of association with Bohemian habits, or with trade – among all the groups whose completed family sizes were below the average for the social class to which they belonged (the Registrar-General's Class I, the upper and upper middle class, for all except the aberrant tobacconists) for all marriages from pre-1861 unions onwards. By the same token, the French letters which a French observer found on sale in Petticoat Lane a little later, in 1883, 'avec le portrait du ministre Gladstone ou de la reine Victoria' were not likely to have appealed to these solid family men: they would be, presumably, for the young Conservative or republican market, no doubt mainly aristocratic and wholly unmarried.

The strong probability is that the wives in these upper-middle-class families remained unemancipated, strong or at least unrebellious believers in the dutiful and subordinate role to which their upbringing had conditioned them, and that the initiative in family limitation came from their husbands; or, since the degree of male dominance in Victorian middle-class life may well be exaggerated in the conventional stereotype, that the adoption of family limitation was a strategy discussed and mutually agreed by wife and husband. What does seem certain is that it was not the consequence of any unilateral drive for independence on the part of wives resolved to free themselves from the trials and burdens of unending pregnancies. It is not certain that the particular uppermiddle-class groups which have been specified were in fact the only ones to begin limiting their families from at least the 1850s, since when the Registrar-General placed individual occupational groups into social classes from the 1911 returns he could only draw on occupational information to construct social classifications. It so happened that only some occupations, chiefly in the professions, could be assumed to be wholly middle- or upper-middle-class; other members of the middle class, for instance cotton manufacturers or ironmasters, were returned for census purposes in the industrial grouping to which they belonged and hence could not be distinguished in the fertility survey from the generality of textile workers or ironworkers. Partial information about some groups of businessmen that can be isolated in the census returns does, however, suggest that the commercial and industrial middle classes may indeed have embarked on family limitation distinctly later than the professional groups. Thus, the upper-middle-class groups who entered the band before 1871 were all still from the professions: barristers, Anglican clergy, and those 'engaged in scientific pursuits'. Those who joined before 1881, however, included bankers, merchants (commodity unspecified), chemists and druggists, who were clearly in the commercial world, as well as dentists, architects, teachers, and law clerks, who were the professional laggards. Colliery owners, moreover, were ten to twenty years behind all these other middle-class groups in opting for smaller families, and at the end of the Victorian period still had larger families than considerable sections of the working classes.

The prominence of the professions in opting for smaller families suggests very strongly that there were some influences or circumstances peculiar to that group in society, or at least impressing them sooner and more insistently than other sections of the middle classes. It might be that some change in cultural or sentimental values or attitudes began to sweep through the professional class in the 1850s, but with the example of Victoria and her nine children before their eyes, and with the cult of the family in its domesticity reaching its height, this appears most improbable. It is more likely that the pursuit of economically rational behaviour was the dominant influence, and the professions as a group can certainly be assumed to have mustered sufficient intelligence to identify the rational course to take. There are no grounds for supposing that they experienced the rising costs of prosperity, in terms of home comforts and luxuries, any earlier or more insistently than any other middle-class groups with similar income levels. It is very possible, on the other hand, that the professional class were more affected, and affected earlier, than other groups by the rising cost of educating their children. Not only were professional men likely to set a high value on a good education, but also if they were keen on their sons following in their footsteps, as so many in fact did, they were excellently placed to know what kind of education or training was currently appropriate for entering their own profession. The decline of 'Old Corruption' and its final dismemberment in the 1830s and 1840s removed the traditional route of patronage and favour as the way forward in the professions – more obviously in some, like the Church, the law, and perhaps medicine, than in others such as the army or the civil service – and more formal and more prolonged education began to be substituted as the avenue of entry. In some cases that meant staying longer at more expensive schools, or going on to university, in others it meant taking articles which had to be paid for and which yielded little or no income for the trainee; in either case the cost of launching a son into an acceptable career had increased. It is, moreover, apparent that businessmen who contemplated having their sons follow them in the family firm did not favour such prolonged or expensive schooling; they did not become patrons of the public schools much before the 1890s, and their sons generally went into business at the age of sixteen or seventeen to learn on the job. The nine ancient public schools, those investigated by the Clarendon Commission in 1864, probably remained very much the preserve of the aristocracy and gentry and were not much penetrated by the sons of professional men. But the great crop of new public schools founded or radically reconstructed from grammar school origins between

1840 and 1870, for example Cheltenham, Clifton, Marlborough, or Radley, of which there were at least thirty altogether, catered primarily for the sons of the professional class. The total cost of educating a son and fitting him to enter a profession was of the order of £1500 to £2000, spread over perhaps ten years; with an outlay of that size in prospect it would be most understandable if parents developed a desire to restrict the number of their children to that which they could afford to educate adequately.

It is true that secondary education for girls, a truly revolutionary departure, made its appearance only a little later, with the North London Collegiate (day school) and Cheltenham Ladies' College (boarding school) in the early 1850s, both of which had the daughters of professional families much in mind. The growth of girls' public schools thereafter, however, was gradual rather than spectacular; Woodard, for instance, began his scheme for studding the country with strict Anglican public schools for boys with Lancing in the late 1840s, but did not move into public schools for girls until the 1860s. It was not until the 1880s and 1890s that there was anything like a rush of foundations of girls' high schools and boarding schools, and until then it is a fair presumption that expensive secondary education for their daughters remained a decidedly secondary consideration with even upper-middle-class parents. Education-based family limitation, therefore, at least in its initial forty to fifty years, was most likely aimed at limiting the number of sons whose future prospects it was desired to maximize, and one would expect professional-class parents to go on having children until a desired number of sons had appeared, a strategy which could well have led to wide variations in the size of families between couples who shared the same family-limitation objectives. This could also help to explain why family sizes, which still remained at over four children for the pioneering professional groups until the 1880s, plunged down to a little over two by 1911, as more equal treatment for the two sexes became more widespread, educationally.

There is little in all this to suggest that the upper middle class was following, after a time lag, the aristocratic example. It is true that some of these groups, especially the army, Church, and law, lived on the fringes of aristocratic society and were prone to seek to emulate aristocratic lifestyles in such matters as servant-keeping and domestic apparatus, as closely as possible. But since the expense of such things does not appear to have been the dominant motive in professional-class family limitation, it cannot have acted as the link in any social diffusion chain. Moreover the educational factor was distinctive to the professional classes, and was not strongly felt by the aristocracy who had long been accustomed to spending rather heavily on the education of their sons and to a lesser degree of their daughters, at least since the early eighteenth century and probably since the sixteenth. As to aristocratic behaviour rendering family limitation respectable, so that the upper middle class then felt free to adopt it themselves without risk of censure, not only is there no evidence that the subject was referred to or commented on by respectable people, but also a section at least of the upper middle class would not have accepted aristocratic behaviour as any guide to respectability. It is more sensible to conclude that the upper middle class had their own good reasons for embarking on restriction of family size, were responding independently to their own circumstances and needs, and were not emulating the class above them.

The rest of the middle classes started to restrict their family sizes from the 1880s, and it is not altogether clear whether they were copying the earlier examples of their social equals, responding to the general movement in educated opinion, or adapting to the arrival in their particular groups of circumstances similar to those which had begun to affect groups in the professions thirty or more years before. Possibly a mixture of the three, with most influence coming from the third factor. Manufacturers and industrialists, as noted earlier, were impossible to identify separately in the census returns; but a family survey carried out privately by Charles Ansell in 1874, a postal questionnaire answered by over 25,000 clergy, lawyers, doctors, merchants, bankers, manufacturers, and peers, showed that the merchants, bankers, and manufacturers had larger completed families than the other groups. Insofar as the merchants and bankers had fallen into line with the professional families by the 1890s, it is not unlikely that the manufacturers had done so as well. It is perhaps excessively determinist to suggest that civil servants, whose families declined sharply in size with marriages made after 1871, responded instantly to the opening of the civil service to competitive examinations in 1870, since that would assume that civil servants hoped to breed future civil servants and began at once to tailor the number of their children to the more elaborate and advanced education which had implicitly been made necessary. Nevertheless, education-triggered family limitation applies as well to them as it does to manufacturers, whose ambitions for gentility for their offspring and more prolonged and modern education were supplying more public schoolboys by the 1890s. The very rapidly growing core of the lower middle class, the commercial clerks, were already restricting their families in all post-1861 marriages and from 1871 onwards their families were only fractionally larger than the upper-middle-class mean; yet these were miles away from being customers of the public schools. The clerks formed one of the fastest growing occupational groups of the second half of the nineteenth century, male clerks quadrupling in number between 1861 and 1891, from 91,000 to 370,000, and female clerks making an appearance from 1881 onwards. This expansion was sustained only by massive recruitment from other, largely manual working-class, groups, and the essential qualifications for entry were literacy, good handwriting, accuracy, and respectability. Recruitment was, therefore, likely to attract the working-class children from the top of the class who had performed best and benefited most from their schooling, and were likely to put a high value on getting as good a schooling as possible for their own children in turn. Moreover, clerks distanced themselves from those they regarded as their social inferiors less by any income differences, since they earned scarcely as much as many skilled workers, than by careful cultivation of status differences expressive of moral superiority, which in their own estimation included shunning public elementary or Board schools for their children and sending them to local private, fee-paying, schools. Here, at a lower level of incomes and standards, was the same category of motives for having fewer children.

The clerks could well have added that it was important to their social self-esteem to make it clear that they were different from the working classes who bred like rabbits, and that far from there being any question of emulating their superiors they were engaged in underlining contrasts with their inferiors. The working classes, however, were far from homogeneous in their family habits; they were not all big breeders; and it is more than doubtful if they were in the business of emulating the middle classes themselves. Although unreflecting and vulgar Malthusians had spoken as though the lower orders were an undifferentiated, uneducated, and unbridled mass, heedlessly indulging in imprudently youthful marriages and insupportably large families, it is fairly obvious that there always had been different groups within the working classes, with different attitudes towards marriage and children. The apprenticeship system in the traditional skilled trades had always been regarded as a check upon headlong breeding, since the rules stipulated that an apprentice might not marry until he had served his term, normally seven years. The decay and erosion of the apprenticeship system has often been cited as a factor stimulating population increase in the eighteenth century, via earlier marriages. On the other hand, while formal and enforceable apprenticeship may have been withering, the enforcement of effective substitutes continued to be a prime aim of the trade societies not merely in the older crafts but also in the new skilled occupations generated by industrialization. Insofar as boilermakers or engine-makers were successful in controlling entry into their trades through monitoring the flow of trainees, and older trades such as those of compositors or masons succeeded in maintaining their traditional practices, similar effects in restraining early marriages might have been expected to continue. In any case, the skilled tradesmen of the labour aristocracy had powerful motives of self-respect and status-protection, quite aside from any possible sexual or marital frustrations imposed by their training conditions, for wishing to confine their families to sizes which they could afford to support in respectable conditions. The difficulty is that the earliest firm foundation for observations on family sizes, the 1911 fertility census, does not give clear support to any such simple explanation and classification in terms of economically and socially rational behaviour.

The situation reached by 1911 was, indeed, one of apparently orderly and rational progression in average family sizes in a league table of working-class occupational groups that ran from the textile workers with the smallest families of 3.19 children to the miners with the largest, 4.33 children, the intermediate steps being occupied, in ascending order, by skilled workers, semi-skilled workers, unskilled workers, and agricultural labourers. It has been readily assumed that this hierarchy was not a recent development, but reflected differential behaviour that had long been established. In particular, it has been inferred from the 1911 position that textile workers were the pioneers among the working classes in family planning, and explanations of behaviour patterns have been focused upon them, and upon the opposite extreme, the miners. Before becoming unduly impressed by circumstantial evidence drawn from the 1830s and 1840s – that textile workers were exceptionally exposed to birth-control literature and ideas and exceptionally responsive to them because of their distinctive employment patterns – it is however as well to reflect on the prehistory of family limitation in specific occupational groups which is revealed by the 1911 census. This shows that for pre-1861 marriages, whose couples were still living in 1911 (a sample biased by above-average longevity), the largest families of around eight or more children were indeed produced by coalminers and agricultural labourers, but masons and boilermakers were within a decimal point or so of producing the same number of children. Similarly, the smallest families were those of spinners and weavers in the woollen and worsted industries, of six and 6.86 children; but their comparative, although not outstanding, frugality was matched by other groups with fewer than seven children, domestic gardeners, domestic indoor servants, and railway signalmen and porters. The families of cotton spinners and weavers of this vintage, often regarded as in the vanguard of liberation or depravity – depending on how family limitation was regarded – were in fact of middling size, around 7.5 children. There was nothing to distinguish them, in this respect, from many other working-class groups, ranging from printers and compositors through railway guards and railway labourers to dock labourers; they were exceedingly average couples in their reproductive performance.

Mine owners and managers, as well as miners, had families of more than eight children in the mid-Victorian years during which the children of these pre-1861 marriages were being born. So also did butchers and master builders. There was, therefore, nothing peculiarly working-class about large families, even if it had already become rather peculiar for groups with middle-class status or pretensions to breed to this extent. It is indeed probable that an average score of something like eight children born alive was the normal tally for families regardless of social class or occupation, until particular and differential influences began to operate to encourage limitation. The average, of course, embraced individual families running up to twelve or thirteen children as well as childless couples; and it included all children born alive, so that infant and child mortality with their differing impact on different classes winnowed down the number of children who survived into their teens in proportions that were not socially uniform. Nevertheless, it is wildly improbable that colliery managers or butchers, coalminers or textile workers, had the remotest idea of the relative risks they might face from infant and child mortality, and implausible to imagine that they thought of controlling the number of their conceptions with a view to ending up with some target number of grown-up children. On the contrary, it is likely that pregnancies were allowed to happen as they listed, until such time as motives for trying to limit pregnancies became insistent.

Occupational distinctions do not point to any single, simple explanation for those motives becoming insistent when they did in different sections of the working classes. The vanguard in the move to smaller families included most railwaymen, but not the engine drivers; most domestic servants, but not gamekeepers; most textile workers, but not cotton spinners; printers and compositors, but not cabinet-makers. It is difficult to see what these groups had in common. It is easier to observe that the groups which started later but had caught up by the 1880s – engine drivers, fitters and erectors, cabinet-makers, and shoemakers – were predominantly skilled workers, although this observation tends to undermine any notion that skilled workers had always been predisposed to restraint on grounds of preservation of their superior status and job-training constraints on early marriage. It is also easy to see that those who were still producing comparatively large families right up to the end of the nineteenth century, of more than five children

– and in the case of coalminers, more than six – were mainly those engaged in heavy manual labour. They were agricultural labourers, builders' labourers, dock workers, and of course, the coalminers themselves. But gamekeepers, boilermakers, and masons were in the same league clinging to large families for longer than the rest of society, and these were clearly not occupations characterized by lack of education or skill.

If this varied and complex pattern of behaviour was the result of rational decisions by thousands of parents, and if their decisions were primarily influenced by some ingredients of their economic circumstances, then the one thread linking the great majority of these occupational groups was the extent, and timing, of their exposure to the processes of industrialization. Thus, machine technologies, large-scale organization, or factory methods, came earliest to textiles, railways, or printing; much later to furniture- and shoemaking; and not at all to building, dock, and farm work, and in the sense that coalmining remained essentially a labour-intensive industry using traditional methods, not to that industry either. Such a model cannot accommodate the exceptions, the engine drivers who were not among the early starters on family limitation, and the boilermakers who remained out of kilter with their large families; but the exceptions are not numerous. It could be that engine drivers, the cream of railway workers, felt that they could afford larger families than the rest of their industry, and that boilermakers responded in similar fashion to their high pay and status among the generality of engineering workers.

The low-scoring and high-achieving domestic servants are the apparently awkward exception to an explanation framed in terms of the influences of industrialization on family life. Domestic servants, however, have been cast in a central role in the general process of 'modernization', a conveniently vague concept intended to sum up the whole shift from traditional, rural and agricultural, customs and lives to modern urban living, without implying that industrialization in any narrow sense was necessarily the chief or only motor in the process. Domestic service was indeed a very important and busy highway for shifting country girls and farm girls into the big city and giving them a view from below stairs of the habits of middle-class households, and a slice of urban living on afternoons off. It is conceivable, but not probable, that female domestics, especially ladies' maids, not only observed the results of family limitation by their employers but also learnt the secrets of the techniques from their mistresses; in this way they could have acted as an important channel for the diffusion and emulation of middle-class habits and attitudes among the generality of the working classes, particularly as they tended to marry respectable town-dwelling workingmen and not dockers, miners, or farmworkers. Given the extreme reticence of Victorian middle-class women, however, who could scarcely bring themselves to mention sex to their own daughters, it is rather absurd to imagine mistresses chatting to their maids about birth control. It would be more plausible to suppose that young female servants, almost daily faced with seduction by their employers or the sons of the house according to popular literature, were obliged to work out for themselves some sex knowledge and contraceptive methods as an essential part of job- and character-preservation.

Leaving specific experience and skills acquired on the job to one side, it is very likely that domestic service inculcated general notions of prudent and careful management, which would be applied to the conduct of their own lives when servants left to get married. A reputation for knowledgeable and competent household management, plus a nest-egg of savings, were after all commonly held to be the major attractions which domestic servants brought into the marriage market. It would not be surprising if, as wives and mothers, ex-domestic servants applied principles of prudence and domestic economy to their own childbearing. How widely ex-domestics diffused such attitudes among the working classes can only be surmised, since there are no records on which to base any conclusions about the occupations of their husbands. Most girls who were in service for some part of their lives did eventually get married, probably at least 80 per cent of them, although they tended to be slightly older at marriage than other women and this in itself would tend to have limited the number of children they had. Very few married male servants and remained in domestic service, because the openings for married couples in service were limited. Since something like one in seven or one in eight of all females over ten years old were domestic

servants throughout the Victorian period, they presumably provided about the same proportion of working-class wives and
mothers; and although female servants were thought to have
strong predilections for marrying shopkeepers and skilled tradesmen, if only because those were the groups with whom they came
into contact most in the course of their duties, it seems likely that
the sheer pressure of their numbers meant that many married
outside those circles. They could, therefore, have been a most
powerful agency in spreading attitudes, or a 'mentality', in which
family limitation formed a natural part, although it must be
emphasized that it is far from clear that such attitudes were
absorbed from their middle-class employers rather than being
self-generated.

The domestic servants whose small families were recorded in the
1911 fertility census were, of course, male servants, since all the
occupational information concerned husbands' occupation, it
being thought of no importance, or impossible, to seek information
on the wives' previous or continuing occupation. Male servants
who married and managed to remain in service, some of them for
over fifty years by the time of the 1911 census, were a somewhat
special and peculiar subcategory of servants since the opportunities
for their employment were very restricted. Servants such as
coachmen, grooms, or gardeners were indeed frequently married
men; but they normally lived away from the house in their own
separate quarters, and were not ranked as indoor servants. It is the
indoor male domestic servants who turned in a better family-
limitation performance than the upper and middle classes, or at
any rate had fewer children. The reason may well have been that
these were upper servants of some distinction and special value to
their employers – stewards, butlers, chefs, or specially trusted
manservants – who were given the privilege of being retained after
marriage. Such special male servants would tend to marry late, and
would be well aware that if they wanted to keep their jobs they
could not afford to have many children, since both space in the
house and tolerance for nursery noise would be strictly limited.
Alternatively, only those married male servants who turned out to
have small families, for whatever cause, might have contrived to
remain in service, the large-family men being forced out into other

occupations. Either way, the male servants cannot have been important agents of 'modernization', and their small families were a consequence of peculiar occupational requirements rather than of the influences of industrialization or urbanization.

There was a widespread feeling among contemporary observers of the early Victorian scene, especially among critics of the factory system, that the influences of industrialization were most strongly at work among textile, particularly cotton, workers, and that they were deplorable, immoral, unnatural, and subversive of the social order. The sight of women and girls working in the mills, as well as children, was found particularly shocking and offensive, the more so when it led to a reversal of gender roles, with the man doing the housework and child-minding while the wife toiled in the factory. Friedrich Engels saw in this not just class oppression and exploitation, but the approaching end of the natural order of the sexes, the dethronement and humiliation of men. 'One can imagine', he wrote, 'what righteous indignation this virtual castration calls forth amongst the workers and what reversal of all family relations results from it, while all other social relationships remain unchanged.' Whether achieved by castration or not, it was widely believed that the millgirls produced fewer children than other women. Mill work in childhood and adolescence was held to arrest and distort physical development, impairing the fecundity of the women or making them sterile. There is no evidence that the millgirls who were young in the 1830s and 1840s were not producing perfectly normal numbers of children in the 1850s, and no reason to suppose that childless couples were any more common in Lancashire textile towns than elsewhere. Married women working in the mills were thought to raise fewer children than normal, because they worked until the final stages of pregnancy and because they returned to work within two or three weeks of childbirth, damaging their own health and leaving tiny babies to neglect and probable swift death. This, if it had been true, might not have affected the demographer's concept of completed family size, since that measures the total number of children born alive to a couple; but it would have affected the effective family size of children surviving beyond the age of one. In any case, there was little substance for such alarmist beliefs. Married women formed a small proportion of the female cotton workers, between a fifth and a quarter, and the great majority of these factory wives were either those who had not yet had any children or those whose children had grown up. The normal situation in the mill towns of the 1840s and 1850s seems to have been that only one tenth or so of all the wives went out to work in the mills; that most mothers with babies and young children stayed at home looking after them; and that the small minority of mothers with small children who did continue to work in the mills made adequate arrangements for baby-minding and child care, preferably with neighbouring kinfolk.

There was, then, an adaptation of family life and child caring to the factory environment, but it was neither on a vast or general scale nor did it necessarily cause any reduction in family sizes. More telling, perhaps, was the view that turning the sex roles within the family topsyturvy, the woman on top so to say, led women to repudiate their childbearing functions at the same time that working in the mills put them in touch with the means of doing so. The notion that birth-control literature and information circulated freely and extensively within the mills was current from the 1820s, and was confirmed by the testimony of Lancashire and West Riding medical men at the official enquiries into factory conditions in 1831 and 1833. One witness agreed 'that certain books, the disgrace of the age, have been put forth and circulated among the females in factories', and that 'the circumstances of there being fewer illegitimate children [should be attributed] to that disgusting fact'. A Leeds doctor claimed that 'books or pamphlets, which are a disgrace to any age or country have been offered for sale' outside the mills; and another doctor asserted that 'where individuals are congregated as in factories, I conceive that means preventive of impregnation are more likely to be generally known and practised by young persons.' The sense of moral outrage shown by the doctors, and shared by the clergy and much of the middle class, is of more significance than any practical effect of the birth-control propaganda. The contraceptive methods being advocated – a sponge pessary 'as large as a green walnut or small apple' – were too complicated and too reliant on careful anticipation, as well as being too indelicate, to stand much chance of taking root among the millgirls. There was a strong current of working-class opinion which repudiated all birth-control ideas on ideological grounds, as a Malthusian–capitalist ploy designed to attribute all the social evils of poverty and destitution to overpopulation and to divert attention from improvement through social and institutional changes. The chance that the mill population retained an aversion to any artificial birth control on moral and religious grounds should not be overlooked, despite its reputation for 'irreligion' in the sense of non-attendance at church or chapel, since its outlook and customs were traditionalist in many other respects.

Above all, there is the evidence that male cotton spinners and weavers continued to have rather large families, of more than seven children, into the 1850s, and did not begin to limit them significantly until after 1871. This is, of course, at best only indirect evidence of the attitudes and behaviour of the mill women; but given that the mill was a meeting place of the sexes, it is probable that a high proportion of marriages were between cotton women and cotton men. It is possible that abortion, rather than contraception, was widespread in the textile areas. It was certainly denounced no less vehemently by the doctors, and perhaps with more reason since the risks of illness and death from illegal back-street abortions were extremely high. Abortifacients, of dubious efficacy, were prominent in the armoury of traditional remedies and popular self-medication, and in the course of the nineteenth century were taken up, commercialized, and heavily advertised in thinly disguised terms. Davies's Emmenagogue Mixture of the 1890s, for example, was billed as 'the best medicine . . . for all irregularities and obstructions, however obstinate or long standing . . . Perfectly harmless, never fails to bring about the desired result, as testified by thousands of married and single females.' How many unwanted pregnancies were terminated, with knitting needles or drugs, is not known or knowable. All that can be said is that there is no evidence that abortions were more common in textile towns than elsewhere, and that if they were at all frequent among cotton women the data on family sizes indicate that they must have been the refuge of unmarried girls, not of wives.

There is a certain irony in the fact that the doctors, who continued to denounce all forms of birth control including coitus interruptus until well into the twentieth century, and the clergy who were scarcely less vociferous, were themselves averaging families of 2.81 and 3.04 children respectively by the 1880s and 1890s, while the textile workers whom they had so uprighteously rebuked were averaging from 3.78 children for wool and worsted weavers to 4.80 for cotton spinners. Some would cáll it hypo-critical; or at the least the muted development of a double standard of family morals, one for the rich and another for the poor. If textile workers, or indeed any other workers, were modelling their behaviour on any members of the middle classes, they were unlikely to have had much cause to emulate the doctors. Judging by results, those who did follow the preaching, but not the practice, of the medical profession were the miners; but they had good reasons of their own, that had nothing to do with outside influences, for persisting with large families for longer than any other members of society.

Coalminers were a people apart, fiercely loyal to one another, seeing little of other members of the working classes, and conscious of the presence of other social classes chiefly in the shape of their boss, a few shopkeepers, and perhaps a local parson or minister and a doctor. Some collieries, it is true, were in towns such as Wigan or Barnsley, where miners might rub shoulders with a larger and more mixed community; but the single-industry and isolated mining villages of Lanarkshire, the north-east, the West Riding, or the valleys of South Wales were their typical habitat. Within these communities they were far from immune from religious influences, as the numerous chapels of South Wales bear witness; and the miners of Northumberland and Durham were already thought to be better educated than most workers, in the 1840s, although labelled irreligious, meaning non-Anglican. But by and large they worked out their own standards and values for themselves, not greatly influenced by the example or competition of other working-class groups, or by their masters. This mentality accepted large families as normal and did nothing very much about reducing them, largely for the negative reason that no compelling motives emerged for easing the childbearing burden of their womenfolk or reducing the number of children's mouths to be fed. Coalmining was a continuously and rapidly expanding industry throughout the Victorian period, its expansion largely achieved by simply increasing the numbers of miners. There was always room down the pit – barring occasional years of recession – for all the sons of mining families, and indeed the growth in demand for labour was such that natural increase was rarely sufficient to supply it, the difference being made good by continual immigration from rural areas. After 1843 the law forbade the employment of women and children underground, and such work had in any case all but died out before then, save in parts of Scotland. A few brawny women continued as surface workers, sorting coal on the pithead bank, throughout the century, but they could be reckoned in thousands against the hundreds of thousands of men. In general there was little if any employment for women and children in mining communities, and they were a clear drain on financial resources, unable to add to family incomes.

There was, of course, an extra amount of unpaid housework for the womenfolk in mining villages, given the large appetites of miners, their exhaustion after a shift and disinclination to help with the chores, and the occupational needs for extra washing and laundry. Women and girls were no doubt kept busy in mining homes, but with no prospects of local employment the girls who did not marry young miners had little choice but to move away, probably into domestic service. Having so little else to do, mining girls may very well have married young, thus helping to perpetuate the tradition of large families. Some historians have argued that in the early Victorian years it was economically rational for the generality of the working classes to have large families because 'children raised frugally and put out to work were valuable assets'. This implies that the economic utility of children declined thereafter in some areas and occupations sooner than in others, explaining the fertility differentials within the working classes; but the argument in fact confuses this point with a different one which asserts that fertility fell first in areas where there was a good deal of female employment but remained high in the mining and heavy industry areas where there was little, because women who had worked outside the home were more interested in protecting their family's economic stability and their own personal freedom, than women who had not. If the reasoning of women, or of married couples, had worked in this way it ought to have caused miners to lead the way towards smaller families, since the economic utility of their children, especially the girls, was low and decreasing, and they should have readily grasped the need to keep the number of their children within the capacity of the husbands' wages. The rationality of miners' wives, and miners, was rather that they might as well continue to reproduce much as they and their forebears had always done, since there was so little else to do, even if the result was a strain on the family budget and a spell of penury while their numerous children were too young to be earning or to leave home. It was, in other words, a consequence of the failure of urbanization to reach the mining villages, since it was town life that generated the alternative pleasures and distractions and provided a clear incentive to save on children in order to spend on other indulgences and leisure.

Overlapping with differences in the timing and degree of exposure to industrialization as a factor explaining the fertility differentials within the working classes were differences in the availability of new forms of consumer goods and services. These, whether in the form of more varied clothing, clocks or pianos for working-class homes, commercial entertainments, organized sport, or seaside day-trips or holidays, were increasingly available from the 1850s onwards, were chiefly to be found only in sizeable towns, and needed quite a lot of cash. The higher paid workers in regular employment, with steady incomes, could afford them; these included not only the skilled workers in both traditional handicraft trades and new engineering occupations, but also many textile workers particularly where there were two wages in a family, many railwaymen, and many domestic servants. The low paid included the dockers, builders' labourers, and, right at the bottom, agricultural workers; these, together with the miners far from the city lights, were the last groups to start limiting their families. Such a response, while in many ways it mirrored the presumed middle-class response to growing affluence and proliferation of home comforts, did not necessarily derive from it by way of example or imitation. It might be argued that these material and costly temptations were placed before the working classes by middle-class capitalist interests anxious to civilize or emasculate the workers, as well as to make profits. It is less far-fetched to suppose that those workers who could afford it were simply pursuing their happiness and pleasures in ways of their own choosing.

Nevertheless, economizing on children in order to be able to increase parental enjoyment was accompanied by, and reinforced by, changes in attitudes to the children themselves. There had been a time when very young children, from the age of five or six, had been widely expected to start contributing towards their keep – in agriculture, textiles, mining, chimney-sweeping, straw-plaiting, and most domestic and cottage industries – even if few had ever been really valuable economic assets. That time may have been coming to an end before legislation took a hand from 1833, with the prohibition of factory work in cotton, woollens, worsteds, flax, and linens, but not in silk mills, for all children under nine years old, and limited the work of nine- to thirteen-year-olds to nine hours a day. At any rate, there were less than 42,000 children under ten years old recorded as having any kind of employment in any occupation in 1851, a number which had fallen to 21,000 by 1871; there were 2½ million children in Britain in the five to nine age group in 1851, and over 3 million in 1871, so that child labour had become negligible for the very young. Factory and workshop legislation came to define a child as anyone under fourteen, and sizeable numbers of ten- to fourteen-year-olds were employed in most industries throughout the Victorian period. The half-timers in the textile industries, defined by the 1844 Factory Act which limited them to a six-hour day, numbered 32,000 in 1850, increased to 105,000 by 1874, and then declined to 21,000 by 1901. And when education became compulsory, to the age of ten from 1876 and eleven from 1893, it was assumed that school-leavers would normally go out to work. Still, from the point of view of an imaginary economic parent the prospect of feeding and nurturing a child for ten or eleven years, after which it might begin to earn a few shillings a week, can scarcely have made procreation look like an attractive investment.

Calculation of the distant future earning capacity of children may be ruled out as a force regulating marital sex, though calculation of the benefit of having some child alive when the parents reached old age may have been a good reason for wishing to have some children, but not an indefinite number. It is sometimes supposed that compulsory elementary education was itself a decisive factor in bringing home the advantages of family limitation to the working classes, on the grounds that it increased the costs of upbringing per child, even after schooling was made free from 1891. This change, however, came too late to explain the early limiters who had begun reducing their families from at least the 1860s; and in any event the opportunity costs of having children at school until they were ten years old were exceedingly small, seeing that there were so few jobs for that age group. Moreover, the majority of working-class parents did not need the state to persuade or compel them into sending their children to school, but voluntarily found the weekly schoolpence to send their children to the voluntary schools of the pre-1870 era. By the end of the 1850s there were already places in elementary schools of some sort, some of them admittedly of more than doubtful standards, for at least two thirds of the total school age group of seven- to twelve-year-olds, and although attendance was erratic and in many cases barely more than token, something like one third of the age group seems to have been at school for 150 days a year or more. These proportions had been increasing since the early nineteenth century, and increasing rapidly since the state first began giving some financial aid to the voluntary societies in 1833, while factory children working in the textile mills covered by the 1833 Factory Act were obliged to attend schools provided by their employers.

It may well be, therefore, that the very substantial minority of working-class parents who were sending their children to schools well before there was any compulsion helped to create the pool of pioneers in family limitation. After all, the mentality which led parents to feel that schooling would in some way benefit their children would also be likely to lead them to feel that they could not afford to provide schooling for an indefinite number of offspring. The burden of the direct costs may not seem very heavy, a typical threepence a week for schoolpence in the early Victorian years representing an outlay of around ten shillings a year per child at school. A family with four children simultaneously of school age – which could have been normal even when completed family size reached eight or more – would have had a peak outlay of £4 a year on school fees. That would have been a very considerable, and indeed unthinkable, sum for the lower paid workers whose annual incomes, if there was only one wage-earner in the family, scarcely totalled £25; but for the higher paid with earnings of £50 a year or more it looks at first sight like a possibly supportable expense. There were, however, indirect costs: the presentable and respectable shoes and clothes which the moral pressure of neighbourhood opinion made necessary for schoolchildren, for example; and, particularly before the 1850s when child labour was more widespread, the opportunity costs of forgone child earnings. All in all, the impact of schooling on the family budgets of even the highest paid workers was sufficiently large to make some family planning of birth intervals, in order not to have too many children at once of school age, a minimum prescription of prudential behaviour. Planning for a restrained ultimate family size was only a step away from this.

Children tend to grow up and become parents in their turn. It is entirely possible that the distinction between those who had had some schooling and those who had had none, which was a very marked distinction until the 1870s and 1880s, carried over into adult life. If it did not, it is hard to see what the purpose of education was. One relevant distinction was that the educated tended to get better jobs, or at least different ones, compared to the uneducated. Some, noted earlier, became commercial clerks; and some, usually the brightest pupils of the voluntary schools, became schoolteachers, mistresses as well as masters. Both of these groups were limiting their families from the 1860s, sharply so by the 1870s. Occupational mobility within the working classes, rather than upward social mobility into the lower middle class, was, however, probably the most common experience for the educated working-class children, a move into the more skilled and less heavily manual jobs to join those whose parents were already in them. Broadly, these also were occupations showing early signs of family limitation. Whether the connection lay in the nature and circumstances of the job, or in the general parcel of values and mentalities derived from the schooling, it is impossible to tell; probably both strands of influence combined to produce the desire for smaller families.

It is also impossible to tell what weight should be given to first-generation educational influences, acting on cost-conscious parents, and what weight to second-generation influences, acting on parents who had themselves been through school. Information on both the precise chronology of family limitation and of school-going habits is insufficiently exact to sort these out, and there is no reason why both stages should not have been at work. In broad terms, however, the educational cap fits. The latecomers to family limitation among the working classes were precisely the latecomers to schooling, the dockers, builders' labourers, and agricultural labourers who needed the spur of compulsion before their children went to school, and whose families only began to shrink significantly in the 1880s. The miners, as always, remain an exception, since they had not neglected their children's education but still continued to have a lot of offspring.

In the schoolroom, as with the piano or the trip to Blackpool, there is a mirror image of a sort of middle-class habits and pastimes and middle-class sexual-reproductive responses. But there is very little to suggest that the formative working-class experience was in some way communicated by or copied from the middle classes, or that the working-class response was a matter of adopting habits or attitudes disseminated by the middle classes. That there were some influences working like a yeast in society at large, which emanated from the middle classes, is not to be denied; and these undoubtedly included general exhortations to prudence – although nothing so vulgar and unseemly as specific birth-control advice – which were relevant to the adoption of family limitation within the working classes. The weight of the evidence and its interpretation, however, leads to the conclusion that the middle classes and the working classes each took their separate paths, for their own separate reasons, which led, with different timing, towards the small families of the twentieth century. Broadly similar responses to broadly comparable circumstances, occurring at different times and places, were more in the nature of womankind and mankind than in the fabric of the class structure. In this fundamental matter of the family the classes worked out their own destinies and their own controls, from a common pool of techniques, and any appearance of a percolation downwards from the top of society to the bottom was a mirage of chronology rather than a fact of emulation.

CHAPTER THREE

————•————

Marriage

Many early Victorians supposed that they were witnessing a 'crisis of the family' that threatened, unless successfully tackled and resolved, to undermine the entire fabric of society and to sweep the nation into turbulent, uncharted, and perilous times of chaos and anarchy. Other social problems might be more visible, more specific, more readily identifiable, more immediately insistent, and apparently more soluble: child labour, women's underground labour, chimney sweeps' boys, agricultural gang labour, even massive problems like poor relief, urban sanitation, or illiteracy, all these seemed to fall into that category. But for many the most menacing, because the most insidious, problem of all was what they saw as the disintegration of the family, eating away like a worm at the very foundations of all social order. Disintegration, it was thought, was being produced by the factory system, by large-town living conditions, by irreligion, and by the weakening and destruction of traditional moral and social bonds and restraints on the unbridled and irresponsible indulgence of individual lusts and selfish appetites. Feminine rebellion against the duties and functions of childbearing and home-keeping seemed to be looming; and with the approaching collapse of parental, particularly paternal, authority, the end of the family as the basic unit of education and social training, or socialization, which transmitted all the habits and standards that enabled society to function, seemed to be in sight. Such were the views of Peter Gaskell or Friedrich Engels on the left, Richard Oastler or Michael Sadler on the right, William Greg or James Kay (Shuttleworth) in the centre, and they came to form part of standard educated middle-class opinion at the time, in varying degrees of intensity and alarm.

The family, plainly, did not collapse. It persisted as an

institution cherished, tolerated, or accepted by the vast majority in all classes of society, certainly into the final quarter of the twentieth century. At this point awareness of the prevalence of single-parent 'families', of the incidence of divorce, of the large proportion of children with broken-home backgrounds, of the pervasiveness of permissiveness, and of the rebelliousness of teenagers, bid fair to make alarm over the approaching disintegration of the family part of standard educated conservative middle-class opinion in the 1980s. What happened in the intervening 150 years was that the family adapted itself to changing circumstances and functions, in a way which possibly it had always done, although it had never before been called on to adapt so rapidly and so radically. The mutual attraction of the sexes, the desire for companionship in 'pair-bonded' arrangements, and the wish to have children for their own sake and not merely as an unfortunate, and now dispensable, by-product of copulation, are probably sufficient to ensure that the family will continue to adapt, adjust, and survive. Well-meaning or interfering people were not lacking, in the nineteenth century, to help the family – meaning the working-class family – on its way to adaptation and survival, and their agency should not be ignored even if it may be doubted whether it was crucial for the purpose in mind. Religion, evangelicalism, education, factory acts, children's acts, all these undoubtedly had some influence on the ways in which family life and family behaviour changed and developed, and contributed to making the family of 1900 different from the family of 1830. The major determinants of change, however, were the material circumstances of the men and women trying to bring up families, and the social influences of their kin, their neighbours, their workmates, and their inheritance from their own upbringing and ancestry. Well-meaning people, or busybodies, will not be lacking in the 1980s, peddling their recipes for rescuing the family from disaster. The future is quite capable of looking after itself; Victorians, in all classes, looked after themselves, but some classes were more bombarded with advice, instruction, and orders than others.

A multitude of observations, arguments, inferences, and pre-judices converged to form the apprehensions of the alarmist early Victorians. There was the 'virtual castration' and transvestism of the wife as breadwinner wearing the trousers, noted by Engels as the consequence of the demand of the mills for female workers, and echoed by Ashley (Lord Shaftesbury). Engels in fact derived his view that 'when women work in factories the most important result is the dissolution of family ties' from Gaskell and his writings of the early 1830s in support of the campaign to regulate factory working hours and conditions. Gaskell asserted that 'the chastity of marriage is but little known among them [factory workers]: husband and wife sin equally, and a habitual indifference to sexual rights is generated which adds one other item to the destruction of domestic habits', the other items including, one imagines, the 'parental cruelty, filial disobedience, neglect of conjugal rights, absence of maternal love, destruction of brotherly and sisterly affection' which he listed in a slightly later book. Such views were the stock-in-trade of the 'factory movement' which aimed at improving factory conditions through legislation, and while they made excellent propaganda for audiences and readerships that had no personal knowledge of factory life, they were not therefore necessarily true or grounded on fact. Closely associated with these views was the variant which held that all female employment outside the home, whether of married or unmarried women, whether in factories or elsewhere, made women into bad house-wives and mothers because it deprived them of domestic training or inclination, and hence weakened the family. From the other end of the generational telescope it was held that family ties and parental discipline were being eroded by the premature, and immature, financial independence of youths who could earn a living wage from the age of fourteen or fifteen in the mills. Millgirls were further spoiled for future family life and motherhood, it was supposed, by the presumed bawdy licentiousness of their working lives, constant deflowerings in the carding rooms or lunch breaks, as it were. Sexual harassment by overlookers or foremen was widely believed to be common, and Engels thought that 'the factory owner wields complete power over the persons and charms of the girls working for him', a belief shared by the French liberal journalist Leon Faucher who visited Manchester in 1844 and solemnly accepted local yarns and pub gossip about the mill-owners' seigneurial rights over the bodies of their millgirls. Engels, at least, who had shacked up with his millgirl Mary Burns, ought to have known better; but the pornographic appeal of a slice of brutish capitalist eroticism, even if totally fictitious, was obviously too good to miss.

Mingling with the presumed anti-family influences of female employment, especially factory employment, were apprehensions about the converging pressures of large-town life. Housing conditions, unsavoury courts, rookeries, and cellar dwellings, and overall chronic overcrowding, were denounced throughout the nineteenth century as inimical to domestic family life and as breeding grounds for all manner of vice and unnatural practices, as well as of misery. Where an entire family, husband, wife, and children of all ages and both sexes, lived in one room any notions of modesty and decency were grotesque, and chastity was thought to be an early casualty. Constant murmurings of incest reached the ears of polite society in the reports of slum visitors and parish clergy, the images of brother-and-sister, father-and-daughter relations thinly disguised in references to 'these breeding places of disease and vice and all manner of abomination'. If incest was at all common or prevalent, which seems most unlikely, its consequences at least must have been massaged away into conventional and respectable forms; the illegitimacy rate, never at all high, was tending to fall from around 7 per cent of all births in the early Victorian years to 4 per cent or less by the close of the century. This must have been in the main the fruits of premarital and extramarital, rather than incestuous, intercourse. Similar goings-on, whatever they may have been, were probably more characteristic, and traditional, in rural areas than in the large towns, where in any case overcrowding was quite as prevalent as in the cities. Nevertheless, promiscuity, whether incestuous or not, was felt to be encouraged by urban housing conditions and to be further stimulated by the pubs, gin palaces, music halls, and other resorts of doubtful reputation which flourished in the larger towns, partly at least as refuges from the inadequacies and unattractiveness of home life. If to all this is added the virtual breakdown of organized religion in the larger towns, of which the more earnest of early Victorians were acutely conscious, then the full force of the supposedly pernicious effects of large-town life upon the institution of the family can be appreciated.

Whether or not any or all of these apprehensions were well grounded, they were the perceptions which induced, or contributed to induce, a whole range of movements, campaigns, moral crusades, religious, educational, and political endeavours, that were intended to reform or correct the material and cultural environment so that, among other objectives, the family might be preserved from the perils which appeared to threaten it. These efforts, very largely but not totally misconceived and misplaced, will be considered more fully in later chapters, as external influences on working-class lives. They were, of course, very much internal influences on the lives of the middle classes, in the sense that they were largely generated by middle-class moralists and social reformers and presumptively reflected what were thought to be already existing habits and conditions within middle-class families. To this extent the content and aims of missionary efforts intended to save the working-class family are most informative about actual middle-class precepts and practices, and most of all perhaps about middle-class fears of the fragility of their own family ideals unless these were protected with constant vigilance by elaborate ramparts of morality, modesty, reticence, sexual segregation, parental discipline and authority, and male dominance. Any self-acknowledgement of such fragility was customarily phrased in terms of the need for barriers of privacy and propriety to protect the middle-class family from contamination by chance contact with vulgar and undesirable people and their corrupting habits, people who might include the raffish aristocracy as well as the great unwashed. The defences may also have been required to protect the middle-class family from the self-destructive potential of the desires and appetites of its own members. The double standard, of strict chastity for the girls and condonation of wild-oat sowing by the young men, never more than obliquely mentioned, was a tacit acknowledgement of this.

The family, regardless of the social class to which it belongs, is always subject to actual or potential internal strains and conflicts which threaten breakdown or disintegration unless kept at bay by observance of accepted rules and conventions, and by all members, husband and wife, parents and children – and in some societies, other generations and other kin – playing their expected roles. What is expected and what is conventional varies between social classes, and over time. This is what the family's function in socializing its members, and what the social history of the family, are all about. The question for the Victorian period is not so much whether working-class families were so precariously based that they could not have survived without a reform and stiffening of their values and morals imposed, or nurtured, by official and middle-class-voluntary policy and preaching. It is, rather, whether and how working-class families managed to handle the manifest pressures of physical hardship, and the stresses of an environment almost turned upside down by urbanization, in such a way as to preserve the cohesion of the family and hold in check its self-destructive potential. The extent to which the routes towards this conservation of the essential cohesion of the family were mapped out by the working classes for themselves, were copied from middle-class examples, or were constructed by legislation, institutions, and moral pressures of largely middle-class inspiration, are matters of lively historical dispute, more informed by the ideologies of the participants than by direct evidence, which is far from plentiful.

Marriage is the conventional starting point for families, and there was plenty of it about throughout the Victorian years. There was, indeed, a scare in the early Victorian decades that socialist ideas were attacking the very concept of matrimony. Robert Owen was after all on record as opposing the 'single-family-arrangement' of the traditional social order, and his critics thought that Owenites were indulging in all sorts of sexual experiments and trying to establish new forms of communities in which free-love reigned and there was 'indiscriminate intercommunion of the sexes, according to all the irregularities of temporary libidinous inclination'. But this was not only a misreading of Owen, who in his ideal new-harmony communities looked for some new form of free association between a man and a woman superior to traditional marriage and freed from the subjugation of wife to husband, but still dedicated to motherhood and child-rearing; it was also a grotesque exaggeration of the practical influence of socialist ideas, which was minimal. Ordinary people paid no attention, and the scare about marriage amounted to no more than a flutter in the clerical dovecotes. If, over the nineteenth century, some couples could always be found who ignored the forms of marriage and simply got on with cohabiting, that was not out of high-minded idealism but out of indifference. To be sure, a small number in the poorer classes were obliged to live in illicit unions because divorce from a previous partner remained practically and financially beyond their reach, in spite of the formal legalization of divorce from 1857. Even then, there was a strong likelihood that such couples would go through a bigamous form of marriage, or trust that prolonged cohabitation would establish an effective 'common-law marriage', while there is some evidence that public wife-selling as a form of popular divorce accepted by the community was still being practised until after mid-century: all of these indicated acceptance of formal and legal marriage as the norm, and a compelling need to find irregular substitutes when some impediment made the norm unattainable. Those who deliberately opted out of this norm when there was no legal obstacle to a legitimate marriage were not the irreligious, who probably formed the majority of the working classes, nor the atheists and secularists, who were a small and mainly bourgeois minority, but rather the minute proportion of the residuum, the dregs of the society, which was incorrigibly disreputable.

Those who never married were a small, but significant, proportion of the total population: in England and Wales about 11 per cent of males were unmarried at the age of forty-five, declining to about 9 per cent in the 1870s and 1880s, and rising again to 11 per cent by 1901; for females the proportions were about 12 per cent, falling to 11 per cent in the 1880s, before rising to 14 per cent by 1901; Scotland functioned with greater celibacy, the unmarried males running at 13 to 14 per cent, and the females at nearly 20 per cent. These, it can safely be assumed, were genuinely unmarried in personal and social terms, as well as by legal definition; they constituted a group, especially of the spinsters and especially in the middle classes, of which society became increasingly aware. Working-class spinsters were expected to fend for themselves, merging unobtrusively into the general body of the female labour force if not required to look after ageing parents; it was the middle-class spinsters in families unable to support them in idleness who were perceived as constituting a social problem, because of the scarcity of jobs of acceptable status. There may, indeed, have been considerably more than the national average proportion of middle-class spinsters, given the socially specific marriage habits that prevailed. Only a limited amount of research has been directed to this subject, although the necessary evidence in the shape of marriage certificates recording parental occupations as well as those of bride and groom is massively available, at a high price in search fees, from the 1840s onwards. These data, together with the genealogies of the propertied classes, convey a strong impression that the upper class and the middle classes had an overwhelming propensity to marry only with their social equals, a category frequently defined in restrictive sectarian and locational terms, and that this tendency only began to weaken towards the close of the century. This meant that if a girl failed to find a partner from within her own social set she was likely to remain a spinster. In the working classes, by contrast, habits of marrying within a particular occupational, geographical, or social group were much less rigid, although they were by no means wholly absent. The net result, however, was that both on grounds of social convention and on grounds of economic necessity marriage was the destiny of the vast majority of working-class daughters.

There were well-established traditions by the 1840s of shoe-makers' sons marrying shoemakers' daughters, and this type of craft-based marriage is readily intelligible in terms of propinquity, opportunities of meeting, shared outlook and customs, and the desirability of finding a wife able to assist in the husband's trade. It was a pattern no doubt repeated in most of the traditional skilled artisan trades, where wives had an essential supporting role in the work process: the furniture trades, tailoring, and some of the metalworking trades fall into this category. Spinners and weavers may once, in the domestic outwork and cottage industry stage, have had analogous economic reasons for intermarrying; these were eroded by the advance of mechanization, but were replaced by the social substitution of the mill as meeting place and marriage market, which seems to have produced a fair proportion of factory marriages. In general, practical economic reasons for endogamous unions within the same occupation would seem to have weakened and disappeared with the development of factory and large workshop organization, and never to have been present in the traditional building trades or the new engineering occupations. To some extent the relaxation of technical and economic incentives for marrying-in among the skilled and semi-skilled was balanced by the sustained and increasing sense of social stratification and group identity within the working classes, although the effects of this would be more likely to show up in keeping marriages within a broad social category such as the 'labour aristocracy' or the 'respectable', rather than within a single occupational group. The miners, because of their isolation and lack of opportunities for meeting other folk – except in such newer coalfields as that of the East Midlands, intermingling with the hosiery districts of Nottinghamshire as it opened up from the 1880s – remained in this, as in so much else, a law unto themselves. Miners' sons married miners' daughters, with some slippage of surplus daughters who went away into domestic service and maybe found husbands from completely different spheres. By and large, however, the impression is that marriages crossed the boundaries of social subdivisions within the working classes with relative ease and increasing frequency by the late Victorian years.

The social identities of marriage partners, usually depicted by the social and occupational background of the spouses' families but ideally including the education and jobs of the bride and groom themselves, are among the most sensitive and acute indicators of community or class feelings. Who marries whom, without courting alienation or rejection from a social set, is an acid test of the horizons and boundaries of what each particular social set regards as tolerable and acceptable, and a sure indication of where that set draws the line of membership. It is, therefore, unfortunate that historical insights into acceptability and unacceptability are so largely hemmed in by the nature of the evidence to the views of the educated and articulate, that is substantially to the upper and middle classes. The vast literature on the working classes, even when it is not concerned to establish the existence of a single working class with a distinctive class consciousness – for which purpose any concern with differences in marriage alliances would be a distraction – has only scratched the surface of the subject. Marriage certificates, as already noted, can be made to supply this deficiency; but the labour is immense, and has so far only been undertaken in a few pioneering studies. For the period 1846–56 11,000 marriages have been studied in the three towns of Northampton, Oldham, and South Shields (John Foster); over 8000 marriages for the two periods, 1851–3 and 1873–5, for Kentish London, meaning the towns of Deptford, Greenwich, and Woolwich (Geoffrey Crossick); and about 2000 marriages for 1865–9 and 1895–7 for Edinburgh (Robert Gray). This is a vast number of marriages in comparison with the numbers of upper- or middle-class unions that have been scrutinized for their social messages, but a tiny proportion of the total amount of marrying going on in the working classes; in Britain as a whole there were 180,000 marriages a year in the 1850s, 226,000 a year in the 1870s, and over 250,000 a year in the 1890s, and at least three quarters of these must have been in the working classes.

Even if the methods of analysing and classifying the data in these three dips into the enormous brantub were similar and comparable, which unhappily they are not, it is therefore rash to generalize about the social structure of marriage and its development from the existing evidence, except in very broad and probabilistic terms. There are, however, no obvious reasons why behaviour in these towns should not have been broadly representative of the generality of British urban working-class populations of broadly Protestant sympathies. That is, the marriages of the Irish have been excluded from the count; the Irish Catholics, and other similar highly distinctive immigrant or religious groups, could be expected to intermarry on strongly extra-social grounds, their choices determined by cultural affinities which transcended purely class or status considerations. The investigations were primarily concerned with testing the degree of stratification within the working classes, but they do show, incidentally, that almost complete social exclusiveness in the choice of marriage partners was confined to the upper middle class of the large employers, and remained so. The middle and lower middle classes, of some of the professions, small masters, shopkeepers, and clerks, did substantially follow suit but were consistently less exclusive. There was always a considerable downward traffic of lower-middle-class daughters marrying beneath themselves, finding husbands from the skilled trades mainly, but also from among the agricultural labourers, and this was probably growing larger during the second half of the century. The middle- and lower-middle-class males were probably more selective and class-conscious in their choice of wives, and did not become any less so; but they also consistently found a significant proportion of their brides, between a third and two fifths, from across class frontiers, daughters in the main of skilled workers but not altogether excluding the daughters of urban and rural labourers.

Working-class girls, therefore, could and did marry upwards in the social scale in significant numbers, chiefly into the lower middle class, many of them no doubt making the transition via a spell in domestic service. As a straw in the wind, the marriages of daughters of men in the skilled engineering, metal, and shipbuilding trades in Kentish London do show some changes in the third quarter of the century. The proportion finding husbands from the identical trades remained steady at one quarter, as did the proportion, just below 60 per cent, whose husbands came from the general group of skilled trades. But the proportion marrying upwards, with husbands from the ranks of white-collar workers, shopkeepers, and the gentry, increased from 18 to 30 per cent. Working-class men were apparently much more conservative and had less inclination or opportunity to jump over this social divide: the proportion of skilled workers in Kentish London who married shopkeepers' daughters remained unchanged at 11 per cent, while in Edinburgh it apparently declined from 12 per cent to 8 per cent between the 1860s and the 1890s. Nevertheless, this social frontier between the skilled working class and the lower middle class, although policed with more vigour on both sides by the men than by the women, was not impenetrable and showed no signs of becoming any more difficult to cross during the second half of the century, indicating that at the least social attitudes were not hardening.

Most social historians, however, have been interested in the internal unity or disunity of the working classes rather than in gauging the depth or shallowness of the division between the working classes and the middle classes. Taking the working classes in the widest sense as embracing all manual workers, they clearly had very strong preferences for marrying one another, and could scarcely have done otherwise since collectively they were more than three-quarters of the total population. Within the working classes, however, differences of status and style between different groups were acutely, even jealously, felt and guarded, a matter of routine observation by all contemporary Victorian social analysts. Some social historians have, indeed, argued that the best-known subgroup, the aristocracy of labour, was actually created by the capitalist middle class in order to divide the working class against itself and thus neutralize any threat to middle-class dominance; this untenable theory has now been discarded, but it remains true that many in the middle classes were not averse to approving and encouraging the deserving and respectable 'labour aristocrats' to differentiate themselves from the broader semi-skilled and unskilled masses and the disreputable residuum. If such divisions within the working classes ran deep, then not much marriage across the divides would occur. The available evidence indicates, to be sure, that the great majority of marriages were made within subgroups, not between them; but the question is, how much intermarriage between subgroups constituted a significant degree of social flexibility and a sign of interchangeability of marriage partners, in terms of social origins of bride and groom not of wife-swapping, within the generality of the working classes.

An older tradition from preindustrial times had held that the central core of marriage behaviour was for craft to marry like-craft, occupation like-occupation, in a voluntary version of an attenuated caste system. By the 1840s and 1850s, if not earlier, this had clearly largely disappeared, leaving the vestigial remains that men still tended to find the largest single category of wives from among the daughters of fathers in the same occupation as themselves, although this category had ceased to be the dominant one. The carters of Oldham, transport workers on the margins of the unskilled/semi-skilled, were by this time unusual in marrying more daughters of overlookers than of other carters. In place of craft- or occupation-based unions, marriages within the bounds of the subgroup which was felt to be socially homogeneous had already become the norm. This was socially, emotionally, and culturally comfortable, and understandable. 'The wife of a lighterman', it was said, 'felt that she was with her equals when she went out shopping with the wife of a stevedore or the wife of a shipwright, but never with the wife of a docker or an unskilled labourer.' Roughly half the marriages of sons of skilled workers, from both traditional crafts and new skilled engineering trades, in both Kentish London and Edinburgh, were to daughters of skilled workers; although there were variations in the marrying strategies of particular trades within the skilled group between the 1850s and the 1890s, for the group as a whole this behaviour remained remarkably stable. This constancy suggests that however much the size and composition of the aristocracy of labour may have been changing in the second half of the century as a result of changes in the craft and industrial structure of the economy, its cohesion as a social group remained unaffected at any rate in this key area of marriage choices.

There remains, of course, the other half – or slightly less than half – of the marriages made by the sons of skilled workers. This confirms the stability of the habits and attitudes of the labour aristocracy. In the 1850s, 22.3 per cent of the marriages of the sons of skilled workers were to daughters of unskilled labourers and servants; in the 1870s the proportion was also precisely 22.3 per cent; in Edinburgh there was a slight, possibly statistically insignificant, increase in this ratio from 11.8 per cent in the 1860s to 13.8 per cent in the 1890s, notable in fact not for any change in habits but as an indication of the cultural gap between London and Edinburgh. On the face of it this suggests that the labour aristocracy was growing neither more nor less socially exclusive, and that it had never been particularly committed to marrying-in; on the contrary, it was always reasonably open to finding brides from the unskilled, from the rural world of agricultural labourers, crofters, and the like, and where possible from the classes immediately above it. Such change as did occur may have been among the girls, not the men, and in a surprising direction. A steady quarter of the daughters of skilled engineering, metal, and shipbuilding workers in Kentish London married men in the same trades in both the 1850s and 1870s, and the proportion marrying into the labour aristocracy as a whole also remained almost constant at just under 60 per cent. But whereas only 18 per cent married into the classes above them (white-collar workers, shopkeepers, and the gentry) in the 1850s and 22 per cent into those below, the unskilled, by the 1870s the roles were reversed, with 30 per cent marrying upwards and 14 per cent downwards. At the margin, therefore, a decided upward shift was taking place in the unions of that two fifths of the daughters of the skilled which did not marry within their own class or subgroup. Unfortunately a similar calculation cannot be made for Edinburgh, as the data do not record marriages of or into the middle and lower middle classes. The clear impression is, however, that any erosion of the self-contained character of the labour aristocracy, which had never been all that self-contained anyway, was being engineered by its girls and was in the direction of blurring the boundaries with the classes above and not in the direction of merging the labour aristocracy into a wider, more unified, working class.

Much the same story can be told about the unskilled labourers, operating at lower social levels. Roughly two thirds of the sons of labourers in Kentish London married daughters of labourers and other unskilled occupations in both the 1850s and 1870s, but the proportions marrying upwards increased slightly, 23 per cent of daughters of skilled workers growing, for example, to 27 per cent in this time, and slightly more than a trickle marrying into the classes above them. In Edinburgh the building labourers found 70 per cent of their wives among the daughters of unskilled and rural workers in the 1860s, but only 62 per cent in the 1890s, while their marriages with girls from the labour aristocracy increased from 13 to 28 per cent. It was, however, the girls in this group also who achieved the main breaches of group and class barriers. Over two thirds of the daughters of unskilled workers and servants in Kentish London married labourers or gardeners, members of their own subgroup, in the 1850s, but this had declined to only half by the 1870s; what happened was that a growing proportion of the marriages of these girls was to the sons of skilled workers (27 per cent increasing to 35 per cent), and to sons of the middle and lower middle classes (8 per cent increasing to 14 per cent). Marriage, therefore, in the hands of the wives was becoming an instrument for tying the unskilled into the labour aristocracy at the same time that it was acting as an instrument for blurring the distinction between the labour aristocracy and the middle and lower middle classes. These currents of social mobility can scarcely have acted to forge, or enhance, the solidarity of the working class. And since they appear to be almost the opposite of middle-class attitudes towards their own marriage alliances, it is extremely unlikely that they derived in any way from any middle-class example.

The middle-class image of marriage was clearly one of a union between social equals, with a penchant for welcoming the good fortune of the occasional lucky alliance with a social superior and to be unforgiving if a son or daughter became entangled with an inferior. Special scorn was reserved for daughters who formed attachments, or actually married, beneath themselves; although such regrettable things clearly did happen from time to time, elaborate precautions were taken to ensure that this was highly exceptional. The ideal was never achieved by the lower middle class, as already noticed, although that sad reality did not prevent the Pooters of the clerical world subscribing wholeheartedly to the concept. Precept and practice came close together among the professional middle class, as witness the extreme care with which Arthur Munby, barrister and minor poet, hid his union with the domestic servant Hannah Cullwick from his literary and professional friends, although the relationship lasted for nearly sixty years from 1854, the last thirty-six of them in happy wedlock: he could never tell his mother about Hannah, because 'the shame and horror' of the fact that she was a servant would have killed her. The threat, or better still the fact, of a mésalliance was one of the stock 'shock' themes of Victorian novels. Among middle-class and upper-class readers it was guaranteed to trigger apprehensive thrills of vicarious disapproval and fascination at the fate of social ostracism and degradation which awaited the unhappy couple, and the humiliating gossip which would surround the unlucky parents to the ruin of their reputations also. Life was every bit as harsh as fiction: unsuitable girls would be heavily bribed to overlook a breach of promise by higher-class men, and unsuitable men who had got as far as actually marrying precious daughters would probably be packed off to Australia to keep out of sight.

The marriage habits of the top half of the middle classes are well chronicled in memoirs, autobiographies, and biographies, as well as in contemporary fiction, but have not been blessed with statistical investigations. Impressions that the Victorian period witnessed growing social exclusiveness in these circles, but weakening of sectarian cellular structure, might therefore be modified by future research, although it is likely that this would at most substitute an image blurred at the edges for the clearly focused picture suggested by the sentiments of the literary sources. At the rural and more earthy end of the middle class, farmers observed conventions which were partly those of class, with their concern for conserving property through social compatibility, and partly those of craft, with their concern with practical and functional couplings. The community of farmers, of course, was far from being wholly middle-class in status, and on the contrary contained within it a complete hierarchy of ranks stretching from the near-labourer near-peasant small family farmers up to the near-gentry farmers of the largest farms of East Anglia, Lincolnshire, the East Riding, and Northumberland, some of whom already had incomes of a thousand pounds a year, that is about fifty times those of some of their labourers. Each within their rank tended to marry daughters of farmers of similar rank, usually from the same local district, a custom issuing from social and business contacts and well calculated to bring appropriate skills into the farmhouse and perhaps the farmyard too. Where property was involved, for the small minority of owner-farmers, dynastic interests could obviously be served as well; but in practice no marrying distinctions seem to have been made between tenant-farmer and owner-farmer families, and the great majority of tenant-farmers could equally plausibly entertain dynastic ambitions. Farmers' daughters, when they did not find farming husbands, seem to have married sons of the local agricultural-commercial community, millers, corn merchants, butchers and the like, thus cementing the ties of the rural, localized, middle classes in their various degrees. Small-scale working farmers and their daughters tended, if it were not possible to marry with their own kind, to intermarry with the superior labourers' families, emphasizing that the rural lower class was not simply an undifferentiated mass of landless labourers.

Such a pattern persisted until late in the nineteenth century. Signs that it was beginning to break down by 1900 may have been partly an illusion created by the rapid turnover of tenant-farming families in the hard times after the late 1870s, the newcomers bringing their own 'foreign' connections with them. But it is likely that they were in the main the consequence of increasing physical mobility and the widening contacts that made possible. Localization was being eroded, in the hinterlands of the larger towns the urban business and professional men were indulging their wish to revert to country residence, the social isolation of the farming community was declining, and marriages were more frequently made with school-mistresses, stockbrokers' daughters, and the like: farmers were starting to become more integrated into wider, less inward-turning, social classes, but not thereby abandoning the concept of suitable and unsuitable marriage partners.

Communities of a different kind, held together by religious beliefs, also moved from early Victorian marrying-in to late Victorian mixed marriages. The Anglican laity were so diverse and latitudinarian in their beliefs that the convention of keeping marriages within the Church never imposed any significant restriction on choice, which was left to be determined by purely social considerations. While with the Anglican clergy the determinant was the individual's rank, rather than the calling itself: those from aristocratic and gentry families tended to marry into that class, and the rest married into other clerical families or, perhaps with greater frequency towards the end of the century, into families in other middle-class professions. Catholics were much stricter about marrying only other Catholics, but social segregation within the sect was also strictly observed: the 'old' English Catholic families, largely gentry but with a few in the nobility as well, married amongst themselves, while the 'new' Catholics were overwhelmingly Irish and in an altogether different class which also kept itself to itself, until in the second or third generation of settlement marriages with members of the appropriate indigenous group, usually the unskilled but including some in the higher reaches of the working classes, became quite common. The priests, of course, did not marry at all. It was in the 'old' Dissenting sects, however, that marrying-in was most marked and most remarked.

These, Unitarians, Baptists, Congregationalists, Presbyterians, and Quakers, were the home of the nonconformist middle class. Habits of upbringing and association, as well as questions of conviction, supported the custom of sectarian intermarriage; with Quakers it was the rule, until 1860, that marrying-out entailed 'disownment', that is, eviction from the Society of Friends. The Jews were probably their only rivals in this strictness. Intermarriage had very considerable business advantages at a time when trading and dealing depended a great deal on personal knowledge and contacts and mutual confidence, and when it was difficult to tell how far strangers could be trusted. That time lasted until the more formally organized and bureaucratized forms of modern business, of limited companies, management hierarchies, and accountants, supplanted the traditional and more informal business habits. That in turn did not happen on any large scale until the early twentieth century, and even then the personal network based on personal friendships and family connections remains important in many businesses in the 1980s.

These business considerations, coupled with social factors, meant that the Quakers, for example, were by no means indiscriminate in choosing fellow-Quaker marriage partners. Wealthy Quakers married wealthy Quakers, and did not ally with Quakers 'in humble life', the farmworkers in the north-west, the servants and industrial workers in the chief towns of Quaker presence, who formed a sizeable minority of the membership of the Society. Even within a sect which numbered no more than about 14,000 members in mid-century there was, in other words, a Quaker middle class which kept itself quite distinct from the Quaker working class. There may well have been a Quaker elite, an upper middle class, which further separated itself from all the rest: the marriage strategies of the Barclays, Gurneys, Lloyds, Peases, Procters, Spences, Cadburys, Rowntrees, and Frys suggest as much. Other Dissenters of the old persuasions behaved similarly; the only difference was that the Quakers, because of the smallness of their total numbers and the even greater scarcity of marriageable partners of acceptable standing, had never been parochial in their choices, the kinship networks spreading over wide regions, if not over the whole country. The larger sects, by contrast, tended to remain geographically much more restricted and localized in their intermarriages until the late nineteenth century, by which time their sectarian exclusiveness was in any case beginning to give way to a more class-and-culture view of marriage and more tolerance of marrying-out.

Munby was undoubtedly right to think that it would be above all his mother who would be horrified by his entanglement with a domestic servant. The formal convention of polite society was that a suitor sought the permission of the father to take the daughter's hand in marriage, and this custom enshrined male authority over the family as well as replicating aristocratic practice. Nevertheless, it is clear that the effective determination of marrying standards, and their enforcement, were substantially women's business, with authority and influence being exercised by wives and mothers, and grandmothers. Father, it is true, was directly concerned with the means, income, and prospects of potential sons-in-law, and if a veto was imposed it was more likely to be on pecuniary than cultural grounds. It was womenfolk, however, who devised and organized the whole apparatus of chaperoning, which was designed to channel their daughters' social contacts and marrying opportunities into clearly defined acceptable circles, and to control their behaviour and premarital conduct within them. It was womenfolk who composed the invitation lists for social events, and thus decided which young men came within the pale of the suitable. And it was womenfolk who developed the appropriate classificatory vocabulary to indicate where to draw the line, chiefly for application to young men: 'not out of the top drawer', 'not public school', and 'not our class' were the demarcation phrases of the late Victorian ladies' tea parties where these strategies were discussed and the peopling of the marriage markets was decided.

The idea that only public-school men were acceptable as possible husbands for middle- to upper-middle-class girls could not have arisen much before the last quarter of the century, since until then there were not enough public schools around for it to have made sense. When it did arise it was evidence that the pool from which marriage partners were drawn had become wider, more anonymous, and more nearly nationwide. Having been to a public school was the necessary, instantly recognizable, stamp of approval in situations where contacts between young people were becoming less and less confined to the older enclosed and cloistered circles in which parental families were well acquainted with one another through the long familiarity of cousinhood, shared neighbourhood, shared religion, or common profession. It was also evidence that class was replacing sect or locality as the dominant criterion at this level of middle-class marriage; it was, of course, class as moulded by a particular kind of education and the set of family attitudes and values which could be assumed to lie behind the selection of that kind of schooling, rather than class deriving at all directly from birth, occupation, or income. This means of defining the middle-class field of eligibles accompanied a secularization and broadening of the social occasions which served, amongst other functions, as marriage markets. In place of church- and chapel-based bazaars, evenings, fairs, or outings – and even simple attendance at services could serve as an occasion for introductions – even the more puritanical of Dissenters and evangelicals were taking to theatre-going, concerts, and dancing from the 1860s onwards, and these, as well as such things as seaside holidays, were opportunities for boys to meet girls. Above all, perhaps, the rapid growth in the popularity of lawn tennis from the 1870s, as a game approved for both sexes, and the spread of tennis clubs, served to break down sectarian barriers and introduce a pan-class marriage market for the middle classes.

There are signs that the elite, the upper middle class, was differentiating itself more sharply at the very time that the general run of the comfortably-off middle class was becoming less fragmented and more class-conscious in its marriage strategies. The early Victorian upper middle class of the major provincial towns had patronized public social events such as subscription concerts, assembly-room balls, and public lectures, continuing habits that had grown up in the late eighteenth century. Their late Victorian successors, although they had not entirely forsaken such functions, were nevertheless using their increased affluence to internalize much of their leisure and entertainment. They held large private dances and garden parties, in their own homes and grounds, they had private croquet lawns and tennis courts, and in one or two cases private golf courses. The latter no doubt saw more business transacted than courtship, but the general effect must have been to accentuate the personal and private elements in regulating the flows of their marriage markets. In such fashion the upper-middle-class elite, mainly the most wealthy but including business leaders and leaders in the professions below the private-tennis-court level, distanced itself from the rest of the middle classes, just as the wider public-school set distanced itself from the grammar-school-going leading shopkeepers and smaller employers, a group which in turn distanced itself from the lower middle class. In the last quarter of the century young middle-class men were exposed to increasing everyday contacts with girls of completely different social origins and status, typists of the new office technology, waitresses of the new fashion for respectable eating out, or shop assistants of the new department and multiple stores. But although fiction, not implausibly, records attraction and romance across these divides, it is most unlikely that real-life affairs of this ilk made any appreciable impression on the class and group defences which the middle classes had erected round their daughters and sons.

The middle classes in all their different layers were, indeed, if anything becoming increasingly selective and exclusive right down to 1914, in contrast to the easing of distinctions within the working classes. Whether the middle classes were imitating the upper class, or simply evolving habits and conventions which seemed comfortable and convenient to them and merely happened to be similar to those of the aristocracy, is another matter. Just how similar they were is, in any case, not altogether clear. The standard study of aristocratic marriage habits (Hollingsworth, 1964) indicates 'two significant changes in the social life of the British aristocracy': the first in the 1720s, with a substantial reduction – from around 40 per cent down to about 25 per cent – in the proportion of aristocratic marriages that were confined within this very exclusive social class; and the second in the 1880s, with a further sharp fall in the endogamous marriages to less than 20 per cent of all marriages. If true, these figures would show both that the aristocracy never had been all that exclusive in their choice of marriage partners, and that they became extremely liberal, open-minded, and indifferent to social barriers and conventions, at the very time that the middle classes were tightening up their ideas of suitability.

There is, of course, nothing inherently implausible or paradoxical about the coexistence of such divergent trends. The later nineteenth century did, after all, witness a growing social accommodation between the old-established aristocracy and the new plutocracy of wealth, an incursion into the peerage of 'new' men of large fortunes and little or no land, and a well-publicized wave of noble marriages both to American heiresses, 'trading titles for dollars' as the saying went, and to actresses of the naughty nineties. The trouble is that the figures rest on the ambiguity and imprecision of 'aristocracy' as a social category. The figures in fact record marriages of the sons and daughters of peers to the daughters and sons of peers, that is, those which were confined to the ranks of the titled nobility. The aristocracy as a social group, however, at least for purposes of acceptable intermarriage, was a great deal wider and more numerous than the titled nobility. This was because, on the one hand, the rule of primogeniture in the transmission of hereditary titles meant that within a few generations many or most of those with 'noble' blood were themselves untitled. And on the other hand, the great majority of landed families with sufficient acreages to sustain the style of country gentlemen – even if these were not vast acreages – were plain untitled landed gentry. It is perfectly true that the landed upper class was divided into several layers, from mere gentry to landed magnates, distinguished more by differences in wealth and acreage than by gradations of titles, and that these differences were important in terms of political standing and social consequence. Nevertheless, when it came to marrying, the whole group, which in normal usage might appear almost indifferently as 'the aristocracy' or as 'the aristocracy and gentry', had long been regarded as consisting of more or less social equals. The charmed circle was not, indeed, confined to families which owned landed estates, although those formed its core. It had always included the wider cousinhood of those descended from or connected to landed families, who were most frequently to be found in the Church, the army and navy, the diplomatic service, and the law; and it had also always included a small element of newcomers who were welcomed into the circle, customarily as brides, but occasionally as grooms, by virtue of their wealth and acquired graces.

The best estimates which can be made suggest that about two thirds of the marriages of sons of peers were with daughters of members of the aristocracy and gentry, and that this proportion remained steady through the 1880s and up to the First World War. The remaining third included many girls whose fathers, although not 'aristocratic' by birth, were in closely connected occupations in the army and navy, the public service, and the Church. It also included, for the years 1870–1914, 104 marriages by peers, eldest and younger sons, to American girls, one tenth of all such peerage marriages. Some of these American brides were extremely wealthy heiresses, of the kind who made the contemporary headlines: Consuelo Vanderbilt, who married the Duke of Marlborough, Jennie Jerome, Winston Churchill's mother, or Mary Leiter who married Lord Curzon. Others included seven Gaiety Girls – who should, however, be eyed in the context of the fourteen British actresses, not all of them of humble birth, who became wives of peers in the same period. There was, therefore, some substance in the contemporary press image, but not a great deal. The majority of the American brides were neither heiresses nor actresses, nor even especially wealthy or daughters of businessmen. On the contrary, they came from the American equivalents of normal British 'aristocratic' backgrounds among land and property owners, military and public service, and the older professions. The wave of American matches, such as it was, was more like a ripple; and it washed across the Atlantic more because luxury liners and American affluence were increasing the European leanings of the cultural and monied elites of the United States than because any impoverished sector of the British peerage went on a dollar hunt. It is not without interest that this process suggests the growth of a transatlantic-cosmopolitan upper class on the margins of the specifically British upper class, but it is significant for signs of some crumbling of national barriers rather than for any dramatic erosion of social barriers.

The daughters of bankers, financiers, and industrialists formed about 5 per cent of these peerage brides, some from one side of the Atlantic, some from the other. The proportions of British and American input may indeed have altered radically in the later nineteenth century, since there had been extremely few American brides, of whatever parentage, before the American Civil War. But most probably all that was happening was that the peerage were adjusting the national mix of the new blood and wealth which they had traditionally recruited, in small but not insignificant amounts, through marrying the daughters of successful merchants, bankers, and industrialists. It would be surprising if this kind of recruitment was not somewhat greater in the late Victorian decades than it had been earlier in the nineteenth century, given the undoubted broadening of high society and the growing ease of access to its circles enjoyed by the wealthy and successful who gravitated towards the metropolitan life. But there is no sign of any revolution in the social habits of the British aristocracy, at least insofar as those were expressed in their marriage alliances; at most there was an adaptation and development of practices of long standing, the affairs of a small minority. The central core of the aristocracy continued on its settled course within conventions that defined compatibility and identified social equals of the marrying sort in socially exclusive terms, and the overall impact on the class was no more than a slight liberalization.

Although the aristocratic movement may have been slight, it was nevertheless in the direction of relaxation. There is, therefore, an impression that the upper class and the working classes were moving in similar directions, on different scales and at different speeds, while the middle classes were going the other way, towards greater rigidity. This accords with the view that it was the Victorian middle classes which were most concerned with finding their social identity, since they were expansive, ambitious, uncertain of their place in society, comparatively lacking in traditions, and in need of clear cultural guidelines as they moved out from parochial, sectarian, and provincial nests and clusters on to a national stage. The upper class, by contrast, was so well supported by the assurance of long tradition and its own ingrained clannishness that it had little cause to worry about its identity, but on the contrary could benefit from a little widening of its marriage catchment area without any risk of loss of face. The working classes, on this reckoning, were the most individualistic and least hidebound members of society. They were, indeed, highly conscious of the different strata within the working classes and of their pecking order; but membership of a particular socio-occupational layer was perceived more in terms of the individual adult male and less in terms of families stretching on through successive generations in the same social layer, than was the case with other classes. The result was that marriages across the boundaries were more common than in other classes, and presumably were more often made by free individual choices uninhibited by social or group conventions and restrictions. Whether there were therefore more marriages for love among the working classes than elsewhere in society is a different question, one that cannot be answered from any body of direct evidence.

Love, affection, and mutual attraction can perfectly well form the basis for engagements and marriages when the set of people within which choice is possible and permissible is restricted by powerful conventions and institutionalized rituals, so long as the set is moderately numerous and its social life allows contacts between the sexes. It is, of course, likely that in such controlled situations other factors such as property, birth, common background, shared values, and dynastic interests, as well as love and affection, will enter into the marriage bond, since that is the object of the controls. It is far from obvious, however, that many, or all, of these ingredients are not ingredients of 'love' in any circumstances. And it is not at all clear that the romantic-liberal alternative model in which 'pure' affection and attraction lead to love matches through random and unstructured contacts that somehow enable soul-mates to get together, has any known historical place in any known historical society. It is clear that the upper class and the middle classes operated highly structured arrangements in their social rituals and codes of social etiquette – their morning calls, their card-leaving, their at-homes, their party lists, their private receptions, dances, and balls, their garden parties, and their society press announcing and recording social events, engagements, marriages, levees, presentations, and comings-out – and that a prime object of all this apparatus was to define social sets and encourage and confine marriages within them. These arrangements reached their highest stage of development, refinement, and rigidity, during the Victorian period; their increasing formalization and institutionalization, in comparison to the less regimented formalities of eighteenth-century polite society, was a necessary response to the growth in scale of urban, and especially metropolitan, society which eroded the familiarity of intimate face-to-face friendship networks and called for the reinforcement of implicitly understood conventions by elements, at least, of a written constitution.

Nevertheless, the arranged marriage in which the parents carried out all the negotiations and the bride and groom had never seen each other before their wedding day had no place in any level of British society since the Tudors if not before, except possibly in the case of some royal marriages, which still tended in some instances to approximate to this patriarchal or matriarchal model. Where property was involved, the financial negotiations were normally conducted between the parents and their solicitors, and led to the framing of terms for the marriage settlement which accompanied all marriages in the landed class as a matter of course and a high and probably growing proportion of marriages in the upper middle class and many reaches of the more middling middle class. In the latter cases the marriage settlements dealt with stocks and shares, rather than with landed estates; but all of them had, as one of their objects, the purpose of securing some degree of financial independence for the bride, circumventing the common-law rules on married women's property by trustee devices which gave the wife control of her own personal income. Some assured financial provision for the prospective children of the marriage was also common to most kinds of marriage settlements, but limitations governing the future inheritance of the family property were features largely confined to the landed class alone. All these negotiations, however, were about contemplated unions between couples who had more or less been free to find each other, within the conventions of their appropriate social set, and to make up their own minds about marrying. The degree of more or less individual initiative and choice clearly varied enormously from couple to couple. In principle all Victorians subscribed to the conflicting doctrines that romantic love was one of the important foundations of true marriage, and that mutual affection and devotion could be relied upon to grow naturally as married bliss developed out of post-wedding experience of married life. In practice deliberate fortune-hunters, who took a cynical view of marriage, could be found at any period. Lord Monson, urging his son to pay attention to Clara Thornhill who was just coming out in 1850 and was reported to have £15,000 a year, and advising him that also 'there are two younger daughters of £40,000 each [in capital], not bad but the first is the large prize', spoke not simply for the mid-Victorian but for the scheming parent of all ages. When he continued that 'I should be very sorry for you to marry for money, but a nice wife with it would not be bad', he spoke for the mid-Victorian scruples about naked and unashamed fortune-hunting; and no doubt entertained an unexpressed hope that tuft-hunting on the other side would do the trick, which as it happened it did not in this instance.

Insofar as there was any trend in these matters it was probably in the direction of greater emphasis on love and affection, and more scope for individual inclinations and choice, from the early eighteenth century onwards, and there are no grounds for supposing that such a trend was subject to any Victorian reversal although the terms in which loving couples expressed their devotion may possibly have been purified by mid-Victorian propriety and then subsequently have become more expansive again with late Victorian exuberance. Even that is doubtful, since mid-Victorians relished the language of love, in their poetry and their novels and possibly even in their paintings, every bit as much as their predecessors or successors; their reputation for chaste prudery cloaks an abiding interest in love and sex, but does not prove that it had ceased to exist. Love and sex were certainly thought to be rife among the working classes, but this was an impression derived from the ignorance of the commentators who imagined they spied promiscuity in every mill, pub, or music hall. These did indeed typify the meeting grounds of the sexes in the working classes – but alongside Sunday schools for the young, and chapels for youths, for the more respectable – but they were scarcely the arenas of chance encounters and social anarchy of prudish and puritanical imaginings. The working classes did not go in for visiting cards and at-homes, it is true, but that did not mean that their social networks and social sets were atomized and unstructured, merely that they were more informal, more localized, more bound by street, neighbourhood, and workplace. How far marriages were in effect parentally arranged is probably undiscoverable, and there is an impression that the personal inclinations of couples were less restrained than in any other level of society. Nevertheless, courtship customs seem to have been well established and well observed, and even if the most intimate of these, the highly practical if tempting bundling practices of rural areas in which courting was done in bed with mutual bodily warmth but a separating blanket, was declining and practically extinct by 1900, all of them involved visits to the parents and sitting up in the front parlour at some stage. The scope for parental influence over unions should not, therefore, be underestimated.

Whether as the fruit of bundling or of more exposed encounters in lovers' lanes or meadows, it has been thought that premarital intercourse and premarital pregnancy were common among the working classes and provided the foundation of many marriages. They were, given the tight surveillance of daughters and the high premium on virginity in the higher classes, more common among the working classes than in any other. That is not, however, the same as saying that they were common or normal events. Prenuptial pregnancy has been studied for the centuries before civil registration of births and marriages started in 1838, from parish registers; it appears that from a low point of about one fifth of brides who were pregnant on their wedding day in the early 1700s, this ratio rose to about one third by the end of the eighteenth century, and then began to decline again. Pregnancy may well have caused marriage; and given the chances of conception, such statistics imply that premarital intercourse became normal during the eighteenth century. What happened later is not so clear. For the period when figures for both prenuptial pregnancy and illegitimacy are available there is a strong positive relationship between the two series, implying that illegitimate births were simply the outcome of premarital intercourse which chanced not to be followed by marriage. Figures for illegitimacy exist for the post-1838 period, and they declined from around 7 per cent of all births in the 1840s to 4 per cent by the 1890s, a reversion to the levels of the 1750s. If the earlier relationship between illegitimacy and prenuptial pregnancy held good through the nineteenth century, then prenuptial pregnancy would by the 1890s have fallen back to something between one fifth and one quarter of all brides. The implication is that although premarital intercourse remained fairly normal among the working classes, it was becoming less frequent during the Victorian period. Whether that was a consequence of the moral influences of Victorian preaching and teaching, the influence of the examples of the higher classes, or of the spread of urbanization and industrialization creating more settled and orderly working-class communities, is not a question amenable to resolution from historical evidence. What is clear, however, is that in all social groups marriages customarily produced children; in some, marriage was followed by conception, in others conception preceded marriage, but in all childbearing and the upbringing of children were at the centre of married life.

CHAPTER FOUR

Childhood

The family survived the perils spotted by the early Victorian alarmists, for many reasons. Partly it was because those perils, where not imaginary, were greatly exaggerated: the teenage promiscuity in the mill towns, widely reported in the parliamentary enquiries of the 1830s and 1840s and almost as widely denied, was in any case not a new industrial or urban phenomenon but was to be found in highly traditional rural and agricultural communities, and was less a prelude to lifelong casual sex than an anticipation of marriage. The great majority of the youths who appeared to exhibit 'a want of delicacy or decency' no doubt grew up to be responsible adult parents. Partly it was because the family retained important economic advantages as a work unit and as an income unit. This stemmed from the persistence of cottage, domestic, and workshop industries, in which there were often opportunities for complete families to work together; but also from the openings in the early spinning mills for parent–children work teams, even if those were more limited than sometimes claimed. The benefits of a family income as distinct from an individual wage, with children and possibly their mother earning as well as their father and contributing to a single family budget, were felt principally by the parents, for whom children's earnings frequently made all the difference between poverty and comfort. For working children, however, whether as young teenagers or as young unmarrieds, it probably also made good financial sense to continue living at home; some economies of scale in running a household, and the almost certainly unpaid or underrewarded housekeeping services of their mother, would make this a cheaper arrangement than the alternative of living independently as lodgers. How far working-class family households kept together as

114

a matter of calculation of individual self-interest, however, and how far as an unquestioned effect of sentiment and custom, are questions which it is easier to raise than to answer. It does nonetheless appear incontrovertible that part of the reason for the survival of the family was the affectionate bond between parents and between parents and children; people actually wanted to live in families, largely no doubt from habit and because it was normal, but also because the habit was satisfying.

Babies and infants obviously had no choice in the matter. Helpless and completely dependent on adult care, they either found themselves in a caring or at least moderately supportive family, or on the scrapheap. Very many found themselves in both. Infant mortality, that is deaths of babies and infants before they were one year old, was shockingly high throughout the Victorian period, persistently over 150 per thousand live births which is well over ten times current rates in the late twentieth century. In the early years these high rates were thought to be distressing but largely unavoidable, the natural consequence of the hazards of childbirth and the frailty of babies that had to be accepted with pious resignation. Largely, but not completely, unavoidable; while medical and public-health efforts were aimed at high levels of general mortality rather than at infant mortality specifically, some medical and moralist opinion was directed at detecting peaks within, or on top of, the overall high level of infant mortality, and at assigning responsibility for them to maternal negligence. By the end of the century, when infant mortality for 1899 at 163 per thousand births turned out to be the highest since the Registrar-General's figures had begun in 1839, and when there was sixty years of no progress and possibly even of deterioration to report, the appalling situation had become accepted as perhaps the major challenge facing public-health, medical, and social services. Why infant mortality failed to fall during the nineteenth century at a time when general mortality declined by about 20 per cent remains something of a mystery, as does the delayed fall in infant mortality itself which started from 1900 and has been continuing ever since: already before 1914 the rate had dipped below 100 in one year, and by the early 1920s was less than half its 1890s level.

It soon became apparent to medical and social investigators, from the 1840s onwards, that there were wide differences in infant mortality between regions, occupations, and classes. Signals were flown at the level of crude national averages, which showed that the Scottish rate was always about 20 per cent, and the Irish rate about 40 per cent, below the English rate of infant mortality. No one supposed that Irish incomes were higher than English incomes, and the Scots generally felt themselves to be less well-off than the pampered English, so the better chances of early survival were clearly not due to greater wealth but on the contrary were inversely related to comparative poverty levels. Certain broad differences in national habits of baby care and infant feeding may have been at work: the superior wholesomeness and availability of Irish milk, or the superiority of Scottish oatmeal over English white bread, might have influenced the quality and adequacy of mothers' milk supplies, but this remains simple speculation. What was clear was that Scotland was significantly less urbanized, and Ireland markedly less urbanized, than England, and that irrespective of parental poverty or the squalor of rural cottages, hovels, or cabins, the countryside was a healthier place to be born in than the town. That this continued to be so for such a long time is proof of the slight impact achieved by sanitary measures, medical improvements, social services, or educational efforts. General mortality had shown similar national differences in the 1850s and 1860s, doubtless for similar general reasons, although the gaps were much less; but from the late 1880s, when urban sewage and water systems were functioning and producing effects, and were more important in England than in the other two countries of the kingdom if only because towns were more extensive there, the overall death rate for England dropped below that of the other two, where it has remained ever since. English infant mortality, however, did not fall below Scottish and Irish rates until the 1920s; it was only then that services and facilities for mother-and-infant care, which were themselves predominantly town-based, began to be of decisive importance in saving infant lives.

What was true of the differences between countries was also true of differences between rural and urban regions within England. The healthier conditions of rural living, in terms of greater expectation of life and of lower death rates, were already well established by the 1840s. By the 1860s there was proof from the demographic statistics that enormous differences in infant mortality existed between rural and urban areas. In Dorset and Wiltshire, which were predominantly agricultural counties and moreover ones where agricultural labourers' wages were the lowest in the country, infant mortality was barely half that in London and in the northern industrial towns. Given that for the great mass of the town population 'their wages are higher, their dwellings are good, their clothing as warm and their food certainly as substantial as that of the agricultural labourer', the explanation lay in environmental differences, in the abundance of fresh country air, and not in income differences or degrees of poverty. In all likelihood this town–country differential was of very long standing, merely surfacing into expert social consciousness when it did because of the novel availability of appropriate vital statistics, although the size of the differential may well have been widening in the first half of the nineteenth century with the rapid growth of the very large towns. If that is so, the maintenance of a more or less static rate of infant mortality throughout the Victorian period may have represented some kind of modest success for a variety of influences – nutritional, educational, medical, and sanitary – operating to reduce infant deaths. If there had not been influences working in that direction, given the town–country differential the constant and pronounced alteration in the composition of the total population that produced a continuing increase in the proportion that were town-dwellers ought to have produced an equally continual rise in overall average infant mortality.

It was simplest for Victorian investigators to think in terms of regional differences, since the Registrar-General collected and presented the statistics by districts, and they could thus be readily analysed territorially rather than socially. Nevertheless an independent inquiry by Charles Ansell in 1874 established that infant mortality among the upper and professional classes was only half the national average. At eighty per thousand births it was still an extremely high rate, and showed that money, education, and high living standards could not by themselves buy survival. It also showed that a baby born to a comfortably-off urban professional family had no better chance of survival than one born to some near-destitute agricultural labourer's family. But it was, all the same, an observation that emphasized the importance of class and income differences. It also implied that babies who could by no means reckon on enjoying the undivided attention of their mothers, and who were not nourished exclusively by maternal care and succour, had a very much better than average chance of flourishing. Admittedly the affluent classes lavished a good deal of expense and thought on employing mother-substitutes when their wives did not choose to, or were unable to, look after their own offspring. The practice of putting babies out to a wet nurse may have decayed as a custom among the upper classes by the late eighteenth century, and have continued only in particular individual circumstances where a mother's milk was inadequate and she chanced to disapprove of resort to bottle-feeding. But the employment of a monthly nurse for the first few weeks, and of a nanny thereafter, was almost universal among families that could afford it. At the very end of the century a few voices could be heard advocating the virtues of natural motherhood and the benefits for a child's physical and psychological welfare of plenty of maternal care and affection; but only wealthy cranks, in the stone-ground flour and vegetarian brigade, would willingly have dispensed with nannies as a matter of principle rather than pocket.

This orthodoxy of employing mother-substitutes was awkward for those who laid the responsibility for part of the generally high level of infant mortality at the feet of working mothers, for they too were making use of mother-substitutes. The argument was a particular application of the general criticism and condemnation of the employment of women outside the home because of its tendency to undermine and destroy family life, to wit that working mothers separated from their infants during the working day were bound to neglect them, and that parking-out arrangements were unsavoury routes to early graves. The more extreme, indeed hysterical, denunciations of infanticide by factory work, made by Lord Ashley and others, were put into cooler perspective by the early factory inspectors who showed that in the cotton industry, the largest employer of women outside the home, no more than a quarter of the female workers were married women. A large proportion of that quarter, moreover, were wives who had not yet had children, or were childless, or had only one child; few mothers with two or more children went out to work, if only because the opportunity cost of day-nursing and child-minding would have exceeded the potential earnings. Viewed from a different angle, it seems likely that only about one tenth of the wives in a mid-century Lancashire mill town went out to work in the mills, another tenth had paid employment in the home, and nearly four fifths were plain wives and mothers undistracted by any paid work.

Nevertheless there was a real problem even if it was on a much more minor scale than the lurid outbursts of the 1830s and 1840s had implied. The nineteenth century was punctuated by medical records and medical statistics portraying a strong correlation between high rates of female employment and high rates of infant mortality. Perhaps the most dramatic was the revelation that the Cotton Famine of 1862–4 was accompanied by a decided drop in infant mortality in the Lancashire cotton districts, against the national trend. The shortage of cotton caused severe unemployment, money was short and families had to skimp and scrape; yet fewer babies died. The conclusion was clear that this was due 'to the greater care bestowed on infants by their unemployed mothers than by the hired nursery helpers', and that 'the care of mothers, it would seem, has counteracted the effects of privation, so that the neglect of their homes by mothers at work in factories is apparently more fatal than starvation.' The 1901 census, which for the first time revealed the marital status of women workers, made it possible to demonstrate beyond any doubt that infant mortality was significantly higher in districts, mainly cotton, hosiery, and lace towns, where the employment of married women was usual, than in towns where very few married women went out to work. Even then there were large differences between towns which had similar proportions of married women in their workforces, and at the extremes Sunderland, where there were few openings for female employment and less than 3 per cent of the small number of working women were married women of childbearing age, had a higher infant mortality rate than Bury, where large numbers of females worked in the cotton mills and 45 per cent of them were married and under thirty-five years old. Nottingham, with no more than a quarter of its large female workforce married women of childbearing age, had the same (high) infant mortality rate as Blackburn, which had 64 per cent of that category. The lesson was that the presence of factory-working mothers certainly had some effect in raising levels of infant mortality, but that it was overshadowed in its impact by the general quality, or offensiveness, of the particular urban environment in which a family was living.

That effect, much smaller than the factory critics had supposed, was the result of the means of infant feeding and care open to working mothers; it did not prove the parental neglect or callousness which were frequently alleged. When a mother with a young baby went out to work it was from sheer necessity, to maintain the family income; it is quite possible that in terms of family welfare the harm done to a baby, and the extra risks to which it was exposed, were more than balanced by the act of keeping the rest of the family from falling into destitution. In demographic terms, lower infant mortality procured by abstaining from work might have caused higher child mortality from poorer nutrition. Going out to work can be viewed as a 'caring' act, although the extreme instances in which a young mother returned to the mill within a few days (a few hours was sometimes alleged) of childbirth inevitably appear heartless and pitiless. Generally a working mother would hope to leave her baby in the care of a resident grandmother, or an elder sister, or possibly a neighbour. Only if these family or neighbourhood arrangements failed would the alternatives be considered of hiring a young nurse-girl by the day to come into the home, or more likely of depositing the baby every morning on the way to work with a day-nurse and collecting it again every evening. Such a hierarchy of preferences, with recourse to strangers as a last resort, was informed by maternal love as well as by financial calculation. But although the day-nurses seem to have been a particularly loveless crew, ignorant and callous older women making a bit of extra money as a sideline by keeping their daily charges in crowded and filthy conditions, while they carried on some other business in the home, such as that of washerwoman, it is probable that from the point of view of a baby's physical health there was little to choose between any of these methods of baby-minding.

This was because in the absence of the mother's breast every kind of baby-minding arrangement meant artificial feeding, and every kind of artificial feeding available was likely to be inappropriate and insufficient at best, and positively harmful at worst. It was probably fortunate that feeding bottles were much too expensive to be used by the working classes, for they were large, cumbersome objects, intended to hold an entire day's feed at once, they were extremely difficult to clean properly, and no one thought of sterilizing them before the 1890s. In any case the cow's milk to fill them with was only too likely to be dirty, stale and adulterated. Special 'babies' milk' was sold in the major towns, at a special price, and was supposed to be pure and wholesome. It was too expensive to be used by any of the baby-minders, except in minute amounts. A few special prepared baby foods and powdered milks did begin to come on the market from the late 1860s onwards, but these too were costly and were only bought by the prosperous classes. Condensed milk became widely available from the 1890s, and was within the reach of working-class budgets; it was probably adopted readily in hand-rearing, but although reasonably pure and safe, it had a low nutritional value and no vitamins. For most of the century the only practical alternative to breastfeeding was to feed babies on a bread and water pap, sweetened with a little sugar or treacle, and occasionally coloured with a dash of milk. This was the normal infant diet discovered by the medical and social investigators who reported on such matters; if a mother returned to work shortly after childbirth her baby would be spoonfed with this pap, which was often kept warm on the hob all day gathering bacteria, from three or four weeks old. It made little difference to the baby's chances of thriving, or of catching its death of 57 varieties of disorders and diseases, if the spoon was wielded by a grandmother, an elder sister, the nextdoor neighbour, or a slovenly day-nurse. Bleak prospects were made bleaker by the custom, which appears to have been almost universal, of quieting a crying or fretful baby with liberal doses of Godfrey's Cordial, Atkinson's Infants' Preservative, Street's Infants' Quietness, or some other opiate prepared by a local druggist. The use of such dopes, all containing laudanum, was certainly not confined to the babies of working mothers, but was a normal part of the popular culture of infant-rearing which held that quietness and sleep were essential, and were no less beneficial if induced by opium; it was also far from unknown in upper-class nurseries. But at best baby-doping might mask some of the effects of undernourishment and of the gastro-intestinal complaints it was likely to cause; at worst it was likely to do fatal damage.

The babies of the small minority of mothers who went out to work were, therefore, at greater risk than other babies, but not as a result of the negligence or heartlessness of either the mothers or the baby-minders. The reason, rather, lay in the poverty that impelled the mother to work and which would have been further aggravated, to the detriment of her family's welfare, if she had not brought in a wage, and which prevented the purchase of the few wholesome and nutritious baby foods for hand-rearing that existed. It was, indeed, only the development of new techniques and technologies in the twentieth century, of bottles, teats, sterilization, and powdered milks which made it possible for mothers with young babies to go out to work without exposing them to extra risks. The extra risks in the nineteenth century, though real enough, were not of enormous proportions. It seems likely that something like 80 to 90 per cent of all babies were breastfed, if only because breastfeeding was the cheapest means of rearing. It was not at all uncommon for a child to continue at the breast until it was fourteen or eighteen months old, and occasionally longer, partly to save expense and partly because it was widely believed, in the face of most contemporary medical opinion but with retrospective confirmation, that a woman who was breastfeeding was incapable of conceiving. In some places there was a taboo against intercourse with a suckling woman, which had the same convenient contraceptive effect. Breastfeeding was the best possible succour, provided the mother herself was eating adequately, which meant more than normally. This was a proviso which was probably not very often met in poorer households, given the ingrained habit of always giving the male breadwinner the best of the food available and the largest helpings; it is interesting, however, that towards the end of the century some workhouses do seem to have been allowing extra rations to nursing mothers. Nevertheless, breastfeeding even with a substandard milk supply was far superior to the alternatives for an infant's welfare. Despite that advantage, infant mortality in the larger towns, in families where the mother was at home and not working, was in the range of 150 to 170 per thousand births, and in particularly congested districts was considerably higher.

The direct causes of these rates were largely gastro-intestinal disorders, with diarrhoea and dysentery the most frequently mentioned causes of infant deaths. These in turn were largely environmentally caused, the result of dirt, insanitary conditions, overcrowding, and fly-borne infections for which large concentrations of town horses and their dung may have been the main culprits. Families, and in particular mothers, were powerless to control any of these conditions, except for domestic cleanliness; house-pride was a key feature in distinguishing the respectable from the slovenly and feckless, and although pursued more for status and show in polished front doorknobs and holystoned doorsteps than for hygienic reasons, it could hardly fail to help the family's health. Helplessness in the face of the elements of their living conditions and their consequences, however, did not necessarily mean that people were indifferent to infant deaths. It is often argued that death in babyhood was so frequent and normal that it was accepted with unemotional resignation or even with relief by parents who already had a surfeit of children. There is evidence, it is true, of extremely matter-of-fact, unfeeling, and calculating attitudes, on the lines of the comment of a Middlesbrough mother at the turn of the century, to Lady Bell, on the death of her child, that 'it would not have mattered so much in another week, as by then the insurance would have come in.' Even then, the inference that some burial insurance money might have been available indicates some concern for the infant, as well as for keeping up appearances by giving it a proper funeral. On the other hand there is evidence from diaries and autobiographies, which are admittedly liable to be atypical because they were so often kept for religious or didactic purposes, that poorer parents were just as capable of feeling genuine grief and sorrow over the death of a baby as were any others.

High infant mortality, it has been widely held, served to blunt and deaden all maternal love and affection, on the grounds that it was emotionally draining and eventually pointless to lavish attention on, form bonds with, and endow with individuality, a wee mite that was like to die. For the religious, it might be remarked – and they included very many in the working classes even if many of the working classes were godless – this was a reason for behaving in precisely the opposite way, since if a soul was in mortal peril in its early months, and if it was to be saved, parental affection needed to be concentrated, not withheld. In any case the chances of a baby surviving were not so slim as to make it likely that some rational calculation about emotional investment or expenditure would override maternal or parental feelings among parents who possessed the personalities and dispositions to display such feelings at all. In the very worst districts of the largest towns eight babies out of every ten born would survive until they were a year old. If child mortality, which was also very high by modern standards, is taken into account, then at least three out of every four would survive to the age of five in the early Victorian years, rising to eight out of ten by the 1890s. For each individual child this was an appalling prospect, and for the community as a whole it was a shocking state of affairs. But no individual mother was at all likely to take the gamble of deciding in advance which of her babies was destined to die young and which to survive, and dispose her affections accordingly. Or rather, even supposing that she knew about the vital statistics or at least their general import, any mother would be likely to behave as if these catastrophes were things which happened to other people, not to herself and her family. How she behaved was another matter. But if a mother, or father, wanted children and liked them, then the existence of high infant mortality was no barrier to feelings of warmth and tenderness; and if children were unwanted, or resented, high infant mortality was not a necessary condition or excuse for showing indifference and treating children with harsh neglect.

Some parents had one kind of disposition, and others another, and this has no doubt always been so. The ways in which parental love and affection have been expressed in child-rearing practices have not remained unchanging. The image of the loving Victorian parent, disciplining her child, feeding only at fixed times with no nibbling between meals, teaching obedience and respect for elders, and allowing the child to speak only when spoken to, is far removed from the image of the late twentieth-century loving parent, for whom indulgence and the minimum of rules and restrictions have become the signs of love. Twentieth-century society has become to a considerable extent a child-centred society, in which the needs of children in their physical and mental development, and their need to be able to live through their childhood as a distinct stage in life separate from adulthood in which they are expected to be individuals and not just small adults, or mere appendages of their parents, are widely recognized as of fundamental importance and are reflected in and protected by laws and social institutions. All this is in the main a post-Victorian development, and quite largely a post-1945 development. It has been the consequence of many factors: the force of liberal and enlightened ideas, both at the level of public policy and in family habits; the impact of mass education and literacy on future parents and on children during childhood; the consequent discovery and exploitation of a children's consumer market for literature, entertainment, confectionery, and clothing; smaller family sizes; the spread of information about how other people live, through radio and television, triggering new aspirations. The list could be extended; but already it is sufficient to indicate that such factors were absent, or only dimly foreshadowed, until the closing years of the nineteenth century at the earliest, and hence that the Victorians lacked the means and opportunities, let alone the impulse, to behave in child-centred ways.

The contrasting image, however, of parental domination and child inferiority and repression, comes largely from upper- and middle-class sources: books of advice and guidance on child-rearing, diaries and memoirs, and contemporary novels. These dwelt almost entirely in a world of nurseries, nursemaids, nannies, and governesses; a world in which infants and children had their own separate and segregated quarters within the household, were looked after by their own special servants, and intruded into the adult world of mother and father only at carefully controlled intervals. The complete regime required a very large house, for it would need a playroom and a schoolroom as well as the nursery, and a large domestic staff, for nanny and governess needed supporting servants, almost a separate establishment. Below the level of the landed classes and the upper middle class all this was clearly not feasible; but all families with any pretensions to gentility tried to approximate to the pattern as closely as their means permitted. 'Single staircase' households would go into contortions in devising inconvenient domestic routines that appeared to ensure that separation of servants, children, and parents which only the double or triple staircased house could comfortably provide; and single servants, by elaborate provision for ringing the changes on different uniforms to suit different daily tasks, were made to perform a multiplicity of roles that ideally required a separate specialist for each.

The regime operated by these arrangements was intended to treat children kindly, although unkind, thoughtless, or tyrannical nannies undoubtedly existed. It was also intended to bring children up in a highly structured, orderly, and regimented routine, partly to make life easy for parents by keeping children out of the way except when they were wanted, and partly because this was regarded as the best way to begin to train character and prepare children for their eventual adult duties and responsibilities. The nursery may not have been a nightmarish world ruled over by a female ogre with a rod of iron, but however cosy and gentle it was, it was designed to teach rules of discipline, obedience, honesty, cleanliness, tidiness, and humility, probably accompanied by sternly enforced, premature potty-training. Children of the nursery classes were certainly not denied all fun and games, and a nursery might be quite liberally supplied with toys: toy trains became available within a decade or so of the real thing. But play was supervised for its moral content, and it was very early established that the rougher stuff was for boys, and dolls were for girls. Such children were necessarily distanced from their parents, and many formed close and lasting attachments to their mother-substitutes; but they did not invariably regard their parents as cold and distant figures, to be respected and possibly feared but not to be loved. Even in high society, where the social round perhaps left a mother only an hour a day to be with her children, some mothers used their brief contact periods for warmly demonstrative cuddling, and many remained close to their children as they grew up. The system obviously succeeded in producing many stable and well-integrated families, as well as some that were painfully alienated. Nevertheless, children were left in no doubt that they were far removed from the centre of the world; they were subordinate to their parents, around whose convenience and pleasure the whole household revolved; they obeyed parental proxies, even though they were superior to the lower servants; they learnt almost from the cradle that their place was to be seen and not heard, and that elders were betters. Yet paradoxically they also learnt from an early age that they were superior to those beneath them in the social order: one of nanny's most important functions was to see that her charges were not contaminated by associating with undesirable characters, and when out pushing the perambulator she would not speak to nannies with lower status babies. As children dutiful, meek, and unobtrusive, as grown-ups they were expected, especially if boys, to be decisive, strong, and commanding; a major task of schooling was to handle this transition through working on character-formation.

Outside the nursery classes children were clearly thrown together with their parents or on to their own resources, since there were no intermediaries. Equally clearly, growing up in these conditions was a totally different experience in a material sense from that of the rich. Cottages and houses were likely to be cramped and poorly furnished; all the brothers and sisters in a family might be fortunate to have one bedroom to share between them, and often one or two of the younger children slept in the kitchen; there was quite likely not enough to eat, the food was monotonous, and it might dry up towards the end of every week before pay day; clothes were largely improvised, cast-offs and hand-me-downs continually being patched and mended, and shoes were a particular problem because of their expense; toys were scarce and rudimentary, a clothespeg doll perhaps, a hoop, or some marbles; and the home atmosphere was one of a constant struggle to survive, to keep want, dirt, and filth at bay, with mother calling on the help of her children almost as soon as they could walk. What is not quite so clear is the effect which such material conditions had on parent–child relationships and on the quality of childhood experience. It has been argued recently that the closely knit, affectionate, and caring family, characterized by less harsh treatment of children and growing concern for their health and happiness, developed first in the wealthier classes from the late eighteenth century onwards, and gradually spread downwards to all levels of society by the early twentieth century. It might equally well be argued that the closely knit unitary family, moderately affectionate and caring, existed first among the working classes, and spread slowly upwards as an ideal type to mingle with the downward-filtering ideas of less punitive treatment of children, more care for their health, and acceptance of children as individuals with independent rights, to form a universal family type accepted by all classes as the twentieth-century norm.

Victorian clergy, doctors, or sanitary reformers who peeped in through the window at working-class home life almost invariably saw something nasty, brutish, disorderly, and objectionable. They saw drunken fathers belting their children for petty or imaginary offences; they saw distraught mothers quieting hungry children with Godfrey's Cordial; they saw skinny, stunted, undernourished children with verminous clothes and their hair full of lice; they saw children who did not know how to use a fork and who had never seen a toothbrush; they saw gangs of young children playing rough games in the streets, hurling rude insults at strangers; they saw children who could not tell them who Jesus was, and who probably thought there was nothing wrong with incest. All these things existed. Beatrice Webb had first-hand evidence of incest and the casual attitude to it from her East End workmates in the 1880s: 'The fact that some of my workmates – young girls, who were in no way mentally defective, who were, on the contrary, just as keen-witted and generous-hearted as my own circle of friends – could chaff each other about having babies by their fathers and brothers, was a gruesome example of the effect of debased social environment on personal character and family life. . . . The violation of little children was another not infrequent result.' The National Society for the Prevention of Cruelty to Children, founded in 1883, was within a few years investigating over 10,000 complaints a year. Brutal treatment of children had, of course, existed for a long time before this, and it had long been known about and thought of as cruel and not simply as perfectly legitimate, if extreme, exercise of parental authority. But such was the sanctity of the home that it took a long time for the public social conscience to nerve itself to intervene in the privacy of family life, at first through the voluntary action of the NSPCC and then through the Children's Act of 1889. These steps brought public recognition, perhaps a delayed and reluctant recognition, that cruelty to children did happen, chiefly at the hands of parents, and that it ought to be prevented. They did not establish that cruelty had been increasing down to the 1880s, any more than the fact that currently the NSPCC investigates about 50,000 cases a year proves that child cruelty has been increasing in the last hundred years.

It is understandable that outside attention to working-class family life should have concentrated on its pathological features, since suffering and hardship naturally attract sympathy and efforts to prevent those incidents that are felt to be preventable. In addition, however, the outsiders constructed a general picture of working-class family life from their observations which was starkly disapproving, because what they saw deeply offended the sense of order, authority, decency, morality, and Christianity which most of them held. And many feared that future generations of unruly barbarians who would be uncontrollable social perils were being reared in the uncontrolled heathen anarchy that seemed to masquerade as home for so many children. Even Engels, who did not look on the scene through moralistic evangelical spectacles and who in theory was in favour of as much social upheaval as possible, announced that the children of factory workers 'grow up like wild weeds', and that they 'are utterly ruined for later family life, can never feel at home in the family which they themselves found, because they have always been accustomed to isolation, and they contribute therefore to the already general undermining of the family in the working class'. From the inside, however, as far as may be judged from Victorian autobiographies and memoirs of working-class childhoods, things did not have quite this appearance.

The fundamental feature of most working-class family life was that it had to be lived at close quarters, in very little space, with everyone cheek by jowl; and that resources which were perennially barely sufficient, and quite probably precarious, had to be used carefully and without waste if there was to be any hope of living reasonably, perhaps even of surviving. These were circumstances that called for prudent housekeeping, which critics thought they frequently did not receive because of the ignorance and lack of education of the womenfolk. They were also circumstances that called for codes of family behaviour or well-understood rules of conduct, so that mother, father, and perhaps four or five children could live, eat, and sleep in maybe no more than a couple of rooms without turning the place into bedlam. Such codes were generally present, and since they are usually transmitted from generation to generation, passing strongly from mother to daughter, being no more than modified by the fashions or examples of each generational peer group, it is possible that they were very traditional. The overwhelming weight of recollections of childhood is that only in the most disreputable and slovenly families, which were generally the very worst-off where the father had only casual and irregular work, was there a lack of domestic order and a crop of unruly, badly behaved, and rough children. These might fairly be described as growing up untended, like weeds; and most other children were sternly forbidden to mingle with them.

The respectable majority were regulated and disciplined, rather than pampered or indulged; but that does not mean that they were not cherished. The rules most often recalled were those which prescribed routine household chores for the children to perform, frequently with a clear sexual division of labour. In the more rural areas it was the girls' role to help with the housework, the boys' to help in the garden or allotment; or in towns, where there were fewer outside jobs, the boys might have to fetch coals and carry water, and clean the boots, while the girls had to help with food preparation, and with the sewing and darning. But in many families brothers and sisters shared tasks like potato-peeling or floor-scrubbing. Where there was baby-minding to be done it invariably fell to an older sister; but generally the family lessons in gender roles were less insistent than those in the middle and upper classes; it was not impossible to find small working-class boys sewing on buttons. Next to the daily and weekly routine of jobs the enforcement of manners, particularly at table, bulks large in memories, no doubt because food and eating were very important. This was not a question of not eating peas off a knife, or not talking with a full mouth, but of establishing a basic feeding ritual to stop grabbing and self-helping. The pecking order of serving food by seniority, starting with father, running down the children by age, and ending with mother, was strictly observed, and nothing was to be left on the plate; many recall a stick, strap, or belt always lying on the table ready to enforce the rules. Bedtimes also were strictly controlled, maybe not so much out of concern for their children's health as for the sake of giving the parents some peace and companionship.

Children continued under this regime until at the age of twelve or thirteen they started work. Then childhood was over, they began contributing to the family income, and they were allowed more independence. The impression is that up to that age they were useful, and subordinate, members of a well-integrated family acting as an effective working household unit firmly under parental command. Whether the authority was essentially paternal or maternal is ambiguous; father wielded the strap, but most of the rules emanated from mother. Some children may have been treated as little more than cogs in the household machine, escaping when their chores were done to play in the streets. The most respectable mothers tried to prevent their children playing out of doors, because of the danger of mixing with ruffians and of tearing their clothes. The street life of children, however, was rarely violent or criminal in the way that many middle-class observers supposed, but on the contrary was regulated by the rituals of games passed on from generation to generation, some of them universal like football with a pig's bladder, or five stones, some of them distinctly local like the 'knurr and spell' of northern mining villages, a kind of incipient rounders played with a pick-shaft, or Bolton's 'blind horse and skenning driver' in which a blindfolded boy was driven like a horse through the streets and tied up to a strange front door. Skipping and rhyming games were regarded as mainly for girls, but many games were mixed; it was remarked that boys and girls played together much more in Yorkshire than they did in London. The important point, however, is that street games followed rules and conventions devised by the accumulated traditions of children themselves, and that in general they represented no defiance of parental or civil authority – although police-baiting sometimes became irresistible if a policeman took to disturbing street or alley football.

Play of their own devising and with others of their own age group was not the only form of relaxation in a working-class childhood. Parents may have had little time or energy left over from work and housework, but there are many accounts of fathers making playthings out of odds and ends, or of mothers reading to their children, usually from 'good' and improving books. Sundays, above all, seem quite typically to have been family days when even if the family did not go to church or chapel it would sally forth as a group on an outing to the park, to visit relations, or for a walk in the country. While few accounts mention much kissing or cuddling, and while it may be true that there was generally little open demonstration of warmth and tenderness between parents and children – although plenty between siblings – parents certainly showed solicitude for their children's well-being. The typical concern for appearances, clean face and hands and clean clothes, may have had more to do with maintaining status and not losing face in front of neighbours or strangers than with loving and caring. Concern and anxiety over children's health, however, was genuine enough, even if such things as making a child with 'thrush' (which was probably diphtheria) swallow a live frog seem a trifle quaint; since the medical profession itself did not know any better, it was arguably worth a try. Doctors could rarely be afforded, dispensaries were heavily used where available, and the local druggist could usually oblige with a powder for every illness. Failing these, folk remedies were widely used, some of them traditional like the frogs or the equally unpleasant prescription of eating live snails to ward off tuberculosis, or the possibly more comforting practice of rubbing a cut on a horse; some of them were conjured out of the urban setting, like the belief that a whiff of the air from the local gasworks would cure whooping cough. Most folk medicine was useless, even harmful, superstition, although where herbal remedies were used they could well have been effective. Useless or not, the caring intention behind their administration is apparent. When Edwardian society was shocked by the revelation of the appalling number of Boer War recruits rejected on grounds of physical unfitness, reaching up to 40 per cent of the volunteers from large industrial towns, this was rightly taken to be a reflection of childhood ill-health and stunted, rickety development. That, however, was a consequence of malnutrition, insanitary conditions, and low wages, not of parental neglect or indifference.

No simple generalizations about working-class childhood are likely to be correct. Quite apart from questions of regional differences and of differences between the several strata of the working classes, which cannot be dealt with adequately in a summary account, it is apparent that the available recollections of Victorian childhoods are by definition those of people who survived the experience. Those who never reached adulthood remain silent. Likewise the children brought up in the disreputable families do not speak for themselves in the records, since the recorded memories are always of those conscious of their respectability and proud of their superiority, in status, morality, and behaviour but not necessarily in wealth, over the roughs. Disreputable families doubtless bred children in conditions of squalor, misery, and drunkenness, and were unfeeling and uncaring: such families were numerous, possibly corresponding to the 'submerged tenth' that late Victorian social investigators identified as the dregs of society, possibly a larger fraction. They were definitely less numerous, however, than the third of the working classes found by the poverty surveys of Booth and Rowntree to be below the poverty line towards the end of the century. Partly this was because later surveys quickly showed that the poverty proportion of London and York, the two towns of the pioneer work, was not necessarily representative of all other British towns; and partly because the one-third in any case included elderly families, with no children at home any longer, and families suffering 'life cycle' poverty through having many young children below working age, who might nonetheless be struggling to maintain a respectable, if underfed, existence. It is, of course, true that disreputability was not a simple function of poverty, and that families with incomes well above the poverty line could live in strange, disorderly, and irregular ways which their neighbours found disreputable. All the same, it is reasonable to suppose that the accounts from respectable sources are representative of the great majority of working-class childhoods.

The picture which emerges is one of an orderly childhood, frequently marked by severe treatment and austere conditions, but providing the security of familiar and certain routines and responses which was lacking with parents who veered erratically and irrationally between blind rages and extravagant indulgence. Much of the time of childhood was spent in household chores, but there was time also for play and pleasure, much of it found outside the home. Indeed, a working-class child was more likely than a child higher in the social scale to learn about cooperation, tolerance, and sympathetic understanding of others within the family, and about relationships with others in the local peer group outside the family; but probably less was learnt about love. Parents were not generally remembered as affectionate, but they did on the whole appear to have been striving to do their best for their children, within the means available, and they showed concern to bring up their children in ways of behaviour, manners, and speech that were thought proper and which imparted a sense of right and wrong. Some remembered their childhood with distaste or loathing, as a miserably unpleasant time, painful, joyless and associated with poor food, nasty stinks, and endless dirt. Most, however, recalled it as a happy time, and with the wont of hindsight made a virtue of the humdrum and poor quality of their everyday life to accentuate the pleasures of the occasional high-days and holidays.

One difficulty is that this kind of impression of Victorian childhood gives little sense of any change over time, although when one memoir speaks of being told that tolling bells signified the death of George III, and another recalls the street decorations of Victoria's Diamond Jubilee, there is at least an assurance of time passing. The only change in upbringing that can be discerned with any confidence is a trend towards less frequent and less harsh use of beating, strappings, and beltings over the course of the century, and the partial substitution of verbal correction and non-corporal punishments. This was a trend shared by all classes, and which took the lead it is hard to tell: it is not irrelevant that it was the highly respectable clergyman, Francis Kilvert, who remarked in 1875 on seeing a girl's bare bottom that it was 'in excellent whipping condition'. This may indeed have been the only significant change that did occur, apart, that is, from changes in physical conditions and surroundings. But it is true that descriptions of working-class childhoods are not spread evenly over time, and tend to concentrate on memories of the 1880s and 1890s. It is therefore possible that the predominant regime of child-rearing that has been described was not unchanging or only very slowly changing, but was the product of important developments over the previous half-century or so. The strength of the family mechanisms passing habits and values from generation to generation argues against rapid or radical changes. On the other hand, the values and codes of behaviour which operated within families were in several respects, in their emphasis on orderliness and cleanliness, for example, not far removed from the values and codes of conduct that middle-class social reformers and educationalists were trying to implant through schools. School, after all, figured as a prominent, compulsory part of childhood for all children by the 1890s, and it had not done so in the 1830s. It is thus possible that what the childhood memories of the late Victorian years were recording was the at least partial triumph of the efforts at indoctrination and socialization which were at the centre of Victorian elementary education.

Compulsory schooling to the age of ten was made general in 1880, although it had been anticipated locally by various of the more progressive School Boards that chose to use optional powers contained in the 1870 Education Act under which they were established. The minimum school-leaving age was thereafter raised to eleven in 1893, and to twelve – except for children employed in agriculture – in 1899. In the last decades of the century, then, the school attendance officer, or truant officer, became a familiar figure in working-class neighbourhoods, sometimes respected since many of these visitors were themselves working-class men and women who behaved like social workers, but sometimes feared and disliked as some new arm of the law come to harry the poor. Truancy proceedings gave the impression that schooling was being thrust upon reluctant and resistant parents and children, that sanctions were being invoked to ram lessons in obedience and discipline down working-class throats. For a section of the working class that was indeed so. Some children always go reluctantly to school, maybe because they are scared or bored, find it pointless or find other things to do that are far more interesting; some children find school attractive and satisfying. These differences in attitudes may be taken as more or less constant; what was of practical importance was the attitude of parents. Victorian parental authority was such that if a child was told to go to school, it would go; the phenomenon of children playing truant without parental knowledge and consent seems to be a very modern one. The main reasons for parental refusal to send their children to school were financial. Until 1891 school had to be paid for, although here and there school managers issued free tickets to the very poorest as an act of charity, which of course carried the humiliation associated with acceptance of charity. School fees, ranging from 1d. up to 4d. a week, were in themselves a formidable burden for the poorest families, who might well have four or five children of school age, but it was the associated costs which generally loomed larger. Although there are frequent reports from the classrooms, particularly after 1870, of barefoot children in rags sitting at their desks and scratching their lousy hair, there is even more frequent evidence of parents saying they could not send their children to school because they could not afford boots or proper clothes: for the self-respecting poor it was unacceptably shameful to let their children appear in public inadequately dressed. Above all there were the opportunity costs of schooling: the poorer families were unable or unwilling to sacrifice the wages that their children could earn to add to the family income. It is true that opportunities for anything like full-time employment before the age of eleven or twelve were whittled away in the course of the century by protective legislation and by changes in economic organization, but the openings for young children to pick up a penny or two here and there remained legion. There were errands to run, goods to deliver, street-sellers who wanted young assistants, and where production still went on in the home or small workshop plenty of demand for young help. The family economy could not spare its useful and productive hands to go and sit in school.

None of this was objection to education in principle, on ideological or class-based grounds, and indeed many parents were to be found vigorously disclaiming any intention of wishing to keep their children ignorant and illiterate, pleading the sheer impossibility of letting them get an education. On the other hand there were parents, themselves uneducated, who were apathetic or positively hostile to the whole concept of education, holding it to be quite unnecessary and pointless for children who were going to have to live the same kind of wretched lives as themselves. 'Must it not be, though reluctantly, allowed that they have only too much reason for their apathy?' Horace Mann observed when commenting on the schools census of 1851. ' "Of what avail" – they may, not unreasonably, ask – "can education be to those who must, of sad necessity, reside in these impure and miserable homes, from which, if it were possible, ourselves would be the first to flee?" . . . Such, really if not in words, are the much-too-reasonable questions by which parents, of the humbler ranks, excuse their inattention to their children's education.' Besides this group from among the poorest and most disreputable families, there was a smaller group from the educated and self-respecting working classes that was highly critical of the particular kind of schooling on offer, because its contents were not sufficiently practical, because of its all-pervading religious-moral tone, or because of the objectionable social attitudes of subservience it aimed to inculcate. Such feelings, however, led more often to bottled-up resentment than to refusal to send children to school, although they could lead parents in the better paid ranks of skilled workers to opt out of the 'public' schools of the elementary network, voluntary society or Board schools, and send their children to some local, private, fee-paying school.

It was generally held that the skilled workers were the core of the intelligent and educated working class, who fully appreciated the value of a formal education and took great pains to see that their children attended school. An education was a passport to respectability and a necessary ticket for entry to many trades; many fathers would pay an extra penny or so a week so that a son could be taught some additional subject like drawing, and thus get a flying start in following in father's footsteps as a skilled carpenter, shipwright, or engineer. This group was well accustomed to regarding schooling for their children as normal, well before it became compulsory and well before the 1870 Education Act. That Act, indeed, should be regarded as starting a process of drawing or driving into the schools children from the homes which had hitherto neglected or rejected education. The prospect of swarms of ragged, smelly, foul-mouthed pauper children arriving to dilute the existing school population of respectables, 'raked in from the gutter, the dunghill, and the hedgerow', as it was put, was thought likely to antagonize artisan parents and their clean and tidy children. The solution devised by the London School Board was to develop a system of differential weekly fees corresponding to different social grades of school, so that the parents willing to pay the higher rates could escape 'the unhappy children picked up in the gutter whom no respectable working man would like to see sitting on the same bench with his children, with all the dirt, moral and physical, belonging to them'.

The great unwashed had been, before the 1880s and 1890s, the great uneducated. They were one part of the great divide to which Robert Applegarth, the secretary of the skilled carpenters' union, referred when speaking about educational policy in 1869. 'No one knows better than the men themselves that there are amongst the working people two classes. There is the careless and indifferent man, who has been so long neglected and degraded that he does not understand the value of education; and him the other class, the better class of working men, have to carry on their backs. Those men who do not understand the value of education must be made to understand it.' In the next thirty years or so they were made to understand it, so that by the early twentieth century truant officers were dealing with individual problem families rather than with entire social subgroups trying to contract out of school. Those who already did understand the value of education, before 1870, were however considerably more numerous than just the body of skilled workers, although they clearly included them. There are as many pitfalls in educational statistics, where many took the school age group as unrealistically including all the three- to fifteen-year-olds and where there were yawning gaps between numbers of children on school registers, numbers actually attending school at any one time, and numbers who clocked up a regular attendance for several years continuously, as there are in occupational statistics that attempt to distinguish between skilled and unskilled. Neverthe-less, contemporaries generally thought of the skilled workers, the elite of the working classes, as forming something like 10 to 15 per cent of the workforce. By 1870 it is generally agreed that somewhere between two thirds and three quarters of the school-age children were at school. The Newcastle Commissioners, indeed, enquiring into the state of popular education, complacently satisfied themselves that 'the name of almost every child is at some time or other on the books of some school at which it attends with more or less regularity' already by 1861. Their arithmetic was wildly optimistic, and faulty; but even pessimists acknowledged that about half the children in the country were being educated in schools of a character that they found acceptable. With a more relaxed definition of 'school' to include establishments, maybe unsavoury and ramshackle but also maybe quite clean and respectable, that did not focus on religious and moral teaching, and with a rising proportion of school-attenders, the comparatively large school population of 1870 is readily intelligible.

The conclusion is inescapable that the school-going habit had become deeply rooted in the working classes and spread far beyond the upper crust of the labour aristocracy. It is difficult to categorize these school-conscious parents who so clearly outnumbered the easily identified artisans. Outside the textile districts, particularly the cotton towns, where there was an element of compulsion stemming from the 1833 Factory Act that had institutionalized the half-timers who spent half their day in the mill and half at school, these parents voluntarily chose schooling for their children and chose to pay for it. Income obviously had something to do with it, and the better paid workers – miners, metalworkers, or railwaymen, for example, who were not usually reckoned to be labour aristocrats – were commonly found in the schooling camp. Regularity of employment was important in shouldering a commitment to weekly schoolpence, and a railway porter with a lowly grade and wage but a secure job might be in the schooling class, while a docker with higher overall earnings in the year but violent week-to-week fluctuations from the casual nature of his work might not dream of sending his children to school. Attitudes towards children, aspirations for them, and aspirations for respectability were strongly influenced by financial and occupational circumstances, but not wholly determined by them; influences from kin and from neighbourhood, from church or chapel, could cut across them. Parents who cared for the education of their children did not so much form a distinct economic or occupational group within the working classes as a socio-religious group: the section imbued with self-respect and dedicated to respectability. They were the parents determined that their children should not 'associate with the lowest children of the town, whose habits and language are sometimes filthy, and whose bodies are almost always dirty and often diseased'.

The school-going habit had been actively fostered and encouraged by middle-class moralists and reformers since the later eighteenth century in educational missionary efforts intended to civilize the rude populace. It is possible that the depth of penetration of the habit among the working classes in the next seventy or eighty years measured the success of such crusades in conquering the greater part of the people for Christ and for social obedience. It is also possible that it represented the success of the working classes in exploiting for their own ends whatever facilities were on offer. The Sunday school movement made the earliest impression, and one which lasted well into the twentieth century, beyond the point when religious commitment had begun to decline. Initiated in the 1790s by middle-class and gentry evangelicals 'to train the lower classes in habits of industry and piety' and to lead them through biblical teaching to feel respect for their betters and humble acceptance of their station in society, at a time when fears of social and political disorder fanned by ignorant espousal of subversive radical ideas were rife, the Sunday schools spread and multiplied beyond the rosiest expectations of their founders. By 1833 the Sunday schools were claiming 1.5 million pupils and by 1851 almost 2.5 million, a figure that represented roughly two thirds of the five to fourteen age group; their popularity continued to increase, as church attendance itself declined, to reach a peak of over 6 million pupils in 1906, well over 80 per cent of the age group. In other words it was exceptional for the late Victorian child, of whatever social class, not to go to Sunday school. The children went not because they were driven by the moral persuasion or coercion of their social superiors, although the local parson or minister, the millowner or in country areas the squire, might exert considerable persuasive force; they went chiefly because their parents wished it. Parents wished it because Sunday schools were to a large extent transformed in their first thirty to forty years from being instruments of middle-class evangelicalism for imposing bible-based values on the working classes, to being vehicles of a domesticated, internalized, working-class evangelicalism for teaching a mixture of religious beliefs and more practical lessons. Hannah More, the most zealous of the movement's founders, was early on dismayed by developments: 'In many schools, I am assured, writing and accounts are taught on Sundays. This is a regular apprenticeship to sin. He who is taught arithmetic on a Sunday when a boy, will, when a man, open his shop on a Sunday.' Probably only a few Sunday schools ever taught arithmetic; but very many came to be looked upon as a source of basic literacy. The vicar's daughter was not, perhaps, altogether superseded by the teenage millgirl as the archetypal Sunday school teacher; but especially in the nonconformist Sunday schools there was a considerable working-class takeover of control. Generations of working-class children learnt the values of orderliness, punctuality, industry, and cleanliness in the Sunday schools at the hands of teachers more homely and kindly, and more of their own kind, than most they were likely to encounter in ordinary classrooms; they also learnt bible stories, but whether thereby they acquired piety is more debatable. These values were the same as those instilled in the respectable working-class home, with the added authority of the church or chapel setting. They reinforced each other, as mutually supporting strands in the working-class culture into which the Sunday schools had been incorporated.

Day schools were far less suited for absorption into the body of working-class culture, and even drew further apart from it as the century wore on and they became more standardized, more formally organized, and more subject to bureaucratic control. The parish school of the 1830s was likely to be small, familiar, and accessible even if dirty and inefficient; the Board school of the 1880s was large, remote, and forbidding though clean and efficient. The earlier schools were often under the eye of a local patron, whom it would be impolitic to offend, while the later ones, living on the rates, could not rely on local notables to act as recruiting sergeants. Differences in methods of school provision, in types of control, even in religious denomination, seemed to make little difference to the propensity of parents to consume education. Viewed through the working-class end of the telescope, all the battles over popular, or elementary, education between Anglicans, Dissenters, and Catholics, between voluntarists and state providers, between the supporters of religious and of secular systems, which punctuated the entire Victorian period, were remote struggles over issues that scarcely concerned them, waged amongst themselves by middle- and upper-class partisans with incomprehensible heat and passion. From time to time the conflicts produced some concrete result, which one way or another generally meant more public money for schools; parents happily took advantage of such results without bothering about their origins.

Parents wanted several things from education, and they could get them either from the informal and commercial sector, or from the formal and 'public' sector of schools approved and run by 'authority'; or rather the choice was there until by the 1890s the greatly enlarged public sector finally extinguished the private sector or pushed it firmly upstairs into the middle-class world. Parents wanted child-minding, to get their youngest children out from under their feet and out of the home; they wanted teaching of manners and behaviour in support of home discipline; they wanted practical preparation for early employment; they wanted their children to acquire some knowledge and learning as an accomplishment that might not be directly marketable; and some genuinely wanted their children to be brought up in Christian principles. Many of the private-sector institutions which figured in the surveys of the 1830s and 1840s as 'schools' were in fact child-minding establishments, dame schools looking after toddlers and three- to five-year-olds in conditions of varying insalubrity. They were frequently dismissed as providing no education, and ridiculed or condemned as the last refuge of ignorant old women who could no longer work and who squeezed a few shillings out of hectoring and maltreating the children of young mothers. The Dickensian dame school undoubtedly existed; but not all were noisome and evil places. 'The physical condition of the Dame Schools of Birmingham is much more satisfactory than could have been anticipated,' the Birmingham Statistical Society reported in 1838. 'None of them are kept in cellars, very few in garrets or bedrooms, and they are generally more cleanly and better lighted than schools of the same description in Manchester and Liverpool.' There was, moreover, nothing intrinsically wrong or objectionable about dame schools where parents enjoined that their children 'are not to be worried with learning'. Their prime function, no doubt, was economic, to release mothers for work or for concentrating their attention on educating older children in the home, perhaps with on-job training in the family trade. But they also had a social and socializing function, in accustoming the very young to mixing with their own age group and to acceptable forms of group behaviour. Prized in the twentieth century as nursery schooling, there is no call to dismiss as valueless this form of education and learning without systematic instruction by qualified teachers in the Victorian dame schools.

Some of the approved day schools in the public sector also, unofficially, provided child-minding services, sometimes admitting a three-year-old who had an older brother or sister in the school although their purpose was to educate children from five to twelve, or beyond. These were the schools which occupied the centre of the stage in public discussions of education, and which have been at the centre of educational histories. They were the schools provided for the working classes by their social superiors, for non-profit-making motives, which might be religious, chari-table, social, or political; in the main they were provided and controlled either by the Church of England National Society for Promoting the Education of the Poor, established in 1811, or the slightly earlier British and Foreign School Society of 1808 whose anti-establishment and Dissenting stance was seen as a threat to the Anglican position. These societies raised their funds from sub-scriptions by their respective congregations, and hence their schools were known as the voluntary schools. They did not, however, offer free schooling. Parents had to pay schoolpence, partly from the necessity of some fee-income to cover the costs, and partly because it was considered good in itself that parents should learn the value of education by paying something towards its cost. What was offered was a subsidized education, the societies' funds meeting a large part of the costs of premises, salaries, and equipment. This gave the societies, through their central organizations and through their local school committees, their essential powers over the appointment of teachers and control over what was taught in their schools. That control was diluted from 1833 when the government began making a small annual grant to the voluntary schools, which was followed up in 1839 by the appointment of the first inspectors, to keep some check on how the public money was being spent. It was more drastically curtailed by the Revised Code of 1862 which introduced payment by results as a device for ensuring that the annual grant, grown from £30,000 to around £1 million, should be spent efficiently and effectively, for the financial necessity of qualifying for grants by getting their pupils to pass the examinations for the several standards obliged the schools to tailor their curricula accordingly. Nevertheless, the school managers remained in command, running their schools in the ways they chose so long as the end-products were reasonably satisfying to the Education Department and its inspectors.

Those ways were founded in religious convictions and belief in the necessity of providing a godly and religious upbringing for the children of the working classes. Religious instruction was central to the voluntary schools, doctrinal and catechismal in the National schools, more neutral scriptural teaching in the British schools; and the school day was likely to have a religious rhythm of prayers and hymns. Some, particularly the evangelicals, regarded this as an end in itself. But to many who supported the voluntary societies, the godly and religious upbringing was a means to an end: the end was the preservation of the social order, the protection of property, and the prevention of disturbance or insurrection. This was to be attained through a right-minded and properly conducted education of the children of the poor, who would thus be civilized – or conditioned – into becoming law-abiding, unprotesting adults. Kay-Shuttleworth, the leading educational civil servant of the 1830s and 1840s, held that the answer to threats to property from rick-burning agricultural labourers, and to industry and political institutions from trade unionists and Chartists, was to provide 'a good secular education to enable them to understand the true causes which determine their physical condition and regulate the distribution of wealth among the several classes of society'. Despite his emphasis on secular education which would impart the basic principles of political economy, he too was convinced that religious instruction was the essential foundation on which this desirable superstructure might be built. The atmosphere of acute social unrest and crisis of the 1830s and 1840s passed, and with it the arguments for emergency action on the educational front to hold the social fabric together; but the idea persisted that the purpose of educating the children of the working classes was to fit them for their proper place in society. Only eccentrics thought that education had something to do with developing the talents and capabilities of individual children, or with enhancing the quality of the human resources of society.

It was not surprising that the ruling classes should think of the school as an instrument for conditioning and controlling the lower orders. That was precisely how the upper and upper middle classes viewed their own public schools: they were instruments for conditioning their boys into becoming upright, manly characters who did not cheat, sneak, or whine, and who could lead without being needlessly cruel to animals or servants. That was largely successful, and the public-school type was pretty easily recognizable by speech, manner, dress, and behaviour: if he had not been, Victorian mothers with marriageable daughters would have been in trouble. It was, however, an internal arrangement within the class, a matter of an older generation imposing upon and moulding the younger in the cause of the self-perpetuation of class identity, a process of socialization by equals (or inferiors: public-school masters were often of lower social status than their pupils). It would be much more surprising if the efforts to condition the children of the lower orders had been equally successful. No readily recognizable voluntary-school type emerged, and that was not only because of the great diversity and lack of uniformity amongst the schools in standards and efficiency, but also because their influence was not powerful enough to counter the influences of home, neighbourhood, region, and occupation, and in the end could only work with the grain and not against it.

The will to control was present; the theory was available, that a suitable education could forge a governable people out of the dangerous mass of masterless men cut adrift from their traditional moorings in the apparent confusion of the new industrial and urban society; the means were created in the physical and institutional structure of the voluntary schools; but the sanctions were too weak to make the means enforce the will. Until after 1880 there was no direct compulsion on the working classes to get themselves educated and no way in which their children could be forced by law to attend specified types of suitable schools. There were external social pressures from local squires and clergy, which could be strong and hard to resist without incurring damaging displeasure, but they varied in intensity between parishes and regions, and between country and town. There were internal economic and moral pressures on parents who realized that some formal education was vital for their children's future job, or simply a necessary part of their upbringing, and who were forced to find that education in the nearest school available. These, however, were puny sanctions for enabling the voluntary schools to capture unwilling children or unwilling parents. Indeed, they never did succeed in capturing the children of the poorest and most disreputable families, which were thought of as nests of misery, vice, viciousness, and criminality, and which were most in need of being rendered governable. Those were the children who were only beginning to be brought within the educational network in the 1880s.

Parents who did bring their children within the network quite typically had some choice of school, at least within the larger towns; in the country it was likely that a single village school had a local monopoly. The number of voluntary schools expanded rapidly from the 1840s, when they were teaching perhaps a quarter of a million children, so that by 1860 they had nearly 1.5 million on their rolls and a normal attendance of about 900,000. Even so, it was reckoned that they accounted for only half or a little more than half of all the children who were at school. There were then just under 7000 schools run by the religious societies and in receipt of government grants, the assisted schools. No one knew quite how many unassisted schools there were, but they were thought to outnumber the assisted, perhaps by two to one. Some of the unassisted were managed by the religious societies but for one reason or another had not applied for grant aid, and some were run by the Church of England but were not under the National Society: these might provide the same quality of education as the voluntary schools, in inferior accommodation. A large proportion of the unassisted schools, however, were small private ventures linked to no religious body and run as a way of making a living. They, like the dame schools, were consistently condemned for providing no education worthy of the name; but their great fault was the absence of a religious basis, and because they were therefore held incapable of providing a godly and religious upbringing they were dismissed as unsuitable. They survived only by securing, and therefore earning, the continued patronage of parents, mainly working-class parents. They wanted value for money, and there is every sign that value meant efficiency in teaching a working knowledge of reading, writing, and arithmetic, and perhaps of the elements of religion and of the principles of good conduct. 'They prefer', the Newcastle Commissioners asserted, 'paying a comparatively high fee to an efficient school to paying a low fee to an inefficient one. . . . There can be little doubt that a school which combined high fees with a reputation for inefficiency would soon lose its pupils.' Many of the unassisted schools demonstrated by their ability to survive that they were deemed by their customers to be giving a satisfactory service.

It was reported from the north-eastern coalfield, in 1860, that 'time for school attendance is spared only with a view to its being preparation for work. Parents have no idea that there is any advantage in children spending so many years at school if the same amount of learning can be acquired in a shorter time. In short, they regard schooling, not as a course of discipline, but only as a means of acquiring reading, writing, arithmetic, sewing, and knitting, as a preparation for the main business of life – earning a living.' From the south-west came the view that parents' 'measure of the efficiency of a school is generally a very simple one – the rapidity with which children learn to write well' – and from East Anglia the report that parents were 'perfectly content with moderate skill in writing, and arithmetic, veto superfluous grammar, geography, history, and all that kind of thing'. Parents were demanding much the same things as parents were demanding in Scotland with its vastly different system of traditional (sixteenth-century) parochial schools but fast-growing numbers of private venture schools, from which literacy and numeracy could be acquired at different grades for different fees, uncluttered by the grammar, Latin, and religion of the parochial schools. 'In Scotland they sell education like a grocer sells figs,' Robert Lowe remarked; a remark to make educationalists wince, but a sensible way of meeting the basic demands of the customers.

When these demands could be satisfied by unregulated, commercial establishments there was little chance that the voluntary schools could flourish unless they provided an equally good, or superior, service; and little chance that they could impose an unwanted conditioning regime as part of their price for providing secular learning. Working-class parents were not so dependent on the religious societies to supply schools as the voluntary schools were dependent on working-class parents to supply pupils. The religious societies were in any case excited by their religious rivalry, and their schools soon acquired the kind of autonomous institutional life in which the object was to continue to survive as schools, and not necessarily as instruments of social control. Survival meant attracting and retaining an adequate number of children on their books, a matter of increasing financial necessity as the route to government capitation grants. There are signs that from the early 1850s, under the pressure to keep up their numbers and to meet the competition, the voluntary schools were increasingly sensitive to parental demands and were making their instruction more secular and practical, while reducing the religious and moral element, so that reading primers moved away from their bible base to words and situations closer to everyday experience. The Revised Code of 1862, which made a school's capitation grant dependent on the number of children who passed graded examinations in reading, writing, and arithmetic, and no longer merely on the number who turned up to be counted on the annual inspection day, gave the voluntary schools a massive push towards secularization, albeit on a narrow front. There were complaints at the time, and harsh criticisms since, that the Code was a mean straitjacket that squeezed out the teaching of all other subjects because no grant payments attached to them, so that history and geography withered away in a philistine desert of the three Rs. At the time the grumbles came from school managers fearful of the prospect of losing grant income, and from teachers worried that they were not competent to get their pupils through the examinations. Parents, however, were well content that the schools should be forced to concentrate their resources on doing an efficient job on really useful literacy. Paradoxically the state used its financial power, from narrow motives of economy and elimination of waste and inefficiency in public expenditure, to promote the interests of working-class parents in obtaining directly useful knowledge for their children, and to weaken the capacity of the voluntary schools to imprint their brand of godly and religious instruction on the minds and souls of their charges. This set the pattern for the self-denying role of government later in the century, when a national system of elementary education was cobbled together after 1870 with the Board schools plugging the gaps in the coverage achieved by the voluntary schools. The state certainly used its power to confirm and preserve the existing social structure with schools suited to its social divisions; but on the whole it did not use its power to attempt any social, religious, or ideological manipulation within the schools.

In all the circumstances the voluntary schools could never succeed in fulfilling the intentions of the founding fathers, to use their particular regimen as a means of producing docile, god-fearing adults. The likelihood of success was scarcely increased by the fact that the schoolchild of the mid-Victorian years spent no more than four years in school on average, and those might well be discontinuous; while attendance was more often irregular and interrupted than it was assiduous. These were short periods in which to get at the minds of the young with indoctrination that was supposed to last for life. None of this is to say that conditions in the schools were pleasant or that teaching methods were congenial: they were not. At best school buildings were gaunt, chapel-like structures, furniture was minimal and uncomfortable, and facilities rudimentary: often a bucket was the only sanitation provided. Children learnt by rote, chanting in unison. Discipline was severe, backed by the cane. Pupil-teachers, risen from the ranks of the schoolchildren by brightness or teacher's favouritism and hoping by exemplary performance to earn their passage to training college and qualifications, were only too likely to use their transient authority with more petty harshness than did the schoolteachers themselves. A kindly teacher, who allowed children to dry wet clothes round a stove after a long rainy walk to school, or brewed a hot midday drink of watery cocoa, was long remembered. Boys and girls over the age of five were strictly segregated, using separate entrances, separate schoolrooms, and separate playgrounds if they were lucky enough to have any at all. The schools gave clear lessons in the different gender roles, mirroring the sexual division of labour in society. Mensuration and plain drawing were for boys, relevant it was hoped to future jobs; needlework was for girls, a compulsory subject from the 1870s, and cookery lessons, strangely remote and unrelated to their ordinary life – rock cakes and sausage rolls – were introduced for older girls from the 1890s.

At least it was expected, from the earliest days of the voluntary schools, that girls as well as boys were to be educated. This was more than could be said for the other classes, where the custom of sending their girls to school did not begin to spread until the second half of the century. Before that, if a girl came from a family below the governess-keeping level her education was likely to be badly neglected; for voluntary schools, and later Board schools, were considered suitable only for working-class children, and possibly for shopkeepers' daughters. Patrons and subscribers to voluntary schools regarded them as nurseries for good domestic servants, and that was what many of the girls became. Sometimes their school training was a direct anticipation of domestic service, a form of unpaid putting-out work. Of one school, largely maintained by a 'bountiful earl', an inspector stated that 'the schoolroom had become the workroom of the Castle. There was a liberal display of household articles, and while the third class had sufficed to seam and hem them, it had been found necessary to employ the first class to mark them with coronets.' This was little different from the roundly condemned straw-plaiting schools of Bedfordshire and Hertfordshire, or the lace-making schools of Devon, where children, mainly girls, were employed in the simple stages of commercial production while allegedly receiving scholastic instruction as well as craft training.

It was unlikely that anyone looking back on all this would recall school as a pleasant or happy experience. Nonetheless, there was little about school conditions or methods, apart from the physical segregation of the sexes, that conflicted with the treatment which children expected at home or with the attitudes which non-school experience led them to accept as normal. Discipline, adult authority, corporal punishment, discomfort, different gender roles, all these were familiar inside the home. It does not follow from this that school had no influence and contributed nothing that could not as well have been acquired inside the family. Parents who had previously educated their own children, not from books but through the experience of family living and family work, looked on schools as institutionalizing one of their parental functions. Schools acted as parental substitutes, and may well have contributed more positively to the character of this socialization process by adding to accepted codes of behaviour concepts of cleanliness, obedience, or politeness more developed and more precise than those current in the home, just as they imparted higher levels of literacy and general knowledge than most parents could dispense. School was a significant part of growing up, and an important influence on a child's ideas about the world and how to behave in it. But it was only one strand among many, and for the working-class child with only a short time in school that was likely to end by the age of twelve, it was not the dominant or decisive element; the home and the neighbourhood, and later on the workplace and the pub, had superior influence in shaping the outlook of working-class youths and young adults. The Home Secretary, Sir James Graham, had proclaimed with a flourish when introducing the (abortive) education clauses of his 1843 Factory Bill, at a time when Chartist disturbances were much in mind: 'The police and the soldiers have done their duty, the time is arrived when moral and religious instructors must go forth to reclaim the people from the errors of their ways.' The schoolmaster as policeman did not work. Samuel Smiles, writing in the same year, was close to the mark when he declared that the home was 'the most influential school of civilization', and asserted that 'one good mother' was 'worth a hundred schoolmasters'.

CHAPTER FIVE

Homes and Houses

Home had more influence than school in the childhood experience of the working classes, and although work may have been more important than either in the passage from youth to adulthood, homemaking reoccupied the centre of life upon marriage. It was odd that the Victorian middle classes, who were chiefly responsible for elevating the cult of the home practically into a religious institution, showed apparent lack of confidence in its moral influence by taking pains to send their children away to boarding school for as long as possible. Schools, however, were considered a better training ground for character than the domesticity of home: they were a preparation for the outside world of careers and business whereas the home was designed as a retreat from it. At the same time, homes were very much part of the outside world as affirmations of status. A prime purpose of the home might be to make family life as private as lace curtains or a privet hedge could make it; but an equally important purpose was for its size, appearance, style, and location to be plainly visible as a statement of the owner's precise place in the social hierarchy. The Victorian middle classes were the most home-centred group in British history; but they were easily surpassed as the most house-conscious group by the landed aristocracy, for whom the country house was not only the essential emblem of status but also the grand theatre in which rituals of display and hospitality were enacted. So important were country houses to social and political position, indeed, that membership of the ruling class can be measured through ownership of country houses of specified size. The same principle can be applied through all the layers of society, grading people through the size of house occupied. House structure, therefore, can be seen as a form of social structure; and the home, the type of life lived in the house, can be seen as the means by which the structure was translated into different types of social behaviour.

The enormous country houses with hundreds of rooms and the single-room cellar dwellings lay at the extremes of this structure. The very wealthy could manipulate their environment to suit their personal needs and tastes; the very poor could only accept whatever environment happened to be available and somehow make their life fit into it. Between these two poles lay a complicated territory of different housing types and living conditions, a series of stepping stones that became more elaborate in reflecting the increasingly fine and intricate social distinctions within Victorian society. Social mobility was a matter of individuals or families stepping from one stone to another; social change a matter of altering, enlarging, and regrouping the stones.

The landed aristocracy and gentry, with country houses set in their grounds and parks and supported by the income from the tenanted farms of sizeable estates, were the traditional and firmly established upper class. They were so firmly established that they remained socially paramount until the First World War, their social leadership slightly diluted but not seriously challenged, and politically dominant until a gradual rather than precipitate decline set in from the 1880s. The old order remained, therefore, the top layer of Victorian society, even while all the time a new order was being shaped by the forces of urbanization and industrialization. Many factors conspired to produce this result, economic, political, and cultural, as well as social. Many of the established landed elite not only prospered through the effects of general economic expansion on their estates, which generated buoyant incomes and capital appreciation that were welcome financial sustenance in keeping up their position, but also themselves formed part of the leading edge of economic development by undertaking or encouraging the building of docks, harbours, railways, mines, or housing estates. They did not, therefore, present a blankly hostile or alien face to the capitalist entrepreneurs, even if no member of the aristocracy would have cared to be classed as a businessman. Moreover, while the rules under which the political game was played both in Parliament and in county government left the landed interest with dominant influence, and the habits of accepting landed leadership long outlasted the radical alterations in the rules by the third Reform Act of 1884–5 and the 1888 County Councils Act, the landed elite did not exercise its power in a narrowly self-interested way but took broad account of the needs and wishes of the middle classes, and from time to time of the working classes. This in turn was linked to moral and intellectual influences, from evangelicalism and from political economy, that impressed some of the aristocracy and gave them common ground with some of the middle classes; and with the cultural influence of the public schools, especially by the later nineteenth century, diffusing gentlemanly and public-service ideals among the upper middle class. Socially, however, the country house itself was a prime agent in the preservation of the old order, both as a vehicle used by the landed class to demonstrate that it was keeping abreast of the times and not being ossified into irrelevance, and as a prize which a section of the new wealthy were anxious to acquire or to imitate.

There were less than 5000 landed families in Britain in the 1870s listed in the social registers of the *Peerage and Baronetage* and the *Landed Gentry*; and of those about 1500 families owned estates of 3000 acres and more, ranging upwards to the giant estates, largely moor and mountain, of nearly half a million acres for the Duke of Buccleuch and 1.4 million acres for the Duke of Sutherland. All the families which claimed gentry or aristocratic status doubtless claimed that their residences were country houses, but in reality many of them were small manor houses or were not easily distinguishable from large farmhouses, and lacked the presence usually expected of a country house. On the other hand, many of the magnates owned several large houses, accumulated through centuries of inheritance and marriage, or built to gratify an ambition. Given the subjective nature of any definition of what was and what was not a country house, all that can be said is that the standing stock of country houses in 1830 was more than 1500 but less than 5000, and a reasonable guess is that there were roughly 3000. The great majority of these came through the Victorian period substantially unaltered and unscathed, furnishing the apparent profusion of Tudor, Jacobean, and eighteenth-century houses that are today's tourist attractions. It is misleading to claim, however, as has been done recently, that 'the Victorian building boom is something of a myth'. In fact some 500 country houses were either built or substantially remodelled between 1835 and 1889. Roughly half this activity was on behalf of new families, who were either first or second generation on their landed estate. Major building works were, therefore, undertaken on about 250 country houses that already existed in 1830 and were owned by old-established families; this was quite a large enough proportion for the effects not to be overlooked by contemporaries.

Some of this work was on a spectacular scale. The Duke of Sutherland virtually rebuilt Cliveden House, Dunrobin Castle, and Trentham Hall, giving Sir Charles Barry a handsome run of commissions. But he was outbuilt by the Marquess of Bute who lavished the coal royalties of his Glamorgan estate on Cardiff Castle, Castell Coch, Falkland Palace, Dumfries House, and Mount Stuart, along with many other less costly projects. More restrained were those who limited themselves to the complete remodelling simply of their principal seat: the Marquess of Westminster at Eaton Hall, or the Duke of Northumberland at Alnwick Castle. Enormously expensive projects like these, carrying price tickets of maybe £400,000 upwards, indulged personal tastes for conspicuous display and grandeur, demonstrated the modernity of the builder as patron of architects, artists, and craftsmen, and served to leapfrog the new halls and castles over the slightly older generations of large halls and castles in the more or less friendly rivalry and competition for primacy within the peer group. They also served to outpace older mansions through incorporating the latest notions of comfort and convenience: an adequate supply of water closets, and sometimes of bathrooms, as part of the design; central heating, either hot air or hot water, in some cases; perhaps gas-lighting, although unless there was access to a town supply this meant building a private gasworks; and the harnessing of hydraulic power, for food lifts, luggage lifts, or for turning the spits in the kitchen. On top of this they performed a demarcation function for the landed elite as a whole, restating the division between the landed class and even the wealthiest of the non-landed by showing the near-impossibility of aspiring both to purchase a large landed estate and build a modern super-large country house. The feat was achieved by the banker Samuel Jones Loyd, Lord Overstone, who assembled an estate of 30,000 acres and built a vast house at Overstone Park, Northamptonshire, in his lifetime; but others had to be content with fewer acres or lesser houses, or both.

The more modest building works were equally significant. Victorian additions and alterations were concerned with many different things, often involving plumbing arrangements as attention to smells and to hygiene increased; but two kinds of activity stand out in reflecting styles of living and ideas of comfort. The most common Victorian additions were extensive servants' wings, with separate nursery wings running them a close second. Servants were moved out of the attics and basements into quarters of their own that were clearly separated from the family parts of the house; children and their attendants likewise. This enlargement of country-house space provided more room for the servants – two to a bedroom perhaps in place of six, and separate living rooms for several grades of servant in place of a single servants' hall – and these more spacious conditions in part showed more liberal and considerate attitudes by their employers. An essential part of the arrangement, however, was to reorganize country-house space into clearly defined spheres so that the family sphere should have its domestic privacy uncontaminated by any intermingling with servants' or children's doings. Both were close at hand to be summoned to perform their services or filial duties, but for the rest of the time remained in their self-contained quarters out of sight and earshot. Extreme forms of the doctrine of privacy required that a servant should turn her face to the wall if she chanced to encounter a member of the family while in the main part of the house. When it is added that menservants were as far as possible separated from the maids, with separate male and female staircases and no communication between their sleeping areas, it is clear that prudery, propriety, and fear of sexuality were strong influences on the drive to subdivide country-house space into clearly defined territories. This seems to stamp the whole process of the domestication of aristocratic living as an acceptance of evangelical morality and of the essentially middle-class ideal of domesticity, and to make this vein of Victorian building into the architectural expression of upper-class recantation of previous sinfulness and frivolity, and dedication to a life of earnest righteousness.

Such an impression is strengthened by the observation that sexual segregation was equally enforced in the main part of the house, at least to the extent of arranging the guests' quarters with separate corridors for the unmarried ladies and the bachelors, and possibly with a quite separate bachelors' staircase. The second very common form of Victorian additions, however, cast a different light on the character and depth of evangelical influences. Billiard rooms, smoking rooms, and gun rooms were frequently added, often with their own lavatories. These were all male preserves, and their creation implemented a code of manners that gave increasing emphasis to the supposed delicacy and fragility of female suscepti-bilities, so that ladies were to be protected from seeing or doing anything unseemly, unfitting, or upsetting. The female territory of boudoir and drawing room might also be extended, by adding more drawing rooms for different times of day, but expansion of the male sphere seems to have been dominant. Libraries were indeed normally to be found in country houses, already part of the male territory, but increasingly they were less rooms for reading in, but 'rather a sort of morning room for gentlemen than anything else'. This spatial separation of the sexes, which also appeared to be an orderly and functional subdivision of space, was another form taken by the architectural expression of evangelical morality. Yet the male activities that were thus housed in their specialist rooms, although by no means irresponsibly indulgent, were not ones which were accepted in the stricter and more proper middle-class circles as innocent and harmless pleasures. Top-flight Victorian country houses did indeed incorporate features reflecting a shift in aristocratic lifestyles away from the public, promiscuous, and pleasure-loving ways of the eighteenth century, that had some-times been so uncouth as to provide chamber-pots in the dining-room sideboard for after-dinner use. The move was towards regularity, order, decency, propriety, and the segregation of persons, sexes, and activities in the interests of domestic privacy. These were also qualities prominent in the ideal of middle-class domesticity; but the aristocratic interpretation of them was sufficiently idiosyncratic in its continued attention to pleasure and luxury for it to be clear that each was responding to a common influence, evangelicalism, rather than that one was emulating the other. Significantly, although the bible-reading and morning-prayer habit did spread into some country-house breakfast rooms, very few of the landed elite thought of providing religion with its separate room, a chapel; where billiards ranked above religion the cultural autonomy of the aristocracy was assured.

An underwater billiard room with a glass ceiling, built on the bottom of a lake, is the last word in frivolous extravagance in the application of the principle of specialization. It was the work of a shady company promoter, Whitaker Wright, as part of his country house of Witley Park, Surrey, which was built in the 1890s. This, of course, was well post-mid-Victorian sobriety; but it is only a bizarre illustration of the tendency of some men of new wealth to build or buy country houses, and of a minority within that group to outstrip the traditional gentry in the fantastical eccentricity and opulence of their building. Worth Park in Sussex was described in the 1880s with profound disapproval as 'the ultra-luxurious house of the Montefiores [financiers], where the servants have their own billiard tables, ballroom, theatre and pianofortes, and are arrogant and presumptuous in proportion'. The majority of those new men who did go in for country houses, however, were anxious to be accepted by local gentry society, and this made them as cautiously conservative and conventional in their building as they were conformist in their country-life behaviour: they kept their servants in their place and their houses up-to-date but unobtrusive.

The traditional view, reiterated innumerable times from the sixteenth century onwards, has been that successful and wealthy men put their fortunes into land and strove to found landed families. 'Merchants are commonly ambitious to become country gentlemen,' Adam Smith reaffirmed in 1776; and in the mid-nineteenth century Richard Cobden despairingly agreed that 'manufacturers and merchants as a rule seem only to desire riches that they may be able to prostrate themselves at the feet of feudalism. See how every successful trader buys an estate and tries to perpetuate his name . . . by creating an eldest son.' This concept of a constant flow of money into land has been challenged in the recent work of W. D. Rubinstein and Lawrence and Jeanne Stone. The flow has been made to look more like a trickle, and consequently the social significance of the process, as the high road of social mobility trodden by the very wealthy so that the successful of each generation were grafted on to the old order, has also been called in question. The nineteenth-century trickle was indeed sizeable, since at least half of those who left fortunes in excess of £½ million had also acquired estates of 2000 acres or more. Nevertheless, since the other half of those who had made large fortunes in banking, commerce, the professions, or industry had not purchased land on this scale, it appears that the ambition to set up as landed gentry was not universally felt. Moreover, it has also been shown that no more than 10 per cent of the total body of landowners of the early 1880s consisted of members of new families which had purchased their estates in the course of the previous hundred years, so that the impact of new wealth on the fabric of the landed class appears minimal.

It is, however, misleading to dismiss the phenomenon of fluidity on the upper-class margins too hastily. A rate of change in the composition of the landed class of 10 per cent in a hundred years – especially since there were in addition some marriages of established landowners to bankers' daughters and the like – is evidence of social mobility rather than social stability. In any case the scale of the movement has been measured on too narrow and restricted a frame, which obscures its social meaning. It is true that only very small numbers of the new wealthy moved in one step into the top level of the landed elite by buying or building a large country house and the acreage requisite to support it from the rentals of tenanted farms: a 2000-acre estate of good-quality farmland might be enough for local gentry style, but something more of the order of 10,000 acres was likely to be needed for equality with the county elite. An estate of that size, along with a suitable house to go on it, represented an investment of £½ million upwards at any time before the 1880s, and was therefore a very large financial step that very few were likely to be able to take. A few, all the same, did take it. Arkwright, Peel, Marshall, and Strutt from the first generation of textile magnates had taken it. In the Victorian years they were followed by a couple of Barings, four

Rothschilds, Loyd (all bankers), Boulton (son of the steam-engine firm), Brassey (railway contractor), Guest (of the Dowlais ironworks), Guinness, and Armstrong (engineering and armaments); with the fall in land prices after 1880 Cunliffe-Lister, the wool-combing magnate, was able to outdo even Loyd, by buying up well over 30,000 acres and acquiring the title of Lord Masham. A few others set themselves up as landed magnates, but the entire group was undoubtedly very small in number. It was not, however, a minute and insignificant group that had cut itself off from all connection with the commercial or industrial origins from which it had sprung. On the contrary, it was the summit of a pyramid that reached down through ranks of lesser landowners, country-house owners, and on into the urban upper middle class.

To begin with there were those of the new wealthy who were content with a lesser estate, in the 2000–10,000 acre range, whose country house and country lifestyle probably had to be sustained by business profits or other investments since farm rents would be inadequate. These were about three times as numerous as the new landed magnates. Below this level in the acreage hierarchy, but not necessarily in new-found social status, came all those who acquired a country house and only an apology of an estate to go with it. For them there was no longer any pretence that landed property supplied the income to support country-house living, as it did for the genuine landed gentry; but nonetheless they acquired several hundred or a thousand acres beyond their new park walls in order to make some show of having a gentleman's concern with farming and estate management, and in order to have some private shooting. These were a species of pseudo-gentry, since they made no bones about not living off the land; but they were only a shade more pseudo than many of the new lesser gentry who also lived mainly on profits and dividends, and the lifestyles of the two groups were indistinguishable. They formed the bulk of the 250 or so men of new wealth who built or extensively remodelled country houses between 1835 and 1889, and were thus about five times as numerous as the new lesser gentry. Below them in turn came those who simply acquired houses in the country; large houses, sometimes little smaller than a country house except for the absence of the offices and outbuildings appropriate to an appurtenant estate, but houses set only in their own grounds and perhaps a paddock or two for a house cow and the family horses. These again permitted a lifestyle little different from that of the groups with more extensive property; hunting was relatively easy, shooting was a little more difficult, involving renting a shoot or finding a hospitable neighbour. Such people were upper-middle-class commuters or sojourners in the country, still close in their habits and their city and business contacts to the urban and suburban upper middle class; in this fashion the social chain was completed. The Victorian houses in the country have never been counted, but quite possibly they are to be numbered in thousands rather than hundreds, architectural testimony to the gentrification of the bourgeoisie and a major source of commissions for such architects as Lutyens, Shaw, and Waterhouse.

Victorian country-house building by the new men started at a low level of nine houses in the five years 1835-9, at a time when old-established families built three times as many houses; but their building rate steadily accelerated to overtake that of the old families, and reached a peak of nearly forty houses in 1870-4. Building by both new and old declined sharply in the late 1870s and by 1885-9 was down to twenty-seven houses in all, two to one in favour of the new men. The course of this activity reflects the growing wealth of the economy and the influence of easy rail travel on the living habits of some of the new wealthy, in the strong upsurge from the 1850s, the check to business confidence from the economic uncertainty following the collapse of the boom of 1873, and the enforced caution of old-established landed families when the outlook for agriculture and for land values turned uncertain to gloomy from the late 1870s. Among the new men those whose fortunes came from finance, banking, overseas trade, brewing, and the law predominated until the 1860s, and manufacturers from the new industries of the Industrial Revolution were only a small minority. Such a distribution conforms well with the new orthodoxy that in the nineteenth century large fortunes were made in the traditional activities of banking and commerce, and the older professions, rather than in manufacturing. From the 1860s onwards, however, the men from cotton, wool, hosiery, iron and steel, coal, railways, engineering, even a piano-maker and an

ostrich-feather manufacturer, began to appear in growing numbers
in the countryside, so that over the period 1835–89 as a whole the
numbers of 'traditional' and 'new' fortunes embodied in country
houses were roughly equal. Even the radical cotton manufacturer
John Fielden, who had played a prominent part in championing
the handloom weavers and in the ten hours movement in the 1830s,
produced a son who went in for this kind of building in the 1860s;
while untroubled by radical ancestries, practically all the creators
of Middlesbrough – Bolckow, Vaughan, Lowthian Bell, and Pease
– built country houses in the vicinity but away from the smoke of
their blast furnaces, Bell throwing in one for his daughter as well
for good measure.

It has been assumed that the slump of the 1870s marked the
virtual end of the era of country-house building. But confidence
revived sufficiently after 1890 for the last dozen years of Victoria's
reign to sustain a building rate of six houses a year, far below the
peak of the early 1870s but still far from insignificant. The
composition of the building force altered radically. The old guard
did not drop out entirely, but whereas the established landed
families had been responsible for half the new houses of 1835–89
their share in the crop of 1890–1902 was down to one quarter. It
was the 'new' industrialists who now made the running, possibly in
style as well as in quantity, and they outnumbered the bankers,
merchants, lawyers, and publishers, even though such recent
products of the financial world as a stockbroker or a chairman of an
insurance company now made their first appearance on this
country-house stage. Among the new industrialists themselves,
moreover, soapmakers and papermakers were more prominent
than coal-owners, shipbuilders, or engineers, while textile manufacturers were no longer in evidence. The arrival of retail trade
was, admittedly, a little outside this period, when Lutyens in 1910
began Castle Drogo for Julius Drewe, the founder of the Home and
Colonial Stores. The Peel, Selkirk, built in 1899 was a step in that
direction: it was for a wealthy baker, W. R. Ovens.

In all there were rather less than six hundred Victorian country
houses, rather more than half of which belonged to the new
wealthy. These were small figures both in relation to the stock of
such houses as it stood in 1830 and in the context of the upper

middle class as a whole. Even when conjectural allowances are made for those of the new wealthy who bought existing country houses and did not mess them about with extensive alterations, and for those who were content with houses in the country, it is plain that only a minority of the new men of wealth of Victorian Britain aspired to some kind of place in the country. It may, however, have been a substantial minority. It is probable that between 2500 and 3000 businessmen who died during the Victorian period left fortunes in personalty of £100,000 and upwards, and they can be taken to have constituted the business elite, the top layer of the upper middle class. The country-bound stream from this elite was certainly more than one tenth of the group, very probably as much as one third, and possibly approached one half. The different industries and occupations represented in this minority were extremely varied, so that it formed a reasonably representative cross-section of the business elite. Moreover, its fortunes had been made in all the principal commercial and industrial centres of Britain, so that it showed no discernible regional bias. Even Birmingham, which failed to produce any new Victorian country house at all until 1898, when Thomas Middlemore, a leather manufacturer who had made a fortune from supplying saddles to the army, set himself up in Melsetter House in the Orkneys, had placed Boulton and Watt on large estates in Oxfordshire and mid-Wales, Ryland (wiredrawer), Alston (chemicals), Muntz (metals), Peyton (chemicals), Hughes (bicycles), and Chance (glass) on lesser gentry estates, besides sending many others of its wealthy out into the country after houses, leisure estates, and sporting estates.

This fraction of the upper middle class did not have in common any ambition to join the landed gentry or to become accepted as members of the county elites. That aspiration was the distinctly personal desire of that small band of individuals who set out to play the landed magnate game in earnest. What the fraction did have in common with one another was sufficient wealth to gratify an ambition to live in the country in style, while most likely remaining active in business or professional life and investing only a small proportion of total assets in the country property. That style required a large house with plenty of guest rooms and perhaps a ballroom, for the private entertaining and private dances that were becoming increasingly fashionable by the 1870s; stables and coach-house; scope for a bit of hobby farming and large-scale gardening; and opportunities for riding, hunting, and shooting. This was a hatchet job on the traditional aristocratic lifestyle, slicing out the agreeable and pleasurable elements and ignoring the responsibilities for tenants and labourers, and for local administration, that had gone with them. The landed elite showed signs of going the same way in any case, with the growing passion for hunting, grouse shooting, deer stalking, and mass slaughter of pheasants. The newcomers may have mingled with the traditional gentry on the hunting field, but otherwise the two sets scarcely met. The pursuit of the pleasures of country life and the adoption of some watered-down or scaled-down version of country ways did virtually nothing to narrow the social gulf between new wealth and old landed society, if narrowing be understood as a process leading to intimate social contacts, friendships, mutual visiting, and intermarriage. But if the two sets showed no signs of merging, they did at least speak the same language, the language of sport, and share many of the same values.

From the point of view of the landed elite the countrified section of the business elite posed no threat, because its members deliberately chose not to try to rival the established families in terms of acreage or compete with them as landlords, but conveniently made themselves passably gentrified. From the point of view of the rest of the business elite the country members remained members of the same club; they were not a splinter group which had detached itself and become alienated from the parent group, because those who stayed behind in town sought variants of the same way of living adapted to their residential settings. The usual habit of Birmingham's mid-Victorian business leaders who lived in one of the town's fashionable suburbs, for example, was also to have a secondary residence and small estate out in the country, and this was likely to be something more ambitious than a holiday cottage. Attwood the banker, for instance, lived in Edgbaston but also had several hundred acres in the country; the Kenricks, the hollow-ware manufacturers, also lived in Edgbaston, but kept a small shooting estate in Worcestershire, and by the 1880s also leased a Scottish grouse moor. Even Quakers, like the chemical manufacturers Albright and Wilson, so far outgrew their upbringing and their principles as to have shooting estates in Herefordshire and in Scotland by the end of the century, although they continued to live in the suburbs. Joseph Chamberlain, screw manufacturer and politician, represented a different type of arrangement but a similar set of tastes, choosing to have what amounted to a country house in the suburbs. Highbury, in King's Heath, Birmingham, was an estate in miniature of a hundred acres, which became completely surrounded by suburban development before the end of the century; the house he built on it was of country-house proportions, with a galleried hall suitable for dances for a couple of hundred guests. Here he had grand dinners, great garden parties, and fashionable and political weekend parties. An expert orchid enthusiast, his grounds were well equipped with hothouses; there was also a croquet lawn and tennis courts, and part of the estate was used for hobby farming, with a model dairy. Richard and George Cadbury, the cocoa brothers, similarly preferred country houses in the suburbs. Richard built himself Uffculme, in King's Heath, in grounds of fifty acres, which must nevertheless have seemed quite crowded when as many as 30,000 people came to the annual temperance gatherings; George started at Woodbrooke, standing in seventy acres, but in the 1890s moved to The Manor, Northfield, on an estate of one hundred and twelve acres. The house was ample for the many visitors who came to see Bournville, and the grounds for the 25,000 visitors who came annually, workers from the firm, and charitable bodies on annual outings; but the grounds were also equipped with a hard tennis court, two grass courts, and a private seven-hole golf course, for less public family pleasures. All that the Unitarian Chamberlain and the Quaker Cadburys lacked from the country-life calendar in their suburban enclaves was a taste for shooting; that was supplied in the next generation when sons went off shooting with friends or on rented estates, and daughters took to hunting.

In the suburbs themselves, which were developing on the fringes of all the major towns from the 1830s and 1840s, there were houses of many different grades and sizes, attuned to the many layers of the middle classes. On the highest class of planned suburban developments, where a single landowner or a commercial estate developer designed the layout of a large building estate as a physical and social entity, it was not at all uncommon to find some large and grand houses standing in grounds of several acres. In one such suburb, Edgbaston, there were indeed some houses with ten-acre gardens, deemed adequate to provide pasture for a cow and grazing for a horse and still leave more than enough land for the most exotic horticultural tastes. It was typical also for the fringes of the built-up area of large towns, especially in the most favoured scenic locations, to be liberally peppered with large villas in their own mini-parks that might run to fifty acres and more. Living somewhat precariously on the moving urban frontier, such semi-rural villas might last for no more than a single generation before having their grounds and gardens carved up into building plots, the great houses themselves being either demolished or institutionalized as preparatory schools, hotels, or, as in the case of Kidderpore Hall in Hampstead, as a ladies' college. A few outfaced the passing tide and survived as tiny rural islands embedded in the urban sea; the majority were replaced, and more than replaced, by scores of replicas built further out. It was an unsettling process, but not without its compensations: every now and again there were windfall capital gains when gardens and parks acquired building land values, and similarly there were periodical opportunities to build new houses in the latest style, with the latest fittings, neatly avoiding the social risk of becoming old-fashioned.

Town villas and villas on the outskirts were essential links in the upper-middle-class chain which ran from the suburbs to the houses in the country. In the early Victorian years the latter were set apart from the fringe villas by their greater distance from city centres, since the fringe villas were not weekend retreats or retirement homes but residences for active business and professional men, albeit wealthy ones who did not keep too exacting working hours. The development of reliable rail services, however, meant that by the 1850s and 1860s tolerable commuting distances for the very wealthy for whom the cost of travel was little object had grown to twenty to thirty miles from London – and further for the occasional eccentric – and to about half that radius around the largest provincial centres. This had the effect of making it virtually impossible to tell apart a house in the country and a fringe villa, except through the identity and career-stage of the individual occupant. This was the time when the stockbroker belt first started to appear in Berkshire and Surrey, the time when successful Glaswegian shipbuilders and shipowners started thinking of building castles out towards Loch Lomond, Manchester men headed for the Cheshire countryside, and Birmingham magnates colonized and emparked alongside the road and rail lines to the Lickey Hills and to Warwick. This residential pattern was not in itself a Victorian innovation: it had been practised for centuries by some of London's wealthy merchants, who had spread themselves and their imposing villas out along most of the roads leading out of London until they touched hands with the larger estates purchased by other successful businessmen with longer purses and grander ideas about imitating the real gentry. What was new was the generalization of the pattern to the hinterlands of all the main provincial cities, the incorporation into it of industrial magnates and top professional people as well as the older commercial and financial elite, and the extended reach of rail-borne villadom. It was a style which reached the culminating point of its development in the years just before 1914, when the motor car was beginning to open up for residence or for weekending places that had previously been practically inaccessible, and when labour costs, for building and for service, remained low enough to sustain the economy of large houses.

The very largest of mid-Victorian suburban houses, which might have eight to ten bedrooms, with servants' rooms in addition on the attic floor, and might boast a breakfast parlour, a library, a billiard room, and a music room as well as the standard dining room and drawing room, were as large and spacious as many a fringe or ribbon villa, and frequently were better plumbed and better lighted. They differed in standing on much smaller grounds, typically of half to one acre, and although that was room enough for stables and coach-house, conservatory and hothouse, it did mark a difference in status. They also differed in provenance and in tenure, but these differences had no status implications. Country houses, houses in the country, and fringe villas were customarily owned by their occupants, and if they were newly built they were custom-built, architect-designed, for the individual owner-client. On occasion, indeed, and more commonly from the 1880s onwards, such houses might be tenanted, as owners who had accumulated a superfluity of houses through marriage and inheritance found it convenient to let some of them out, and as impoverished gentry clutched at an income from renting their seats while taking their families off to live more economically at some seaside resort. That might well slightly degrade the lessor, without elevating the country-house tenant into gentry status. It was, however, a marginal matter, while it was central to all other housing, from the urban upper middle class to the most humble, that the great majority was rented and was built on speculation rather than to the individual order of a prospective occupier. There were naturally many exceptions, and it was not unusual for the rich to own their own houses; but so also did quite a number of skilled workers. Owner-occupancy denoted no particular social position, and tenancy in itself had no particular social connotation, although the different grades of tenure, ranging from weekly tenancies up to seven-year leases, reflected very decided class differences.

The proportion of all pre-1914 houses which were owner-occupied is commonly held to have been about 10 per cent, but there is in fact no firm basis for this opinion, there being no contemporary statistics on the matter. It is possibly true that something like 10 per cent of all new houses built from about 1890 onwards were bought by owner-occupiers. At any rate there are signs from some of the new housing developments of this late Victorian period that some of the middle ranks of the middle classes were beginning to go in for house purchase, and that this was a new departure. Previously owner-occupation had been thought of as primarily a quirk of a small minority of skilled artisans who set especial store on thrift and respectability, saw them as ideally embodied in house-ownership, and successfully pursued their ambitions through the machinery of local, terminating, building societies. It was usual, therefore, for mid-Victorians to think of house-ownership as the preserve of a section of the upper working class, who were commendable in themselves for their self-respect and independence, but whose houses were a bit tainted with the fancifully tawdry embellishments and clutter which home-ownership without landlord control could sprout. It follows that the overwhelming mass of house-ownership was vested in housing landlords for whom this property was an investment yielding an income from rents that was more or less reliable and regular, was as secure as an income from Consols, and represented a gratifyingly higher rate of return. Such house-owners were capitalists of astonishing variety and diversity, owning anything from a couple of houses up to several hundred, sometimes in compact blocks and complete streets, but more often in scattered clutches, sometimes specializing in one particular type of house but often spreading their portfolios across a spectrum of types, rental values, and neighbourhoods. They were a numerous band drawn from a wide cross-section of the middle classes, with local tradesmen, shopkeepers, professional people, and small masters especially prominent, with retired people and widows also much in evidence; quite often the builder, having covered his outlays by selling many of the houses he had built, would retain some and set up as a landlord himself. Not infrequently a builder would live in one of his own houses as proof of confidence in the product, and as a convenience while building was going on around, which in the case of a large take, building perhaps half a dozen houses a year, might last him a lifetime. It could also happen that a non-builder house-owner might live in one of his houses while letting the rest, an arrangement which economized on personal housing costs and made personal, as distinct from agency, rent collection handy if not necessarily easy. Here was another strand in owner-occupancy. But it remained a very thin element in the country at large, split up between different social groups and varying in size from town to town, so that owner-occupiers did not constitute a coherent group in society and were not a significant social or political force.

Most Victorian middle-class lives, therefore, were lived in rented houses, although this in itself did not imply that they had anything significant in common with the working classes who also mainly lived as tenants. Typically, the middle classes held their houses on repairing leases for a short but fixed term of years, which gave them the security and responsibility of householders looking after the maintenance of their homes. The working classes, in England, normally had weekly or monthly tenancies, although in

Scotland it was quite usual for tenements to be let on one-year agreements which somewhat paradoxically were a source of some grievance and insecurity because widespread annual rent-raising and annual home-moving resulted. In both countries working-class tenants usually paid their rents weekly, were dependent on their landlords for the repair and maintenance of the fabric, and enjoyed very little legal security of tenure. The landlord–tenant relationship, however, was perfectly familiar to the urban middle classes, just as it was to the rural middle class of tenant farmers, and the fact that it worked well for them disposed them to believe that it worked equally well, at suitably lower social and income levels, for the working classes. That was far from being the case, chiefly because so much of the working class had severe problems in keeping up their rent payments, either permanently or intermittently at bad periods in the lifecycle, at times of personal misfortune, or in times of general economic distress. All the same, the standard middle-class, and ruling-class, attitude to housing was understandably coloured by their own experience. Ordinary market mechanisms, responding to the inducement of prospective rental incomes, could be safely relied on to supply all the housing, in all the different grades and rent levels, which society required. This happened for the middle classes, and broadly it happened for the great majority of the rest of the population, for the total number of houses in Britain kept steadily, if only slightly, ahead of the increase in the number of people throughout the Victorian period; that was not inconsistent with there being patches, in some towns large patches, where overcrowding measured in terms of the number of persons per house or per room actually increased. Moreover, when most middle-class opinion appeared to be on the landlord's side in matters like the legal sanctions for rent collection or the law on eviction, this was not because most of the middle class were landlords, although they could indeed be expected to defend property rights in general. It was also because as house-tenants they recognized that the advantages of the landlord–tenant system depended on observing rules under which tenants as well as landlords met their obligations.

Those advantages were economy, convenience, and flexibility. Renting a house, in a liberally supplied market where there was plenty of choice, almost invariably cost less in annual outlay than buying it on a fixed-period mortgage; or to put it another way, the same annual expenditure could rent a bigger and better house than it could buy. The outlay on a simple mortgage without regular repayment provisions was indeed lower, but in the nineteenth century houses were generally depreciating assets as age and the superior quality and appeal of newer houses knocked down their market value, and they were markedly dwindling assets if, as in many towns, they were on leasehold sites, for then they reverted to the possession of the ground landlord on the expiry of the term. This, in many cases, made it financially more secure and more prudent to put savings or borrowing power into other investments, and not into house purchase. It was, in any case, highly convenient for many middle-class people to keep the largest possible part of their resources available for use in their business or profession, while for others the ease and rapidity with which a family could move house from one part of the country to another was a great advantage of the system. Above all there was the astonishing flexibility which it made possible, not simply geographical mobility, but social and lifecycle mobility as well. Families could move between houses of different sizes as their requirements altered with the arrival, growing up, and departure of children, with the transition from work to retirement, or with the rise and fall of family income. Families could also move between similar sized houses because one neighbourhood seemed more attractive or socially superior to another, or because they wished always to be in the newest possible house, in the latest style and with the most modern fittings. Many families were, of course, not as restless as this seems to imply, for it was perfectly possible to put down roots and remain in the same house for a generation, even if it was rented under a succession of short leases, just as it was very usual for tenant-farming families to remain on the same farm perhaps for several generations, even if that farm was held on an annual tenancy. There were also many families which did regularly move house every two or three years, Holborn one year, Hampstead the next, and Wimbledon the year after, as it were; and in this way there was a considerable section of the middle classes that was pretty much as constantly on the move as a considerable section of the working classes, save that among the working classes the moves tended to be for shorter distances and at shorter intervals.

Just as most middle-class housing was built on speculation, not individually commissioned, so most speculative builders put up houses with a middle-class market in mind, because the middle classes were solid, reliable, respectable, and well behaved, and if they could be induced to become residents they would confer those qualities on the development. It then not infrequently happened that there were not enough of the middle classes to go round, they were overprovided with houses and many had to be adapted for a lower class of occupation, perhaps by tenementing. It follows that for the middle classes themselves there was generally a wide choice of houses to suit all tastes and circumstances. Taste might be a matter of choosing between locations, high and bracing, or equally salubrious but more sheltered, newly fashionable, or safely close to church and vicarage; or it could be a question of Regency, Gothic, Romantic, neo-Classical, Queen Anne Revival, or mock Tudor, mostly as mangled and debased in the manuals of drawings used by speculative builders. The circumstances which counted were largely financial, a matter of what rents could be afforded at what income levels – the middle classes generally reckoned that it was reasonable to spend about 10 per cent of income on rent, and imprudent to spend over one eighth – and as income rose over a lifetime so social pressures dictated moves to better, bigger, and more expensive houses. Family circumstances were also a consideration, and different house sizes with different arrangements of their space were best adapted to different phases in family life: one kind of house for newly marrieds, another for families of young children with nurses and nannies, perhaps a third kind suited to school-age children, and a fourth to cope with resident spinster aunts or grandparents. The Victorians found houses to fit their lifecycle requirements; in the late twentieth century people more often force their lifecycle to fit into the houses they happen to have.

There was, then, a large spectrum of housing for the Victorian middle classes, with rents running from as little as £20 a year up to £150 a year or more, and accommodation ranging from two reception-three bedrooms on two floors and perhaps in a row or terrace, up to eight and ten bedroom detached houses three or four storeys tall, plus basement, standing in spacious grounds. From the 1830s the great bulk of this housing was to be found in suburban developments, for the privacy, seclusion, respectability, and remoteness from business of suburban residence were making it an essential feature of middle-class life. London, as befits its dominant size, had the largest number of these early suburbs: Islington, Camberwell, or Kensington, for example. But Birmingham's Edgbaston, Bristol's Clifton, Glasgow's Kelvinside, Leeds's Headingley, Liverpool's Everton, Manchester's Ardwick, or Sheffield's Broomhall, all testify to the widespread appearance of suburbs in the largest cities at very much the same time in the early Victorian years. Subsequent growth and expansion on a vast scale has, of course, long since turned these places, once outlying and secluded, into central districts; and in doing so has largely obliterated their atmosphere and character as predominantly one-class residential areas. In their inception, however, such places also testified to the power of the social and commercial pressures to make suburbs, or at least large compact districts within them, into architecturally and socially homogeneous neighbourhoods. Social tone, status, and morality, as well as property values, were seen to depend on the exclusiveness of one-class occupation and the vigilant manning of barriers – sometimes literally physical ones, gates guarding private residential roads and housing estates, more often the legal and financial defences of restrictive covenants and house price levels – to keep at bay undesirables whose occupations or habits might destroy the tranquillity or the morals of the residents.

The homogeneity of these neighbourhoods, however, was not the homogeneity of a single social class; it was the physical and cultural expression of the layer upon layer of subclasses, keenly aware of their subtle grades of distinction, which constituted the middle classes. The range of incomes of these layers stretched all the way from the bare competence of the clerks, small shopkeepers, and schoolteachers of the lower middle class, struggling to keep up genteel appearances and often not able to afford a domestic servant, up to very wealthy families with three or four indoor servants and maybe an outdoor staff as well looking after the garden and the private carriage. In between lay groups and social sets finely tuned to a sense of their own standing and their identity, which stemmed from occupational, income, educational, religious, and locational factors stirred in varying proportions, even if such groups have rarely been singled out and given distinct labels by historians. Houses, and the character and reputation of distinct neighbourhoods, mirrored these gradations and helped to define and reinforce them. There was both a physical, spatial, differentiation and a chronological sequence to the residential patterns which emerged. The lower middle class, for example, continued to live in terraced rows, albeit marked off by bay windows and lower densities to the acre from working-class terraces, until the early twentieth century, long after the rest of the middle classes had deserted such conditions, the middling for the semi-detached and the upper for the detached house or villa. Around London the scale of suburban development was sufficiently large by the last quarter of the century for whole districts to bear a distinctive hue: Hammersmith, Balham, or Leyton, for example, were predominantly lower-middle-class, and Camberwell had been largely taken over by clerks; Ealing or Penge were middling; while Hampstead, at least in its upper reaches, was firmly held by the upper middle class. Elsewhere, because of the smaller numbers involved and hence the smaller demand at any one time, it was unusual to find entire districts of uniform character and more normal for an enclave of two or three streets to be the limit of any single influence. Typically, suburban settlement took place in a series of wave-like motions stretching over half a century or more, propelled by the pulse of local or national building cycles, early pockets and islands of higher class settlement becoming in the course of time hemmed in by a rising tide of lower grade and higher density development, or perhaps being overwhelmed by socially inferior infilling. The wealthy moved on and out to sample the attractions of fresh areas, and the whole process got ready to repeat itself. As a result few areas as large as an entire parish or township experienced a uniform quality of development, and were much more likely to display a mixed social character. It was not, however, a random or promiscuous mixture, but the topographically complex and often confusing product of methodical stratification in socially and chronologically distinct layers.

The suburban house, then, the apple of the speculative builder's eye and the object of the middle-class householder's dreams, took many forms; these, moreover, altered over time. The large family house of the 1840s was taller, narrower, and altogether larger than the large family house of the 1890s, quite apart from stylistic differences. Smaller families and fewer servants dictated the elimination of basements, while the pursuit of comfort, convenience, and health pointed to the cultivation of such things as bathrooms, adequate gas lighting (and electric lighting from the mid-1890s), and lateral instead of vertical spread in order to cut down on staircases. Possibly, also, domestic life became slightly more relaxed and informal, requiring fewer and larger rooms than the extremes of spatial specialization and segregation so admired at mid-century. Meanwhile, the lower-middle-class terraced houses of the 1890s were generally more spacious, fatter, equipped with more elaborate porches and bay windows, and supplied with bigger back extensions, than their early Victorian predecessors; here, too, the bathroom had become universal, and a separate bedroom for each child was expected. Suburbia was a shifting and changing collection of such houses and places, loosely laced together by transport services and the ties of church or chapel; it was also a state of mind and a way of life.

Domesticity and the cult of the home as the centrepiece of family life were the hallmarks of this lifestyle; the separation of work from home, non-working and thoroughly domesticated womenfolk, intensely private and self-contained nuclear families, and strict and all-pervading morality, were its principal means of expression. It was a way of life which had its beginnings in the late eighteenth century as the teachings of evangelicalism started to exert their influence, and flowered in the early Victorian years, when morals, manners, and respectability all pointed to this as the domestic ideal. Certain features were very general, without being completely indispensable. Servant-keeping was widespread, even if no more than a single inexperienced and inexpensive young teenage girl was kept, and overworked. But it was possible to have no living-in domestic servant without losing face or status, and many of the clerical lower middle class at most had occasional domestic help coming in from outside; and many households contained a servant without thereby becoming middle-class – artisans and miners could keep an orphan girl from the workhouse at practically no cost, who might do some domestic chores or form part of a domestic work unit. Work was normally separate from the home, but it was still quite possible up to the end of the century and beyond for the tobacconist or grocer on the corner to live over the shop without loss of status. Separate rooms for separate functions and sexes were the ideal, female territory in drawing room and boudoir, male territory in study or library, shared ground in the dining room and breakfast room. But in the 'parlour house' of the suburban terrace there were not enough rooms to permit separate female and male space, and territorial rights narrowed down to mother's chair and father's chair in the parlour. There is no doubt that the houses of the middle classes came to be constructed to suit the requirements of the lifestyle; and that the layout and arrangements of the houses encouraged their occupants to conform to a stereotype of respectability. Nevertheless, provided the decencies were observed, the wife did not work or could not be seen to be working apart from running the household, and proper display were made of privacy, propriety, and prudery, the respectability of some grade of middle-class status was assured.

It is tempting to say that while the middle classes were gradually breaking out of the stifling cocoon of the cellular home isolated and insulated behind its net curtains in the last decades of the nineteenth century, the working classes had never been in one. It would not be wholly true. For some the home and the family were never sufficient in themselves to sustain middle-class culture, and they looked outside to a variety of clubs, societies, and associations as essential ingredients of life; for others a reserved, tight-lipped, unsociable mentality persisted in the new semi-detached fortresses of interwar suburbia despite the influences of radio, cinema, and motor car in eating away at the barriers of isolation. On the other hand, some of the Victorian working classes were themselves very strong on lace curtains and the sanctity of their homes, and only the smallest differences in ornamental brickwork or the detail of window moulding might distinguish their houses from those of the lower middle class. Nevertheless, it is broadly the case that working-class lives were always gregarious, mutually supportive, open, and part of a living community in a way that the closed individuality of the middle-class home seldom was. Only with the massive slum clearance and rehousing schemes of the interwar, and more particularly the post-1945, years was the cohesion of these neighbourhood communities disrupted, and large numbers of working-class families were pitched into the anonymous isolation of new housing estates, frequently with socially disastrous results.

When contemporaries like Chadwick or Faucher looked at the large towns of the 1840s they gave the impression that they were populated by teeming multitudes of rootless and masterless individuals, thrown together indiscriminately by the forces which sucked them in to the sources of work. It has become a common perception that the rapidly growing industrial and commercial towns were not only physically repellent – dirty, smelly, unhealthy, and generally miserable – but were also melting pots in which a mass of miscellaneous individuals were bit by bit fused into a new form of urban society with new forms of social stratification. There is something in this, but the cataclysmic view needs such heavy qualification and restatement that gradualness and continuity emerge as the dominant social characteristics of the urbanizing process, largely explaining why the novelty and abruptness of the physical and economic dimensions of urban expansion were not politically more disruptive and explosive. On the one hand, the great growth towns of the nineteenth century, whether giants like Manchester and Glasgow or middle-order places like Oldham and Paisley, did not suddenly appear from nowhere in the manner of twentieth-century new towns. There were a few exceptions, the railway towns like Crewe or Swindon, for instance, and iron towns of which Merthyr Tydfil early in the century and Middlesbrough towards its end were prime examples, where large urban settlements mushroomed on previously bare sites. In general, however, Victorian towns grew around established settlements that already possessed urban, trading, and frequently manufacturing traditions stretching back maybe for centuries. There were, therefore, existing occupational and social structures to which the influx of new people tended to attach themselves, naturally seeking the security of a place in the living framework of urban society. Larger and larger numbers certainly changed that framework, spatially, occupationally, and socially; but it was slowly unfolding change from within, not the sudden change of a mass incursion of unassimilated outsiders. On the other hand, and complementing this process, the manner in which towns grew was by no means incoherent or unstructured.

It is easy to see that that part of the growth in urban populations which was provided by the natural increase of the townspeople themselves would be absorbed into parental lifestyles without undue friction. Before the 1850s at the earliest, however, that was a very small part, and in many cases a negative part as the high mortality of many towns continued to exceed births. In 1840 William Farr at the Registrar-General's office was expressing a hope for the future when he said; 'there is reason to believe that the aggregation of mankind in towns is not inevitably disastrous', while admitting that in the past towns had been 'the graves of mankind'. The major part of the increase in the populations of early Victorian towns, and in some places the whole of it, came from migration from rural districts and Ireland (there was some immigration from the Continent, particularly of Jews, but this did not become numerically significant before the 1880s). While massive, this migration was on the whole more of a self-controlled movement than a blind stampede. Most of the townward migration was over relatively short distances, say ten or a dozen miles, and this made it comparatively simple for immigrants to flow through family and highly localized networks. Typically, immigrants, whether singly or as families, would make for a base in town already established by relatives or friends from the same village who had moved earlier, and as often as not they would end up living in the same street or even the same building, while the same relatives or friends were invaluable contacts in obtaining employment. In this way towns became studded with little districts sharing common rural origins, perpetuating a shared cultural tradition as far as might be in an urban environment, and reproducing or even creating the extended family, perhaps spread over two or three streets, as a system of mutual affection, sociability, and support. It is well known that Irish immigrants, who moved over much longer distances, followed a similar pattern, since the Irish quarters of London, Liverpool, Manchester, or Glasgow have always been instantly recognizable for the distinctive religion, language, occupations, and habits of the residents. To head for an established Irish bridgehead was an obvious strategy for a newly arrived immigrant from a poor peasant society for whom a large town was a strange, totally unfamiliar, and hostile place. Comfort and self-protection by association with the familiar made migration a less terrifying and intimidating experience than it would have been for lone individuals, forlorn and friendless, and mainland immigrants had similar emotions and motives to the Irish even if for them the contrasts between birthplace society and the urban environment were not so extreme.

Young unmarried girls were the major exception to this pattern of migration, as they poured into the towns in their hundreds and thousands to enter domestic service, forming by far the largest occupational group among women workers and one whose members were, by definition, far away from home and separated from kith and kin. Moreover, at least in London with its maxim that West Country girls made the best servants, many of these girls moved over long distances and came from deeply rural back-grounds. They may, therefore, have suffered more severe culture shock than other urban immigrants, all the more so since they were often pitched into middle- or upper-class households with lifestyles totally different from anything they can have known before. Most, however, came with introductions and with jobs already lined up, so that one of the chief elements of anxiety and uncertainty of migration was removed and the security of food and shelter was assured in advance. Those who travelled simply in hope and arrived in the big city with no prearranged destination were frequently disappointed, and it was thought that many young girls were quickly driven to prostitution to keep alive; the tale soon went around that procurers regularly met the Paddington trains and generally picked up some recruits. Those who did succeed in entering domestic service were often confronted by working and living conditions that were harsh and meagre, even if there were also many employers who were benevolent and comparatively generous in their treatment of their servants. For all domestic servants, however, the occupation in itself provided some sort of position in a household and through that a place in urban society, and prevented them from being mere flotsam on an unruly sea.

Domestic service was, in its own way, one route to urban assimilation; servants, it could be said, were absorbed at a menial and subservient level into substitute families, making the townward move in a peculiarly controlled, regulated, and supervised way.

Servants had their being in urban society but they were not of it: they were not householders, they had little by way of lives of their own, they were largely cooped up in their employers' houses, they were isolated and alienated from other workers, and they rarely took part in communal political or social activity. For them, housing was something provided by an employer, whether it was a mere cupboard in a basement kitchen or an attic room, and their social status tended to be something reflected on to them from their employers. A significant, and largely female, sector of the working classes thus had their lodgings provided for them along with the job, and were effectively removed from the housing market: the fraction was already 14 per cent of the entire occupied population by mid-century, rose to the 1880s, and thereafter slowly subsided to its previous level. The rest of the working classes, with the exception of the unnumbered but perhaps not inconsiderable occupiers of tied cottages and the probably smaller number of living-in farm servants, had to find house-room at whatever rent they could afford. In this they differed from the middle classes in being able to pay lower, often very much lower, rents, in offering less security to landlords because of the frequent irregularity of employment and precarious nature of earnings, and in being obliged to live close to their work – although none of these differences might apply to skilled workers, who could match the lower middle class in incomes and regularity of work. All this pointed to poorer and smaller houses, less space per family, and more bleak discomfort for the working classes, and no one has ever doubted that the housing conditions of the working classes were worse than those of groups with higher incomes. The importance of community life, in street or neighbourhood, meant however that the individual house or home was of lesser social meaning – sometimes perforce, because there was no space in the dwelling – than in other classes. And, simply because the housing was of a lower standard and value, it did not follow that it formed an undifferentiated mass and that there was no range of choice to suit different tastes and wage levels.

Contemporaries were startled, often deeply shocked, by the veritable explosion of information about the abject poverty, misery, and wretched living conditions in the large towns, an explosion of reports and surveys from medical men, statistical societies in Manchester and Liverpool, Poor-Law officials, and parliamentary enquiries into the health of large towns, which provided much sombre reading matter in the 1830s and 1840s. Many historians, rightly or righteously moved by the mass of evidence of this type, have contrived to convey the impression that the entire working class dragged out its existence in cellar dwellings or lived whole families huddled together, or even several families, in the single-roomed quarters of some warren of makeshift apartments or tenements. It is easy to overlook the fact that they have been describing the conditions of the poorest, most unfortunate, or most disreputable sections of the labouring poor or working classes, sections with which those who were above this level of destitution did not necessarily have much sympathy or much in common. Victorian slums were nasty, affronts to the wealth and civilization around them, and it is important to understand what they were like and why they existed; but it is as important to remember that four fifths or nine tenths of the people did not live in slum conditions.

The distinction between slum and non-slum was a social as well as a physical distinction, and the corresponding but somewhat wider difference between the disreputable – who might be feckless, bad managers, or big drinkers, and not simply the very poor – and the respectable was the major line of division within the working class. Respectable working-class families, who paid their rents regularly and took pride in their homes, did not wish to be associated with or live alongside families which abused their homes, defaulted on their rents, and flitted ceaselessly from one despairing landlord to another. Here was a powerful force separating one kind of working-class community from another, leading to the social distancing of physical segregation and tending to find expression in different kinds of housing. Respectability, however, was not the preserve of the skilled workers or the labour aristocracy, but spread through much wider and more numerous echelons of the working classes. Nevertheless, the artisan elite, with its higher incomes, superior skills, and greater independence, had clear aspirations to houses and homes of a style and dignity befitting their status and a tendency to congregate together in their own neighbourhoods. Hence the respectable working class contained two quite well-defined subclasses, and the social and income differences between them tended to produce different kinds and standards of housing and different residential districts. The third broad category of working-class housing, that of the disreputables and slum-dwellers, was not so much built to cater for the demand, as was the case with the other two, as left to tumble down to multi-occupancy and overcrowding when some better class of user had discarded it.

This pattern became reasonably clear-cut from the 1860s with the general development of bye-law housing in all the main towns; that is, houses built under municipal bye-laws, which varied from town to town, regulating the width of streets, the number of windows, the height of ceilings, the size of rooms, and the provision of privies. This sorted out and standardized house types – in regional patterns – regularized street layouts, making homogeneous districts readily identifiable, and made the single-family house, enveloped however thinly in its own privacy, the normal form of working-class housing, at least in England. Some towns had moved along this regulatory path earlier: Liverpool introduced its first building bye-law in 1842, while London had had building regulations since the Great Fire, whose influence on design, layout, and construction can be clearly seen in surviving eighteenth-century terraces and squares. It is, however, doubtful how far anything like an orderly, and differentiated, pattern of working-class housing can be discerned much before the 1860s. This is partly because there was no long tradition of building specifically for a working-class market on a mass scale, and the social cost in health and welfare of what had been built since the later eighteenth century was only becoming glaringly apparent in the 1830s; and partly because little is known about working-class occupancy except for the grossly unhealthy blackspots.

By the second half of the eighteenth century, however, and

certainly by the time of rapid economic and urban expansion in the 1780s, a large-scale working-class demand for housing had developed with significant concentrations in the major industrial and seaport towns. A host of small builders, carpenters, bricklayers, masons, and petty speculators appeared to satisfy that demand by running up housing that was sufficiently small and cheap to be within the means of the prospective tenants. Some of the influx found accommodation of a sort in made-down houses vacated by their original and wealthier inhabitants, and frequently these were made down simply by subletting in single-room apartments in which an entire family would live, without any material alterations or adaptation whatever. Much of the worst overcrowding, dirtiest and most squalid living conditions, for the poorest people, occurred in such properties; and the practice inevitably continued through the nineteenth century, with similar results, and indeed still continues with late twentieth-century squatters. Most of the influx, however, lived in houses built expressly for that particular market. The rents that could be paid were small, from as little as 1s. 6d. a week up to 5s. or in 'high rent' London 7s. by the 1830s and somewhat lower in the late eighteenth century. The house-room that could be provided was, therefore, correspondingly small and of low-cost construction. There was, however, a range of rents, determined both by the wage levels and earnings of different occupations and by the lifecycle stage of individual families, and builders responded to this by supplying a range of house types. The single-room cottage was a possibility: it matched the previous rural experience of many migrants, who took with them to town a habit of single-room living. On the other hand, it was generally not an economic use of expensive urban land to build single-room houses, and most single-room living went on in subdivided older houses or in the notorious cellar dwellings for which Liverpool, somewhat undeservedly, earned the blackest reputation. Complete houses of two rooms, the classic 'one up, one down' possibly with a ladder rather than a staircase, three rooms, one on top of the other in three storeys, and four rooms, 'two up, two down', were being built in all the main English towns from the later eighteenth century, and they formed the bulk of working-class housing in the early Victorian years. Naturally they were not detached houses, but in blocks and rows; they were, to our eyes, diminutive, twelve foot square being common in Birmingham, fractionally larger in Manchester or Leeds; and they were innocent of amenities or facilities, an outside privy in a yard, shared by half a dozen households, being almost a luxury. Nevertheless, they formed a hierarchy of housing matching a hierarchy of incomes and status within the working classes.

The trouble with this housing, to the sanitary reformers of the 1840s, was not the box-like nature of the individual houses so much as the arrangement and layout of blocks and groups of the boxes. The back-to-back developed as the characteristic housing form of the Yorkshire, Lancashire, and Midland towns, although it was almost unknown in Bristol and London and never spread to Tyneside or to Scotland. It could provide the greatest amount of floor area for the lowest cost, and hence the best value for a given amount of rent, since each house, apart from the end-row houses, had only one outside wall, thus economizing on construction costs. Provided the streets, or gaps, between the double rows were kept narrow, it was a building method that lent itself to packing the greatest number of houses on to the smallest area. It was a flexible form which could be stretched from two-room up to six-room size, or squeezed into odd corners of a plot as a half-back, and even perched on the steep slopes of Pennine mill towns as a blind half-back or back-to-earth half house dug into the hillside. To the occupants it offered basic shelter or better, and the advantages of warmth and neighbourliness. To the sanitary reformers it was anathema. This was partly because by the 1840s back-to-backs had become firmly associated with extremely high densities of development with all the consequent disease and dirt and neglect that flowed from congestion, although this was the result of the historical course of development and the effect of the economics of particular land and building costs, and was not inherent in the back-to-back concept. Partly it was because the lack of front-to-back through ventilation was held to be inherently unhealthy, although single-aspect rooms remain extremely common and are not in themselves objectionable; any form of living in one or two rooms is liable to be smelly and insanitary, regardless of the house form. Mainly, however, it was because back-to-backs did not have and could not have any sensible, private, and seemly arrangement for privies or for refuse removal, not at least until indoor closets became feasible, and that in turn meant not until the water closet was sufficiently developed and sufficiently cheap to be installed in low-cost houses, which turned out not to be before the 1880s.

The sanitary idea, therefore, propagated both centrally and locally in the more progressive provincial towns in the 1840s, and percolating through to most other towns in the 1850s and 1860s, condemned back-to-backs and insisted upon the through-house as the essential vehicle of cleanliness, hygiene, and better health. The great thing about the through-house with its back as well as front entrance was that it could have a backyard with a privy, usually an earth closet but more and more frequently a pail closet in the 1860s and 1870s, and even more importantly could be served by a back lane or alley to be used for nightsoil and refuse removal. Thus the through-house, already the normal form of common row houses in London, became the characteristic type permitted by municipal bye-laws of the middle years of the century, and advanced in row upon row, rank upon rank, across the working-class quarters of almost every English town until halted by the garden city idea and the council housing estates of the twentieth century. One by one the cities and towns prohibited the further erection of back-to-backs, until by the mid-1860s only Leeds was left as a back-to-back builder, refusing to outlaw the type perhaps not so much because the Leeds authorities were exceptionally tender towards the interests of builders and landowners or indifferent to those of occupiers, as because they had confidence in the ability of the type to lose its evil reputation and incorporate improvements in standards and quality. Thus in Leeds back-to-backs continued to be built until the 1930s, and the more modern ones continue to be lived in in the 1980s, some of them much sought after by the professional classes. Elsewhere the stock of back-to-backs was frozen at its mid-Victorian size, and declined gradually thereafter as redevelopment became attractive, or in a few areas as clearances were undertaken. They survived, however, as a substantial fraction of the total stock of housing, largely relegated to the lower and more disreputable reaches of the working classes outside the West Riding textile towns; there, with back-to-backs still 60 to 70 per cent of all houses in the pre-1914 years, they contained their own hierarchy of sizes, situations, and services to suit the different social grades.

Equally, or even more, offensive to noses and to sanitary opinion were the dwellings in closed courts that were also a common form of development from the late eighteenth century; most noisome of all was the situation where one court backed on to another so that the sides forming the court were themselves back-to-backs. The court, often with only a narrow tunnel entrance from the front street, was a form of intensive development frequently dictated by plot size and shape where there was a narrow frontage and a long, narrow plot behind it; and it was a form which builders found well adapted to the development of the land lying behind a front house, itself perhaps older, larger, and originally of a much higher class. The individual houses or cottages which made up a court might in themselves be as commodious as or no more despicable than other cottages in rows. Collectively, however, they were guaranteed to breed unspeakable squalor, closed in and airless, with perhaps a single privy for a court with a dozen or more families, a midden heap in the centre of the narrow courtyard which was seldom cleared, garbage everywhere, and no obvious source of water. Middle-class observers also readily condemned the lack of privacy and separate family life, and the promiscuous mixing, which went with living in courts, and which may well have been reckoned positive attractions, or at least compensations, by the denizens. Condemnation on sanitary, if not on moral, grounds is, however, readily intelligible, and the unsavoury courts of Birmingham or Nottingham, Liverpool or Leeds became prime targets of the medical men and sanitary reformers. Many were too gruesome and too dilapidated for anything but demolition; but others survived, frequently improved by removal of the front house so that they were thrown open as narrow cul-de-sacs, to form part of the housing stock of the second half of the nineteenth century. Nothing could improve their social standing, and courts or ex-courts were an element in the bottom rung of later Victorian working-class housing.

Thus the new houses built in the second half of the century did not displace the older ones so much as add new layers on top of them; the older houses were pushed downwards in relative comfort, in rents, and in esteem. Chronological strata of houses of different ages in this way extended and reinforced a social structure that was also embodied in the different types and values of new houses. This was very similar to the middle-class world where the wealthiest and most ambitious were continually on the move to the newest and most fashionable district, and lesser people moved in behind them. From about 1860, when bye-law housing became dominant, there were at least three main regional types in addition to the improved back-to-backs of the West Riding textile towns: the two-storey Tyneside flats, in effect one cottage on top of another, with access by outside steps to the first floor; terraces of through houses without back additions in the Lancashire cotton towns; and terraces of through-houses with back additions in most of the Midlands and the south. Within these regions there were deviant minorities that departed from the standard type; of more moment, each standard type admitted of variations in size, room numbers, internal layout, standard of equipment, quality of finish, and the detail of architectural embellishment. Some of these differences were clearly substantial: the difference between having two bedrooms or three was a material one, as was that between an inside water closet and one outside in the backyard. Others might seem to be more cosmetic: in some houses the front door opened directly into the front room, in others there was a narrow entrance-hall passage with the ground-floor rooms opening off it; the street fronts of some were in fancy brickwork with courses of contrasting colours and qualities, while others were in plain stock brick – all the back elevations were in plain brick, only the fronts were for show; and sandstone door and window lintels were a cut above mere brick. Differences like these did not indicate that one house was newer and more modern than another, although that might often be the case, so much as they expressed fine shades of distinction in status and less subtle distinctions in weekly rents.

Broadly speaking there was a regional hierarchy of working-class housing with the south and Midlands at the top with the largest number of rooms per house – five or six were the most usual – and a steady decline through the normal four-roomed houses of the Lancashire cotton towns and the three- or four-roomed houses of the West Riding textile towns, to the two or three rooms of the north-east. To some extent the fewer the rooms the larger they were, so that the disparities in the amount of living space per family were not so great as they might seem. Nevertheless, domestic arrangements and the whole style of family life are obviously quite largely dependent on the number of separate rooms at the disposal of a family, and habits and standards that rely on segregated space for each kind of domestic activity will simply be impossible when everything has to be done in just two or three rooms. Thus, in spite of the availability of a moderate supply of houses both larger and smaller than the norm in each region, these regional differences in house size are a reminder that social distinctions within the working class, in patterns of living, tended to be superimposed upon regional distinctions between working-class lifestyles, and had by no means eroded those distinctions before 1914.

The south–north housing slope bottomed out in Scotland, where 85 per cent of the houses in Glasgow in 1911 had three rooms or less and the typical apartment consisted of two rooms. Even that was some improvement on the past, for in the 1880s a quarter of Glasgow's families lived in one-room apartments and earlier in the century that had probably been the most common form of urban living. These apartments were radically different from the English house intended for single-family occupation. They were in tall tenement blocks, four or five storeys in Glasgow, more in Edinburgh, each block containing eight or more sets served by a common central staircase. Tenement building and tenement living were already well established in Edinburgh and Glasgow before the Victorian period, and their continuation throughout the nineteenth century was perhaps due to the ingrained custom of living in tenements – which in Edinburgh at least extended to the professional classes as well as the populace – as much as to any other factor. The whole of western Europe, except for Belgium, was like Scotland in featuring tenement blocks and multi-storey living as the typical form of city life, and the concierge as the typical custodian of the common services and facilities, and possibly morals, of each block. Belgium, the first to follow England in industrialization, followed England also in housing its workers in cottages, although whether that was cause and effect is difficult to say. The English worker had a rooted dislike of tenements, and indeed the wealthier classes themselves only took to flats, which were highly superior forms of tenements, very gradually during the last quarter of the century. In London the philanthropic housing built from mid-century onwards by such bodies as the Peabody and Waterlow trusts and several artisans' dwellings companies was usually in tenement blocks. These were widely regarded with suspicion and distrust as being no better than barracks, an analogy helped by the strict discipline and battery of restrictions which housing managers imposed on the tenants.

Each nation clung to what was customary, the potential occupiers no less than the builders. But when and why England diverged from most of western Europe, or more parochially, when and why Scotland diverged from England, are questions easier to ask than to answer. Many explanations for the tenement/cottage divide have been tried; none is altogether satisfactory. Fortifications and town walls survived in Europe into the second half of the nineteenth century, penning in urban development and making high-density, high-rise building the only way of fitting more and more people on to a fixed quantity of land. By the later eighteenth century, however, Scottish towns had long since abandoned their walls, and there was no more physical or military restraint on their outward spread than there was on English towns whose walls had fallen into disuse in the sixteenth century. In Scotland, it has been argued, building land was more expensive than in England, as a result of the Scottish system of land tenure known as feuing, under which a proprietor parted with his land in return for a fixed annual feu duty, or rent. Since this was in effect a perpetual lease at a rent which could never be altered, the owner had a powerful incentive to fix the highest possible rent at the outset, with the effect of pricing building land above the level at which it was economic to cover it with cottages. Scottish towns did indeed have tenements built on feued land. But European cities had tenements built on freehold land whose ownership passed outright from landowner to builder; and several English towns, such as Sunderland, Oldham, Stockport, and Bristol, were developed with cottages although their tenurial arrangements of perpetual leases at fixed annual chief rents were remarkably similar to feuing. All that can be said with certainty is that building land was more expensive in Scotland than in England, and that this differential did encourage tenement building. Moreover, in the Victorian age of building regulations – and most Scottish burghs had in fact an unbroken tradition of civic or guild regulation of building operations – the rules were intended to produce structurally sound and sanitarily approved versions of the prevailing type, the tenement block. The side effect of these regulations, whose specifications of building materials, types of construction, or street widths, were appropriate for tall tenements, was a set of requirements that made the building of cottages prohibitively expensive.

The worst conditions in early Victorian Britain were to be found in the Glasgow tenements, the smelliest, the dirtiest, the most unhealthy, the most overcrowded, and the most offensive to evangelical morality. The usual arrangement was to group the tenement blocks in small courts which opened off a narrow wynd, barely as wide as a cart, that gave access to the main street. In the middle of each court was a dunghill, where with luck the excreta and detritus of perhaps twenty or thirty families accumulated; much of it, however, got lodged in the common staircases, which were unimaginably filthy. A one-room apartment was all that an unskilled labourer, at least, could expect; everything, cooking, eating, sleeping, procreation, childbirth, death, perhaps urination and defecation, went on in the one room. The room was probably slightly larger than the average English room, but that hardly made the family life in it any less squalid and disorderly to southern eyes. It helped to explain, but not to excuse or condone, this rough, tough life that it was no rougher or tougher than the life in Highland bothy or Irish cabin from which many migrants had come, and that Scottish rural emigrants had generally brought a tradition of one-room living with them to town.

Improvement in Glasgow from the mid-century meant tidying up and sanitizing the tenement, not scrapping the building form. Above all, in pursuit of the great Victorian quest for light, air, and cleanliness, it meant outlawing wynds and courts and ensuring that all tenements had a proper street frontage. But it also meant increasing differentiation, frequently within a single block, of one-, two-, and three-room sets. Even in two- and three-room apartments the rooms had no clearly defined or specialized functions; one would be called the kitchen, but was likely to have a bed in it, and the others were general-purpose rooms. By the 1880s all the rooms were likely to be provided with a distinct bed recess, often with a built-in bed or a bedstead supplied by the landlord; and many newly built tenements had internal water closets, opening off the kitchen, a feature also found in the one-room apartments that were still being built. Glasgow remained at the end of the century the city with the worst overcrowding in Britain, measured by the essentially English definition of the census authorities that more than two people per habitable room in a house constituted overcrowding. Glasgow's rating certainly recorded great congestion, but it was also a reflection of the differing customs of Scottish and English urban living. Overcrowding, in Glasgow's eyes, was a matter of cubic foot of air space per person rather than of persons per room, and with that in mind efforts were made to prevent it by 'ticketing' each block with a metal plate recording the permissible number of occupants, sometimes to the discomfiture of families that exceeded the ticket.

Thus the general level of working-class housing in Glasgow improved considerably in the last forty years or so of the nineteenth century, as it did with variations on the theme in major Scottish towns, Edinburgh, Aberdeen, Dundee, and Stirling, all of which had the tenement habit; and as it did in the rest of Britain. The improvement was the work of the building industry and the housing market, steered it is true by municipal bye-laws but powered essentially by the demand exerted by the working classes and the supplies of funds and construction which that evoked. The resultant living conditions were drab, cheerless, cramped, and unimaginative, manifestly inferior to those of the better-off classes and inadequate in terms of late twentieth-century standards and expectations; but if not spacious or gracious they were at least passably decent, and a long way short of being a disgrace to a civilized and wealthy nation. Surveys conducted by the Board of Trade in the early years of the twentieth century showed, indeed, that British workers were better housed than those of any other European country and, in terms of the proportion of wages devoted to rent, more cheaply housed. For the great majority of the British working classes at the end of the nineteenth century there was no housing problem; that was something which concerned the minority at the bottom end of the market and on the lowest rung of society. That problem produced periodic outbreaks of anxious investigation and flurries of legislative and philanthropic action by well-meaning or scared Victorians, with negligible results. When the housing problem was 'solved' by subsidized council housing after 1919 that was because the problem itself had been radically changed by the First World War, not because of any long-term inadequacies of Victorian mass housing.

Behind the grimly depressing and featureless landscape of ranks of terrace houses arrayed in repetitive gridiron patterns, and the tough, grey cliffs of tenement blocks, lay the variety and individuality that gave physical expression to differences in status and social position. In England the layers within the working classes tended to separate themselves out through the social distancing of one-class neighbourhoods, while in Scotland all groups tended to get jumbled together in the blocks, although vertical layering of the kind more familiar in Continental cities was possible. Even so, in late Victorian Glasgow it was well recognized that a one-room apartment was suitable for an unskilled labourer's family, at least until the children began to earn, and that skilled workers needed a three-room set to maintain their dignity and self-respect. The essential differences between the two countries did not lie in the pecking order of the groups and classes, which was broadly similar, but in the customs and habits of domestic life, which helped to shape the different housing forms in the first place, and which were strongly influenced by those forms and the way in which living space was arranged. In England the separate house intended for one-family occupation encouraged the domestication of the family by emphasizing the concentration of activities inside the house where they were not shared by strangers, and reducing the opportunities or necessities for conducting everyday personal and domestic functions in public. This was especially noticeable in the insistence on having a separate privy for each house, an ideal made easier to attain with the widespread introduction of the pail closet in the 1860s and easier still with the wave of cheap water closets that started in the 1880s; noticeable also when piped water was brought into the house, as it was into most new houses from the 1860s (although older houses could well still be without at the end of the century), eliminating the communal standpipe or well. The individual through-house in particular, with its own backyard providing its own clothesline space and its own ashpit as well as its own privy, encapsulated under individual family control the basic resources needed to draw a sharp line between private domestic life and the public face worn by people as members of a community. Release from the necessity of doing one's dirty washing in public was literally the path to respectability.

Privacy and domesticity were not cultivated by the working classes to anything like the pitch attained by the lower middle class especially, for whom the cult of keeping oneself to oneself became an obsession. Perhaps particularly in the older and less reputable districts the womenfolk and children were continually in and out of each other's houses, far from cocooned in separate cells. And in the newer world of backyards the back lanes or back alleys designed for the sanitary removal of nightsoil and refuse were appropriated as the private space of the residents and their children, an arena for a semi-private community life of a clearly identified community and a kind of half-way house between the disorderly living in public of the old courts and the sealed-in privacy of middle-class gentility. Nevertheless, the privacy and domesticity developed and refined as part of the way of life of many layers of the English working classes was of an altogether different order to anything within the reach, and perhaps within the aspirations, of most of the Scottish working classes. Whether Scottish people did not want a domesticity arranged in a setting of functionally distinct rooms and family-controlled private space, or whether they shaped a way of living to fit the accommodation available, the effect of tenement living was that life within the home appeared chaotically unstructured and casual to English eyes, and that much of life which had been internalized in England continued to be lived outside the home in semi-public.

In nothing was this difference more apparent than in the incorporation of the cult of the parlour into the pattern of respectable working-class living, for it was a style virtually incompatible with the tenement form where even in three-room apartments every room was likely to do duty as a bedroom and thus be in daily use. To be able to set aside the front room as a parlour required a four-room house with the front door opening on a separate entrance passage as a minimum; a front door opening directly into the front room was useless for the purpose, and a five-room house with an adequate scullery as well as a large kitchen-living room was decidedly superior. The essence of a parlour was the elevation of the front room to the status of a household shrine, a special room withdrawn from daily use and consecrated to special occasions. Much love and care was lavished on the parlour, it was the repository of the best possessions, the best furniture, and the most respected prints and pictures – mainly religious until the 1880s, then joined by reproductions of royal portraits. Most significant of all, it was the home of the piano, finding its way into working-class homes by the million in the last quarter of the century, valued as an instrument but above all prized as the status symbol of the age. The great thing was that the parlour was for display rather than use, and this constantly puzzled and angered late Victorian middle-class observers to whom the deliberate exclusion of a whole room from everyday use by families that were crowded and short of space seemed wilful and stupid extravagance. Raymond Unwin, leading architect and planner in the garden city movement at the end of the century, regarded it as his mission to eliminate useless parlours from working-class cottages: a cottage needed 'a living room large enough to be healthy, comfortable, and convenient, [and] it is worse than folly to take space from that living room, where it will be used every day and every hour, to form a parlour, where it will be used only once or twice a week'. It was the once or twice a week, however, which gave the parlour its place in the popular culture of the home, and everyday use would have negated its special character of solemnity and sanctity.

The parlour by being set apart from the sweat and toil, noise and dirt, of everyday domestic life could impart an aura of solemn ritual to those less frequent occasions on which it was used. Sunday dinner with the whole family sitting down together was frequently one such occasion, the special surroundings emphasizing family unity in contrast to the dispersal and staggered mealtimes of weekdays. Special visitors, particularly those from a higher social class, were received in the parlour, and relatives and neighbours on feast days or when formality needed to be observed. Courting might be carried on, but this was as it were an underhand use of the parlour because it happened to be secluded; more in keeping with the true spirit of the parlour, it would be used for discussing marriage arrangements and for wedding teas, and more sombrely for funeral bakemeats. The parlour habit spread vigorously in the second half of the nineteenth century, growing on those habits of keeping best rooms with cherished possessions of cased clocks and a few books which had already been observed among some artisans and better paid millworkers in the 1830s and 1840s. It was not confined to the urban working classes but spread to rural and agricultural workers wherever there was the opportunity. 'If two dwelling-rooms of the same size are provided,' the Duke of Bedford observed disapprovingly of rural cottages in 1897, looking back on the previous thirty or forty years, 'one is often kept idle as a parlour, where china dogs, crochet antimacassars, and unused tea-services are maintained in fusty seclusion. This idle parlour adds nothing to the comfort of the cottagers.'

Housing and homes nurturing this parlour-based culture of respectability and domesticity covered much of the English working class by the end of the nineteenth century, certainly much more of it than merely the labour aristocracy, and much less than the whole since the poorest were untouched. Town and country alike were affected. Much had changed from Chadwick's Britain of courts, alleys, and wynds of the 1840s, and while the changes could be viewed as a general all-round improvement of conditions, they were also a process of social differentiation marking off group from group. The parlour-house of the superior artisan did not differ fundamentally from the parlour-house of the commercial clerk at the bottom end of the lower middle class, except possibly in the matter of front and back gardens; and their ways of using the space – their domestic cultures – differed more in mutual disapproval than in actual substance. Thus was the link forged in the chain which ran without any sharp breaks from the meanest cottage or one-roomed hutch all the way to the grandest country mansion. The Victorian nose – and eye and ear – for fine social distinctions was reflected in the housing structure, where the development and refinement of different house types tended to accentuate the multi-layered nature of society as urbanization progressed. An industrialized society polarized into just two or three distinct and conflicting classes was not a product of housing or home lives, and insofar as it was more than a myth invented by intellectuals it was a social structure issuing from the workplace and from political life that coexisted with the much more complicated and hierarchical social structure of the home.

CHAPTER SIX

Work

Victorian middle-class culture was dedicated to separate spheres: separate single-family houses, separation of work from home, and separation of women from work. They were features increasingly incorporated into the public image of working-class living, because that was the kind of house provided, that was the kind of work available, and that was the ideal of working-class leaders. In 1877 the Trades Union Congress resolved that one of the aims of trade unions was 'to bring about a condition . . . where wives should be in their proper sphere at home, instead of being dragged into competition for livelihood against the great and strong men of the world'. Aspirations, in this case of men using an appeal to femininity to cloak their fear that women would take their jobs, and forgetting about the importance of family earnings, were not the same as achievements. The working classes appeared to conform to patterns at least broadly similar to those of the middle class, but their private practice was but loosely related to their public appearance. Houses built with the normal family of parents and children in mind frequently housed more than a simple family. Some kinds of work, in the clothing and packing trades, for example, continued to be performed in the home to the end of the century and beyond; and even though employment outside the home was the increasingly typical mode, the workshop or factory could have an intimate and family-based subdivision of the workforce which made it socially not dissimilar to the outworker's home or the weaver's cottage, however different it was in physical structure and mechanical contents. Women worked as a matter of course, in paid employment if that was available and compatible with their family situation, and otherwise at the unpaid work of the household. Work was not socially unthinkable, as it was for

197

middle-class women for whom posts as governesses or ladies' companions were virtually the only jobs that could be taken, around mid-century, without degradation and loss of class. Skilled workers may have come to share these ideas of gentility, for their wives; not for their unmarried daughters, who were expected to earn their keep. The 'respectable workingman', that favourite figure of Victorian social reporting, understood by 'respectability' something different from the values the middle classes attached to it: the differences flowed from different experiences of work as much as from obvious differences in income levels.

The respectable workingman became a key mid-Victorian figure, the character on whose good sense hopes of social harmony were based, and whose example of independence and self-respect would inspire a whole class. Hard-working, reliable, reasonably sober, and a dependable family man, he set great store by a regular job, and although by no means obsequious to his masters he had no intention of overthrowing them or of subverting the economic and social system which provided the job. Such attitudes appeared to be in stark contrast to those of the turbulent and disorderly 1840s, when the rhetoric of Chartism and the atmosphere of mass meetings had vibrated with anti-master feelings and workers seemed so far from being reconciled to the capitalist industrial order that revolutionary changes seemed not at all impossible. The mid-Victorian social tranquillity was indeed such a contrast that some historians have only been able to explain it by inventing a cunning and fiendishly successful conspiracy by the employers to subvert the true path of working-class consciousness. According to this theory the employers bought the allegiance of their skilled workers by conceding them a special status which protected their control of entry into the craft, their control of the work process, and their pay differentials. They became a privileged, highly paid elite, the labour aristocracy, attached to the established industrial order which nourished their privileges, essentially collaborationist and non-militant. The labour aristocracy was thus detached from the main body of the working class which was left insecure, exploited, and leaderless. Since the labour aristocracy creamed off the resources of talent, intelligence, and education in the working classes, the rest were left almost powerless to organize or to articulate their interests and were helplessly swept along by the great tide of mid-Victorian industrialization, surfacing in the 1890s as a mature industrial proletariat ready to resume the class struggle where it had been left off in 1848. Schematically neat, this view bears little relation to reality: respectable workingmen were far more numerous than just skilled workers or labour aristocrats; the labour aristocracy was created by the nature of the job, not by employers' strategies; high wages and secure employment were not the preserve of the skilled alone; the skilled were more radical than the unskilled; and the proletarians of the 1890s, however cohesive socially, were conspicuously indifferent to fighting the class war.

Middle-class and official Victorians who delighted in classifying and categorizing the working classes used occupational and wage criteria to distinguish the superior artisans or skilled workers from the rest. Many historians have followed this lead in seeing 'the skilled artisan, separated by an abyss from the "labourer" ', and have seized upon the testimony of Thomas Wright, the skilled metalworker writing in the early 1870s: 'Between the artisan and the unskilled labourer a gulf is fixed. While the former resents the spirit in which he believes the followers of "genteel occupations" look down upon him, he in his turn looks down upon the labourer. The artisan creed with regard to labourers is, that the latter are an inferior class, and that they should be made to know and kept in their place.' This functional and status distinction had a real enough existence in the world of labour, although it was by no means a simple and straightforward matter to say who was an artisan and who possessed skill. An alternative approach is to employ cultural or moral criteria, and by these standards the great majority of the mid-Victorian working classes were thought to be independent and self-respecting, that is far more than the 10 per cent or so of the labour force who were skilled craftsmen. They may not have been independent in relation to their work, in the way that a cabinet-maker or a carpenter was independent in setting his own pace and standards, but they were fiercely self-reliant and determined to live on their own resources and not to suffer the indignities of poor relief, charity, or ruinous debt. By this reckoning it was only a minority, many of whom may indeed have been unskilled, general labourers, who were not respectable:

destitute or poverty-stricken, feckless or idle, disorderly or drunken, scrounger or disabled, this minority was variously estimated at from one tenth to one third of the whole.

The ultimate disgrace for a Victorian worker's family was a pauper burial. Having the means to avoid it and to provide for a decent funeral that would preserve the family's standing in the community was the measure of basic respectability; around this minimum core could be built all the other defences against degradation and all the other displays of status and comfort which stretched all the way up to the comparative ease and security of the superior artisan. Getting the means was a matter of resolve, regular habits, and social motivation, rather than of any particular level of wages. It meant making a regular contribution, perhaps of no more than a halfpenny or a penny a week and perhaps at a sacrifice of food for a hungry family, to an insurance fund that paid out funeral money. This might be a burial club, usually local and short-lived, often linked to a particular trade or calling, which had been very common at least since the late eighteenth century and were thought to be specially numerous in Lancashire. It might be a friendly society, either a local and trade-related club or fellowship of the kind which were already common in the eighteenth century, or one of the national affiliated orders, of which the Manchester Unity of Oddfellows was the prototype and the Ancient Order of Foresters the close rival, that were growing extremely rapidly in membership from the mid-1830s onwards. In either case these, the 'true' friendly societies, offered many other benefits besides death or burial insurance; sickness, accident, possibly unemployment and old age, were likely to be covered, while the local lodge or court of the society (a 'tent' in the case of the Rechabites) had an active social life of ritual, ceremony, feasting and drinking. Another type of institution, somewhat confusingly known as the friendly collecting society, was beginning to flourish in the 1850s. This merely collected weekly contributions, through its agents, and was run as a pure insurance operation with no social or convivial functions. The Royal Liver, of 1850, and the Liverpool Victoria rapidly became the largest of these collecting societies, concentrating on burial insurance and the poorest part of the population; others, however, might go in for high subscriptions and an extensive range of benefits. The Hearts of Oak was of this type. The last main road to a proper funeral was the industrial assurance company, a profit-making company specializing in life insurance, on infant as well as adult lives, for small weekly premiums, whose policies were commonly used for funeral expenses. The Prudential, founded in 1854, quickly became the giant in this field, and by the early 1870s had over one million members.

Any of these could confer the basic badge of respectability, although membership of a friendly society with its higher subscriptions, extensive benefits, and club life denoted markedly higher status than minimal decency. The numbers involved were large, but impossible to determine accurately since although there was from 1793 a body of statute law to encourage and help friendly societies, neither registration with the Registrar of Friendly Societies (from 1846) nor the submission of returns by the societies were obligatory. It was thought that there were 600,000 to 700,000 members of friendly societies in 1801, a little short of one million in 1815, a full million in 1835, and not far short of 1.5 million by 1850. If these figures are anything like correct, they imply that about one quarter of the adult males of Britain were in membership, a proportion which had begun to increase from the 1830s. After mid-century the increase was very rapid, if a much-quoted estimate of the Royal Commission on Friendly Societies of 1874 is to be believed, for its statement that there were then 4 million members implies that 60 per cent of adult males belonged. The 1874 figure is in some doubt, since the estimate included membership of burial clubs, and if the concern is to measure the importance of the 'true' friendly societies then it seems that a few years later, in 1880, there were 1.6 million members of ordinary or unitary friendly societies and 600,000 members of the large affiliated societies. With 2.2 million members, however, friendly societies had grown to embrace 30 per cent of the adult male population; and since it was clear that very few people indeed outside the working classes ever joined friendly societies, the proportion of all male workers who were in membership was even higher. On the other hand, if the object is to try and gauge the possible extent of the respectability net then the burial clubs and the full 4 million deserve to be reinstated. Moreover, something needs to be added for those who covered themselves through the collecting societies and industrial assurance companies. In 1880 these institutions had a total of 7.8 million separate policies in force; while these represented a good deal less than that number of insured people since many individuals accumulated several policies over their lives and insured with more than one institution, and while these insured and members of societies and clubs were not mutually exclusive categories, nevertheless some millions should be added to the friendly and burial society members in order to arrive at a plausible view of the size of the provident population. It seems likely that by the 1870s this was easily three quarters and possibly as much as 80 per cent of the total adult male population. By 1915 after more than thirty years of further growth there were 6.6 million members of friendly societies, and 45.5 million policies were in force with collecting societies and industrial assurance companies. These numbers are so enormous that making every allowance for duplication and for the spread of policy-holding to women (though few became friendly society members), the conclusion is inescapable that at least half the male workforce was in friendly societies, and it becomes hard to imagine that more than 10 per cent of the population can have been without some level of protection.

Before concluding that this mounting tide of thrift and providence signified a thriving and contented working population, it is well to recall that the future happiness being bought by the weekly pennies and sixpences and shillings ranged all the way from security against all the major hazards and accidents of a working life down to nothing more than a fitting burial and funeral feast after one's death. The minimum level of security brought a certain peace of mind and anticipation that self-respect would not be mocked in death, but did nothing to alleviate the hardships and miseries of life and may indeed have increased them. Nevertheless, totals and proportions of this magnitude create considerable difficulties for those who believe that prudence and independence were the preserve of a small privileged minority of workers, the skilled, and that membership of friendly societies was a particular hallmark and defining characteristic of the labour aristocracy. On the contrary, these figures suggest that from the 1830s onwards there was a considerable broadening out through different working-class strata of the friendly society habit, with all that that implied in the way of regular savings, defence of living standards, and awareness of a status and standing in the community. From the 1830s to the 1870s this broadening process was perceptible, even though broadly speaking real wages were only growing unsteadily and weakly in these years; after the 1870s the process accelerated greatly, and in the last quarter of the century real wages increased by roughly 50 per cent. Concurrently with this movement more and more of the lower ranks of the working classes, implicitly the lower paid, were drawn into the basic respectability net until by the 1900s it looks as if only the bottom 10 per cent, the residuum, were left out. Having money to spare after providing for the bare necessities clearly had much to do with this movement, and it received a strong push from the rise in incomes towards the end of the century. It can be argued, however, that the crucial steps towards forming a broad-based respectable working class were made in the mid-Victorian years, with the later accelerated expansion building on these foundations; and further, that these crucial steps were less a response to rising disposable incomes, since there was no marked rise, than a deliberate reordering of family budgets to make room for 'respectability' or 'security' payments.

This was a cultural change, a sign that sections of the working classes were settling down to urban living and to industrial work, incorporating these conditions into a normal and accustomed pattern of living, carving out for themselves an honourable place in the new society. As the pattern of work became familiar and stable, and built up its own traditions of customs and practices, so it provided the essential cultural, as well as the more obvious financial, underpinning of a stable way of life. Skilled workers in the traditional crafts had long possessed a well-defined relationship to their work enshrined in elaborate rules and customs for each trade marking out the territory of the artisan, and ensuring his control over specific parts of the work process. The new skilled workers generated by machine technology had little difficulty in establishing in relation to the making of machines a position similar to that which joiners, for example, held in relation to the making of furniture. There was no fundamental problem here of social assimilation, although there was novelty in the technical skills involved and there were economic problems and frictions in evolving satisfactory forms of work organization and relations between workers and employers. All this amounts to saying is that the engineers and the fitters, the boilermakers and the gas-fitters, were absorbed into the ranks of the labour aristocracy almost as a matter of course, by virtue of the training required, whether by formal apprenticeship or by several years of experience as juniors, by virtue of the variety of different specific skills comprised in the job, and by virtue of reliance on the individual worker in choosing the appropriate methods for the task in hand and in setting the pace of working. This was a significant new departure in the sense of a successful grafting of new growth on to old forms of social organization. The momentous departure and striking social innovation, however, came with the social stabilization of the new industrial workers whose work could not be assimilated to the traditional craft models, but who nevertheless secured a place in the social order without becoming mere factory drones and without being beaten down into submissive subservience.

At times in the troubled 1830s and 1840s it seemed that the textile industry produced both the most desperate and distressed workers, in the handloom weavers, and the most dangerously disturbed, in the mill operatives. It was no accident that Engels caught a whiff of the class struggle in the air of Manchester, or that mass torchlight meetings on northern moors bred fears of uprisings and attacks on the mills. There were no risings, more because the people were extremely doubtful about the wisdom of resorting to physical force than because they were overawed by the troops of northern command, which were handled very discreetly. The fear of social breakdown was nonetheless real enough. The contrast between the turbulent and disorderly northern manufacturing districts in the Chartist years and the peaceful and harmonious social order found there in the 1860s and 1870s somewhat overstates the turbulence and the harmony, but is a broadly correct picture. This contrast was the result of many factors. Contemporaries thought it little short of miraculous, and if direct divine intervention seemed implausible were inclined to credit religious and moral influences, or at least education, for conquering the unruliness of ignorance and error and spreading the orderliness of knowledge and sound doctrine. Historians have preferred to look to the operations of the trade cycle, to the post-Crystal Palace fruition of earlier investment in structural changes in the economy, and to the cumulative effects of factory discipline spreading down the generations.

The concept of people being broken in to obedience to the unnatural rules and routine of the mill, as a young horse is broken in, has something to recommend it; and by 1850 some of the millworkers were of the third generation in the factory, with no folk memory of any other mode of work. Still, familiarization, whether it is described in the emotive language of breaking the spirit or not, is an acquired rather than an inherited characteristic, and occurs with each individual – powerfully conditioned no doubt by the quality of the family environment of upbringing – and not with family trees. Moreover, although by mid-century the long-settled factory population, descendants of those who had come into the mills in the 1790s, formed a significant nucleus of people to whom mill work was traditional, they were still a minority. Even the cotton towns, which had been longest of all in the factory business, continued into the third quarter of the century to have new migrants as the majority of their working-age populations, and hence it is likely that the majority of their millworkers were incomers. In the industries where factories developed later and more slowly it is, therefore, all the more likely that the great majority of workers belonged to the first generation in the factory, and indeed in the town, in the third quarter of the century. Yet this was the time when the tranquillity of maturity, not the disturbance of rawness, appeared as the mood of the industrial districts. It was not so much that a new generation of workers became reconciled to a factory culture which the generation of the 1830s had resisted, as that work, working practices, and workers all changed together to produce a restyled factory culture.

These changes are at their clearest in the Lancashire cotton industry, whose workers were chided by John Bright in 1842 for their error in opposing the masters and striking for the Charter, and praised by Gladstone in 1864 for the example they had given in public responsibility through their 'self-command, self-control, respect for order, patience under suffering, confidence in the law, and regard for superiors'. They are principally associated with the definitive entry of the menfolk into the factory and the consequent reunion of the family in similar working conditions and often in the same workplace; and secondarily with the consolidation of the authority of adult males, not indeed in control of their work process since they were subject to the authority of employer, overlooker, and machine, but in relation to their own dependants. Men had early on displaced women as spinners, for as soon as the frame and the mule made spinning into a factory process these became male-operated machines, with women doing inferior work in the cardroom. The mulespinners grew so powerful and confident in their skill, indeed, that it was said that during a long strike in 1824 several manufacturers went to Richard Roberts, a well-known Manchester engineer, and asked him to devise something to 'render them in some measure independent of the more refractory class of their workmen'. Roberts obliged with the self-acting mule, whose relatively automatic operation threatened to deskill the mulespinner's job. Self-actors came in rather slowly, and were only generally adopted by the industry in the 1840s. But many shared the view of the Glasgow manufacturer, Archibald Alison, that they offered the one bright hope of avoiding submission 'to the present system of coercion and ruin imposed upon them by the workmen'. 'There is the self-adjusting mule,' he said, 'which had been known, but it had not spread to any great degree in Glasgow; but since the late strike of the spinners in 1837, the number of persons who have given orders for self-acting mules, or for double wheels, which reduces the number of spinners to one half, is so great, that already it has had a very serious effect in throwing cotton-spinners out of employment; and I therefore think it very probable that in five or seven years the cotton-spinners will be reduced to the same destitution as the hand-loom weavers are now.' It did not happen so.

The self-actor raised productivity and reduced costs to such an extent that demand, and output, grew faster than before and the number of spinners did not decline, but increased. Of more importance, the mulespinners who had seemed to face loss of status and relegation to the ranks of the unskilled reasserted their position and authority as key men in the mill community. In part this was a consequence of the mechanical limitations of the self-actor. It was true that one self-actor served double or treble the number of spindles of the hand mule it displaced, but it was some way short of being a precocious piece of full automation, and skill, experience, and judgement, as well as dexterity, were still needed for its operation. In part it was a consequence of employers and foremen accepting the managerial convenience of allowing mulespinners to remain responsible for recruiting and controlling their own assistants. Each mule required a team of assistants, or piecers, generally children or teenagers, whose job it was to piece together broken threads; two or three for the old hand mule, perhaps five or six for the self-actor. The usual custom was to leave it to the mulespinner to find his own piecers, and to pay them out of his earnings. This piece of subcontracting saved the millowner a certain amount of bother, and since each mule was in any case effectively a self-contained production unit which the spinner was bound to supervise, it saved him a certain amount of supervision as well. The price, from the employer's point of view, was a degree of independence for the spinner. 'In the spinning department', as a guide to factory management of the 1830s put it, 'there are men who have the charge of their own work, and are paid only for what they do, and responsible for both the quantity and quality of their work . . . and hence it is not necessary that the spinning master should be always present.'

For a while it seemed that the introduction of the self-actor, by radically altering the ratio between spinners and piecers, would disrupt the established custom, and that masters might seize the opportunity to go over to direct employment and control of the piecers, thus reducing spinners to a fully dependent position. The threat, if it was ever a serious one, had gone away by the end of the 1840s, any dilution of complete managerial authority throughout the mill more than compensated by the smooth running of the spinning department and by the good labour relations which the custom encouraged. There were some spinning mills where the piecers were hired by the master or the overlooker, but predominantly the mulespinners remained in charge of hiring, training, and supervising their own piecers, and it stayed that way until the end of the century. This little bit of patronage gave mulespinners a certain amount of prestige and power both within the factory and in the community from whose families the piecers were recruited. When possible a spinner would employ his own children, and this was undoubtedly the most effective way of keeping the family together in the factory as a work unit, especially when his wife worked in the cardroom of the same mill. In the course of his working life a spinner could well see all his children through their early steps in the mill, under his own fatherly eye; but it would have to be one by one, as his children in turn reached the right age for piecers – nine years old for part-timers after the 1833 Factory Act, and thirteen for full-time work – and in turn became too old to continue as piecers and at fifteen or sixteen had to move on to different jobs or perhaps out of the mill altogether. At any one point in time, therefore, most of the children working as piecers were not working under a parent, and most spinners had teams of assistants consisting largely of other people's children. Spinners frequently used their patronage to employ the children of relatives, and in this way it is easier to see the extended family being held together, or created, in the factory, than the simple nuclear family. Neighbours' children, however, were probably the largest category, and the main social importance of the system lay in the position and influence in the local neighbourhood community which it conferred on the spinner, rather than in any capacity to project family life into the workplace.

The other side of the coin was that there was much more employment in spinning mills for women and children, in the preparatory processes and as assistants, than there was for men. This highlighted the special position of the mulespinners, but it meant that many of the heads of families in the cotton towns stood no chance of ever becoming one of them, even though their wives and children might be in the mill. At the same time it should be remembered that the majority of millworkers continued at least into the 1870s to be fresh arrivals from the country, with no traditions of factory work in their backgrounds. It is true that there were some grades of distinction among farmworkers, with ordinary labourers at the bottom of the pile and at the top the more skilled, and better paid, ploughmen, horsemen, cowmen, or shepherds. It is also true that there was much child and female labour in agriculture, probably considerably more than the census record states. But the children and the women generally worked at their own distinct and separate tasks, not alongside the men and not in family teams; it was only on the 'family farm' employing no hired labour that an agricultural family was likely to be found functioning as a work unit. The mills may not have offered a great deal of scope, in practice, for transplanting the family into the factory as a working team serving a mule, but they did afford some scope; since there was little or no preindustrial tradition of family-group working (as distinct from experience in domestic industry), this was more often than not a creation, not a transplantation, of the family as a work unit and may be construed as a positive contribution to family cohesion and authority resulting from the social or customary processing of the labour requirements of machine spinning.

The Lancashire way of speaking of a man 'getting his wheels' when he became a spinner in charge of a mule reflects the absorption of the machine into common language, but more than that it expresses the importance of the step as a rite of passage, a landmark in the life of a man as he moved into a position of some consequence. As befitted someone at the top of a small hierarchy, the mulespinner was well paid, getting 30 to 50 per cent more than most other adult workers in the cotton industry. As in other occupations with a scarcity value, spinners aimed to entrench their industrial power by controlling entry; at various times efforts were made to restrict the job to those who were sons or nephews of mulespinners, but without success. Instead, the rule was widely recognized by employers that no one could become a mulespinner who had not previously worked as a piecer, and this made perfectly good operational sense as this work served as suitable training. It is these characteristics of status, pay differentials, and entry conditions, which have led many historians to regard the cotton spinners as labour aristocrats. They figured in Archibald Alison's 1838 list of examples of skilled workers: 'By skilled labour, I mean the labour of those peculiarly difficult trades to learn, which have got an organization of trades' unions, such as cotton-spinners, iron-moulders, colliers, iron-miners, and so on.' Interestingly enough, this list did not mention any of the craft or artisan trades, those with apprenticeship; the significant point about the spinners, indeed, was that they enjoyed a special position without conforming to the labour aristocrat model.

The spinners were indeed an elite of sorts, thanks to their superior pay, but they were not an elite separated from and confronting a mass of inferior labourers since not only had they themselves risen from the ranks of junior labourers in the mill, but also their wives, children, friends, neighbours, and relatives were likely to be working in 'inferior' jobs in the industry, probably in the same mill. Spinners were indeed men with a skill, but it was the skill of a machine operator acquired by experience and needing dexterity and intelligence, and was not in fact a 'peculiarly difficult trade to learn'. Mill mechanics, who had to know how to repair and service the mill machinery, were more obviously in the traditional skilled labour class; they were a subgroup of the engineers, formal or informal apprenticeship was needed to learn the trade, and they commanded wages 20 to 30 per cent above those of the spinners. Finally, spinners owed their jobs less to their own qualifications and merits – in comparison, say, with mill mechanics – than to the fact that the overlooker or master noticed them and chose to give them their chance with 'the wheels'. In practice, by the mid-Victorian years, it was common for spinners to be the sons of spinners, but this manifestation of the hereditary principle was evidence of the masters' concern for the harmony and welfare of the mill rather than of successful pressure by spinners on reluctant masters. All these qualities of the spinners, indeed, pointed to the integration and cohesion of the whole workforce of the spinning mills, across all the different grades, and to the importance of the individual mill as the focus and the means of forging a sense of community.

In the mid-Victorian mill towns life centred on the mill, not simply because it was the source of work and wages but because it formed a distinct community and attracted specific loyalties. The individual mill was not a rival centre to the home but a complementary one, precisely because so many other activities besides work were based on the mill. The workers at a mill might play together, possibly pray together, sing together, celebrate together, go on holiday together, and vote together – not only after 1867 when all the householders among them became entitled to vote, but also before that when a few of the better paid and more thrifty were electorally qualified as £10 householders. Such group solidarity in social behaviour was not in defiance of the master, but was actively encouraged and fostered by the employer. Voting patterns indeed suggest that the workers of a mill adopted the politics of their employer, by virtue of the mill's identity as a social entity rather than through intimidation or coercion: the workers of an Anglican millowner tended to vote Tory, and those of a Dissenter, Liberal.

The mid-Victorian millowners, in contrast to their predecessors in the 1830s, tended to tolerate trade union organization among their workers, which was led by the mulespinners; the days of union-breaking and refusal to recognize unions were past. Employers found it highly convenient, in fact, to have union officials with whom to negotiate the complex lists of piecework rates on which untroubled labour relations in the industry depended. The lists, indeed, which needed constant alteration to take account of small changes in technology, became the hallmark of spinners' union activity and the chief instrument of a long period of industrial peace from the early 1850s to the late 1880s. Employers, however, did not simply buy better labour relations through a more enlightened attitude to wage-bargaining than that of the early Victorians. They also very generally adopted the philosophy of benevolence in the conduct of their businesses, taking over some of the ploys of the earlier cotton paternalists like Thomas Ashton of Hyde, Henry Ashworth of New Eagley, or Samuel Greg of Quarry Bank, without taking over their stern and authoritarian manner. The new mid-Victorian paternalists were more relaxed, less comprehensive in the range of provisions they aimed to make, and less demanding in the kind of disciplined obedience they expected in return. Entire mill villages, with cottages and houses suited to every grade of worker, and complete with chapel, church, school, and dispensary, were no longer the order of the day. Cradle-to-grave services and supervision, smothering the independence of the workers, were likewise beyond the aims of the new paternalists. They were also beyond their needs.

Once the mills moved into towns and away from isolated rural sites, the infrastructure of the working communities – the housing, shops, and basic services – could be left to market forces and civic action to provide. Employers were free to concentrate their resources on more directly profitable investments; the giants of the early years of cotton, insofar as they had been reluctant paternalists, were revealed as products of the special needs of a particular phase in the industry's development. The mid-Victorian masters pursued profits like any other capitalist. They wanted a successful business to hand on to the next generation, founding a cotton dynasty with the family firm in much the same way that the gentry founded landed families. This objective perhaps tempered the sharpness of the profit motive at the same time as it suggested the scope for paternalism as a paying proposition whose long-term dividends were manifested in loyalty to the firm, harmonious labour relations, a well-behaved workforce, few disruptions in production, and low wage costs as well as low labour costs. Symbolic of the dynastic elements in paternalism were the elaborate celebrations in the mill to mark the coming of age of the employer's son, or a family wedding, when the flowers and bunting decorating the machines and mill yard, the feast, and the loyal and deferential speeches closely echoed the rituals of the landed aristocracy. These ceremonial occasions were becoming common among the larger employers from the 1850s onwards, and the habit was by no means confined to the millowners, being found among ironmasters, brewers, engineering employers, shipbuilders, and many others.

The more humdrum and everyday version of these grand but occasional feasts was the annual works outing or treat, which also appears in the 1850s. Sometimes this was a visit to the employer's residence, with tea and improving games in the grounds, and no strong drink; the enormous parties which Richard and George Cadbury gave in the 1890s in the grounds of their homes not far from the chocolate factory were simply jumbo versions of normally more modest affairs. Sometimes it was a trip in the firm's wagons or hired horse buses for an afternoon in the country. With larger employers the grander gesture of an all-day railway excursion to the seaside, in special trains and with the entire workforce parading in procession behind the firm's band, became popular from 1850 onwards. A typical works outing in the 1880s by Bass, the Burton brewers, required nine special trains leaving from the firm's own sidings at ten-minute intervals from 5 a.m. onwards, bound for Skegness; workers and their families from different sections of the brewery were allotted each to their own train, and the discipline and precision of the entraining operation was no doubt expected to cast its air of orderliness over the whole holiday. The annual outing came to extend far down the business scale, as readers of *The Ragged Trousered Philanthropists* will recall. There, the small builder's firm went on an annual summer beano, largely financed by the men's own weekly subscriptions but grudgingly supported by their employer, who went with them on the excursion in the hired brakes. This beano collapsed into drunken brawling and the outpouring of pent-up bitterness against the employer and foreman; it is a reminder that the outing did not necessarily do anything to encourage orderliness, cement loyalty to the firm, or enhance respect for the employer.

Works treats might be convivial. The more substantial and enduring forms of paternalism were more expensive and more confined to the larger industrial firms whose workers were sufficiently numerous to provide some demand for specialized or recondite amenities. From about 1850 it became increasingly common for the big employers to provide a newspaper room, a reading room, or a library at the mill; those who were particularly impressed by the association of cleanliness, good health, morality, and steady working habits, went in for mill bathhouses, and a little later in the century for gymnasia. Works sports grounds did not come until the 1890s, but works canteens were known by the 1860s. Some works activities were purely utilitarian, like the mill fire brigade, but still engaged pride and enthusiasm outside the workplace itself. Others, of which the works brass band became the emblem of dedicated factory patriotism throughout the northern factory towns, may have originated from below from the workers' urge to collective music-making, but frequently attracted enthusiastic support and finance from the employer. The brass band, indeed, was the point at which employer paternalism designed to make the mill or factory a social institution and something more than a mere workplace met the tendency of the employees to use the mill or factory as the framework for their social life. Thus, the mill, factory, or colliery, was seen as the natural basis for forming clubs or societies of those interested in glee-singing, in growing roses or marrows, in keeping pigeons, or in cycling. Mills had their own committees organizing holidays, collecting holiday money, and arranging social evenings. It would be misleading to suggest that the mill ever totally monopolized the social as well as the working lives of the operatives, sucking them into an all-encompassing embrace and isolating them from the rest of the community and from independent influences. The street neighbourhood was unlikely to be peopled exclusively by operatives from the same mill; and the most puritanical and authoritarian employer never succeeded in keeping his workers out of the pub, in which all sorts of mixing went on. Nevertheless, while mill and factory remained much less than total institutions, there was a marked social division between those workers who lived in the orbit of the mill, and those who did not work in large units and therefore regarded their employers simply as a source of work and wages and nothing more, and were completely reliant upon and exposed to non-employer and non-firm provision of amenities and recreations.

The most works-centred communities of the third quarter of the century were in the cotton-spinning towns of south-east Lancashire, and in the handful of company towns which owed their existence and prosperity to a single company like the railway towns of Crewe, Swindon, Eastleigh, or Wolverton, or to one or two dominant employers as in St Helens, Middlesbrough, Barrow, Merthyr, or Aberdare. Towards the end of the century Port Sunlight and Bournville joined this company, earning a reputation for novelty that was justified by their physical design and layout rather than by their social character. Elsewhere and in other kinds of working conditions the elements of a mill culture and of the firm as a cohesive social unit grew weaker and more difficult to discern across the spectrum of industries and occupations, until they disappeared entirely in the atomized world of outwork and casual labour. In the equally atomized structure of the workplace stretched out across the fields, the isolation of the workers who were increasingly treated as inferior farmhands by their farmer-employers was offset by the traditional, paternalist, community-building functions of squire and parson. In the great middle ground which stretched between the factory communities, freshly knit together in the mid-Victorian years, and the village communities, strained but not broken by the commercialization of agriculture, the workplace and the nature of the job exerted their influences on individual, group, and class perception and consciousness more or less undeflected by paternalist employers pursuing a nascent form of welfare capitalism.

Cotton-weaving, closest both geographically and socially to the spinning towns, did indeed have mid-Victorian employers, such as Hermon of the giant Preston firm of Horrocks, who may well have outpaced the spinning-mill owners as benevolent paternalists. There were, however, significant differences between the weaving and spinning sections of the cotton industry in labour and work practices which made the weaving mill a less closely integrated social unit than the spinning mill. Weaving moved into the factory much later than spinning, the period of rapid and widespread adoption of the powerloom coming in the 1830s and 1840s. The aversion, not to say hostility, of male handloom weavers to the machinery, coupled with the employers' desire for a docile labour force, meant that the women moved first into the new weaving mills and took charge of operating the powerlooms. Male weavers began to join them from the mid-1840s, but by then women were too well entrenched to be shouldered aside and it became established that the responsible adult job in weaving of being in charge of a loom could be performed equally well by women or men. The normally clear-cut Victorian distinction between what was women's work and what was men's work, even when both sexes were employed in the same industry as in spinning, was decisively broken in weaving. The female weavers of the late nineteenth century were virtually the only group of women workers doing the same job as men, in roughly equal numbers, for roughly equal pay, and with roughly equal participation in the powerloom weavers' union; little wonder that Lancashire working-class women supported the pre-1914 suffragette movement. Equal piece-rates were the rule, but equal earnings were rarely achieved: men were frequently allotted more looms than the women, men tuned their own looms, and were paid for it, while women did not, and men tended to produce more per day than women. The rough equality, therefore, still left female weavers inferior to males in earning power. Moreover, this reassertion of male superiority in the weaving mill was only a partial sop to male esteem. The female weavers were among the highest paid women workers in the country, but the male weavers, because they were in a job whose wage rates were affected by the prevailing differential between male and female rates, were poorly paid in comparison with other men.

Weaving was a good job for women but not one of high repute for men. A weaving household, although it might enjoy high family earnings if, as frequently happened, husband and wife were in the same job, was unlikely to enjoy the same social standing as a spinner's household. This reflected the inability of powerloom weavers to achieve the same status as the mulespinners who established a customary control over entry into their own occupation. The masters retained control over the recruitment of weavers, partly because of the late arrival of the factory, and partly because employers could play off men against women. This difference between restricted and open occupations showed through in the greater strength and bargaining power of the spinners' trade societies. It also showed in the hiring of children as assistants to the weavers, known as tenters. In the earlier days of the weaving mills, either side of mid-century, the model of spinners and their piecers was followed, and it was common for weavers to employ, and pay, their own tenters. This practice seems to have declined during the third quarter of the century, with little sign of objection from the weavers, so that it became normal for the master to employ the tenters directly. This not only diminished the power and influence of weavers in their local communities, as sources of employment for children, but also weakened their independence, and hence authority and self-respect, within the mill. This was relative weakness, in comparison with spinners; weavers still had a fair degree of control over their own work process in settling the speed at which they worked, within the limits of the power drive, and in showing the skill and competence to attain the dignity and higher earnings of being in charge of a bank of four looms, where the more lowly had just one or two. There remained, too, a reasonable chance of having their own children as their tenters, when they were of the right age, even when tenters were directly employed. Weavers were not so much of an elite group as the spinners, but they also were at the top of a cohesive workforce which did not have any sharp lines of division between superior and inferior workers. It was a workforce for which the mill became an extension of the home and family, doing much to heal the scars of the miserable decline of the handloom weavers even if it did nothing to rescue or rebuild the lives of individual handloomers.

It would be wrong to suppose that all was happiness and harmony in the mill towns, with no special tensions and no class conflicts. The social order was hierarchical, the patriarchal cottonmasters expected, and received, deferential behaviour from their operatives, not always given without resentment, and there were disputes, sometimes extremely acrimonious and bitter as in the Preston strike of 1853–4, the particularly violent 1878 Blackburn strike, the long Oldham strike in 1885, or the great Brooklands lock-out of 1892–3. Strikes, however, were rare and 'trouble at mill' infrequent in comparison with the highly disturbed 1840s, and were occasional flarings of anti-employer resentment when normal habits of negotiation and compromise broke down. Industrial peace was the normal condition of Lancashire in the second half of the century, frictions between masters and men were sporadic not endemic; a certain identity of interests between masters and operatives was recognized, with an appreciation that the livelihoods of both depended on retaining the industry's overseas markets; and the operatives protected and advanced their interests by talking rather than by confrontation. Some of this was due simply to the expansion and prosperity of the industry, though the peacefulness held up well through the adversity and distress of the 1864–5 Cotton Famine. Much was due to the integration of the mill into the cotton operative's world, and above all its integration in a way which embraced all workers and did not create sharp lines of division between different grades and skills.

The special character of Lancastrian social harmony is well

illustrated by the contrasting experience across the Pennines, where the essentially very similar spinning and weaving technologies did not underpin similar social results. The differences were partly a matter of differences in timing, and partly a matter of differences in business structure which in turn derived from differences in the end-products between cottons, and woollens and worsteds. Power-driven machines were generally adopted, with adaptations, in the West Riding textile industry some decades after they had been pioneered in cotton. The only truly significant native innovation was the wool-combing machine, which had devastating effects on the 'aristocratic' hand-combers who had been the princes among the worsted workers, and which created a factory industry with great rapidity in the 1850s, concentrated into a few large firms in Bradford, which worked on commission for spinners. No other branch of this or any other industry moved so smartly into the factory, with the result that in order to survive, the hand-combers had either to follow the machine into the factory, which many did, or leave the industry and probably the district altogether. In other branches the move into factories was generally a gradual and drawn-out process, with the older hand methods and domestic organization continuing alongside. The men were, therefore, inclined to remain in their traditional trades, and the new factories were filled disproportionately with children, youths, and women. By the time men followed on into the spinning and weaving mills, ten to fifteen years later and never in numbers to equal the females, workplace customs were already set. By far the most important was that the hiring of child assistants, the piecers and tenters, generally remained in the employers' hands, probably because the women workers were never strong enough in bargaining power or in continuous employment by the same master to be able to follow the Lancashire example. This greatly weakened the capacity of West Riding mills to function as extensions of family and neighbourhood communities through the intimacy of self-regulated work units.

The second main difference from Lancashire was that, on the whole, the production of woollens and worsteds was not fertile ground for the growth of large firms. There were, indeed, many varieties of finished cotton piece goods, but in comparison with woollens and worsteds they seemed like standardized and homo-geneous products suited to very large production runs, amenable to economies of scale through the greatest possible subdivision and mechanization of manufacturing processes, and hence condu-cive to large firms. In contrast the varieties of type, quality, grade, and pattern in woollen and worsted goods were positively kaleidoscopic, the market tended to support only a limited run of any one product, the need for flexibility in production made investment in highly specialized machinery risky or worse, and in this situation the lightly capitalized small firm continued to flourish. This is not to say that the West Riding produced no large firms. There were household names like the carpet-making Crossleys and Akroyds of Halifax, and in worsteds Titus Salt with his model mill-village of Saltaire. These and others like the Holdens were great figures, as formidable as patriarchs and as benevolent as paternalists as any Lancashire counterpart. There were relatively few like them, and those few tended to be found in the worsted industry. The normal mid-Victorian worsted mill was between two and three times larger than the woollen mill. The smaller mills tended to run older, less elaborate, and more primitive machinery, to rely on low wages and 'hard driving' of their workers to keep production costs down and profits up, and to have millowners who were financially incapable and tem-peramentally indisposed to acting as grand patrons of their workpeople. Labour relations, which in the domestic industry set-up had been generally amicable, and particularly in the more remote valleys characterized by an atmosphere of social equality between masters and men, became embittered in the mill, which magnified and emphasized differences between employers and workers. The West Riding mill, because of the general weakness or absence of paternalist employers, because of the greater bleakness of working conditions within it, and because of the absence of family and kin groups, did not fashion communities in the manner of the cotton mills. By the 1880s the differences were enshrined in the common view that the West Riding towns were marked by low wages, social instability and bitterness, and disturbed industrial relations, while Lancashire was highly paid, peaceful, and untroubled by serious class frictions. It was no accident that the Independent Labour Party found early support and nourishment in Bradford.

Textile mills were the only factories where men and women worked alongside each other in similar numbers, with large supporting contingents of child assistants. Hence they were the only factories where there was any possibility of the separation of workplace and home having little effect on family life. There were other industries in which all the workers in a firm were socially undifferentiated, remaining essentially unstratified despite there being a hierarchy of pay rates for different grades. But in these, being all-male, the social effects were not the same as in textiles. Coalmining was the largest of these industries, well-known for the close-knit character and solidarity of its mining communities, in spite of the gulf which separated the earnings of the hewers from those of other underground workers, let alone the surface workers on the pit-bank. Hewers were the highest paid miners, earning 40 or 50 per cent more than the underground hauliers, or the putters who filled the coal-tubs, and enjoyed earnings of around £2 a week in the 1870s and 1880s which put them on a par with, or above, men in the skilled trades. They did not, however, form an elite that was socially separated from the main body of colliery workers. Victorian coalmining was a pick-and-shovel operation. There were considerable changes in mining technology during the second half of the century, but these concerned power-driven ventilation, the substitution of pony haulage for human haulage underground, and improvements in winding and pumping gear, and did not reach the coal-face itself where mechanical cutting, although talked about, was still virtually unknown in 1900. Cutting coal needed a pick, physical strength, experience of local geological conditions and local working customs, and the skill to undercut the seam at the right place to produce a controlled fall. In these senses hewers were certainly skilled workers, but they did not undergo any long training or apprenticeship, and they did not exercise a craft which put them in any position to control entry to it. They were, in effect, a distinct age-group in the mining community, not a distinct or superior stratum.

In general the hewers were the adult males of the mining community in the prime of life, between their early twenties and their early forties; when they were younger they had worked in various supporting jobs underground, and when they were older they moved to less physically demanding, and less well-paid, jobs, often above ground. Different coalfields developed different customs, which to some extent modify this picture. It held true in the north-eastern coalfield where boys entered the pit as drivers of the pit ponies, moved up in their late teens to be putters manhandling the tubs from the face to the main roadways, and then after a few months or a year working alongside a hewer they became hewers themselves in their early twenties. In South Wales, by contrast, this career pattern was modified by different recruiting practices in which hewers took on their own young helpers, frequently sons or kin, who in due course became hewers, while those who entered the pits as hauliers were quite likely to find that they remained in the less well-paid haulage job throughout their working lives. The north-east was distinctive also in developing a double-shift system for the hewers, who by the 1870s worked shifts of six to seven hours while the haulage workers kept the colliery running with a working day of ten to eleven hours. The method of working in the north-east created small stalls or 'bords' at the coal-face, each worked by a single hewer and separated from adjoining stalls by pillars of coal that were left to support the roof; when an entire section had been worked in this fashion the coal pillars were removed in a retreating operation, leaving the roof to collapse behind them. The effect of the double-shift system was that each hewer chose a mate, or 'marra', and the pair shared the working of a stall shift and shift about. This was a close working partnership, for each depended on the other for good workmanship in the stall and their earnings depended on the quantity of coal hewn, generally shared equally between them. Trust and friendship at work formed an important social relationship, one of the ties which held a mining village together. Independence and self-reliance were other characteristics of mining villages, fostered by the considerable independence at work of the hewer, shielded in his solitary stall from any constant supervision. This was less so in districts with the longwall system of working in which the coal was mined in one continuous face formed of a succession of hewers' individual pitches, and where it was essential that the entire face advanced in unison; even so, the cramped and confined conditions made close supervision difficult, and hewers were very much left to their own devices compared to the closely controlled haulage workers.

From coalfield to coalfield the precise texture of social relations undoubtedly varied with differences in working conditions. Overall, however, trust and confidence among the entire workforce was essential in dealing with the physical danger, and isolation, of mining. These qualities were accentuated by the isolation of most pit villages, and by the social self-sufficiency which miners had to cultivate. Colliery owners were not, in general, the callous, brutal, and reckless employers depicted by Engels; their own self-interest in protecting their sunk capital and securing its continuous operation ensured that they looked after the safety of their mines reasonably well. Explosions meant costly stoppages, as well as lost lives. But colliery owners were not notable for welfare or paternalist activities; apart from miners' free coal, an unavoidable concession more than an act of generosity, and in some places the provision of free ground for allotments, they provided few amenities outside the colliery, and even within it such things as pithead baths were a twentieth-century development. Housing was not uncommonly provided by the colliery owners, often perforce with the more remote pits. Equally often it was of poor standard, and was openly used by employers as a means of disciplining and controlling their workers, preventing strikes by threatening eviction. Tied colliery housing was, therefore, widely resented by the miners, and only in the exceptional cases where it was of superior quality, as with the cottages Earl Fitzwilliam provided for his South Yorkshire miners at Elsecar, could it be regarded as an expression of a caring paternalism which might excite some signs of gratitude or attachment from the colliers.

'So soon as these men leave the pit-bank, the authority of capital ceases,' it was said of the South Yorkshire miners in the 1860s. Not all miners felt as free and independent as these, and in the Lanarkshire field in the 1870s, for example, there was a fairly clear-cut distinction between the 'honourable men of Larkhall' and the 'degraded and willing slaves of Gartsherrie, Rosehall and Carnbroe'. The honourable men were colliers who clung to their traditions as independent hewers, exercising special skills, sharing workplaces and stints equally among themselves, and endeavouring to restrict entry and prevent dilution of their trade by inexperienced and unskilled labour; they were mainly strong union men. The degraded slaves were under the employer's thumb, working longer stints for lower wages with little sense of fraternal solidarity with their fellows, newcomers to the industry with no sense of the mysteries of mining, mainly Irish who were frequently used as blacklegs, living at the mercy of employers in insanitary company housing; they were largely ununionized. The untrained Irishman fresh from his potato patch, it was said in the 1880s, was a menace to everyone else in the pit: 'he does not know when his Davy lamp is out of order; he does not know what the indications of gas are; he does not know anything of the strata, the setting of coal may rumble its warning, but to his ear it has no meaning.' Such distrust and suspicion of raw recruits was perfectly understandable; established workers are always likely to resent intruders and interlopers. But in an industry expanding as rapidly as coalmining, which practically trebled the size of its workforce in the second half of the century, there were bound to be large numbers of raw recruits since the natural increase of the already existing mining population, though large, was not large enough to sustain expansion on this scale. The influx might contain a large Irish element, as in Lanarkshire, or might come chiefly from agriculture, as in the north-east or with the Welsh hill farmers and the agricultural labourers from the bordering English counties who flocked into the South Wales valleys. The actual occasion of particularly large and locally prominent influxes was prone to be strike-breaking, when in boom conditions employers were anxious to increase production and the established miners were equally anxious to use their scarcity value to improve their conditions. Newcomers, therefore, quite frequently started their mining lives under the shadow of blacklegging. In the course of time, however, they were absorbed into the workforce and integrated into the mining community, and next time round would themselves be part of the regular band of colliers denouncing a fresh wave of blacklegs. None was more fierce in their local pride and patriotism than the South Wales miners of the 1900s who were descendants of immigrants from Gloucestershire and Herefordshire.

At any particular moment colliery districts, or even individual mining villages, might well exhibit sharp social divisions, between honourable men and degraded slaves, union men and blacklegs, native mining families brought up in local work traditions and newcomers with the hayseeds hardly out of their hair. Although they were sharp at the time, such divisions were temporary. The main influence of working in the pits was to tend to produce integrated mining communities, to heal divisions and smooth away the roughnesses of different origins and backgrounds, and to emphasize the values and sentiments of brotherhood, in community life as at work. Such effects were most pronounced in settlements where mining was virtually the sole occupation; there the independent, self-sufficient, inward-looking mining community, detached from and rather suspicious of the outside world, was most highly developed. Not all mining districts were like that. In the fast-growing South Yorkshire field of the 1870s and 1880s, for example, the majority of miners probably lived in villages in the Barnsley and Rotherham districts where they were but one amongst several groups of industrial workers, and much the same was true in the West Midlands. The great majority, however, were male-dominated societies in which the fraternalism of the miners had a strictly literal application. There were no openings for female employment in the industry after the 1842 Act, apart from the few groups of pit-brow lasses who remained, mainly in Lancashire, tough and resilient but numerically small examples of female colliery surface workers, until well into the twentieth century. Even before 1842 and the prohibition of female work underground, the presence of girls and women down the pit had been a sign of technically backward districts, as female labour had generally been phased out when underground pony haulage had been introduced.

Typically, there were no other kinds of female employment in the mining districts. Girls either left, mainly to become domestic servants, or got married. There was no shortage of marriageable young men, reaching their peak earning power in their early twenties, and miners' daughters generally married young and brought up large families. The fact that they could not contribute to the family income was no hindrance to the large number of children which miners raised, their family size remaining well above that of the rest of the population and of any other occupational group until after the First World War. It would be wrong to suppose that this was because there was little else to do in spare time in mining villages, apart from drinking; the probable cause was the low age at marriage of miners' wives. In an exceptionally dirty industry the womenfolk were kept exceptionally busy in keeping husband, clothes, and household clean, and the slipper-bath was a badge of respectability in a miner's home. It was only in untypical districts, however, such as parts of the Nottinghamshire field, which were developing strongly in the 1870s and 1880s in the hinterland of established towns, that there were plenty of jobs available for women. In this instance the miners' womenfolk worked in the hosiery industry, and the presence of working daughters and some working wives modified the masculinity of the society and gave it much closer daily contacts with the rest of the working world than was usually the case. The more common pattern was one of tightly knit communities, revolving round their male members, not very strongly influenced by their employers, and suffused by notions of neighbourliness and brotherhood stemming from an occupation which was hazardous, cooperative, and devoid of marked structural or status subdivisions. This generated a group or class consciousness that reflected a clear social separation from the colliery owners, but it did not necessarily reflect a sense of permanent or underlying confrontation and conflict between masters and men. The reputation of the miners as the vanguard in the class conflict and as the elite brigade of organized labour was won in the twentieth century. In the nineteenth century they were more often peaceful and conciliatory than militant, more taken up in negotiating sliding-scale wage agreements than with striking, more concerned with their regional differences than with class solidarity.

The other great Victorian growth industry in which the workers were socially homogeneous notwithstanding the existence of large wage differentials was ironmaking. The mouldmakers and pattern-makers were, indeed, skilled men who stood apart from the main body of workers. They exercised a craft, learned by apprenticeship, which gave them a strategically powerful position in the whole production process since the marketability of the final product depended on the accuracy, quality, and reliability of the moulds into which the iron was poured. They were well paid and they had their own exclusive craft union; like many other labour aristocrats they felt threatened towards the end of the century by new technology, in stamping and pressing, which might displace their skills. Their earnings, however, were not very different from those of gantrymen who loaded ironstone into kilns to be calcined, mine-fillers who barrowed the calcined ironstone from kiln to blast furnace, chargers who worked on platforms at the top of the furnace seeing that the right quantities of ironstone, limestone, and coke to make up a charge were loaded into the furnace at the right intervals, or furnace-keepers who kept an eye on the whole operation and made the critical decision when to tap the furnace, which he and his helpers then carried out by knocking out a fireclay plug with main force. All of these could well be getting between £2 and £3 a week towards the end of the century, and the puddlers who stirred the molten metal in the works producing malleable iron might be earning £4 a week and more. These were rates between two and four times higher than those of labourers in the same works. Yet all these jobs required physical strength and practical experience of the smelting process, rather than skills which were acquired by specific training or apprenticeship. The point at which experience, which involves lives no less than the quality of the product when great masses of material are being handled at extremely high temperatures, becomes skill may be left to students of semantics. Contemporaries were clear that the main body of ironworkers were not skilled, in the sense that artisans were skilled. The crucial feature, socially, was that the best paid and most physically demanding jobs were filled simply from the ranks of the main body of ironworkers. They were held, moreover, by individuals at a particular stage in their lifecycles, after which they would fall back to less strenuous and lower paid jobs.

The effect was that in an ironworks the workers were stratified by wage rates, and to a considerable extent by age, but not by status. There was little sense of social separation between the labouring men who humped the pigs from the casting floor to the trucks or barrowed away the slag to tip it, and the furnace-keepers; they might easily be members of the same family, or live in the same street. Ironworkers were not very different from coalminers in their social cohesion, and although the iron and steel towns were much larger than pit villages and tended in some cases, like Sheffield or Barrow, to attract the metal-using industries, like them they had little female employment to offer. Ironworking communities were tough and masculine, and their cohesion gave them a common social identity. It was not, however, a class feeling directed particularly against the employers, with whom conflicts were infrequent; rather, the sense that each man had a chance of holding one of the highly paid jobs in the works at some time in his life served to individualize the workplace tensions and aspirations, and to stifle the accumulation of any head of resentment of the masters.

Resentment was rather more likely to be found in the sections of the working population which were out of reach of the social and cultural influences of mill and mine, either because their work long remained technologically traditional, or because it was dominated by groups of skilled artisans. Either way the resentment was not wholly or continuously directed against capitalist employers. There were three broadly different types of work situation involved, tending to produce three broadly different types of social response. Where working methods and commercial organization remained traditional, and there was no upper layer of skilled workers, pay tended to be low, competition for jobs was fierce, employment was insecure and irregular, friction with middlemen and small employers was normal and occasionally acute, but the absence of large workplaces to serve as arenas for forming friendships and associations, and of large employers to oppose, meant that a common group culture that could be identified in ways of living did not easily develop into a common group, let alone class, consciousness. This typified the situation with farmworkers, domestic workers in hosiery, boot- and shoemaking, clothing, and other domestic industries, dockers, carters and carriers, and domestic servants; although each of these groups should be the subject of qualifications and subdivision, at least between the regular and the casual workers in each. Where traditional methods and organization remained, and there was an upper layer of skilled workers with a measure of control over the work process, the gulf between the artisans and the unskilled labourers yawned in its most traditional shape, a gulf of pay, a gulf of education, a gulf of manners, a gulf of self-respect, and a gulf of social esteem. The labour aristocrats were as vigilant to protect themselves from encroachment or infiltration from those below, to keep the unskilled in their place, as they were to prevent their employers eroding their privileges; the unskilled workers, for all their lowly position was part of long-established practice and therefore sanctified as custom, were obviously more likely to be resentful of the artisans who were directly responsible for holding them down than of the more remote employers. The building and construction industry was the largest occupation in which this pattern held true throughout the century, and beyond, where a large and shifting population of labourers, some of them notoriously tough, wild, and unrespectable, confronted an aristocracy of tradesmen well entrenched in their craft unions. Furniture-making and the closely allied trade of vehicle-making were in the same mould, along with the upper end of men's clothing, piano-making, watch- and instrument-making, printing, and some of the old metalworking crafts such as the cutlery trade; these, however, did not have the same mass of labourers in relation to skilled men.

In the third situation there was an upper layer of skilled workers, but the work, the technology, and the organization were all new, developed to make the machinery and equipment of industrialization. In contrast to the older metalworking craftsmen who worked in small workshops under masters who could have risen from their own ranks, and sometimes, as with country blacksmiths, worked independently, the new engineers who made the steam engines and the machines for other industries, and often operated them as well, worked in large factory-like units of production. It is true that the large units generated supporting rings of small specialized works producing components, but it is more significant that even the large works were typically called engineering shops or workshops, and were rarely referred to as factories. The work which went on within these shops depended on highly skilled manual labour using hand tools for finishing, fine adjustment, and assembly, while the powered metalworking machinery available from the 1820s and 1830s in the form of lathes, drills, planes, slotters, or hammers, was in effect a vast extension of hand-tool capacity, since it did not operate automatically and it needed skilled manual setting-up and control. The men who acquired these skills, either by transference from the older crafts of the millwrights or blacksmiths, or from scratch, had by the 1840s formed a new craft with its own internal specialist subdivisions into turners, fitters, and erectors, and its product divisions into boilermakers, engine-makers, pump-makers and the like.

The engineers had a scarcity value based on skills which could only be acquired through regular and long training. They had little difficulty in establishing formal apprenticeship systems, and if these were not self-devised they were in any event imposed by large employers, such as the railway companies, whose own interests demanded properly trained workers for their locomotive or carriage works. They were, therefore, in little danger of competition from untrained and unqualified interlopers, who were simply incapable of doing the job, in comparison with some of the older trades where some semblance of the work of a carpenter or bricklayer, even if shoddy, could be picked up in a week or two. Their chief concern, at least until the last decade of the century, in protecting their high pay, status, and privileges, was to prevent the market becoming overstocked with trained engineers; in a generally vigorously expanding market this was not difficult to do, and although cyclical recessions posed problems for engineers no less than for other workers, control over entry through regulation of the number of apprentices was normally achieved without friction with employers through the basic requirements of the work process itself. For the other characteristic of the engineers, which marked them off from the skilled building trades and made them more like the workshop-craftsmen in coach-building, printing, or silver-smithing, was that they did not generally work directly alongside any large body of unskilled labourers. There were no doubt general labourers employed in the big engineering shops on fetching and carrying, but the young hands who helped directly in the work of production were apprentices, novitiates and probationary members of the club. The beginnings of large-scale bicycle production, from the 1880s, marked the first time when skilled engineers worked in the same firm with large numbers of less skilled workers who stood no chance of ever joining their ranks, and the division was established between the skilled men who set up and maintained the machine tools, and the semi-skilled production workers who ran the production line.

This was the warning signal for the end of an era, and the approach of a fourth situation where the technology and organization were non-traditional, and there was no need for skilled workers in the old-fashioned sense of those with specially acquired manual skills. The virtual extinction of all the traditional skills, and the demotion of the bulk of engineering workers to semi-skilled status, has been the tendency of all the main changes in industrial technology since the late nineteenth century, but it has taken most of the twentieth century for British industry to reach this position, usually lagging behind its international competitors. The reason was that Britain industrialized with a technology that was heavily reliant on manual skills to make it and to keep it running, and that in the half century after 1830 the skilled workers became entrenched in positions of strength in possession of particular strategically placed jobs from which it proved exceedingly difficult to dislodge them. The threat of displacement tended to pitch skilled workers into confrontation with employers, with whom they had previously lived in reasonable harmony; and insofar as all workers were suspicious of unfamiliar machines and new working methods, resistance by the skilled workers propelled them into the unaccustomed role of leading the class.

This was the core of the profound changes in the social significance of the work process, which can be discerned in the 1890s but which took the following half century and more to work themselves out. Where differences in working methods and in the organization of work had acted to separate the working classes into dissimilar, disconnected, socially distanced and sometimes hostile sections, a number of changes in the mature industrial economy acted to bring them closer together. Arguably the crucial changes came in engineering, where technical developments which had been in progress since at least the 1860s quickened and converged to produce a sense of crisis among the skilled workers in the 1890s. Developments in machine tools and the processes of metal machining which substituted the precision working of the machine itself for the inevitable variation and imprecision of manually controlled operation, however skilled, had been underway at least since the 1820s and 1830s with Maudslay's use of slide rests instead of the artisan's hands to hold cutting tools, and such devices as Nasmyth's self-acting nut-milling machine, and Whitworth's machine for cutting bolts and screws to the standard threads and sizes which carry his name. These early steps towards mechanically controlled operations that supplanted manual skill were, however, small and piecemeal, and were reliant on manual skill to sharpen and set the cutting tools and apply the gauges, so that the role of the skilled worker was enhanced rather than diminished. Much the same was true of the turret lathe, developed in the 1840s but coming into widespread use in the 1870s; these lathes, with turrets holding up to eight different cutting tools, were capable of carrying out complicated shaping operations with minimal supervision, but were absorbed into the artisan framework. The introduction of milling machines for the automatic and accurate shaping of parts, and of grinding machines for automatic finishing to microscopic tolerances, many of them coming from America in the 1870s and 1880s, together with the development of special high-speed steels for cutting tools, provided a cluster of new technology capable of upsetting the craft control of the engineers.

The full array of machine tools needed for the economical production of interchangeable, standardized, parts was now available. It had indeed been available, in more primitive form, for several decades, as demonstrated in American small-arms manufacture, to a more limited extent in some British small-arms production, for example by the Birmingham Small Arms Company in the 1860s, and in the Singer factory at Clydebank which by 1885 was turning out 8000 sewing machines a week. With interchangeable parts assembly of the final product no longer required the fine tuning and individual adjustment by a highly skilled engineer, though with a complicated product that was itself a machine, it certainly required intelligence and the ability to follow diagrams and instructions to fit the pieces together.

Moreover, with each part being produced in quantity there was scope for the subdivision of machines into highly specialized repetitive functions and a corresponding division of labour to look after them. A machine operator on the production line needed to know no more than how to operate one specific kind of machine, something which could be picked up in a week or two; he was no more than semi-skilled in comparison with the engineer who had served his time. Employers, understandably, saw no reason to pay skilled rates for semi-skilled work, and indeed could not afford to do so and remain competitive; while the skilled engineers, also understandably, saw the erosion of their control over work processes regarded as customarily their own preserve as undermining their security and their craft ethos. This was the essence of the deskilling which formed the ground of uneasiness and grievance among engineers in the 1890s, culminating in the great Engineering Trades Lock-out of 1897–8. The craft union, the Amalgamated Society of Engineers, tried to convince the general public that the conflict was primarily a struggle to obtain the eight-hours day, a cause likely to attract sympathy. But the Employers' Federation of Engineering Associations in fact took their stand on the issue of 'preserving or relinquishing of their right to manage their own business' on the question of their right to employ whom they chose to work their machines, without the prior approval of the union. That is, the employment of semi-skilled, non-union men under the production system of the subdivision of labour, was at the heart of the dispute; even more so was the union attempt to assert a 'one man, one machine' rule in an effort to halt the slide of skilled craftsmen in the face of banks of several interlinked semi-automatic machines each of which could be easily worked by a single semi-skilled operator. The employers locked out the men, and won.

This was the first major industrial dispute to be fought over the issue of managerial control, harbinger of the twentieth century in which industrial relations have been littered with such disputes, and portent of the end of Victorian industry in which skilled or privileged workers in command of key stages in the production process had established customary control over their workplace and their working rhythms, and hence a measure of independence and equality with management. The defeat damaged the pride and self-respect of the engineers, and narrowed the range of jobs that they could reserve for qualified 'society' men. Perhaps even more damaging to the craftsmen's sense of pride were the effects of the new special tool steels and the new grinding arrangements. With these, tool-sharpening itself became a specialized activity carried out by a specialist worker, and engineers found themselves deprived of some of their personal tools and of their individual responsibility for keeping them in good order. Employers assumed that the engineers were merely sulking over the loss of their customary grinding time, which had provided pleasantly sociable breaks from work. In fact, personal possession of the tools of the trade, and personal care of their condition, were the marks of the skilled tradesman – carpenter, joiner, plumber, or mason, no less than engineer – and emasculation of this was a direct emasculation of independence and status, a move towards stripping the artisan of both symbols and objects which distinguished him from other workers. Indeed, when a set of tools could well be worth between £30 and £40, the equivalent of well over one year's wages of most agricultural labourers, its possessor combined the independence of the petty capitalist with the position of wage worker.

In the event, alarming as the prospect seemed in the 1890s, the deskilling and degrading of the engineers did not proceed far before 1914. The reason was economic, not technical. Massive investment in product-specific machines, and employment of the semi-skilled operators who went with them, was on the whole only profitable when the product was a consumer good with a mass market. Producer goods, even when as with textile machinery there was a regular demand for considerable numbers of the same machine, could not be produced and sold in sufficient quantity to dispense with the skilled men. Sewing machines were unique in being at the same time producer goods for the clothing industry, and consumer goods in the home, and the size of the market amply sustained the economies of the new organization of production. Bicycles were another such product, and the mass demand put the bicycle industry in the forefront of these changes in the 1890s. But there were few other examples. In heavy engineering the number of locomotives or marine engines built annually remained low, with such variety of size and design that a batch of a dozen or so of any single type was rather large. The most efficient railway workshops, for example, introduced the latest milling machines to speed up work and increase its accuracy; but with each engine in effect custom-built the skilled men were unruffled and were certainly not knocked off their perch. In the shipyards skilled tradesmen squabbled with each other, and the demarcation dispute between fitters and plumbers was one of the long-running acts of the 1890s, with the plumbers extending their empire from lead and brass pipes into iron piping, and the fitters, who regarded iron as essentially their material, defending the frontier of flanged joints in all large pipes while grudgingly conceding that plumbers might make certain screwed ferrule joints.

Shipyards had indeed already become, as they were long to remain, the classic breeding ground of demarcation disputes. As was explained to the Royal Commission on Labour of 1893–4, 'the demarcation of work occurs wherever two trades work in the same materials, as, for example, shipwrights and joiners; engine-fitters and plumbers; engine-fitters and drillers; engine-fitters and caulkers and hole-cutters; engine-fitters and blacksmiths who are not in the same societies; plumbers and tin and ironplate workers; tin and ironplate workers and platers belonging to the Shipbuilders and Boilermakers' Society; angle-iron smiths and blacksmiths; iron-shipwrights and caulkers; platers and caulkers; . . . caulkers and drillers; painters and red-leaders.' The apparently highly disputatious condition of the shipyards arose from the rapidly developing complexity of iron ships and their fitting-out which was making the building of ships into an intricate assembly operation calling on many different materials and skills. Given the background of craft loyalties and organization from which these different skills were recruited it was inevitable that each trade should fight to secure and mark out its own patch in the new territory. All this was no doubt very tiresome for the employers, and in a different kind of labour market without the strongly entrenched craft tradition of one particular type of work for each specialized skilled tradesman a different kind of skilled labour force, tailored to the needs of shipbuilding, using transferable and flexible skills, might have been assembled. Nevertheless, even if its use of skilled labour was inefficient, British shipbuilding remained competitive and internationally dominant, producing over 60 per cent of the world's mercantile tonnage at the end of the century. Friction between the tradesmen perhaps hurt themselves more than their employers; it did little apparent harm to the industry, and it did nothing to displace skilled workers or to deskill the nature of their work.

In engineering, and in lesser degree in shipbuilding, it was only the First World War which brought deskilling on a considerable scale. The massive demand for arms and ammunition was precisely the kind of mass market which called for new production methods based on extreme subdivision of labour and machinery, and, coupled with the flow of skilled workers into the armed forces, it led to the 'dilution' of the workforce with large numbers of semi-skilled and unskilled women, as well as men. In return for their agreement to this dilution the skilled men received a promise of post-war reinstatement from the government. At the end of the war the women promptly left the industry, or were pushed out; but the old working practices were gone for good. The displacement of craft practices and the erosion of cultural differences and barriers between artisans and other workers in this key sector was, therefore, a long-drawn-out process. The skilled engineers did not lose their particularism and their attitudes of superiority all of a sudden in the 1890s and hurry to exchange their elitist image for some standardized working-class kit. Rather, the 1890s should be seen as the start of a rearguard action, or of a more intensive phase of a long-continuing rearguard action, in defence of craft practices and privileges, in the course of which the terrain changed around them as novel branches of the industry making new products developed from time to time, and slipped away into the hands of the semi-skilled. In the old familiar parts of the terrain the old core of traditionally trained engineers remained very much in charge, though less confident about the future security of their status. This disposed the men to place less reliance on acceptance of the 'custom of the trade' in individual plants and by individual employers as sufficient protection, and more reliance on the collective and political actions of their trade unions. Herein lies the significance of the developments of the 1890s: they did not sweep away the sectionalism and stratification of the working classes and create a culturally unified working class, but they did impart a strong impulse to the politicization of the class leadership.

Similar developments took place in the building trades, where there were no comparable technological innovations but the 1890s produced a pronounced switch from appeals to the custom of the trade as the means of preserving the position of the skilled workers, to reliance on the more centralized and political action of trade unions through collective bargaining. A few of the building trades had been faced with the competition of machinery since the 1840s and 1850s, and had learned to live with it without losing their status. Carpenters were the most seriously affected, and machine-made joinery captured a whole slice of their former work; the solution was to surrender this area, for example of window frames for standardized and repetitive housing, to machine-operating carpenters, and to retain craft control at the upper and more individualist end of the market. Masons were also affected, and throughout the second half of the century they continually reverted to attempts to ban the use of 'worked stone' which had been dressed, or partially dressed, at the quarry by stone-sawing and planing machinery. Other trades, however, bricklayers, plasterers, glaziers, painters, or plumbers, had no shadows thrown over their skills from machinery. For them, and for the masons and carpenters, the dangerous shadows were cast by the untrained and unskilled interlopers who purported to do the same work, and by the employers who used them. Preservation of craft standards, craft privileges, and a high quality of workmanship, meant resistance to builders who employed cheap labour and did shoddy work; it also meant hostility towards the interlopers who worked in 'unfair' and 'dishonourable' ways, and hence contributed to social divisions within the broad ranks of building workers.

The bricklayer's skilled status and good workmanship depended on his own control over his pace of working, which was embodied in customary limitations on the number of bricks to be laid in a day. In the 1830s the rule of the trade was of the order of 800 bricks a day, at a time when many masters held that 2000 a day was perfectly attainable; by the 1870s the trade norm was 600–800 a day, and by the 1890s it had been sharply reduced to 300–400 a day even though employers thought 1200 a day was possible without any skimping. What employers held to be restrictive practices deliberately designed to restrict output, keep up employment and wages, and hence inflate labour costs, were indeed partly that and were therefore most effective during building booms when orders were plentiful and workers were in a strong bargaining position, and least effective during building recessions. But they were also the way in which the exercise of skilled workmanship was expressed, the touchstone for distinguishing between fair and unfair working methods; as such the recognition of such rules was a constant objective of the artisans, though the precise form of the desired rule might alter over time as the economic circumstances of the industry altered. Thus, the masons' drive to prohibit the use of worked stone of the 1860s had become, by the 1890s, a demand to ban the import of worked stone from any district with lower wage rates than those in the place where it was to be used. And the plasterers, who in the 1860s had been trying to enforce a rule that all jobs should be given three coats, were by the 1890s concentrating on a demand for full control over the number of apprentices they took on, and were making themselves most unpopular with the employers.

The distinction between the honourable and dishonourable workers in the building trades was not one simply between union and non-union men. No union men were dishonourable, since the union regarded itself as the guardian of the rules and customs of the trade even if members did sometimes break some of the rules when work was especially difficult to get. Many non-union men, on the other hand, were honourable workers equally strongly attached to the customs of the trade; some were dishonourable men who skimped, did bad work, and worked too fast and too hard, and these were obnoxious to union and non-union honourables alike. Numbers and proportions are impossible to state; but with between 10 and 20 per cent of the building workers unionized in the 1870s, it would seem not unreasonable to suppose that as much as half of the remaining 80 or 90 per cent were on the honourable side of the divide. The control over their own work rates, methods of working, and working conditions which trade rules and customs gave to the men was successfully reasserted in the boom of the

1860s, after setbacks in the 1850s, largely by the concerted action of union and non-union men at the local and site level, invoking 'the trade' rather than union muscle-power. Ground was once more lost in the building depression from the mid-1870s, and then pretty much recovered again in the boom of the 1890s, but this time using union initiative and leadership as the major instrument for winning concessions. The tactics changed because of the great expansion of opportunities for employing dishonourable and obnoxious labour, especially in subcontracted work, stimulated by the scale of the boom, and the conclusion that united and coordinated action was the best way to contain this expansion. The emphasis on union action and on the power of union officials swung the building trades into line with the engineers in their conduct of industrial relations and in their struggle for control of the work process. While on this score a shift towards working-class solidarity is suggested, the struggle was in fact the defence of an elite's standards and pay differentials against the mass of inferior labourers; it was inherently divisive, and further fragmented the general body of building workers by putting pressure, for the first time, on the non-union honourables. It was also essentially a cyclical phenomenon, and the power of the building unions swiftly weakened, along with the superiority of the tradesmen, when building activity began to sag from 1901–2. There is a twin reminder here that the changes in work practices and attitudes to work of the 1890s did not lead unambiguously towards eroding sectionalism and divisions within the working classes, and were not necessarily enduring structural changes.

The 1890s may, indeed, be conveniently taken to mark the point at which the cotton operatives clearly emerged from the shelter of their mill-based culture into a more calculating and commercial relationship with the employers, as the advance of limited company organization into the industry displaced the mid-Victorian paternalism of the family firm. Equally, by the 1890s the hosiery industry had completed its mechanization and the boot and shoe industry was poised for its final move into the factory, in the face of the competition of factory-made American shoes and with the use of American machinery for sewing soles, and then for machine welting. These moves completed the extinction of the outwork system in two of its largest outposts, the culmination of a decline that had been in slow progress since the 1850s. With it the traditional family economy of the outworkers disappeared, and also the traditional grievances of extortionate frame-rents extracted by bag-hosiers and exploitation of women and girls working in the home hand-sewing, or closing, the uppers of boots and shoes in competition with the early upper-sewing machines. Indeed by the early 1890s bootmaking and hosiery trade unions were actively campaigning for all-factory working because they could not organize or control the scattered and fragmented surviving outworkers, and thus were unable to prevent them undercutting factory workers and undermining factory work practices. In this sphere also, then, workers were being drawn out of the cellular and familial structure of domestic and outwork industry and into the common pattern of factory work, and the industrial relations which governed their working conditions were increasingly in the hands of the unions.

Agricultural labourers and domestic servants were untouched by any equivalent changes, and numerically these were large exceptions to any generalization about the transformation of the working classes in the 1890s. Some contemporary opinion indeed held that domestic servants were not part of the working class at all, but were servile and degraded appendages of the class of the householder for whom they worked. It is true that they were unorganizable and therefore worthless from a trade union standpoint; but such a view is unjustifiably dismissive of women who were drawn from working-class families and mainly returned to the working class on marriage, bearing important cultural messages from their period in service. Agricultural labourers, on the other hand, had made their bid for unionization in the early 1870s, and although it was briefly not unsuccessful, by the 1890s their union had dwindled to almost nothing in the face of agricultural depression. Their ranks were thinning fast, through voluntary migration to better jobs in the towns at home or overseas, rather than because of displacement by machinery. Mechanization of harvest work with horse-drawn hay-mowers and reapers had in fact spread considerably from the late 1850s, and accelerated in the 1890s with the adoption of combined reaper-binders; but the effect was more to diminish the demand for seasonal labour than to displace regular workers, and in other farming tasks – apart from threshing, which had long been mechanized – the impact of machinery was negligible. Agricultural wages were increasing in the last quarter of the century, in money as well as in real terms, and even in the lowest paid English county, Dorset, late Victorian labourers were noticeably less miserable and wretched than their predecessors of the 1830s. Agricultural labourers, nevertheless, stayed at the bottom of the heap in the pay league in the largely rural parts of eastern, southern, and south-western England, and in rural Wales and Scotland. They were certainly not all cowed, dejected, or lacking in spirit, but their work tended to be isolated if not solitary, they were denied the companionship of working in family units, and their resources for sustaining dignity and self-respect against the authority of their farmer-employers or the patronizing proprietorship of the squire and his lady were meagre. Agricultural labourers might become more like other members of the working classes when they became known as farmworkers, in the twentieth century, mechanically minded, riding about on machines, using factory methods of production. Meanwhile, in the 1890s, they remained separate and apart.

Some of the unskilled and semi-skilled, however, did begin to break out of their bonds of inferiority in the wave of 'new unionism' of 1888–91. Coming at an opportune point in the trade cycle when unemployment was exceptionally low and the demand for labour strong, this wave was heralded by the strike of the Bryant and May matchgirls in 1888 and arrived with Will Thorne's successful organization of the London gasworkers and the great London dock strike of 1889 for the 'dockers' tanner', or minimum rate of 6d. an hour. The novelty lay in unions for the unskilled, with open entry, low weekly subscriptions, and no friendly society functions; moreover they attracted much public attention, from the support of socialist agitators such as John Burns, Tom Mann, and Ben Tillett, the intervention of Cardinal Manning in the dockers' dispute, and the fact that they received help, not ridicule, from more skilled and already organized workers like the stevedores. New unionism was, however, something of a flash in the pan, its reputation in the annals of labour history generally inflated far beyond its real importance. Its only successes were the gasworkers and the dockers; their imitators among general transport workers and general labourers, let alone among domestic servants, failed to get unions going. And when the trade cycle turned downwards after 1891 even the gasworkers and dockers lost many of their gains, their unions faded sharply and had a struggle to stay alive. In 1888, on the eve of the new unionism, total trade union membership was estimated at 750,000 or about 5 per cent of the labour force; by the end of 1891 total membership had doubled, to 1.5 million, and the 'new' unions contributed perhaps a quarter of this total. By 1900, however, when total union membership had climbed to 2 million or about 12 per cent of the labour force, 'new' unionists were less than one tenth of the total. The old unions of engineers, building tradesmen, shipbuilders, printers, cotton operatives, miners, and boot and shoe operatives, remained, therefore, very much in command of the trade union scene. The new unions, although not unimportant, were clearly powerless to bring about a decisive transformation of the trade union movement, or to act as an institutional expression of some newly revealed working-class solidarity. Their importance was more limited. They brought some sections of the unskilled out of obscurity, into the limelight, and into contact, through union leaders, with the upper levels of the working classes.

They did not reflect any widespread assimilation of different types of work and levels of skill to a common pattern, since the technological and managerial developments tending in that direction were not very strong. Neither did they initiate any real blurring of distinctions within the working classes. As John Burns said of the 1890 Trades Union Congress: 'Physically the "old" unionists were much bigger than the "new". . . . A great number of them looked like respectable city gentlemen; wore very good coats, large watch chains, and high hats and in many cases were of such splendid build and proportions that they presented an aldermanic, not to say a magisterial form and dignity. Amongst the "new" delegates not a single one wore a tall hat. They looked workmen; they were workmen.' It may be doubted whether many miners, who were after all 'old' unionists, were ever much in the habit of wearing tall hats; but the contrast between the dignified and exclusive craftsmen, and the rough and horny-handed unskilled, was fairly drawn. It was a contrast which permeated the archetypical new Victorian occupation, that of the railwaymen, created by management as a requirement of the job, not inherited from any previous craft traditions. Running trains needed a disciplined labour force, and in the key places on the footplate and in the signalbox highly trained men capable of working independently far away from managerial oversight. Railway managers, initially often ex-army officers, drew on military experience and military ideas of a hierarchy of ranks, to organize their large and scattered bodies of men and to set up their chains of command. The ranks and grades remained, but by the time railway practices settled into a regular structure of secure – and therefore prized – employment in the 1850s, they had sorted themselves out into less paramilitary categories: footplatemen and signalmen were skilled and greatly superior to porters, shunters, cleaners, loaders, carters and the like who were unskilled, while guards occupied a somewhat uneasy intermediate position. The white-collar workers, the railway booking clerks, felt themselves to be lower-middle-class and a cut above all those who had dirty hands. In terms of chronology railwaymen possessed 'old' unions, albeit of modest size and little power since the railway companies consistently refused to recognize trade unions, on the grounds that they interfered with the discipline and obedience of their workers and jeopardized safety, until the great disputes of 1907 and 1911 ended their resistance. The Amalgamated Society of Railway Servants dated from 1871. It was exclusive, looking to the better paid for its membership, but not exclusive enough for the engine drivers, who broke away in 1880 to form their own Associated Society of Locomotive Engineers and Firemen. The Railway Servants adopted some of the 'new' characteristics in the 1890s by making themselves into an all-grades union, thus preparing the way to become the nucleus of the National Union of Railwaymen, formed in 1913 by combining with some smaller societies. ASLEF remained as the institutional expression of the railway aristocracy, as separate from the main body of railwaymen in its recruitment and lifestyle as it was in its organization and its labour relations. The rather less aristocratic society of the United Pointsmen and Signalmen, however, did decide to throw in its lot with the NUR, evidence that the common interests uniting all railwaymen had been growing stronger and were capable in some instances of overriding sectional differences.

There were, then, important changes in the 1890s affecting the working classes, but they were mixed in character and certainly did not point unambiguously towards the levelling of sectional divisions and assimilation to a common pattern of working conditions. Technical and organizational developments in hosiery and boot and shoe manufacture, for example, were coming to fruition and turning their operatives into factory workers, at much the same time as the distinctive cohesion of the mill communities of the cotton towns was weakening and, in turn, making their operatives more like other factory workers. In engineering also, factory work by the semi-skilled operating self-acting machines was beginning to make a mark. There is a definite sense in which factory workers sharing many experiences in common in employment conditions, in the general type of work they did, and in relations with employers, were emerging as the largest coherent section of the working classes, different both from the skilled, dignified and aloof, and the unskilled manual labourers. In mining and building, on the other hand, on the railways, in the docks, and in much of shipbuilding and engineering, there were no radical changes in the 1890s in what people did and the way that they did it when at work, no marked discontinuities in the pace of technical change sufficient to make the end of the century sharply different from the rest of the Victorian period. Much continued as it had always been. It was in 1915 that the great sense of craft pride and style of the carriage finishers in the Swindon railway workshop was noted by Alfred Williams: 'The carriage finishers and upholsterers are a class in themselves, differing by the very nature of their craft, from all others in the factory. As great care and cleanliness are required for their work, they are expected to be spruce and clean in their dress and appearance.' These were decidedly superior, undoubtedly tall-hatted, workers, not easily to be distinguished from the coach-builders of the 1830s, of whom it was said at the time: 'The body-makers are the wealthiest of all and compose among themselves a species of aristocracy to which the other workmen look up with feelings half of respect, half of jealousy. They feel their importance and treat the others with various consideration: carriage makers are entitled to a species of condescending familiarity; trimmers are considered too good to be despised . . . ' And it was in the 1890s that the printers' union, tightly organized, exclusive, restrictive, with firmly entrenched control of their workplace, compelled the employers – mainly in the newspaper sector – to employ only skilled and highly paid printers to operate the new linotype machines, notwithstanding the fact that it was within the capacity of any reasonably efficient typist to work the machine. The concept of pseudo-skill, of forcing the employment of skilled workers on work where the skill was not needed, had a long run ahead of it.

What did happen in the 1890s was not so much the long-delayed emergence of a coherent and homogeneous factory proletariat, as a surge in collective activity, particularly trade union activity, across a broad cross-section of the working classes and across the boundaries of skill and status. This was accompanied by a shift in the character of union activity from dominance by the concerns of individual workshops and plants, to control and leadership by union officials in pursuit of more general industry-wide strategies. It was a move welcomed and encouraged by most large employers, who, aside from the railway companies, saw the advantages of collective bargaining conducted with responsible union leaders for securing peaceable labour relations, uninterrupted work, and predictable production at settled labour costs. These managerial advantages were becoming increasingly important the more British industry was faced with German and American competition. This unionization with its emphasis on negotiation with employers and necessary decline in the importance of the friendly society and benefit functions of the older unions, was a politicization of the working classes whose direct results in terms of parliamentary politics were shortly seen in the formation of the Labour Representation Committee in 1900, the start of the Labour party. It was, however hesitant, indecisive, and weak the Labour party may have been for its first twenty years, a definite manifestation of a working-class consciousness. The class consciousness, however, was a sectional consciousness, expressive at most of the common identity of the 10 to 20 per cent of the working classes who belonged to the organized labour movement. The claim of that fraction to speak for the whole has always been denied at the polls, although the fraction of course grew considerably larger in the twentieth century. The possibility that it could establish a claim, towards the end of the Victorian period, to be the articulate and politically aware representative of the inarticulate and unorganized masses, was already unreal. The masses may have been unorganized, but they were no longer inarticulate. Above the residuum, at least, the 10 to 15 per cent of the population who were utterly wretched and held to be unemployable, they were literate, they had at least a little spare money above bare subsistence, they had some sense of self-respect and of respectability, and they were opting for a popular culture that was increasingly independent and increasingly apolitical.

CHAPTER SEVEN

Play

Group and class identities were shaped by different work experiences; the distinctive and separate social building blocks produced by this process in mill, factory, and workshop, were fused together with varying degrees of cohesion and in a different set of patterns by more widely shared common interests and activities outside the sphere of work. It was only in completely enclosed communities that all the ingredients of a culture, all the values and attitudes, were provided by and controlled by the institution. Monasteries and nunneries are prime examples. Prisons, boarding schools, army regiments and naval ships came near to being total cultural institutions in this sense, but rarely exercised their sway throughout a lifetime, and could not live without contacts with the outside, unregulated, world. Similarly, the mill communities of paternalist employers, although they built up loyalties to the mill and provided many facilities for non-work time, could not insulate the operatives from the wider neighbourhood and town communities and the outside world of pubs and clubs. The complete compartmentalization of the life of individuals, so that what is done at work and what is done with leisure seem to have no connection with one another, is a product of the boredom and monotony of twentieth-century assembly-line work. Leisure or non-work time and their influences cannot be so simply separated from work time in the lives of the Victorian working classes, when leisure was so often what a group of workmates did when they were not at their workplace. Nevertheless, the social or cultural meaning of non-work activities attracted much attention from contemporaries, anxious that these were taking place out of the sight of and out of the control of employers or responsible authorities, and are key elements for any understanding of Victorian society.

One very large group, the domestic servants, worked so that another group of women, chiefly middle-class wives, could be leisured. It is an oversimplification to suppose that all domestic servants worked in middle- or upper-class households, or that all middle-class families were servant-keepers. Some, perhaps a great many, of the girls in rural areas described in censuses as 'domestic servants' were in fact living-in farm servants, and some in the towns were in working households, working in the business of shop or workshop rather than doing household chores. Again, some families of clear middle-class status had no living-in servants, but probably employed daily or part-time charladies and made use of outside washerwomen. The central core of the group of domestic servants, however, were working for middle-class wives, although we do not know how much smaller this core was than the million female domestics recorded in 1851 or the 1.4 million of 1901. Wealthier middle-class households kept more than one servant, and the landed classes typically had large domestic establishments with a hierarchy of servants with specialized duties; but the typical domestic was to be found in a one-servant family, and was more likely to be a hard-driven drudge and maid of all work than a well-treated friend of the family. Country girls were preferred as recruits to service, daughters of small farmers or agricultural labourers, although in the second half of the century a growing proportion were town-born. Few women regarded domestic service as a lifetime occupation, and those who did make it a career probably did so unintentionally, because they had failed to get married in their twenties. The normal pattern was for a girl to go into service as a teenager and leave to get married after perhaps a dozen years in service, maybe finding a partner through contacts made in doing her mistress's housekeeping business, and maybe having saved up a nest egg which could propel her into the lower middle class.

For reasons such as these domestic servants were by and large a group without an identity, not incorporated into working-class culture, organization, or politics, and lacking a culture of their own. Although their earnings were high in comparison with many other unskilled or semi-skilled occupations, male as well as female, since board and lodging and perhaps their working clothes were found and their money wages were pure spending or saving money, they enjoyed very lowly status in the eyes of the rest of the working classes. Their work was regarded as servile and degrading, they were trained to be subordinate, deferential, and obsequious, their manners and morals were by definition derivative and imitative, and they lived and worked as isolated individuals in a middle-class world with no opportunities to get together and assert their existence as a distinctive subclass. Moreover, at any one moment the great majority regarded themselves as transients, looking forward to the time when they would cease to be domestic servants, so that the chances of forming a corporate identity were minimal. Little wonder that here was a numerous body of workers which labour leaders and thinkers preferred to forget when they spoke of the working class. Only a tiny minority of this body, perhaps no more than 5 per cent of the whole, lived and worked in the great houses in country and town of the aristocracy, landed gentry, and the very wealthy upper middle class, and experienced the group customs and traditions of the servants' hall. Here virtually all the male domestic servants – roughly one tenth of the total workforce, and a declining proportion from mid-century as the occupation became more feminized – were concentrated, serving as butlers, stewards, footmen, valets, and as coachmen and grooms who were sometimes indoor and sometimes outdoor servants, according to the size of the establishment and the arrangement of accommodation and stabling. The servants' hall had its own rules and its own hierarchy, not entirely reflecting male dominance since the female housekeeper or cook commanded her own chain of obedience, and not only reflecting its own functional subordination to the needs of the employing family since within it the servants had a social life of their own. In such households there was a group life, there were the elements of a career structure within domestic service, there was varied experience in moving from country to town, and there were opportunities to meet other servants, the valets and lady's maids of house guests. Here if anywhere was the breeding ground of a servant ethos, here if anywhere a servant class had its being. With its mixed loyalties to its own members and to the interests of master and mistress, its capacity to combine deference with an ability to live well, and its airs of condescending superiority towards everyone else, it was not a class that could be fitted comfortably into any working-class social analysis. It was perhaps a replica of the military world in a multitude of small units, each with its officer class of master, mistress, and family, its NCOs of cook and butler, and its other ranks living in a private world that combined strict discipline, much cleaning and polishing, separate messes, some relaxations, and some camaraderie.

Servants in the grand establishments had a certain amount of leisure, and a distinctive culture. They had nothing in common with the vast majority of servants who were solitary workers, had no leisure, and nothing which could pass for a self-generated or self-sustained culture. If they were lucky and had a good employer, servants might, towards the end of the century, get an afternoon a week off duty, it is true; but most had to spend all the time in the house, constantly at beck and call, and with no regular hours of work beyond the knowledge that the day started at 5 a.m. and went on until bedtime. As for their cultural equipment, it was the aim of elementary schooling, especially in the voluntary schools, to turn out girls at the age of twelve or so who were well suited through habits of cleanliness, neatness, and obedience, and through their training in moral principles and sewing, to make good domestic servants. With this grounding, if it had been obtained, a girl might start in a household where a junior kitchenmaid, scullerymaid, or general dogsbody was kept, and after a year or two of training on the job move on to employment as the chief, and only, servant. Here, in servicing a middle-class house and family to suit middle-class habits and values, she had a worm's eye view of middle-class ideas of propriety, cleanliness, decorum, dress, eating customs, morals and every ingredient of middle-class family life, and precious little opportunity to compare these values with anything else. It is, therefore, extremely likely that domestic servants absorbed middle-class values and attitudes, and it has indeed been argued that this was the major agency for the transmission of notions of respectability and concepts of 'modern' behaviour, via marriage, to the bulk of the working classes.

This is undoubtedly an exaggeration, for although the marriage patterns of ex-domestics have yet to be established, it seems possible that they were beamed towards the lower middle class of publicans and small shopkeepers rather than towards the working classes at large; and in any case the capacity of sections of the working class to produce their own internally fostered canons of respectability, without the aid of imported domestic servant influence, is abundantly documented. Still, the domestics themselves may well have acquired a veneer or pastiche of bourgeois culture, a hybrid style in which performance of manual labour continued amid a display of genteel manners of the cup-and-saucer, home-centred, variety of refinement. For whatever other tastes domestics acquired from their employers, they had no chance of adopting the freedom from manual work, and the leisure, which it was the object of their existence to provide for others. The middle-class wife and mother, with a single servant to do the cleaning, the fires, the washing, and perhaps some of the cooking, might still not have much time on her hands while she had young children to look after as well as the duties of overall household management. But at many stages in the lifecycle, and at all times in families that could afford more than one servant, or a nurserymaid or nanny, servant-keeping meant that there was time and energy to spare from the basic routines of keeping a family fed and clothed and a home clean and tidy. The uses made of this surplus time and energy set the shape of middle-class culture. The distinctive contribution of the Victorian middle classes was to legitimate or even sanctify those uses of this time and energy that were approved, as being the performance of duties and responsibilities, and to classify those that were disapproved as being selfish, and sinful, pursuit of pleasure and personal gratification. It was an attitude which readily led to censorious interference in the leisure of other classes.

Middle-class culture was shaped by the moral revolution of evangelicalism, allied to the older puritan traditions of Dissent, launched in the closing years of the eighteenth century and reaching its greatest influence in the early Victorian years. Evangelicalism was a call to public and political action in almost every sphere, from bible-teaching to church-building, prison reform to the abolition of slavery, from the prevention of cruelty to animals (and, perhaps, children) to the suppression of lewd and licentious entertainments, from the propagation of the gospel in foreign parts to the curtailment of drinking at home. It was also, and first and foremost, a creed and a code for the conduct of personal and family life. The ideal of a Christian home, ordered by a morality that enshrined piety, chastity, sobriety, filial obedience, and charity, and shunned displays of luxury, sexual transgressions, and all diversions which were not improving or uplifting, was the secure base from which the public manifestations and campaigns of evangelicalism were mounted. The private ideology was not conceived as exclusively applicable to families with enough affluence to have some leisure, and indeed was well suited to the work-and-thrift ethic of male business and professional family heads. Still less was it intended to imply that religion and the Christian spirit were luxuries available only to the comfortably off who had time for leisure pursuits. Nevertheless, it supplied a pattern of total behaviour excellently fitted to the middle classes keen to differentiate their status from uncouth lower orders and frivolous aristocracy, a pattern that could be adopted without necessarily accepting wholeheartedly its religious foundations. And it was undeniable that the implementation of the ideology, both in the home and in the field of charitable works, was primarily the work of the womenfolk, a product of their servant-keeping leisure.

Religion was at the centre of middle-class lifestyles. How typical or normal was its penetration to the core of domestic life, in regular daily bible-readings or morning prayers for the assembled family and domestic staff, is not known. It may be that these were the customs only of the most devout, and then mostly Dissenting, families; but many examples exist from early and mid-Victorian family journals. Regular church- or chapel-going was universal among the middle classes, often to two or three services each Sunday; not to attend was scandalous or bohemian. It was vital to build a church or a chapel on a new housing development, as an early priority, to ensure its respectable and middle-class character. Only towards the end of the century did this custom begin to break down, a sign of growing irreligion blamed on the spread of the practice of living in flats, held to be inherently immoral, and the growing popularity of weekending away from home. Religious sentiments and precepts saturated the home in pictures, biblical texts, and moral injunctions, and insofar as there was a social life outside the home it too revolved round the church or chapel. There was church music, church choirs, church teas, and church outings; there was helping with Sunday school, and with church bazaars, and later in the century there might be church brigades to run, for boys and girls; also by the 1880s and 1890s there might be church socials, pandering to the growing secularization of attitudes with singing and dancing that were patently not religious, though they were emphatically decorous and respectable. Above all, there were charitable works, either organized through the church or inspired by religious faith and teaching. There were so many Victorian charities and so much philanthropic activity, local and national, institutionalized and purely individual and personal, sectional, sectarian, and indiscriminate, that raising and spending the money involved could easily have taken up all the spare time that middle-class women had left after running their homes. Caring for the sick and the poor were the major areas of charitable concern, either by good-neighbourly impulse or through parochial and other organizations: visiting and nursing, finding and distributing food, clothing, and fuel in time of need, running local dispensaries, helping to save the souls of the dying and comfort the bereaved, all these things were to be done. There were hosts of other good causes to support, all needing funds to be raised, all relying on voluntary helpers to do their work. There were orphans to care for, fallen women and unmarried mothers to provide for, ragged schools to be run, and missionaries to be supported; while caring for horses, providing them with drinking troughs in town and old-age homes in the country, and looking after stray cats and dogs, probably excited as much sympathy even if the resulting ministrations did not engage so many voluntary helpers as the plights of distressed and impoverished humans.

The closest the Victorians came to having an apparatus of social services was not, as has sometimes been suggested, the result of legislation and official action through the Poor Laws and support for education, but the consequence of the largely unsystematized efforts of vast numbers of individuals and voluntary organizations, mainly inspired by religious motives, and sustained by the work of armies of middle-class women. In this there was a clear separation of male and female spheres. It is perfectly true that the tasks of publicizing, recruiting, and organizing evangelical congregations or major charities were almost exclusively a male preserve, with some interventions by women writers on philanthropy. These men, commanding the armies of middle-class women, were the professionals, the clergymen and the ministers, and their authority was unchallenged. The armies of rank-and-file female voluntary workers, however, were not matched by equivalent numbers of rank-and-file men. The menfolk, the husbands of these women, were out of the home at work in the office while their wives and daughters were out of the home doing their visiting. The men no doubt shared the same religious outlook, and were certainly the main source of the charitable giving. But they were much less directly involved in philanthropic service, and their lives were much less circumscribed by the church or chapel network, for quite apart from their place of business as a source of values they had access to social institutions that were male, secular, and independent of any church; clubs, literary and philosophical societies, or masonic lodges, for example. The separation of work from the home, while it meant that middle-class women were increasingly excluded from any participation in the breadwinning process, did not mean that they were housebound in a purdah of antimacassars and domesticity. The replacement of gainful or productive employment by voluntary work may have been an exchange which did more for the status of the class than for the status of women, but it did nonetheless take the women out of the home more frequently and regularly than in the premodern 'home as workplace' situation, and it did mean that the women tended to have more contacts with and more experience of other sections of the community than did their menfolk. Whether these contacts increased understanding between the classes and eased social tensions, or stoked up resentment of the patronizing superiority of charitable ladies, is another matter.

The claustrophobia of middle-class housewives, housebound and bored, was a product of the interwar spread of anonymous suburbia and the encroachment of salaried social workers, particularly in health care and visiting, on the voluntary sphere; it was not a Victorian malaise. All the same, the cult of domesticity was a powerful cultural force in respectable, God-fearing, middle-class families, tending to internalize relaxation and pleasures and to regard permissible outside activities as matters of moral duty, not enjoyment. Not that enjoyment was the chief aim of the use of leisure in the home. All activities, in the best-regulated families, were designed to be edifying and uplifting, contributions to the improvement of character and expressions of the purity of thought. Music-making and singing were much encouraged, especially for the females: demure, chastely romantic, tragic in a spiritual way, never strident, vulgar, or hot-bloodedly passionate. Pianos and sheet music poured into middle-class homes, and in due course into working-class parlours as well; the same instrument could render 'Oh for the wings of a dove' in one home, and pick out a music-hall ditty in another. Much reading went on, frequently with sessions of reading aloud in the family circle; a seemingly endless stream of moral and uplifting tales, for every age group, supplied this market, although the great names, particularly those like Dickens or Trollope who appeared in serial form, were also known in such households. For the women there was much needlework and embroidery, for hands should never be idle, and for the men a newspaper, or, greatly daring, *Punch*. The strictest families did not allow playing cards in the house; children's toys were for instruction, as it might be in the alphabet or in gender roles; and there was no question of going out to pubs, theatres, or dances.

The stereotype of the austere, stern, unbending, puritanical Victorian family did no doubt actually exist in all its uncomfortable glory in the privacy of some homes, but it is not an accurate picture of the culture of the middle classes. Quaker domestic culture came closest to the strict model, plain in speech and dress and shorn of all frivolity, ornament, or display. In strict Quaker homes at the beginning of the century there were no pictures or portraits, and only plain serviceable furnishings and utensils; music, singing, and dancing were not allowed, and imaginative literature was rigorously vetted because of its immoral tendencies. Theatres, gambling, immoderate drinking, and field sports were emphatically out. This regime probably reached the height of its influence in the 1830s and 1840s, but even then was already being challenged by the more wealthy and successful Quakers, often known in the unaffected vocabulary of the time as 'gay Friends', who liked pretty clothes, fine china and glass, elaborate dinners, music and dancing, and the latest novels. By the 1860s and 1870s the simplicity and rigour of the way of life were everywhere eroded by worldliness. Music was being taught in Quaker schools and widely enjoyed in Quaker homes, concert-going and theatre-going were no longer scandalous, and a Quaker could appear on the hunting field without risk of disownment. The *Westminster Review* recorded the change in 1875, with an eye admittedly to the manners of the · wealthiest: 'Influential Quakers . . . are the owners of the choicest paintings, which are exhibited to the world after the costliest entertainments, amidst the melody of operatic performances. In the hunting-field, in the ball-room, at the whist-table, some of the very best performers of our acquaintance are gentlemen who are to be found every Sunday sitting under their hats . . . waiting for divine illumination.'

Quakerism, which was a tiny sect (about 16,000 members in 1840, falling to under 14,000 in 1860 and thereafter rising gradually to about 17,000 by the end of the century) spanning all levels of the middle class from clerks and small retailers, through farmers, millers, and professional men to great bankers, merchants, and manufacturers, may well have responded to worldly and hedonistic influences more readily than larger and more solidly lower-middle-class–upper-working-class groups like Congregationalists or Methodists. Nevertheless, theatres and concerts were never without middle-class patrons in such numbers that they can only have been drawn from every sect, and none; many evangelicals, while adamant on the wickedness of plays, approved of oratorios as being sacred music and condoned orchestral concerts as long as they were approached as culture and not as simple amusement. Provincial theatres and halls, started in the eighteenth century for the local gentry and county society, seem to have suffered a decline in the early decades of the nineteenth century, and then enjoyed revival and expansion into many of the newer industrial towns in the 1850s and 1860s, chiefly for middle-class family audiences. Holiday resorts, again pioneered in the eighteenth century for the aristocracy and gentry at Bath or

Brighton, Tunbridge Wells or Scarborough, were by the early Victorian period being rapidly developed for a solid middle-class family clientele, rather than for fashionable society, for instance at Ramsgate and Margate, Southport or Torquay. Although the socially most significant feature of the great mid-Victorian expansion of resorts was the spectacular rise of the working-class seaside playgrounds, such as Southend, Cleethorpes, and above all Blackpool, the greater number of holiday towns, new like Bournemouth or Eastbourne, or expanding like Folkestone or Hove, were catering for a massive middle-class demand. A class which took regular summer holidays, albeit strictly *en famille*, in the privacy of family lodgings or a quiet family hotel, with the full decorum of bathing machines and respectable promenades, and no naughty promiscuous gregariousness, was not a class which abjured pleasure and amusement. Nor was a class which invented football by codifying it, took up croquet, and invented lawn tennis, in the 1870s, as a game for both sexes to be played at clubs which rapidly became rivals to church or chapel as a source of marriage partners, a class which confined all its leisure to home and family. The middle classes, whose publicists often appeared as kill-joys towards the rough lower orders, were not kill-joys towards themselves, and it seems probable that the puritan-evangelical blueprint of family conduct was adopted in its entirety by no more than a small minority of the middle classes, even in its early Victorian heyday.

Indeed, the fact that the mass of early Victorian literature seeking to prescribe codes of behaviour and conduct was unanimous in preaching the puritan message, occupying itself with such fine doctrinal questions as the extent to which playing card games with elderly or sick relatives might entail a fall from grace, should not be taken as a ground for inferring that normal or majority middle-class behaviour actually conformed to this model. The very persistence of the propaganda could indicate less the triumph of the ideal than the persistence of large numbers of unregenerates happily sampling the pleasures and amusements of the world. Membership of the middle class emphatically required an unsullied reputation in the community, and that rested on conformity to a code of behaviour in public and in the company of strangers which was carefully defined in the etiquette manuals which multiplied prodigiously in the early nineteenth century to meet the hunger of the upwardly mobile for social instruction. The solid, industrious, and prudent middle classes understandably sought to differentiate themselves from the idle, dissolute, and thriftless, whether the extravagant undeserving rich or the rough undeserving poor. In the age of the Benthamite felicific calculus, however, when it was acknowledged that the pursuit of pleasure was the prime force in human behaviour and that it could be harnessed by suitably contrived pains and penalties into serving as the prime force for social harmony and betterment, it was only the strictest of evangelicals who held that the rules of propriety dictated abstinence from all forms of enjoyment. For most of the middle classes it was a matter, rather, of confining their pleasures to those which were permissible because they were rational, not morally corrupting, and not recklessly extravagant.

A stark conflict of public morals and private behaviour is, however, enshrined in the notorious double standard of female chastity and fidelity, and male indulgence and unfaithfulness. The roots of the hypocrisy with which the succeeding generation taunted their Victorian predecessors, as they gleefully showed that the great and the good had had feet of clay, lay in their sexual behaviour. Others have seen in prostitution, which had the dimensions of a grave and growing social problem in much Victorian religious and social thinking, a case of double exploitation: of females by males, and of lower-class girls by their social superiors. The numbers of prostitutes were certainly very large, although there is no means of telling whether they were closer to Henry Mayhew's guess of 80,000 or more in London in the early 1850s, or the 8000 or so recorded as known to the police at that time. The overwhelming majority did come from working-class backgrounds, with the possible exception of a few of those in the fashionable West End trade and its provincial equivalents. The overwhelming majority of their clients also, however, were from the working classes, notably the soldiers and sailors of the port and garrison towns that were the objects of the notorious Contagious Diseases Acts of the 1860s, designed to curb venereal disease by compulsory medical inspection of common prostitutes and forcible detention in hospitals for the diseased. Some of the custom undeniably came from middle-class and aristocratic men, with solicitors, local merchants, and respectable gentlemen figuring occasionally in the police records of prosecutions of prostitutes for stealing from their clients. Even though the traffic was not in practice a straightforward matter of men of education and property buying the bodies of working-class girls, its toleration by society was justified by an ideology which was as much a class as it was a sexist statement. This held that male sexuality was far greater than female, pure and well-bred women being indeed almost devoid of sexual desires, though lower-class girls might possess strong animal lusts natural to those of lesser intelligence. It followed that it was a physiological necessity for this excess in male sexual impulses and needs to have an outlet in premarital and extramarital intercourse. Finally, it was argued that the postponement of marriage to the late twenties or early thirties, which was an essential element of middle-class business and professional life, made these outlets peculiarly necessary for middle-class men. The evangelical doctrines of abstinence naturally embraced abstinence from sex, the obvious solution to the problem created by the economics of middle-class careers; but it is not clear that such moral teachings ever succeeded in doing more than dent the attractive arguments that this particular kind of abstinence could be damaging to physical health, or even worse might cause grievous mental, physical and moral damage simultaneously if denial of natural sex led, as it so easily could, to masturbation, the sin of onanism being one of the worst in the Victorian book.

The mainly medical pundits, who served as the Victorians' sexologists, probably had the sons of the upper classes and the fashionable young men of London society in mind, when they rationalized the indulgence of male sexuality and condoned the arrangements for its satisfaction, so long as respectable society could pretend that they did not exist. The opportunities for sexual initiation through seducing servant girls were more plentiful in upper-class than in middle-class households, and the general tenor of aristocratic culture was more indulgent and permissive. Yet it is clear that the world of promiscuous, illicit, and commercial sex was by no means an exclusively aristocratic, or a dualistic upper- and working-class subculture: it was only that those of the middle classes who enjoyed the pleasures of this world had a more acute sense of sin, were more ashamed of themselves, and took more care to cover their tracks. The frailty of the Victorian middle-class males, and disreputability of their sex lives, should not however be exaggerated. There was never the remotest possibility of any imitation of the French rules of the marital game, where it was understood and accepted that a wealthy bourgeois would keep a mistress. Reticence in mentioning sex was in all likelihood accompanied by reticence in practising it, and there is no reason to suppose that the average middle-class Victorian did not have a satisfying married life that conformed to the professed standards of sexual morality. Equally, there is some reason to suppose that sex within marriage was not invariably the joyless and purely functional operation which the 'legs apart and think of England' image suggests. In an area where the direct evidence of diaries, journals, and correspondence is necessarily extremely scanty there is, at any rate, room to believe that the great public parade of straitlaced prudery and apparent sexlessness, which for many is the essence of Victorianism, was an effort to subdue and direct into manageable channels, but not to suppress, what were seen as naturally exuberant and devouring passions, which left to themselves could cause social chaos. Some critics of late twentieth-century permissiveness are inclined to see the point.

It would be tempting to try to divide the middle classes into two groups, those who acknowledged the pleasure and amusement they derived from entertainments, games, books, and even the marriage bed, and those who had to convince themselves that everything was done purely out of a sense of duty and for the sake of self-improvement. There is insufficient evidence of private lives or group behaviour to do this, but in any case the division would be unlikely to coincide with the income, occupational, and educational boundaries between the several bourgeois subclasses, though it might well correspond more closely to denominational differences. Amidst considerable uncertainty in the delineation of middle-class leisure culture, two points are reasonably clear. The evangelical ideology was in the ascendant in the 1840s and 1850s, but while its grip on the language of public discourse on manners and morals became very nearly total, its hold over actual behaviour was partial and vulnerable to the pressures of affluence and self-indulgence. Second, the long-run tendency of the wealthy to acquire a taste for some of the delights of aristocratic living was, at most, slightly moderated during the phase when the rhetoric of puritan disapproval resounded from press and pulpit, and in all likelihood continued unabated on its course. At any rate by the 1860s and 1870s the tendency had resurfaced into public visibility, intensified in scale by the growing adhesion of wealthy manufacturers to the ranks of the culture-conscious and pleasure-seeking upper bourgeoisie of bankers, merchants, and professional men, and extended in its impact by the ready access to the countryside and its special variety of pleasures opened up by the railways. The result was that the culture of the late Victorian middle classes, in the age of Gilbert and Sullivan, Sherlock Holmes, and Rider Haggard, had shed the husk of earnestness and self-righteousness and embraced the notion of fun, its pursuit constrained by strict adherence to the secular rules of etiquette governing social relationships rather than by religious scruples. The mantle of moral rectitude, sanctimonious piety, and austere recreations lugubriously endured, had shrunk until it no longer fitted any but the lower middle class, their ultimate weapon of respectability in the struggle to distance themselves from the seaside-postcard vulgarity of the better-off workers, with whom they might otherwise have become confused.

The story of Thomas Cook's travel agency captures these trends and illustrates, in the key holiday sphere, how the commercialization of leisure aided and abetted the displacement of high moral purpose by the pursuit of pleasure in middle-class relaxations. Thomas Cook, wood-turner by trade and Baptist bible-reader by faith, first revealed his flair for combining good causes with shrewd business deals when he negotiated one of the earliest special excursion trains at reduced fares to take a party of over five hundred temperance workers from Leicester to a big temperance rally near Loughborough, in 1841. Realizing the potential demand for cheap travel in organized groups at cut rates, and his own power as agent representing this demand in negotiating terms with railway companies and other suppliers of travel services, Cook devoted more and more of his time to the travel business, seizing the opportunity of the 1851 Great Exhibition to enlarge his operations to the national scale with veritable fleets of special trains converging on the metropolis. These were excursions largely for the respectable working classes, and were viewed in a high-minded way as essentially uplifting educational visits that would help spread the enlightened message of the Exhibition, of material, cultural, and moral progress and peaceful international competition, throughout the land. Polite London society was indeed pleasantly surprised by the good behaviour of the crowds, having feared the worst in drunken brawls from the invasion by the rough provincial masses, and even invented public lavatories for the occasion to head off the risk of an uncontrollable flood of indecent exposures.

The charms of profitable philanthropy always endeared themselves to an influential section of public-spirited Victorians, who cheered themselves with the thought that if good works produced a small but steady profit it proved that the works were good, because no recipient would willingly pay a remunerative price for bad works. Thomas Cook felt that he was doing good in this sense, spreading enlightenment through cheap travel and gaining himself a living in the process. Much of the expansion of his domestic tours business in the 1850s did continue to cater for the huge popular, and essentially working-class, demand for travel revealed by his, and similar, enterprising feats of organization, dealing, and advertising. Some of the imitators, forming travel agencies more towards the end of the century, were in the missionary tradition of Thomas Cook: John Frame, notable for opening up the Highlands to tourism, was an ardent teetotaller who enforced temperance rules on his customers, an unlikely and unrewarding task in the land of whisky, and Sir Henry Lunn was a Dissenter keen on promoting free-church reunions through the unifying medium of cheap and companionable travel. Others, notably the railway companies who took to arranging and marketing their own special excursions, felt no call to look further than the extra revenues and profits to justify their entry into the excursion business. Whether the excursionists embarked on their trips intent on self-improvement and eager for an uplifting experience, or with less complicated ideas about adventure, curiosity about strange places, and simple pleasure at getting away from dreary surroundings, it is perhaps impossible to tell, although it is reasonable to suppose that enjoyment – of food, drink, and a bit of a lark – was what the great majority had in mind.

When he turned his talents to foreign travel, however, Thomas Cook put them at the service of the middle classes. The Paris International Exhibition of 1855 set him off in this direction, and the set-piece special trips he arranged for this, and its 1867 sequel, retained the popular, classless, and educational image. At 36s. for four days in Paris, including accommodation and the return fare from London, the package cost rather less than one week's wages of a skilled worker, and intelligent artisans mingled with inquisitive clerks on these instructional jaunts. These, however, were the occasional highlights, for Cook and adventurous artisans alike. The ordinary tours which he organized to Paris, and to French, Swiss, and Italian resorts, from the later 1850s and early 1860s, were middle-class affairs with middle-class fares. This trend, and the emphasis on the commercial rather than the philanthropic character of the travel agency business, became more pronounced when his son John took over the direction from 1865. He concentrated on developing the system of through bookings to holiday destinations which his father had originated, introducing the travel coupons covering journeys over all the separate railway systems and shipping lines that figured in an individual itinerary, a great convenience for individual and group travel. He negotiated agreements with most of the European railway companies to this end, and with American ones too by the 1890s; these arrangements were confined to first-class passengers. In the 1880s he set out to make Egypt and the Nile safe and comfortable for English tourists, which in that unhygienic and unreliable land meant investing in hotels and river steamers under direct Cook ownership and management. Seeing the Pyramids was a cultural experience of the highest order; it was one which the working classes had to do without, unless the twists of imperial policy and the fortunes of war chanced to take some of them there at Her Majesty's expense. A Nile cruise would cost two or three hundred pounds, a once-in-a-lifetime treat for a prosperous middle-class couple. Nearer home a six weeks' package tour for two people, starting from London and taking in the Rhine, Switzerland, and France, cost about £85 in the early 1870s, three to four months' salary of a senior clerk at the height of his career. Conceivably such a person might have aspired to take his wife on such a tour just once in his life; but it is plain that for the most part Cook's Continental tourists came from the comfortably-off middle classes.

It would be wrong to suppose that the middle-class character of this tourism in itself negated the moral and cultural purpose of travel and revealed it in its true colours as indulgent pleasure-seeking. The lower orders were not the only people needing and deserving help and encouragement from persuasive leaders to steer them towards desirable goals, and it was not unlikely that the middle classes who promoted the gospel of rational recreation for others might on occasion practise what they preached. There were plenty of serious reasons for visiting the treasures of the Continent: there were art galleries, churches, architecture, and antiquities to be studied, opera and music to be appreciated, while Switzerland came into fashion for health and exercise, and Alpine mountaineering was pioneered by a fanatical minority of the English intellectual and professional classes. Mid-Victorian tourists had a reputation for being earnest and extremely proper, always correctly if rather inappropriately dressed as they went round with a Murray's guide or a Baedeker in hand, careful not to miss the approved sights just as they were perpetually on guard against unboiled water and the innate knavery of all foreigners. They marked themselves off from the frivolous aristocracy which ignored the art treasures and headed straight for the comforts of Le Touquet, Nice, Baden Baden, or Biarritz. They took their holidays very seriously indeed, and expected to return home mentally, spiritually, and physically refreshed and enriched. Holidays with a serious purpose, a purpose often imbued with moral force, were certainly not carefree jaunts; but they were escapes from ordinariness into exciting new worlds of well-regulated and carefully rationalized pleasure and happiness. There is no sign that these middle-class adventurers were mortifying the flesh or practising self-denial as they fanned out across Europe. As Thomas Cook had hoped, they widened their horizons and maybe became better citizens; but this form of self-improvement was a source of enjoyment, not one to be undertaken in a spirit of self-sacrifice and out of a stern sense of duty. The boat-train, the cross-Channel steamer, and the book of Cook's coupons were the symbols of the entry of the pursuit of happiness into middle-class culture, placing the mid-Victorian holidaymakers a good deal further away from the joyless evangelical stereotype than they were from the topless customs of late twentieth-century Mediterranean beaches.

Seen from above, this guidebook culture skimmed uncritically from a dash through Europe in a week or two seemed ludicrously shallow, vulgar, and meretricious. In no time at all high society was laughing patronizingly at cartoons of Cook's tourists leaping about in the Alps in their imitation mountaineering gear, swarming over Vesuvius, and relentlessly 'doing' Cologne cathedral oblivious of the service going on around them. The spectacle of clerks and tradesmen solemnly appraising old masters and painstakingly studying the distinctive characteristics of romanesque architecture may have struck the upper classes as irresistibly comic. The ridicule, however, was a defensive reaction designed to protect the preserves of good breeding and good taste from invasion by inferiors who might get above their station if they deluded themselves that a veneer of refinement picked up in a few weeks' sightseeing was a substitute for a culture absorbed from birth and developed over a lifetime. This was an assertion of social exclusiveness rather than cultural superiority, for many of the middle classes were undoubtedly better read and better informed than many of the aristocracy whose intellectual interests barely extended beyond racehorses or gaming rooms. Complaints of vulgarity, superficiality, bad manners, debauchery and lechery had also been levied against young milords doing the Grand Tour. The middle classes were doing in groups, at cut rates and at railway speed, an edited and abbreviated version of what aristocratic youths had done before them, with results that were very much the same, sometimes good and sometimes deplorable. Technical innovation in the shape of railways and steamships, commercial organization in the shape of Cook's and other travel agencies, prised open the treasure-chest of elitist pleasures, enabling the middle classes to imitate or borrow some of the trappings of the aristocratic good life. The elite responded by retreating from their

former haunts and becoming ever more expensively out of reach in
the luxury hotels of the Riviera or their private villas in Italy,
distancing themselves from emulation in the transatlantic luxury
liners of the 1880s and the East African big-game hunting of the
1890s. A trip to Paris or a voyage up the Rhine did nothing to
narrow the social distance between clerk or shopkeeper and the
aristocracy; but they did help the wealthier middle classes, who
could afford to borrow more extensively from the aristocratic
wardrobe in other ways, to become more and more gentrified.

This process began at home rather than with foreign travel, and
was more concerned with a gentrification of tastes and manners
than a gentrification of possessions, to which only a minority of the
wealthy aspired. The families of wealthy merchants, bankers, and
lawyers in the City and Westminster had for long contained men
and women of sophisticated tastes and cultivated minds, patrons of
artists, musicians, and architects, collectors of pictures and books.
All that was new in the nineteenth century was that successful
provincial manufacturers adopted a similar cultural style. By the
1830s it was becoming common for prominent industrialists to
have fine houses with fine furniture, to adopt polite London habits
for mealtimes and for drawing-room etiquette, to buy pictures,
generally by safe and well-established artists, and to form well-
stocked libraries. The culture was derivative, borrowed or copied
from London and from the aristocracy, not the homegrown
product of an independent industrial elite; but the core of the
culture had in any case been derivative in the first place, largely
borrowed or copied from the French and the Italians by the
aristocracy, and the manufacturers were doing no more than claim
a place in the descent of European civilization. By mid-century
some manufacturers had built up sufficient self-confidence to
escape from reliance on conventional taste in buying minor and
fake old masters, and backed their own judgement in collecting
works by living artists. 'The principal support of British art
proceeds from wealthy Lancashire,' it could be asserted in 1857.
'Some twenty years ago, the merchants and manufacturers were
collectors of "Old Masters", they paid large sums of money for
"names" with bad pictures.' G. F. Watts, breakaway pre-Raph-
aelite and extremely successful in the 1850s and 1860s with his

portraits and his allegorical subjects, flourished under the patronage of C. H. Rickards, Manchester merchant and son of a cotton spinner. The National Gallery of British Art, better known as the Tate Gallery, was built in 1897 with a gift from the sugar refiner, Sir Henry Tate, and his private collection formed the nucleus of the new gallery. In the 1850s Karl Hallé launched a symphony orchestra, destined to become of world class and to earn him the recognition of the Establishment with a knighthood in 1888, with the support of the Manchester commercial community, particularly that of the German colony – including Engels – which was prominent in the cotton trade. These were exceptional individuals and exceptional cases, but for all that they were not so rare as major individual contributions to high culture by members of the Victorian landed elite. Of those perhaps only the gift of the Wallace Collection to the nation in 1897 by the widow of Sir Richard Wallace, Anglo-Irish landowner, baronet, and illegitimate son of the Marquess of Hertford, stands comparison. They are, rather, straws in the wind, a wind that was blowing away the charge of money-grubbing philistinism which Matthew Arnold levelled at the millocrats, before he even made it.

Wealthy Victorian businessmen may have tended to acquire their culture wholesale, with more than a thought for its possible resale value. Joseph Gillot, the largest pen manufacturer in Birmingham and possibly in the world, for example, was the owner of the 'largest and finest' collection of Turners in private hands, acquired by buying the entire contents of the artist's studio at one go; by the time he died in 1872 he had a collection of 527 pictures, including many Gainsboroughs as well. He also collected musical instruments, at one time declining the offer of a Stradivarius with the comment, 'Nay, lad, I shan't buy any more fiddles; I've got a boat-load already.' There are two sides to art as investment, however, sellers and buyers. By the 1890s it was the old aristocracy which had grown bored with its art treasures; engrossed in the pursuit of comfort and luxury, more intent on collecting stocks and shares than pictures, aware that there were greater social returns from money spent on a well-run shoot or a well-stocked cellar than on books, the great country-house owners were indifferent to the fabulous contents amassed by their predecessors, momentarily aroused from their fashionable ignorance when an art dealer chanced to put a tempting price tag on some item for the market. The slow stripping of the country houses, and the build-up of the great American collections amongst others, had begun. The eighth Duke of Devonshire, as Lord Hartington the last of the great Whig politicians, bored with everything except racehorses and the Duchess of Manchester, his mistress, was typical in his ignorance. One of the duties of the Chatsworth librarian was to 'tour the principal rooms with the Eighth Duke and his Duchess the day before a house-party began, and tell them a few outstanding facts about their principal possessions', which they had always forgotten again before the next lot of guests came. By the late Victorian age the role reversal was complete. The aristocrats were the philistines, impressed only by the cash value of their stock of art. The guardians of the values of high culture were the intellectual and professional middle classes, backed by the money, and often the appreciation, of businessmen.

There was another role reversal, with different implications. At the beginning of the century the business and professional communities of the provincial centres had shown no interest in the field sports of the gentry, and leading Dissenters had positively condemned them as wicked. Before the end of the century prosperous industrialists and merchants were amongst the most enthusiastic sportsmen in the field, hunting and shooting with as much determination as any country landowner. By the 1840s the change was under way, the fumbling and maladroit intrusion of the *nouveaux riches* into the hunting field observed with delightful humour in the sporting novels by R. S. Surtees, the Durham squire. It was in 1839 that Mayer Rothschild formed his own pack of staghounds, renting kennels for them at Tring Park and thus planting the seed of the territorial empire of the Rothschilds in the Vale of Aylesbury. In the 1850s Engels rode regularly with the Cheshire Hunt on a hunter given to him by his father, evidence possibly of no more than his love of exercise, although such a gentrified form of exercise was possibly evidence also that the regrettable necessity of making money out of the cotton business in order to support Marx in the work of constructing socialist economics was not incompatible with socializing with the detested bourgeoisie and gentry. Thereafter the popularity of hunting spread rapidly among city businessmen. By the 1890s a Midlands sporting journalist could report: 'Thirty years ago, the Warwickshire, Staffordshire and Worcestershire Hunts received little support from city men; today hundreds of Birmingham magnates and business men devote a large amount of their leisure to the prince of sports.' Shooting became an acceptable, and then a favourite, sport of the upper middle classes at much the same time.

This was most striking, and most noticed by contemporaries, with the spectacular growth of deer stalking, whose attractions were barely known outside the Highlands before the 1830s and whose nineteenth-century fashionability dated from 1842 when Prince Albert shot his first two stags. Royal interest led to settlement at Balmoral, and court and aristocratic interest followed suit; in 1845, for example, the Marquess of Salisbury bought the isle of Rhum specifically in order to have his own deer forest. By 1866, however, an experienced Scottish sportsman could write, 'the English squire first drove the poorer Scotch one out of the market and he, in his turn, has been superseded by millionaires from London, Manchester and America. Incredible prices are given by the latter for all our first class deer forests and shootings.' And in 1877 Peter Robertson, who had been forester on one of the Argyle deer forests for fifty years, recorded that 'for great part of the kind of sportsmen we have now is cotton manufacturers, coal proprietors, ironmongers etc. so that the most of our Highland chiefs are gone and many do not know what real sport is except conceit to show themselves marksmen and the less chance for their game the better'. In fact the vast majority of the deer forests were still owned by the aristocracy at the end of the century, chiefly by the Scottish aristocracy with some infiltration by the English such as the Marquess of Salisbury, the Duke of Portland, Lord Ashburton (Baring's bank), Lord Wimborne (Guest's Dowlais iron), and Sir J. W. Ramsden (owner of most of Huddersfield); amongst the owners only Michael Bass, Burton brewer, and John Fowler, Leeds steam-engine and steam-plough maker, stand out as first-generation representatives of new wealth. The lists of shooting tenants were less exclusively aristocratic, but were still dominated by the traditional landed classes. Nevertheless, the exaggerated impression of an industrialist incursion was pardonable, since some manufacturers were early on the scene and their presence was clearly conspicuous. Already by the mid-1850s the tenants of deer forests included an Akroyd from the Halifax woollen industry, a Meux from London brewing, a Vaughan from Swansea copper-smelting, and a Jardine from Jardine-Matheson the Far Eastern merchants. In the next fifty years there were more shooting tenants from brewing, Bass, Buxton, Guinness, and Whitbread; from cotton, Coats, and Hermon of Horrocks, Preston; from chemicals, Allhusen, and Tennant; from engineering, Perkins, and Platt; from iron, Guest, and Crawshay; from the Russian trade, Loder; from contracting, Betts; and from retail trade, Shoolbred, the most fashionable Tottenham Court Road furniture dealer of the time.

Deer stalking was a very expensive sport, and it was only the wealthiest of the business elite who could afford the outlay, although those few who became owners or shooting tenants very likely shared its delights with numerous family and friends as their guests. It was a field of interests shared by plutocrats and aristocrats, even if that in itself did not necessarily breed close or harmonious relations between them. It was even the setting for a nascent international upper class, the American millionaires announcing their arrival in the Highlands with the appearance of W. L. Winans, son of an American railway magnate, in the early 1870s. By 1883 he controlled 200,000 acres of deer forests in the west Highlands, making himself thoroughly detested by his ruthless efforts to clear all crofters out of his forests, and by his unsportsmanlike methods of slaughtering stags and deer by the score. Fellow Americans who followed in the next few years, W. K. Vanderbilt, Bradley Firth, and Bradley Martin, were less controversial figures, and were more readily absorbed into the fraternity. Deer stalking was also rough, tough, and physically demanding unless pursued on the Winans model of a round-up and deer drive which negated the whole object of the challenge of the stalk; it was unlikely to become more than a minority taste even of those wealthy enough to afford it. Less arduous, and on the whole much less expensive, ways of killing animals were offered by grouse shooting, developing from the eighteenth-century localized interest of moorland owners into the great Victorian institution of the 'glorious twelfth', and by pheasant and partridge shooting, which ceased to be the legal privilege and monopoly of landed proprietors in 1831. By the 1850s businessmen were taking to these sports with great enthusiasm and it was becoming fairly common for them to rent or purchase small shooting estates, perhaps a small farm or just a few acres of rough land, within a day's journey of their work; and by the 1860s they were not uncommonly to be found leasing or buying grouse moors in Scotland. It was at this time that the LNWR began running 'Grouse Specials' from Euston, complete with horse boxes and carriage flats, and third-class compartments for the servants, expressing entire city, and aristocratic, households to the Highlands.

Riding to hounds or shooting pheasants and grouse did not in themselves convert a businessman into a country gentleman, and did not necessarily indicate an aspiration to join the landed gentry. That ambition, and indeed its fulfilment, was confined to a minority who bought sizeable landed estates, usually of around a thousand acres and upwards, and made provisions for founding a landed family in which the eldest son, or other heir, could withdraw from business and live in the country on an investment income supplemented by a little rent. This minority, it should be noted, included the great majority of the super-wealthy, those Victorian millionaires from banking, commerce, industry, and transport who were both more numerous and probably more intent on founding landed families than their eighteenth-century pre-decessors. Here was a line of division in the behaviour and culture of the upper middle class marking a point at which a segment peeled off to seek assimilation in the landed classes. The majority of middle-class sporting types, however, worked out their own distinctive lifestyle in which they combined active involvement in business with their country pursuits, probably keeping up a town house as the centre of business, professional, and an urban social life, and a country establishment for occasional or holiday use. This was in its way an independent, upper-bourgeois culture, rather than a poor imitation of the aristocratic way of life, for no Victorian aristocrat, however hard he might work at supervising the management of an estate and its multifarious resources, would have dreamt of mastering the detailed management of a bank, counting house, factory, or department store for his living. On the other hand many aristocrats who had extensive mineral, industrial, urban, or transport interests growing out of their landed estates, while they may never have sat behind an office desk or had direct personal dealings with production workers or with customers, were nonetheless familiar with the two worlds of town and country, business and rural leisure, in roughly the same way as these superior bourgeois commuters were at ease in both worlds. Cultural distinctions on this borderland of social divisions were thus blurred, and became increasingly indistinct from the 1850s onwards as it became socially acceptable for peers and heads of old-established landed families, especially if they were politicians serving spells in opposition, to sit on the board as company directors.

This particular version of an independent culture, with its dual aspect and appropriation of rural sports, differentiated one set of the upper middle class from another, which sought to live entirely within the resources of an urban civilization. It was from this second set, broadly speaking, that the urban elites were drawn which discovered the ethic of civic pride in the 1840s and 1850s and set about conferring some dignity and presence on their Victorian cities, with town halls, libraries, museums, galleries, and parks of self-confident grandeur. Although powerful enough to achieve this, they were prone to continual defections to the hunting and shooting bourgeoisie; the industrial, commercial, and professional middle classes, although not given to serious quarrelling among themselves, lacked the strength and cohesion, because they lacked agreement on common standards and values for their ideal lives, to produce a dominant or robust urban culture. The implications for Victorian politics and government, for success in avoiding class polarization and in maintaining a pragmatic approach, were far-reaching. Among them ranks the failure to impose a puritanical ideology of leisure on the working classes. The middle classes not only lacked the control of the machinery of legislation and administration for the effective implementation of a programme, they also had different ideas about the desirable goals. Rational recreation for the working classes was a slogan on which all might agree: but when one section of the middle classes thought it natural to enjoy themselves they were unlikely to give much support to another section of moralizers who held that only recreations that improved the soul and the mind were permissible. The route of the working classes to self-expression and the development of an independent culture adapted to an urban society was thrown open by the divided counsel and ineffective power of the middle classes.

The evidence on working conditions all suggests that early Victorian workers had no leisure, unless it was the enforced leisure of the unemployed. The great enquiries of the 1830s and early 1840s into employment in factories and mines all spoke of extremely long working days of twelve to fifteen hours, six days a week. Hours of work in workshop, domestic, and outwork trades were at least as long, possibly longer, than those in the mills; and in agriculture, though lack of daylight brought a shorter working day in winter, the labourer's average working week was the longest, as well as the hardest, of all. On Sundays, generally, no work was done, but many observers held that the day of rest was swallowed up in feeble recovery from physical exhaustion, leaving no strength or energy for going to worship, let alone for recreation. Yet the time when the life of the labouring classes was being portrayed as one of unremitting toil was also the time when there were loud denunciations of the undesirable and vicious habits of the poor at play, and strenuous efforts to steer workers' recreations into approved and rational courses, implying that there was quite enough free time around for the guardians of society to be worried about its use.

The explanation is that hours of work were never so long, so continuous, or so regular as the employers might have wished or the opponents of the exploitation of labour might make out by presenting peak-period workloads as the workaday norm. At one extreme there were groups of workers who habitually had short hours, like the north-eastern hewers who enjoyed a seven-hour day by the 1850s well over half a century before other miners achieved the eight-hour day. At the other extreme was the world of casual labour, typified by the dockers but also including most of the unskilled labourers in building and construction work, where men were hired by the day, or hour; or agricultural labourers who were hired by the week. For such groups the number of working days in

a year was unpredictable, and annual earnings were correspondingly uncertain and precarious; their interest was to maximize the
amount of work they had, but in practice they had an excess of free
time, unsought, undesired, unpaid, and unenjoyed, which they
would gladly have seen reduced. In between fell the bouts of free
time seized by workers in full work because it was customary and
they felt like it, or conceded by employers because they were
frequently powerless to resist the force of local custom and
tradition. The most widespread tradition, carried over from the
eighteenth century and earlier, was that of Saint Monday:
prevalent in pre-factory occupations, workers would frequently
decide to take the day off on Mondays if they had enough money
left over after Sunday and could reckon on making up their usual
earnings by a bit of extra effort on the remaining five days of the
week. Inconvenient and irritating as this was to employers, who
could not tell how many of their workers would turn up on a
Monday, the habit was a long time in disappearing and Saint
Monday was still common in the workshop industries of Birmingham or Sheffield in the 1850s.

More occasional time off, but more energetically devoted to
popular amusements, came from the habit of leaving work on fair
days, for local sporting events, during parliamentary elections, or
to see a public hanging. Such irregular absenteeism was highly
objectionable to factory owners, who could not maintain production when their machinery was only partly manned. But although
the factory workforce was much more tightly disciplined than the
rest of the labour force, and was subjected to strict time-keeping, it
is notable that millowners found it impossible to assert complete
control over the holiday traditions inherited by their operatives; in
the 1840s, if not sooner, many cottonmasters were shutting their
mills for the wakes, for their operatives simply took the day off
anyway whether the mills were open or not. Wakes, originally
religious festivals surrounding the annual renewal of rush flooring
in the parish church, had evolved through ritual parading of
elaborately dressed and decorated rush-bearing floats into purely
secular celebrations. Some wakes were attached to what had
become the cotton towns themselves, some were in neighbouring
villages. It was to these that cotton workers went in their thousands

for a day's fun and entertainment, incorporating into an urban and industrial popular culture an essentially rural tradition through the sheer force of custom.

In ways such as these early Victorian workers, whether working in factories or not, did have a certain amount of free time, time which either legitimately or by prescription was not spent in working, sleeping, or praying, time in which they could amuse themselves, or, in the eyes of moralists, get up to untold mischief. The comfortable classes held several different attitudes towards this popular leisure. There was a strong, puritanical, strand of moral disapproval of idleness as a source of temptation and cause of depravity and disorder, which held that there was too much of it. There was a commercial view which did not object to the amount of leisure so much as to its irregular and unpredictable incidence that disrupted the efficient conduct of business. And there was a welfare view, not unconnected with the enlightened self-interest of some employers, that the physical health and general well-being of the workers required adequate leisure and relaxation, that the general working patterns of the early nineteenth century allowed pitifully insufficient free time, and that more of it would amply repay through more productive workers any loss of working time.

In the long run this last view prevailed, the force of the argument aided by the strong interest of organized labour in fighting for reductions in the hours of work, but also blunted by the reluctance of organized labour to adopt and formalize the traditional leisure-preferences of individual workers and campaign collectively for extra rewards to be taken at least partly in the shape of more leisure rather than entirely in more pay. By the early twentieth century, however, workers generally had considerably more leisure, of more regular and reliable a character, than fifty years earlier, although it should be remembered that such things as the eight-hour day were not generally achieved until the 1920s, and that holidays with pay, while spreading fast in the 1930s, did not become well-nigh universal until after 1945. In the short run, until the 1850s and perhaps until the 1870s, it was by no means clear whether the amount of free time was declining or was simply being restructured into orderly patterns suited to the rhythms of urban and industrial life. Half-day working on Saturdays, for example, was established by law in 1850 for the textile industries, in the Factory Act which stipulated that mills must cease running at 2 p.m. on Saturdays. Several mills had half-day working on Saturdays in the 1840s, so that 1850 marked a step in generalizing best practice rather than an entire novelty. The half-day was rather rapidly taken up in other trades and industries, without any statutory compulsion, again suggesting a managerial and social more than a political and reformist origin. By the end of the 1850s the five-and-a-half-day week, 'la semaine anglaise', was well on the way to becoming an immemorial custom, an Englishman's birthright; by this the French remarked, according to taste, on the greater liberty or the greater laziness of the English. Saturday afternoon and evening moved into the place they have occupied ever since as the high spot of the workers' week, the time for exercise and sport, for spending and bargain-hunting, for drinking, fighting, and loving, for sociability and enjoyment. Habits were in effect switched from a boisterous, unofficial, unregulated Saint Monday to a less chaotic, official, and uniform half-day on Saturdays, and this exchange suited the employers' interests as there was more work and production to be got from a steady five-and-a-half-day week than from a week which veered erratically between five and six days at the whim of individual workers. It did not follow, however, that the exchange was against the workers' interests. The casual and individualistic nature of Saint Monday was ill-suited to machine industry, where the interdependence of groups of workers meant that an entire team had to be present before the production process could run at all. Voluntary absenteeism by one could well prevent many others from working at all, forcing them to lose a day's pay that they had no chance of making up later. A steady half-day's free time was to be preferred to the possibility of sneaking a full day off now and then, which only the independent skilled craftsman could do with impunity. An adjustment of the pattern of working time and free time was taking place which was mutually convenient and mutually advantageous to both workers and employers.

A similar restructuring of leisure time can also be seen at work in the replacement of casual breaks for fair days or unusually attractive sporting contests such as a particularly hard-slogging prizefight or an evenly matched foot race, by an orderly pattern of fixed holidays recognized by employers and workers alike. Sports themselves were drawn into the new Saturday routine, or withered as popular attractions if they could not adapt to this regularity. The fairs which survived did so in part because they conformed to regular local holidays, for a great objection to them, quite apart from their alleged rowdy and disorderly character, had been their disruption of ordinary working days. The most successful timing for a fair came to be on one of the bank holidays; instituted in 1871, these quickly spread beyond the bank clerks and within a few years had been appropriated by the whole working community. Beyond the Saturday half-day and the bank holidays there were considerable regional and occupational differences in holiday practices. In the Lancashire cotton towns the day for the wakes which the employers had begun to recognize in the 1840s was growing into a mini-break by the 1850s by having one or two extra free days tacked on. By the 1880s many millowners had expanded this into a full wakes week; mills closed down for repairs and maintenance, whole towns became almost deserted, and workers streamed off to the seaside by the trainload. In the 1870s two or three of the largest railway companies began giving their workers an annual week's holiday with pay, and some clerks in central and local government were similarly treated. Otherwise, employers were less generous and workers less able to establish longer holidays by simple absenteeism. In the Black Country and the Potteries Saint Monday persisted into the last quarter of the century, and was often extended into two or three days' play at the time of a wake. In Birmingham, however, Saint Monday had disappeared by mid-century, and slightly extended holidays were won by tacking an extra day on to the August bank holiday, a technique also used to good effect by London's skilled workers.

In general most working people enjoyed more free time from the 1870s onwards, although the increases were unevenly spread and for some were slender, and even the most favoured groups could not have been said, before 1914, to have been overindulged with leisure. The interesting point, however, is that the more leisure the working classes had, the less censorious and alarmist were the propertied classes about the ways in which the workers used it. The poor at play in the 1820s and 1830s were widely regarded as idle, feckless, dissolute ruffians engaged in mindless, brutal, and semi-criminal activities that were individually damaging and corrupting, a threat to order, and a danger to society. The masses at play in the 1890s were generally accepted as reasonably well-behaved, exuberant maybe but essentially harmless, engaged in legitimate and necessary relaxation and recreation in ways that might not be to the taste of the more genteel and educated classes, but were tolerable as long as excesses were avoided and a proper separation of the classes was preserved. What changed was partly popular behaviour itself: roughness, violence, drunkenness declined, so that conduct became more respectable. What changed was also the concept of respectability: the formerly unacceptable became acceptable as the working classes became somewhat better understood and as they asserted their powers of self-expression.

The traditional popular pleasures, against which disapproval had been mounting from the late eighteenth century, came under their heaviest fire in the couple of decades after Waterloo. Fairs were denounced as the resort of pickpockets, prostitutes, and villains, and the occasion of reckless extravagance and debauchery; festivals, such as some Whitsun, Guy Fawkes, or Boxing Day celebrations, with their saturnalia, role reversals, and lords of misrule, were seen as pagan and socially subversive; massed games in which village was pitched against village in an indiscriminate rough-house that was known as football seemed to be merely senseless, uncontrollable, disorder; sports like bull-running, where a bull was goaded through the streets along a traditional route, bear-baiting, cock-fighting, or ratting, where dogs chased and killed large rats selected and kept for their fierceness, were attacked for their cruelty and for the dishonesty and viciousness encouraged by the heavy gambling which they attracted. Only prizefighting and race meetings, both of which attracted gambling, drinking, and many shady elements, and the first of which was violent even if not cruel, were spared the full volume of condemnation, because each had the protection of aristocratic patronage. Much of this criticism expressed fear of large, uncontrollable, turbulent gatherings of people in a state of high excitement, who might cut loose and turn riotous. Some of it expressed the employers' view that business was being interrupted, the virtue of labour was being challenged, and profits threatened. Most of it, however, derived its philosophy, its vocabulary, and its moral force from evangelicalism.

The three-pronged force was a powerful combination which exerted much influence on legislation, magistrates' actions, and public sentiment, and produced decisive changes in popular recreations by subjecting them to moral, social, and police discipline. The most successful organized pressure group, which in the long run was largely responsible for a major change in national attitudes, was the Royal Society for the Prevention of Cruelty to Animals. It was founded in 1824 and in 1840 obtained the royal patronage of Victoria, who had a great personal concern for animal welfare so long as that did not inhibit the killing of stags or grouse. The inspiration for forming the Society was predominantly evangelical, and several bishops, many country clergy, and sympathetic local magistrates were its most ardent supporters and informers; but it also attracted the support of many prominent utilitarian radicals, and some leading industrialists and peers who were not normally in the evangelical camp. Other leading figures, however, for example Peel and Bright, although undoubtedly humanitarian, declined to be associated with the Society, or were actively hostile, from doubts about the wisdom or feasibility of interfering with individual liberties or local customs. It was a broad-based association, but by no means a simple institutional articulation of latent majority opinion. Rather, it was a crusade by an enlightened minority against a mass of custom, indifference, and thoughtlessness.

The mission began with the recent 1822 Act making it an offence to inflict cruelty on cattle, promoted by an evangelical private member, as the sole piece of legislative protection of animals and the only legal weapon for dealing with offenders. This law could be, and was, invoked in efforts to control and suppress sports featuring cattle, bull-baiting and bull-running, but it had been designed chiefly with the treatment of cattle in mind, on their way to, and inside, Smithfield Market. The initial impulses of humanitarians were indeed directed primarily towards the treatment of horses and cattle in their ordinary working lives, or deaths, and aimed at reforming the habits and practices of those who worked with them. Cruelty to horses working in the city streets, in cabs, buses, wagons, carts, or vans, was particularly visible and shocking to humane feelings; its eradication remained a constant concern throughout the Victorian period, just as the supply of sufficient horse-troughs or adequate rest periods remained a constant care of horse-lovers. The RSPCA, therefore, was very much concerned with the world of work. With the extension of the 1822 Act, in 1835, to cover wanton cruelty to animals, and to make it illegal to keep places for 'running, baiting, or fighting any bull, bear, badger, dog, or other animal (whether of domestic or wild nature or kind), or for cock-fighting', its sphere expanded to take in popular sports as well.

The RSPCA itself was the chief agency for enforcing these laws, through its more active subscribers who acted as informers and sometimes brought prosecutions, and through its private police force of full-time salaried constables or inspectors, which grew from an initial two in 1832 to 120 by the end of the century. By the 1890s it was bringing over seven thousand prosecutions a year, and the police, with whom the Society always worked closely and who were kept vigilant by constant promptings and tip-offs from the Society, made up to twelve thousand arrests themselves for animal cruelty cases. These offences, however, were overwhelmingly those of individuals against their domestic cats and dogs, or of drivers against their horses; organized, and popular, cruel sports had been broken up, suppressed, or driven underground long before this. It is true that cock-fighting, for example, still goes on, but it has long been a rarity, a clandestine activity of a tiny minority relegated to secluded barns in remote parts of the country. The cruel sports with bulls, badgers, dogs, or cocks had to all intents disappeared before the end of the 1850s, or were in the final stages of decline. The scene was set for the English to acquire a reputation for being sentimental animal-lovers, and to busy themselves with a certain self-satisfied officiousness in discovering cruelty in the habits of other nations.

It was a remarkable transformation of national attitudes, for which the RSPCA was largely responsible. It also bears many of the signs of a grand success for the methods of social control, augmented by the strong arm of the law. The agents for propagating kindliness and prosecuting vice were all middle-class or upper-class: the Society relied for its influence and income on the support of the royal family and members of the aristocracy, especially on aristocratic ladies who were particularly sentimental about animals. Moreover, the objects of the campaign almost all belonged to the lower orders. This was partly because the self-interest of the Society, and the inbred assumptions of its members, made it impolitic and unthinkable to attack the aristocratic blood sports, which it could be plausibly argued only involved wild animals that did not share the feelings or obligations of domesticated animals. It was also because the reformation of the lower orders, rather than the simple protection of animals, was the conscious purpose of the Society's leaders. The idea was to civilize the rough and brutish manners of the lower classes by forcing them to think about and deal kindly with creatures even lower than themselves, as a step towards showing consideration for others and thus coming to religion: in this sense the movement was just one weapon in a whole armoury which included Sunday schools, temperance, popular education, and personal hygiene, that was intended to persuade or compel the working classes to adopt approved standards of behaviour rooted in religious belief. Here were all the elements of class discrimination: from its earliest days critics of the animal lobby charged it with promoting class legislation, and the fully functioning late Victorian Society was not uncommonly viewed as an upper-class organization acting hand-in-glove with the authorities in harrying the workingman.

In due course the workingman was harried, or converted, into being kind to animals. To claim this as an unqualified success for the techniques of social control would, however, be misleading. To a considerable extent the anti-cruelty movement was swimming with the tide, not creating it. Bull-baiting and bull-running were the most public and most popular of the animal sports, in many places the central features of traditional local holidays and thus the focus of annual celebrations. They were also the prime targets of reforming opinion, because they were such open and public exhibitions of cruelty, on the streets and village greens, and because they drew whole communities into a kind of pagan ritual accompanied by much drinking and uninhibited enjoyment of tormenting the bull. Yet they were already in decline in the early nineteenth century, well before there was any legislation, any considerable body of reforming opinion, or any organized anti-cruelty movement. Decline, and in some regions of the north and of the South Midlands virtual disappearance, were being reported in the 1790s: since there is no evidence of direct suppression by the exercise of authority, the decline is likely to have been caused by the more indirect influence of social and cultural changes. Refusal by the more substantial members of local communities, squire, farmer, or butcher, to provide a bull, without which there could be no sport, may well have played a far greater part in the decline than any growth of popular distaste or revulsion. Such refusals could have been caused by many things: the rising cost of bulls, a change in sentiments, a weakening or breakdown in the ties of community, or growing disapproval and anxiety about the roughness of crowd behaviour, are some of the possibilities. The result was that the disintegration and collapse of a popular sport and festival, once supported by all members and classes of a local community, was well under way in the early decades of the nineteenth century. The role of the animal lobby and the RSPCA was to push this collapse along more rapidly and to mop up the most stubborn survivors by mobilizing the full power of the law, central government, and troops. This was notably so in the notorious Stamford affair, where most of the townspeople and many of the borough magistrates clung tenaciously to their annual November bull-running which they held to be rooted in the town's charter as well as in immemorial custom, and the RSPCA enlisted the aid of the Home Office and detachments of Metropolitan Police and dragoons to force its suppression in a series of paramilitary campaigns between 1837 and 1840.

The bull business, in any case, was an affair of country towns and villages, an essentially rural amusement. There was never any hint of a possibility that it could be formalized, institutionalized, and acclimatized in a city arena after the Spanish model. It is rather less true that cock-fighting and dog-fighting were exclusively rural sports, for there was no technical difficulty in translating them into the large towns and they had taken some root in the East End and in some of the Lancashire towns by the 1840s. Nevertheless, they were plainly rural in origin, and it was the country clergy and the country magistrates who were most anxious to root them out, as marks of depravity and wickedness as well as cruelty, and who were most zealous in making the RSPCA the effective means of suppression. Certainly, city cockpits were raided and suppressed from the late 1830s onwards, by RSPCA constables or by the police; but these were pure exercises in law enforcement unsupported by any pressure of local opinion. Most of the work was done in country areas, where most of these sports were to be found. By the 1860s and 1870s they had dwindled to negligible proportions. Insofar as this decline in traditional recreations represented a change in popular attitudes brought about by a combination of educated local opinion and enforcement of the law, it was a change which substantially concerned rural society only. Admittedly, rural society formed at least half of the nation until mid-century, and thereafter remained numerically of much the same size even while forming a fast-shrinking proportion of the whole, so that its habits and manners were far from being of negligible importance. It was, however, the portion of society whose lower ranks had from time out of mind been subjected to the moral as well as the physical authority of parson, landowner, and farmer, tempered to some extent by the liberties and sanctions of even more immemorial local custom. These, the rural labourers and country workers, had always had their lives shaped by a very direct and personal social leadership, which may be termed the traditional form of social control. In stamping out the cruel sports from the range of traditional popular rural recreations, the Victorian reformers demonstrated the power of the existing means of social control when reinforced by laws capable of chipping away at customary practices. They further disciplined an already disciplined body of people. This was an important, but limited, moral and social victory; the evangelicals had looked for greater triumphs than that.

Reaching out beyond rural society the animal lobby registered an impact on working habits more than on leisure, through the horse rather than the bull, and struck not so much at any inherent callousness or brutality among drivers or others who worked with animals as at the consequences of commercial competition and management requirements, which virtually obliged employees to be harsh and ruthless in order to terrorize their horses into performing their allotted stints. Improvement, when it came from the 1840s and 1850s onwards, came less from any profound reformation of manners than from the growth of larger-scale firms in the omnibus, carting, and carrying businesses, whose sense of self-interest prompted proper care and maintenance of their principal assets, the horses, more readily than was the case with small operators who had to cut their costs to the bone and who worked with low-value secondhand horses that could be flogged to an early death without troubling pocket or conscience.

The countryside was swept clear of many of its traditional popular amusements by the force of opinion and legislation inspired by class. Yet the ability to organize and sustain a nationwide movement that has flourished ever since speaks of a sincerity and conviction in the opinions which reaches far beyond any narrow expression of class feelings, and which before the end of Victoria's reign had clearly come to reflect attitudes and feelings held in every layer of society. Animals were one thing: amusements, however boisterous, provided by and for the common people were another matter. Fairs and the goings-on at them were denounced, from the early nineteenth century, for their disorderliness and gross immorality with even more lurid vehemence than the cruel sports. They were traditional, customary, in many cases legitimized by local charters, inevitably mainly rural and small-town from their preindustrial origins but by the 1820s of equal, or greater, importance to town-dwellers than to the country population. The impulse to suppress and abolish was evangelical and dissenting, aided by particular local property interests and the guardians of order, and many fairs were indeed suppressed, the main casualties coming in the thirty or forty years after 1820. Yet many did survive and flourish: there was never any consensus, no general or united anti-fair movement, no weaning of the common people from their amusements. The zealots carried the day, broadly, so long as there were general fears of public disorder and doubts about the capacity of the authorities to contain it. Thereafter, particularly in the last quarter of the century, the surviving fairs and a few new ones were left alone to prosper or wither as popular demand might determine. Central government and police forces became tolerant and neutral: the remaining objectors, as articulate and shrilly moralizing as ever, were reduced to the isolation of puritanical sectarians out of sympathy with the weight of official and public opinion, not so much as the voice of a class or a subclass, let alone of the nation. An important form of popular recreation had survived, purged and adapted to urban needs, but not taken out of the control of popular tastes. It had been subjected to police control, regulation, and influence intended to secure orderly behaviour in public; it had not yielded to the reformers' designs for the eradication of immorality and of frivolous and unedifying pleasures.

The weighty objections to fairs in the early years of the nineteenth century were that they had become the resort of thieves, pickpockets, prostitutes, and ruffians, scenes of drunken debauchery, and occasions of hooliganism and breaches of the peace. Most of them had arisen as periodic markets for horses, farm livestock, or labour, all things which it was convenient to sell annually to a body of consumers gathered from a wide locality. They had built up a surrounding glitter of entertainments, booths, peep-shows, exhibits of natural and unnatural rarities and monstrosities, food and drink stalls, and the like, attractions which drew the crowds and made fairs into popular festivals. The crowds in turn attracted their natural predators, the pickpockets and prostitutes. The market functions declined, bypassed by the development of direct trading or in the case of hiring fairs rendered obsolete by the decline in importance of those workers who had normally been hired by the year, the living-in farm servants, leaving behind the enjoyable bits which, because they had become customary, expected, and eagerly anticipated, had acquired self-sustaining vitality. The reformers contended that there was no reason for holding merely pleasure fairs, once the market functions had decayed, and that the pleasures were at best frivolous and empty-headed and in most cases were depraved and indecent, and hence ought to be suppressed in the cause of improving public morals. Since fairs were undoubtedly noisy, drew throngs of strangers from outside the neighbourhood, encouraged drunkenness, horseplay, and holiday-mood sexuality, and presented a concentration of petty crime, local householders, property-owners, and ratepayers tended to regard them as a nuisance and were glad to assist in their abolition. This combination set to work getting rid of a large number of fairs from 1819 onwards, acting through petitions to local magistrates who from 1822 had special Police Act powers to declare fairs illegal. Long-established fairs vanished particularly from the fringes of London, where the moral pressure was highly concentrated and the Home Office was particularly sensitive about public order, but also in other parts of the country, for example from the neighbourhood of several Lancashire towns.

This was a classic confrontation between the uncouth and the respectable, the humble and powerless and the influential and powerful. Yet the mighty failed to sweep all before them. This was because they had underestimated the continued economic vitality of some kinds of fair, and because government and police proved to be no more than temporary allies. Farm servants and the hiring fairs which went with them were indeed in full decline in eastern and south-eastern England in the early nineteenth century, or had already vanished, and this easily gave London-based opinion the impression that they were completely moribund institutions. In fact in parts of the west, in the north, especially in Northumberland, and in Scotland the practice of keeping farm servants who were hired by the year, particularly those who were working with livestock and in dairying, persisted strongly well into the last quarter of the century. The hiring had to be done at hiring fairs, and with the hiring fairs went the jollifications, diversions, and games of the unmarried men and women who were there to be hired and who had a change of masters to celebrate and their hiring shillings to spend. No one was powerful enough, however strong their moral convictions, to strip these occasions of their customary fun and games and reduce them to the drabness of mere labour exchanges; they were, and they remained, the annual holidays of a significant part of the northern English, and a major part of the Scottish, farming population, and they were immune from control from above. Some of the livestock fairs and horse fairs persisted too, surrounded by their bustle of showmen, entertainments, and refreshments, withstanding the competition of functional, unglamorous, cattle markets and select country horse-sales of well-bred stock. These generated considerable incomes from tolls, which gave borough treasurers, as at Barnet, a vested interest in resisting pressure from householders and moralists for abolition.

Those country fairs which survived held on to their place in the popular holiday calendar largely because they were still under-pinned by serious economic functions, until relief came from the improved technology of steam traction which was bringing travelling funfairs and circuses into country districts by the 1890s. For town fairs a stay of execution and continued vitality did not come from the support of the solid economy, for by the 1830s virtually all of them were unabashed funfairs, but from the sheer weight of popular support and the development of police tolerance. There was no doubting the popularity of the Easter and Whitsun fairs that were within reach of large centres of population. Shoreditch and Edmonton fairs were said to attract 30,000 and 40,000 people in the early 1820s, the railway alone took 35,000 to Greenwich on Whitmonday in 1839, and Stepney was reported to have been visited by 200,000 on Easter Monday in 1844. Hamp-stead Heath, one of the new fairs with no charter or ancient lineage, drew around 100,000 visitors to the equally new August bank holiday fairs in the 1870s. Crowds of this size could clearly be alarming, and it is understandable that residents were scared by these regular invasions of hordes of what they took to be savages with scant respect for persons or property. Understandable also that the new and inexperienced police forces of the 1830s did not look kindly upon these large assemblies with their unknown potential for disorder and riot. The pressure of popular demand was not enough in itself to ensure survival, and many of these fairs were suppressed when still near the height of their popularity, with the active assistance of the Metropolitan Police and the Home Office. Considerations of public order, morality, and crime apart, the grounds on which fairs were traditionally held had often become more valuable for building, and the open spaces simply vanished. Denied their accustomed stamping grounds, holiday-making Londoners simply surged elsewhere, to new sites like Hampstead or to old ones further afield like Croydon and Barnet.

With growing experience and increasing familiarity with crowd behaviour the police in time ceased to agree that all fairs were necessarily evil. Men, women, and children off on a family outing made crowds altogether different in mood and character from the all-male gatherings of strikes or Chartist meetings. Relaxed and in holiday mood, noisiness and high spirits did not mean that they were not peaceable and well-behaved, as the police came to recognize. Confident in their ability to control crowds and maintain order, the police no longer routinely agreed, by the 1840s, with local residents' petitions for closures. There were setbacks, with more closures in the 1850s and again in the 1870s, but by then the police were arguing strongly that these amusements and pleasures of the poor were harmless, with no more than an easily containable fringe of petty crime, and were socially beneficial as legitimate outlets for playful energies and agencies for spreading contentment. By the 1880s the Home Secretary was declaring 'that a fair was not to be discontinued merely because it was no longer needed for business and gave trouble to the police, if it still provided once or twice a year a popular amusement for poor people', and ordered that there was to be no interference with 'these innocent amusements of the poorer classes'.

The amusements may have become more innocent over the previous fifty years. They had certainly become more highly commercialized. The supply side of fairs moved out of the hands of dozens of individual stallkeepers and showmen, who besides being suspect as strangers to the places where they popped up to do business were inevitably classed as petty, insubstantial traders of no account, beneath the small-shopkeeper level. In their place came much larger-scale operators, showmen with considerable capital and several employees, owning specialized transport, elaborate swings, and by the last quarter of the century steam roundabouts and steam organs. They may have been showy and vulgar characters, hardly identified with the sober frock-coated business community, but they were nonetheless substantial businessmen with a lot of money at stake and a lively interest in seeing that their customers both enjoyed themselves and behaved in an orderly manner, and hence disposed to cooperate with the police, not to antagonize them. What they provided was more innocent in the sense that it was less brutal and, for example, avoided shows that involved cruelty to animals, although travelling menageries, performing bears and the like remained very popular. It was, however, no more educative, edifying, or uplifting than it had ever been; arguably it became less so with the decline of the little theatrical shows, sometimes crude melodramas but sometimes popular moral tales, that had still been common at the fairs of the 1830s. The commercial amusements were vulgar, exciting, thrilling, pleasurably scary, vaguely erotic: they were for pure enjoyment with no concealed messages. They were what the people wanted, and if they were not then the people did not come. Ordinary people, the working classes, were trusted to choose their own amusements, expressing their choices through the roundabout and hurdy-gurdy market, and the authorities no longer tried to tell them what they ought to want. Those who continued to disapprove were left stranded on their sectarian limb.

The commercialization of popular entertainment and leisure was a prominent feature of the second half of the century. It was perhaps most obvious and most commented upon in the music hall, which developed out of the self-entertainment and sing-songs of Saturday evening free-and-easies in the pub, from the end of the 1840s, and whose aura of drink, promiscuity, and bawdiness was a ripe and prime target for puritanical critics. It was seen among the literate working class, who were supplied with *Reynolds News*, the *News of the World*, penny dreadfuls, and towards the end of the century with Harmsworth's *Daily Mail*, by commercial publishers, because that was what they liked to read rather than the religious stories and improving literature which the early Victorian generation of educationists had hoped to teach them to want. It was seen in the organization of daytrips to the seaside, and seaside holidays, serviced by hosts of petty capitalist landladies and boarding-house keepers, and by much larger transport interests. And it was seen in the professionalization of sport, notably football, and the associated commercial organization of spectator sports.

Commercial organizations needed orderly conditions and security for their property in order to function, and hence were on the same side as the police in wanting their public to behave peaceably; they needed to stay within the law, for the risk of being closed down was not worth running; and they were against unruly or violent behaviour as bad for business, although they were not always able to prevent it, for example at some of the great football matches of the 1890s and early 1900s. Commercial provision meant, on the whole, quieter, more civilized, and in a sense more disciplined leisure behaviour. It did not mean business control or dictation of popular tastes. People paid for what they liked and enjoyed, for what they found entertaining, and if the leisure industry did not supply the right mixture it did not prosper. Leisure entrepreneurs certainly innovated from time to time and created new popular tastes, but novelties only worked if they were skilfully placed within the ambit of existing appetites, and the capacity to get the people to consume anything sharply unfamiliar or alien to their habits was minimal. The capitalist system itself, therefore, operating through the openings which the entertainment market presented to entrepreneurs, emerged as the guarantor of popular sovereignty over the use of popular leisure. Admittedly this sovereignty was not absolute. It was limited by the rules which the suppliers had to observe, laws governing public entertainments and meeting places, conventions about public decency; and it was limited by the ability of the customers to pay. Within such limits, however, control of popular leisure was in the hands of the people themselves, protected from the imposition of middle-class values by the collective power of the working-class purse.

The commercialization of leisure depended on the size of the popular market, and the amount and proportion of working-class incomes that could be spared for entertainments plainly differed between occupations as well as changing over time. Thus the relatively high-earning and regularly employed cotton operatives were the first group of industrial workers to generate a demand for seaside holidays, unless they were anticipated by the better paid East End artisans who already in the 1820s were joining with Cockney clerks in their thousands on excursions to Gravesend by paddle-steamer, and some of whom were resentfully noted as lowering the tone of Margate by the 1830s. Cotton workers were going for daytrips to Blackpool or Southport for the sea-bathing in the 1840s, encouraged by the cheap excursion fares offered by the new railways; in the 1850s weekend visits became popular, and before 1870 the habit of staying for a full week was taking hold, along with the self-help institution of the holiday club back at the mill, with its weekly subscription, to finance it. By 1870 Blackpool was well set on its course of development as an essentially working-class resort, investing municipally and privately in facilities, amenities, and amusements for both staying visitors and daytrippers. This was exceptional. Only Southend, drawing on the vast pool of higher paid workers in London, could compare with Blackpool in vigorous mid-Victorian development as a predominantly working-class resort. The West Riding textile workers, for example, were nearly a generation behind the Lancashire cotton operatives in developing the taste for seaside excursions and holidays, perhaps because they lacked any similar tradition of sea-bathing habits, but more likely because family earnings were lower. Indeed, there were no other large and concentrated groups of workers, outside London, at mid-century with family earnings large enough to rival the holiday expenditures of the cotton people. Much of the working class, of course, had little or no surplus income for indulgences, and something between a tenth and a third lived in poverty. In its early stages the popular market for commercially provided amusements of any kind was necessarily restricted and far short of being a mass one.

The mid-Victorian seaside was largely the preserve of the middle classes, earnestly consolidating their possession of the holiday habit which had been pioneered with somewhat more frivolity by the aristocracy and fashionable society half a century earlier, fitting out Brighton, Ramsgate, or Scarborough with a plentiful variety of creature comforts to absorb the invigorating effects of bouts of sea-bathing. The middle classes believed no less strongly in the healthiness of sea air and sea-bathing, but sought to internalize the beneficial effects within the privacy of the family, and looked on the holiday as a duty, for recuperating health and energy for renewed hard work, not as a period for mere pleasure or abandon. The mid-Victorian seaside resorts which grew and proliferated mainly in response to middle-class demand were, therefore, solid and sober places, comfortable but decorous and highly respectable. It was a time of propriety, of strictly segregated bathing, of bathing machines and the freezing out of bathing in the nude – which had been usual but not usually mixed – by the force of stern

disapproval backed by some local bye-laws. There were promenades for exercise, convenient for the massed Sunday church
parades that were a feature of all the better-class resorts as a means
of publicly establishing respectability, there were public gardens
for botanical instruction, and there were piers, also for exercise and
possibly with some seemly middle-brow music at the end. There
were little boat-trips to explore the natural history and geology of
the area, and immense quantities of shells, rock specimens, and
fossils were shipped back from the Victorian seashore as witness to
holiday educational achievements. Within their lights the middle
classes no doubt enjoyed themselves and had fun while improving
their bodies and their minds. They did so without benefit of street
vendors, stalls, side-shows, peep-shows, and funfair-style
amusements, which were rigorously excluded from such middle-
class resorts as Eastbourne or Bournemouth which were being
rapidly developed in the 1850s and 1860s; and they shunned anything sexually exciting like mixed bathing, or the indiscriminate
mixing of the sexes in public dance halls.

The more raffish and vulgar delights were introduced to satisfy a
lower class and popular demand, and before 1870 were to be found
only in those very few resorts that were not under the middle-class
hegemony. The breakthrough to the mass flight to the seaside came
in the last quarter of the century, a consequence of the sharp rise in
real wages by between one third and one half. Excursions came
within the reach of most of the urban working classes who lived
above the poverty line, which the surveys of Booth and Rowntree of
London in 1886 and York in 1899, as currently interpreted, suggest
meant that between 70 and 85 per cent of working-class families
might have been able to afford such pleasures, at least from time to
time, towards the end of the century. A rather smaller proportion
were able to follow the cotton operatives in acquiring the taste for
staying for several days by the seaside. It may be doubted, however,
whether either daytrips or seaside holidays came within the mental
horizons of agricultural workers at this time, even though they
experienced a similar increase in real wages: in any case, despite
this increase, the majority outside the northern counties were probably still living at or below the rural poverty line in 1900, except
when there were working children adding to family income.

The great influx of plebeian excursionists transformed the social and physical map of the late Victorian coastline, and by its example helped to liberate sections of the less deeply religious middle classes from their holiday inhibitions. Some of it went to swell the business and hence the resident population of places already established as predominantly working-class resorts, notably Blackpool, Southend, and Weston-super-Mare. Another stream flowed into new resorts built expressly for the working classes, such as Cleethorpes and Skegness, or virtually appropriated older resorts like Margate, Great Yarmouth, or Whitley Bay, which had quieter and more genteel origins. A third stream, probably the largest in total, invaded virtually every middle-class resort within striking distance of large centres of population, and the clash of cultures resulting from this, easily the most widely experienced set of middle-class encounters with the working classes often literally in the flesh, sent ripples of consternation and conflict through the coastal towns. Responses were various. In some resorts, for example Eastbourne and Folkestone, respectable middle-class interests were so well entrenched in a local economy and society geared to a large resident community of the retired and invalid, as well as to long-stay visitors, that the great unwashed were successfully excluded by the simple expedient of refusing to permit or provide any of the attractions demanded by trippers. No whelk stalls, no German bands, no nigger minstrels, no pleasure piers ruffled their sedate and stuffy serenity. All proposals to introduce trams were squashed, because these were a low-class form of transport. The working classes were not wanted in places like these, and they stayed away because there was nothing for them to do there.

In most of the larger resorts, however, there was no united front of municipal authority, local business interests, and residents, against excursionists. There were always plenty of businessmen, many of them small traders but some fairly substantial capitalists, ready to provide whatever the market wanted and to argue, if they had any qualms, 'If you can't beat 'em, join 'em.' And always in the background were the railway companies, keen to maximize traffic with special fares and indifferent to the feelings of the inhabitants or regular visitors at the trippers' destinations. Even Bournemouth, staid pride of the mid-Victorian middle classes, tastefully decked out with municipal efforts to entice and please them, municipal pier and pavilion, pleasure gardens, overcliff and undercliff carriage drives, and deck-chair service, succumbed to the trippers by the 1890s and gave them a grudging welcome. Trams were installed, under municipal management for fear that unscrupulous private enterprise might exploit their vulgar potential to the full, discreet street trading was allowed, and popular but well-regulated music on the pier. At the same time the municipality fortified the resort's middle-class appeal by providing golf courses, installing electric cliff-lifts, taking over the winter gardens, and establishing the first municipal orchestra in the country, destined to reach world class. Middle-class attractions were preserved and enhanced, but in directions which reflected a shift in middle-class habits from the high Victorian valetudinarian and high-minded towards pleasure-seeking and 'palm court' tastes. What the late Victorian middle classes found agreeable and acceptable at Bournemouth remained more polite, refined, and sedate than anything the working classes fancied. But the gulf was narrowing, and in any case Bournemouth only attracted a better class of popular excursionist, with airs of respectability, precisely because it did not offer the full blast of boisterous or bawdy entertainments.

Few general-purpose or multi-class resorts adopted in full the exuberant satisfaction and stimulation of popular appetites that was pioneered by single-class Blackpool in creating the candy-floss holiday economy of Tower, pleasure palace, seafront trams, illuminations, ballrooms, funfair-style piers, mutoscopes ('what-the-butler-saw' machines), and popular variety shows and music hall, in a world of fun, fantasy, and fish and chips that already drew an estimated 850,000 visitors in the 1873 season and swept on to nearly two million in 1893 and approaching four million in 1913. Many, however, were a good deal more welcoming than Bourne-mouth, and developed a section of Blackpool-type features, usually scaled down in brashness, to cater for working-class visitors. More often than not this was accommodated in distinct working-class sectors, achieved by self-zoning more than by municipal regulation or exclusive club-style institutions, with certain beaches, certain piers, and certain sections of esplanades becoming the recognized preserves of the masses. Brighton, Clacton, and Scarborough, for example, developed this two-sector structure as the means of capturing a share of the working-class trade without alienating their middle-class custom. Other resorts, too small to be able to afford to duplicate facilities and major items of holiday capital, aimed to have their cake and eat it by staggering the holiday seasons, August for the working classes and the other summer months for their middle-class clientele. This worked, but usually only by some slippage in the grades of middle-class visitors towards the level which might buy, along with the August folk, the comic seaside postcards whose immense popularity and particular nuances of vulgarity represented the semi-respectability and semi-naughtiness of these holiday styles. The classes, then, frequented the same places but did not mix; they were highly visible to each other, but they did not touch.

The spatial accommodation of the differing cultures and their partial reconciliation was helped by the differences within the classes in holiday expectations and behaviour. Not only were trippers bound for Bournemouth a good deal more subdued and deferential than the Blackpool crowd, a difference perhaps explicable by differences in their places of residence, types of work, and levels of pay, but also all Lancashire and West Riding working-class families did not necessarily welcome full-frontal exposure to the rumbustiousness of Blackpool. For those of them who liked something less noisy, jostling, obtrusively commercial, or blatantly bawdy, Morecambe appeared, almost next door, quieter but not much less carefree or more straitlaced. Similarly, those of the middle classes who could not stand the transformation of their old stamping grounds into multi-class resorts took themselves off to smaller, newer, or more remote places. In Frinton or Cromer, Aberystwyth or Lytham, they could continue to savour austere and uplifting experiences without any distractions from commercial or daytripper intrusions; while those who did not like the turn which Brighton was taking had only to move a mile or two to Hove, where the retired and the invalids ensured that the bath-chair brigade remained visibly in command of the seafront.

The late Victorian seaside was a thing of many colours, home for two cultures each of which contained many different flavours of holiday tastes and habits, running from the exclusive and sedate to the chummy and boisterous. It was the scene neither of class conflict nor of jolly class harmony and mixing, but of class coexistence, a condition in which the classes did not allow themselves to become seriously annoyed with each other, and in which one class did not try to dominate or dictate to another. Many of the working-class trippers, paddling with rolled-up trousers, absorbing huge quantities of beer and shrimps, wearing funny hats, remained far from respectable by middle-class notions. But most polite observers were, condescendingly, surprised and amused by the behaviour of the workingman and his family at the seaside, not shocked, and commented on the general good humour, non-violence, and orderliness of the crowds. This was respectability by working-class standards, on their own terms. It was the sensitivity of the holiday industry, from railway companies and advertising agents to landladies and publicans, from street traders to music-hall managers, to market forces and commercial opportunities which gave the working classes the setting in which they could display these qualities to the public gaze in a manner and on a scale that were impossible in the workaday environment.

Commercialization in other spheres of popular recreation and entertainment had broadly analogous effects, at the same time and for the same reasons, the great rise in real wages in the last quarter of the century. The rise of mass spectator sports, played by professionals, financed by gate-money, and calling for large investments in specially equipped grounds in prime urban sites, came suddenly and dramatically in the 1880s and 1890s. Association football, soccer, was the leader on the national scale, becoming the ruling passion of the working classes of the Midlands and the north, of Scotland – which was already the source of imported professionals for Lancashire clubs in the 1870s – and of parts of London. Locally, other sports might outrank soccer in their following: in the poorest parts of London, the East End and Southwark, professional boxing was the most consistently popular and accessible spectacle. And in Wales, for reasons which are obscure, the people took rugby football, rugger, to heart and made it into the national sport. Soccer, however, undoubtedly drew the largest number of paying spectators in aggregate in Britain, had the largest amount of press coverage, with the possible exception of racing, in the new mass circulation papers, and came closer than any other sport to generating a popular national cult with nationally observed rituals and ceremonies.

Soccer had a prehistory, partly as an inchoate rural rough-house between rival villages and partly as a game played by aristocratic and middle-class boys at school. In its modern form it dates from 1863 and the foundation of the Football Association, from which the game takes its name. This body of middle-class officials from middle-class amateur clubs codified the rules of the game out of the many individual variants current in the public schools, thus making possible games and competitions between all clubs which adhered to the Association. The inauguration of the annual FA Cup competition in 1871, open to all clubs that used the rules, undermined the fiction that it was essentially a gentleman's game and exposed the superiority of gentlemen's clubs to direct challenge. Thereafter the landmarks came rapidly. In the 1883 Cup Final Bolton Olympic, a team of northern workingmen, defeated the Old Etonians, a defeat which signalled the retreat of the gentleman amateurs. The working-class players, unable to afford travelling expenses to matches or to take time off work for training, were necessarily semi-professionals, subsidized by their clubs or by supporters even if not paid a regular football wage. In 1884 the FA sought to uphold the amateur status of the game, many thought in revenge for the humiliation of 1883, by banning professionals from the Cup. The outcry was such, and the formation of a break-away association in Lancashire so damaging, that within a year the FA had climbed down and publicly authorized professionalism in the game. This, in effect, acknowledged the superiority of working-class players with their massed ranks of working-class supporters, superior in skill and superior in financial resources. Amateur teams and gentleman players withdrew from what had become unequal competition, and either continued to play soccer only amongst themselves, or, more frequently, took refuge in rugger where there was no awkward class rivalry. By 1888, when the Football League was established, there were no middle-class clubs of good enough quality to stand a hope of inclusion even if they had cared to apply. In the short space of little more than ten years all the essential features of soccer's place in popular culture had been put in place: professional players and recruitment of talent by transfers of non-residents, full-time managers, the Cup Final and the annual pilgrimage of the fans to London, intense interest in positions in the League table and extreme, sometimes violent, partisanship in support of the local team, and some gambling on the results. A few finishing touches remained to be added later: the customary royal presence at the Cup Final, and football pools, date from the 1920s. These were embellishments of a great popular, national ritual which was already fully functioning by 1890.

By the 1890s commentators were freely denouncing professional soccer for its commercialism, rowdiness, and general barbarity: the players were mercenary and unsporting, fouling when they could get away with it and abusing the referee when caught out, and the crowds were rough and blindly partisan. It was a game fit only for mechanics to play and hooligans to watch. They had already forgotten that there had been a time when soccer was a middle-class and upper-class game regarded, not least by the clergy, as an ideal vehicle for the exercise of leadership by instructing the working classes in the principles of fair play and healthy recreation. The lessons had been too exciting. The game had become not only dominated by working-class leadership in technical skill and mastery, but also the almost exclusive preserve of the working classes as a spectator sport. The effects of organization, professionalism, and commercialization in soccer were to separate the classes, just as they were kept separate on the beaches. This was a disappointment for the school of muscular Christianity which had hoped that athletics and outdoor sports would promote better understanding between the classes through interclass participation and contact. By the same token it was a boost for popular control of popular recreations, a significant step in the formation of a working-class culture independent of middle-class direction or tutelage.

Class segregation was not so clear-cut in all other sports, although there were signs of it in most. Amateur rowing, an extreme case, was kept in the hands of the gentry by rules which expressly excluded mechanics and labourers from the rowing clubs that competed in the major regatta at Henley, because gentleman oarsmen did not care to face unfair competition from professional boatmen. Amateur athletics, however, which had similar mechanics clauses, went the other way under the pressure of popular interest in competing, and in 1880 passed under the control of the new Amateur Athletics Association founded on the principle of admitting allcomers regardless of occupation or status. These sports concerned participants rather than vast numbers of spectators. Racing, on the other hand, had attracted crowds ever since the first organized meetings in the seventeenth century, and became popular among the urban and industrial working classes. It was matter for comment that Manchester races were held on Kersal Moor immediately after Peterloo, attended by the usual crowds, and passed off peaceably; while Derby Day was something of a Londoners' holiday celebrated by a mass trek to Epsom Downs by a motley social mixture of carriage folk and tramping artisans. The attraction of race meetings, apart from love of horseflesh and the atmosphere of excitement, was the betting, and predictably racing came under attack from the evangelicals for its drinking and gambling. This, however, was the sport of royalty, aristocracy, and county society, and they had little difficulty in protecting it, and the plebeian racegoers, from puritanical onslaughts; indeed, the number of regular race meetings increased in the early and mid-Victorian decades, spread over most parts of the country. A Select Committee of the House of Lords argued in 1844 that racing 'serves to bring together for a common object, vast bodies of people in different parts of the country, and to promote intercourse between different classes of society'. The social mixing, however, if it had ever existed except at the superficial level of mere casual propinquity, declined. Off-course betting, through betting shops, was the major object of working-class enthusiasm for racing. When betting shops were made illegal in 1853 and the poorer class of punter was forced to rely on illegal street runners, much harried by the police, it could not help seeming more like class legislation than moral policing, calculated to discriminate specifically against the working-class obsession with horses, the more so since the gentry could continue to place their bets in their private clubs with impunity. On the course, also, social segregation grew in the second half of the century. Traditionally racecourses had been more or less improvised on available open spaces of heath, moor, and common, and it had been impossible to control admission. Increasingly, Victorian racecourses were enclosed, on private land, charges were made for admission, stands and enclosures were erected, the unwashed were sorted from the gentle and the two were kept apart. Some territory slipped out of upper-class hands as polite society gave up going to some of the large town meetings, such as Manchester and Newcastle, leaving them in lower-class possession. Mainly, however, the working classes were tolerated at the races so long as they stayed in their own pens, out of smell if not out of sight of the fashionable racegoers in their stands.

The working classes had their racing and betting set, just as did the aristocracy. From the standpoint of the self-improving working class with its emphasis on thrift and sobriety, it was far from being respectable. Since it survived and flourished under the protection of aristocratic attachment to the sport, it was also far from being as disreputable as moralists tried to make out. Here was one major popular recreation, traditional in the sense that it long antedated industrialization, which adapted successfully to large town society and preserved its continuity, and expansion, with only relatively minor concessions to Victorian morality and propriety. Cricket was another, a game already spreading beyond the village greens and beginning to attract spectators in the very early nineteenth century, and becoming a favourite in the towns and cities of Lancashire, Yorkshire, and the Midlands, as well as in the southern counties, during the Victorian period. It was a very considerable spectator sport in the last quarter of the century, although never a mass spectator sport on the soccer scale. Cricket did not attract much gambling, although drink was a different matter, and gentlemen could continue to play without risk of being completely outclassed by workingmen at the crease. For these reasons it retained the participation and support of all classes, and in the opinion of the quality newspapers at least had an unchallenged claim to being the national game of the late Victorians.

The early Victorian evangelicals did their bit in rooting out Sunday cricket, which did not enhance their popularity, but otherwise found nothing morally objectionable in the game; on the contrary, it was much advocated as the ideal school for learning fair play, the discipline of observing the rules and accepting disappointment and hard decisions with good grace, and praised for its contribution to social mixing. Nor did professionalism present any threat to respectability. Professionals had been recruited from very early days, initially from estate workers and farm labourers, to play in mixed teams with their masters, and by the time of the inauguration of the annual Gentlemen v. Players match in 1806 some of them had national reputations. Professionals, from lower-class backgrounds and accustomed to hard work, were highly suitable for the sustained physical exertion of bowling, while gentlemen were freed to enjoy themselves with the bat; the gentry produced no fast bowlers of note. Mixed teams of amateurs and professionals were so well established that the transition to employing full-time, or seasonally full-time, professionals with the growth of programmes of regular fixtures and then, from 1873, the organization of the county championship, presented no problems. Status and class distinctions did require, however, that amateurs and professionals had separate changing rooms and did not mingle in the pavilion. County cricket grounds, many of them as close to city centres as the major football grounds, tended to separate the classes of spectators through admission charges in much the same way as racecourses, though perhaps less sharply. The main stand tended to be reserved for members of the county cricket club and their friends, exclusively gentry and middle-class, but everyone else mixed indiscriminately on the public stands and terraces. Lesser grounds, especially those of festival cricket, had no spectator equipment more elaborate than a few tents, including the vital beer tent, and the atmosphere was generally relaxed, friendly, and informal.

Football and boxing produced their stars who enjoyed enormous local popularity and adulation; but it would have been W. G. Grace, the cricketer, and Lord Rosebery, racehorse owner, Derby winner, and prime minister, who figured on any late Victorian list of national celebrities. These four sports mark out the field of popular games and their relationship to working-class culture. Two fell largely into the hands of the working classes and, abandoned or shunned by other classes, were incorporated into a manifestly independent culture. Two were watched and followed by large numbers of working-class enthusiasts, with some small direct participation as jockeys and cricketers; these two were multi-class sports, reliant on aristocratic and gentry finance and patronage, and although the working-class element was well integrated into the class leisure culture it was not incorporated into the sports on terms of equality, and remained inferior and deferential. It would be mechanistic to suppose that these four represented distinct and different sections of the working classes at play, or even that the two broadly contrasting types corresponded in their followers with the difference between assertively independent-minded workers and deferential conservative workers. It is just as likely that the four appealed to four different moods, or suited the four seasons of a workingman's life, for the composition of the crowds, in individual detail, is unknown territory. What is known is that these were essentially male occasions: women were firmly excluded from boxing matches and were only just starting to go to cricket and football games in the early twentieth century, though race meetings were always considered suitable for family outings. In the main, the family man went to funfairs, the seaside, and perhaps the music hall, but not to matches except on his own.

The self-respecting workingman, indeed, with his principles of self-improvement, thrift, and sobriety, was unlikely to approve of any of these sports with their association with drinking and gambling, except that cricket matches might have been found acceptable. His recreations were more likely to be active than passive, creative rather than mindless and undemanding, associated more with the family than with the assertion of masculinity. Such was the model, to which there were many exceptions. For the skilled man with resources to spare for leisure, angling, mainly coarse fishing, developing at the end of the century, and the more traditionally popular pigeon-fancying and pigeon-racing, though both gentle and tranquil sports, were ideal excuses to escape from pestering wives and children, or opportunities for the display of manliness. It has been suggested, also, that skilled, not unskilled, workers formed the pool from which football players were recruited. Nevertheless, there is much evidence that skilled workers preferred recreations which called for individual skills, intelligence, and application; there is no contradiction here. The principle of the busman's holiday was quite widely observed. Carpenters and joiners often made furniture for the home or toys for their children, decorators painted their own homes, and tailors helped in making clothes for children or dolls. Such activities were, no doubt, obvious and utilitarian contributions to the family economy; but the fact that DIY only spread among the middle classes in the late twentieth century is no reason for dismissing its qualities of relaxation and enjoyment when found among the Victorian working classes.

The most striking case of leisure as a direct extension of work did not directly concern skilled workers. Allotments, or field gardens, were advocated from the 1830s as the ideal means by which agricultural workers could supplement low wages, and keep themselves away from poor relief and the beerhouse, by honest toil in their spare time. The number of allotments and plots available, through the parish or direct from farmer or landowner, increased considerably; doubtless the majority of the 691,410 allotments reported to exist in 1881 were dug by agricultural labourers. All the same, there was a considerable demand for allotment gardens in the towns, and the general opinion was that the best kept and most carefully tended allotments were in the hands of non-agriculturalists, and that agricultural labourers, from fatigue and boredom, were liable to neglect theirs. Railwaymen and miners were often singled out as particularly keen gardeners; it was from this level of the better paid working class, and from skilled workers, that the passion for growing prize chrysanthemums, marrows, or leeks, received its impulse, just as in the late eighteenth century it was the enthusiasm of the weavers of Spitalfields, Lancashire, and the west of Scotland for flower growing which produced the development of the show auriculas, many-coloured and many-headed derivatives of the primula, well suited to small spaces and window boxes.

All these activities, gardening, angling, pigeon-racing, and the closely associated breeding of pigeons, canaries, and dogs, needed access to space and spare cash for special equipment and stock, which effectively limited them to the better paid and the skilled before the 1880s. They provided the pleasure and satisfaction of individual achievement, but they were not solitary pursuits. Mutual help, swapping of information and stock, rivalry, and competition were necessary elements in the pleasure. These entailed discipline, organization, and association, arising informally from within the fraternity and not imposed from outside. The appearance of the gentry as patrons of local horticultural and flower shows was a matter of spreading this meritorious competitive habit to areas where it had not taken root on its own, notably to rural villages, not a question of wresting control from the artisans in their own territories. Here was fertile ground for early and mid-Victorian clubs and associations, formed and run by the participants themselves and for many much more prominent in their ordinary daily lives than any skilled trade society to which they might happen also to belong. In the 1880s and 1890s many of these local societies were federating and forming national associations to govern national events and competitions; but while this meant more formality and bureaucracy, the self-government and popular appeal were not lost.

Music and singing, which were very important parts of working-class culture in some regions, were perhaps rather more interclass activities, although this was less obvious with brass bands than with choral singing. By the late Victorian period most towns throughout Britain could muster at least one band – in Scotland it might be pipe and drum rather than brass – and the popularity of band music was one good reason why the Salvation Army advanced behind its brass when it set out to conquer and redeem the dregs of society in the 1890s. Brass bands had first taken hold, however, in Lancashire and Yorkshire and the colliery districts in the 1830s, and these remained the heartlands of numbers, excellence, and popular following. Many bands were attached to individual mills or collieries, of which the Black Dyke Mills Band is an internationally known surviving example, and millowner support was a typical feature of mid-century factory paternalism. Other bands, however, sprang from local communities in more purely voluntary fashion. The bandsmen, whether playing with middle-class patronage or not, were all workingmen, and bands of both types played together in the concerts and regional contests that became popular, to largely working-class audiences: a special performance by the Black Dyke Mills Band was reckoned to have drawn a crowd of 10,000 in the 1890s.

Choral singing was rather different. It was, again, a much-loved activity in both Lancashire and Yorkshire textile districts from the early nineteenth century, and was to become closely identified with the mining valleys of South Wales when they experienced their late Victorian expansion. Glee clubs and choral societies were to be found in even the smallest textile villages in mid-century, and in the middling-sized and larger textile towns middle-class and working-class men and women sang together in the same choirs. This sign of friendliness and good feeling between the classes, singled out for welcome and praise at the time, was not all that surprising. The choirs sang mainly oratorio and cantata, and Handel's *Messiah* was the most frequently performed work. The religious character of the music naturally won approval from moralists. It also meant that the choral societies recruited heavily from church and chapel choirs, and were drawing upon congregations, particularly nonconformist ones, in which religious observance already provided a common bond that overrode some class differences. Both in chapel and in choral society the working-class element was self-selected to be respectable, probably skilled, clean and tidily dressed, well-mannered but not necessarily excessively deferential; it was unlikely to be a cross-section in depth of all levels of the working classes. The choirs were, in other words, to a considerable extent Sunday religion carried on by other means, means which brought pleasure and enjoyment to performers and audiences alike, and which were secularized with admission charges, festivals, and competitions. The social mixing, while present, was less remarkable than the sectarian mixing of Anglicans and Dissenters, which was cautious but not unknown. Musical standards were high, probably way above those of contemporary mid-Victorian orchestral music, and popular appreciation was manifest in the large audiences, up to a thousand strong, and in the local patriotism excited by local prize choirs. The Huddersfield Choral Society, formed in 1836, or the Leeds Philharmonic Society, were simply the largest and most renowned late Victorian choirs, towering above the hundreds of societies which testified to the region's lively musical culture.

Choirs and band music did not obliterate class differences, however warm the middle-class approval of the singers and players. Nor did that approval mean that singers or bandsmen were declassed in the eyes of their fellow workers, regarded as toadying to the masters. There is no sign that they were conspicuous among strike-breakers in any of the occasional great confrontations of capital and labour that punctuated the normally amicable industrial relations of the textile industries. Along with the other activities like marrow-growing or pigeon-racing, they absorbed much energy and much of the spare time available, they engendered pride in talents and skills patiently applied, and they gave pleasure and happiness. When the labour movement became active, and actively class-conscious, in the late nineteenth century these things were seen as diverting interest unnaturally away from political activity, distorting class loyalty and solidarity, and reflecting a conservative ideology of acceptance of the status quo insidiously fostered by the middle classes. Astute socialists set out to capture and politicize these interests by forming socialist choirs, without much success, just as others sought to capture working-class religious habits with labour churches, also without a great deal of success, or mobilize the great new cycling enthusiasm of the 1890s into socialist cycling clubs. In fact the lack of interest in political activity was not due to any conspiratorial diversionary efforts inspired by the middle classes, but to the clear preference of the people concerned for devoting their spare time, cash, and energies to the pursuit of happiness through the recreations which they found rewarding.

In due course, in the 1880s and 1890s, broader masses of the working classes manifested their intense interest in apolitical pleasures, and their addiction to football matches or seaside holidays was deplored as political apathy and wilfully ignorant acquiescence in the capitalist system, when it should have been recognized as the expression of an independent popular culture. In the interval between the decay and suppression of the traditional, rural, popular recreations, and the rise of the commercially provided mass entertainments, roughly between the 1830s and the 1880s, the brunt of the task of sustaining an independent culture was borne by the choral societies and brass bands, the marrows and chrysanthemums, the pigeons and canaries. These were the recreations of skilled workers and the better paid workers with regular employment. They were not acting as the standard-bearers of a working-class culture, keeping the flag flying through lean times when the majority of the class were unable to afford such relaxations, but simply as exponents of the tastes of their own groups, a reminder that sectional differences within the working classes extended into leisure just as they did into the organization of work or patterns of housing. The one taste which ran through all sections, or produced abstaining minorities in all, was the taste for beer. The one culture which embraced all the working classes and which survived all attempts to stifle it was the pub culture.

CHAPTER EIGHT

Authority and Society

Drink and sex were the most popular pastimes of the working classes; possibly of all classes, although the devout sections of the middle classes fostered an impression that they were sparing in their enjoyment of either. Inevitably, both had always attracted the attention of authority, civil and religious, for such basic areas of social activity could not be allowed to go unregulated. The treatment of both was typical of the general nineteenth-century approach to questions of conduct and behaviour: law and government prescribed the ground rules according to which the game was to be played, but the actual form and content of the game was left to the influence of voluntary associations, local communities, and custom. Thus, the law supported the institution of marriage, said who might not marry whom, ruled that heterosexual intercourse alone was lawful, between males and females above a stipulated age of consent, kept prostitution in a twilight zone of unacknowledged toleration, and prohibited abortion. Sexuality was hemmed in by other rules, notably those on obscenity, and Victorians were particularly prone to believe that sexual passions were liable to burst out all over unless kept under strict and vigilant control.

The control, however, was mainly that of religious teaching and the conventions of acceptable behaviour of different social groups, not that of the law itself. Sex was not confined to the marriage bed by law or police, but by moral codes backed by religious sanctions. Publicly these were most frequently addressed to the lower orders, but in practice it was the middle classes who most closely observed the rules. Premarital sex, although probably not normal in the sense of being universal, was not a matter of disgrace among the working classes, and was socially acceptable so long as it was followed by marriage; promiscuity and the desertion of unmarried pregnant girls were the sins. Extramarital sex was favoured by the upper classes and was tolerated in society; the sin was to create a scandal by public exposure or public humiliation of one of the partners. Abortion, while illegal, was not considered wrong in many of the poorer neighbourhoods, where it was accepted as a necessary expedient for protecting marriage chances, female employment prospects, or family living standards, while it was also attempted, more surreptitiously and privately, by some middle-class women.

In much the same way all classes drank, but only the working classes went in for public drinking. There had been little of this segregation in the eighteenth century, when merchants and lawyers often had their own parlours customarily reserved for them in city taverns, and village inns were reputedly the scenes of convivial, socially mixed drinking. By the 1850s no respectable middle-class man would enter a public house, although in country towns farmers and dealers kept up their tradition of meeting in inns on market days. It was only in the interwar period, tentatively and stimulated by the roadhouse phenomenon, and more confidently after 1945, that the middle classes rediscovered the pub. These were changes in social habits, not greatly influenced by changes in legislation, and they did not signify the abandonment of social drinking to the populace. Gentlemen took to their clubs, and the non-temperance part of the middle class, which was considerable, took to drinking at home in their increasingly large and comfortable houses. The working classes, their homes small, crowded with children, often cheerless, were left in possession of the field, the pubs their only possible meeting places. No small part of the class reputation for comradeship, conviviality, and companionship derives from the fact that their meetings and their drinkings of necessity took place on public territory, in public view.

Governments were interested in the sale and consumption of alcohol for two reasons: the customs and excise revenue which could be raised, and the public order problems which could be caused. Evangelicals, much of Dissent, and many self-improving workingmen added a third reason: the immorality of drink, with its capacity to undermine character, religion, the work ethic, and family responsibilities, and to lead to destitution. In the 1820s and 1830s the immorality was reserved for spirits, and beer was seen as harmless, almost a benevolent ally of temperance; but increasingly from the mid-1830s the teetotallers with their single-minded crusading zeal and their theatrical displays of pledge-signing, born-again, redeemed reprobates, elbowed aside the advocates of moderation or spiritlessness; and statutory prohibition, or local option as a first objective, were the aims of the politically formidable United Kingdom Alliance when it was formed in 1853. These incompatible concerns, for maximum consumption to produce maximum revenue, for limited and regulated consumption to prevent disorderly behaviour, and for no drinking at all, and the contending political and trade organizations which formed around them, ensured that it was difficult to alter the law on drinking and the drink trade. They also meant that popular drinking habits were not threatened by the overwhelming force of united, repressive action by political and moral authority.

Drinking possibilities, if not drinking customs themselves, were indeed remarkably enlarged by the 1830 Beer Act which inaugurated forty years of free trade in beer. This Act was the result of a long campaign against the monopoly powers of the large brewers and established publicans, and the restrictive and arbitrary practices of the licensing magistrates, fuelled by alarm at the apparent increase in drunkenness and gin-drinking. The 'free trade' consisted in enabling any ratepayer, on payment of an annual duty of two guineas, to obtain direct from the excise a licence to sell beer for consumption on or off the premises. The theory was that unrestricted competition from large numbers of conveniently accessible beershops, their numbers limited only by the size of consumer demand, would divert demand from spirits, available only in the restricted number of public houses licensed by the magistrates, to healthy and wholesome beer. The theory was helped on its way by the abolition of the duty on beer in the 1830 budget. Although the tax on malt, the chief raw material, remained, the price of a pint did fall by nearly one fifth and Victorian beer was duty-free until 1880 when Gladstone repealed the malt tax, thus removing a long-standing grievance of the farming interest, and reimposed a beer duty to produce an equivalent revenue. This was unsurprising, since at the time the malt tax yielded considerably more than the income tax, accounting for nearly one tenth of total public revenue, and a loss of revenue on this scale was unthinkable on simple Treasury grounds even if a dramatic reduction in the price of beer had been politically conceivable when half the Liberal party and many Tories were pledged to contain the demon drink. The result was that neither producers nor consumers were much affected by the 1880 tax changes, with the one difference that future governments found it much easier to increase the rates of duty on beer than it had been to vary the rates of the old malt tax.

Meanwhile the cheap beer and unrestricted beershops of the post-1830 regime had permanently altered the terms of public debate. They were responsible for the hardening of temperance attitudes into a strictly teetotal position, which introduced a new criterion of respectability that marked a divide within the middle classes as well as setting them against the labouring classes. Within the temperance ranks the hypocrisy of much Victorian puritanism seemed to be confirmed, for some of the leaders held that moderate wine-drinking in their own homes was quite permissible, and argued that drink should be allowed in hotels because residents used them as substitute homes. Hence the class character of the teetotal mission was readily apparent, for the prime aim was the regulation and elimination of public drinking places which were the sole watering-holes of the working classes before the rapid development of portable bottled beers in the 1890s. In fact the temperance movement was much more of a religious than a class movement, given its Dissenting and evangelical basis, and from the 1860s onwards politically it was essentially the cause of radical nonconformity working within the Liberal party and seeking to put pressure on Liberal governments. There were, indeed, many working-class leaders from Francis Place onwards who deplored the evil effects of excessive drinking on the lives of working men and their families, on the prospects of working people being accepted as self-respecting responsible citizens, and on the chances of self-improvement. The formation of sectarian groups of teetotal Chartists in the 1840s, the well-publicized parades of repentant drunkards which included the Preston plasterer who coined the word 'teetotal' in 1834, or the success of the Salvation Army in the 1880s in saving some of the very poorest from drink and damnation, all indicate the existence of teetotalism in the working classes. Nevertheless, drink and especially social drinking remained of central importance in popular culture, and it would be no exaggeration to claim that the canons of working-class respectability, although they outlawed excessive drunkenness and the abuse of wives and children by habitual drunkards, positively enjoined a due amount of ritual, ceremonial, and companionable drinking.

Beer can thus be seen as both symbol and source of many of the complexities and contradictions of the Victorian social structure, and as the proving ground for the ascendancy of religious over class divisions. All the same, the effects of the 1830 changes on habits and attitudes were superficial and symbolic rather than profound. The newly created, excise-licensed, and unregulated beerhouses certainly multiplied with great speed. Within a couple of years there were over 30,000 of them and their numbers moved steadily upwards to peak at around 50,000 in the 1870s, declining slowly thereafter to some 40,000 at the end of the century. They were highly visible, single-class, drinking places or handy off-licences for filling the beer jug; they were suspected of being run by a lower-class, more venal and disreputable, type as beersellers than the publicans who had to be sufficiently respectable and well-behaved to hold on to magistrates' licences; and nationally they were in direct competition with the traditional public houses, of which there were just over 40,000 in 1830, for part of their trade, although locally the beerhouses flourished best in the poorer districts of towns and more remote or straggling villages that were some distance from a local. Understandably it became a prime temperance aim, shared by much moderate opinion, to get the beerhouses under control. This was achieved temporarily from 1869 when the licensing of all new beerhouses was made subject to magistrates' approval, interestingly on the motion of a Tory private member; and more permanently from 1872 when Bruce's Licensing Act placed all drinking places, beerhouses as well as public houses, under the licensing justices, to which control of off-licences was added from 1882.

After forty years of freedom, therefore, the number of permitted outlets was brought under the control of established authorities who measured the public interest in terms of good order, good management, and effective supervision rather than individual liberty, maximum competition, or maximum revenue. There is little sign, however, that the forty years were years of unbridled indulgence or dramatic increases in drinking or drunkenness. In the weeks following the passage of the 1830 Beer Act there was indeed fierce competition between established pubs and new beerhouses, and free beer flowed in the streets as the rivals strove to attract or retain customers. It was during the widespread and public debauchery of this short-lived trade war that the Beer Act acquired its reputation of being 'an Act for the increase of drunkenness and immorality' and that Sydney Smith coined his 1830 aphorism: 'The sovereign people are in a beastly state.' But after this initial period of excessive enthusiasm consumers settled into the new pattern and the amount of legitimate drinking, of alcohol or its ingredients on which duty had been paid, showed quite the reverse of any tendency to get out of hand. The English were the chief beer-drinkers of Britain, and the nineteenth-century peak in their beer consumption per head (literally their malt consumption per head, and the number of gallons of beer produced from a bushel of malt varied with the strength of the beer brewed and with changes in brewing techniques) fell between 1800 and 1815. After a sharp drop which made 1817 probably the driest year of the century, beer-drinking per head went into a rising trend in the 1820s, which was indeed continued after 1830 for a few years. The result was to make 1835 a peak year for beer, although this peak was 25 per cent below the levels of the record years, 1802 and 1803, which in turn probably fell considerably short of the drinking feats of much of the eighteenth century when a smaller population had frequently put away as much malt, and hence beer, as the larger population of 1802.

It could be argued that the Beer Act gave a boost to consumption which was already on a rising trend, although it could equally be maintained that rising consumption was a response to good harvests and a fall in the price of barley, circumstances clearly associated with earlier surges in particular years. In any case the increase in beer-drinking was modest by past standards, it hardly attained scandalous proportions, and it was short-lived. For from the second half of the 1830s beer-drinking went into a declining trend, gradually falling to a low point in 1855 which was one third below the 1835 level and only half the 1802 level. Then, following the mysterious rhythms of a twenty-year cycle, it gradually rose once more to a fresh peak in 1875, 37 per cent above the 1855 trough but 10 per cent lower than 1835 and 30 per cent lower than 1802. After falling back slightly to 1880 beer consumption remained broadly steady for the remainder of the century until it started on its prolonged twentieth-century decline shortly after 1900. For what they are worth, the figures suggest that there were indeed some groups of years when the amount of beer being drunk was rising sufficiently for it to have been noticed by contemporaries who did not care to appeal to statistics of annual consumption per capita, notably between 1820 and 1835, and between 1855 and 1875. By the same token the decline between 1835 and 1855 was large enough to have been hailed as a sign of the onset of general sobriety. For the Victorian period as a whole the secular trend was gently downwards, roughly from levels that fluctuated either side of 36 gallons a head in the 1830s to ones fluctuating either side of 30 gallons a head in the 1890s. These are relatively low levels of consumption in comparison with those of serious beer-drinkers like the Belgians or Germans, or with eighteenth-century Englishmen, and suggest that the Victorian drink problem existed in the minds of the beholders rather than in the bellies of the people.

The figures cannot be pressed far, for calculations of consumption per head of total population clearly cannot reflect the fact that most children did not drink at all, that most women drank less than men, and that some unknown and possibly growing fraction of the adult population was teetotal. Nevertheless, the behaviour of regular drinkers, whose individual consumption might easily soar to four or five times the per capita average, could hardly fail to be reflected in the long-term trends and was likely to have dominated them. The long-term trend in spirit-drinking was simply a straight line from 1830 to 1900, with year-to-year variations influenced by the state of employment and wages of roughly 10 per cent above or below an average annual consumption of about a gallon a head in the United Kingdom. It is true that this average masked a slow but reasonably steady growth in English drinking, mainly of gin, a more erratic but slightly larger Scottish decline in the drinking of Scotch, and virtually no change with the Irish. The Scots, however, began this competition by drinking very nearly five times as much spirits per head as the English in the 1830s, while the Irish, whose duty-paid drinking may well have been more depressed by illicit distilling than anyone else's, were drinking more than twice as much. In terms of hard drinking the Victorian drink question was first and foremost a Scottish question, probably an important part of the Irish question, and only in third place an English one. Understandably the anti-spirits movement was founded in Scotland and Ulster in the 1820s, and it was Scots who brought the idea of an organized temperance movement to England, to the Lancashire and Yorkshire textile towns, in the 1830s. It should be noted that separate excise returns were not compiled for Wales, so that Welsh drinking habits remain statistically unknowable; the very strong temperance feeling in Wales which was apparent from the later 1850s onwards was almost certainly due to the growth of nonconformity and association with nationalist aspirations, not to any pattern of notably heavy drinking.

The hard evidence on drink consumption, therefore, does not disprove the free-traders' theory that the removal of restrictions on beer-selling would encourage more moderate and harmless drinking habits. Nor does it prove that the theory operated in practice to do more than increase the number of permitted drinking places; the effects on the volume of drinking are uncertain. A long-term decline in drunkenness, such as several contemporaries claimed to discern in the 1820s and 1830s when looking back over the previous thirty or forty years, could not be attributed to policy and legislation; it was the result of movements in real wages, the claims of new articles of popular consumption like tea on working-class budgets, changes in manners which made public and private drunkenness less acceptable spectacles in most social groups, and many other influences on personal and group behaviour. By the same token the effects of the temperance movement on the volume of actual drinking cannot be measured with any confidence, but were probably negligible; the social effects of a sectarian movement which attempted to attach a moral stigma to drink, and of a much wider body of opinion which held that popular drinking was immoderate and ought to be restrained, were more serious.

Temperance had to wait a long time for its one great legislative success, the 1872 Licensing Act, which even then was a bitter disappointment because it was hard to see as a step towards the goal of total prohibition. Nevertheless, the United Kingdom Alliance, with its great electoral importance to the Liberals, was a main spur to legislation. The Act created a virulently anti-government stir in the licensed trade that was somewhat out of proportion to its specific provisions: concentration of licensing powers in the hands of the magistrates, a rather mild general restriction of opening hours, and an increase in the penalty for public drunkenness to a 10s. fine. The trade, however, saw a threat to its property and livelihood, fearing an intention to reduce the number of licensed premises and to make licence renewals more seriously contingent on good behaviour. The fears were not ungrounded, since after 1872 the number of licences ceased to grow in line with total population, so that the ratio of drinking places to people fell from 1:200 to 1:300 by 1901; any actual decline in licences, however, fell almost entirely on the beerhouses, with public house numbers remaining stable. It was still widely felt in both political parties that this process of natural attrition left excessive numbers of pubs, and the prime purpose of Balfour's 1904 Licensing Act was to establish the right to compensation on non-renewal of redundant licences, and the machinery for paying the compensation from a levy on the trade. Thereafter, to the accompaniment of protests from the temperance, local option, and nonconformist lobbies that the drink trade had been endowed by statute, the number of public houses declined steadily, reaching a level of 1:668 people by 1961.

The restriction of opening hours was of more moment for the drinking public. The principle of statutory control had been introduced with the new beerhouses in 1830, which were allowed to be open on weekdays from four in the morning until ten at night, with two short drinking periods on Sundays in the early afternoon and in the evening that marked the first small appearance on the English scene of the divided and policed drinking day. These restrictions do not seem to have been much noticed at the time by the public, absorbed by the novelty of the beerhouses themselves; and public houses were free to stay open for as long as the publicans chose. Legal restrictions were applied to public houses from 1854, when sabbatarian sentiment with temperance approval succeeded in passing a Sunday Beer Act which extended to them the beerhouse regime of a short and divided drinking Sunday. The feeling that the religious and temperance busybodies were using the law to interfere with the publican's liberties and discriminate against the workingman's rest and recreation took root. Sunday closing of parks, museums, and art galleries, and the attempts, although unsuccessful, of extremists to prohibit Sunday trains, were all resented as discriminatory assaults on working-class leisure. But the new curb on drinking was at the seat of the serious rioting in Hyde Park in 1855, although it was triggered by Lord Robert Grosvenor's extreme, but abortive, sabbatarian Bill to prohibit all Sunday trading in London. The government response to these riots, which were paralleled by less tumultuous protests against Sunday restrictions in some provincial towns, was a prompt increase in Sunday drinking time from the six hours allowed by the 1854 Act to eight and a half hours from 1855.

Thus alerted to the intensity of popular feeling about opening hours and the danger of disturbances on the streets, the government made careful enquiries about the risks of rioting when framing the 1872 licensing legislation; the 1855 riots were still being cited in the 1890s as evidence of the dangers of tampering with Sunday drinking. They account, no doubt, for the mildness of the restrictions imposed by the 1872 Licensing Act, which slightly reduced Sunday drinking time and introduced statutory weekday closing times for all public houses, alongside those that already applied to beerhouses. These, which allowed drinking from dawn to midnight in London, to 11 p.m. in other towns and 10 p.m. in country districts, may not seem like serious infringements of liberty. But their symbolic importance as the first general, weekday, restrictions on public houses was immense and they met with a hostile reception; there were massive protests up and down the country, riots in Liverpool, troops called out in Ashton and Maidstone, although London appears to have accepted its fate without major disturbances. The restrictions also accelerated the politicization of the drink question. The Tories, many of whom sympathized with the temperance cause and the desirability of bringing drink under control, were happy to let the Liberals take all the blame for the unpopularity of the 1872 Act and to accept the support of disaffected publicans. One of the first acts of Disraeli's new government in 1874 was to reward the publicans with an extra half-hour on the Londoner's drinking day. By the 1880s it was generally accepted that most of the brewers and distillers, and publicans, were firmly on the Tory side, just as the Alliance was a Liberal pressure group.

After 1874 it always turned out to be politically inexpedient to meddle further with opening hours. It was only under the cloak of wartime necessity that temperance made its next, and last, advance, when in 1916 Lloyd George, on grounds of the need to combat the dire effects of heavy drinking on the efficiency of munition workers, made the Sunday regime into the everyday rule, thus introducing the late morning opening time and the afternoon dry gap which have subsequently become accepted as one of the quaint traditions of English customs. The years 1872–4, therefore, marked something of a watershed in party divisions; the Tory alignment of the drinking classes, and the sensitivity of working-class voters on the issue, inaugurated a long period of official inaction, broken only when Balfour misguidedly felt strong enough to make a pro-drink move in 1904. The same years were a landmark in class divisions as well. Much of the heavy drinking, in sporadic bouts when funds or credit chanced to be available, had for long gone on in the poorest sections of society. The uneducated, the unwashed, the casual labourers, the slum-dwellers, these took 'the quickest route out of Manchester' to the pubs and early Victorian gin palaces as the only form of escape and enjoyment, apart from sex, within each. Such groups, the core of 'the brutish masses' or 'the residuum', did not easily lift their eyes above their own small world of the immediate neighbourhood to identify with any wider community or class; but they formed fiery material whose primitive religious and nationalist prejudices were easily fanned into the ugly eruptions of the 'Church and King' mobs in the 1790s, the no-Popery demonstrations of 1850 against the 'papal aggression' of re-establishing Catholic bishoprics in England, or the notably savage Murphy riots of 1867–8 in Lancashire when the Orange demagogue Murphy roused the rabble against the Irish. These groups were preordained by their own traditions to become Conservative working-class cannon fodder when some of them, as householders of a sort, acquired the vote either in 1867 or 1885: the drink question did little to alter their identity as a subclass, for it was already firmly shaped by their destitution, insecurity, and hopelessness.

Matters were rather different with other classes. The upper classes, it is true, did produce one or two prominent temperance individuals who felt it incumbent on them to set a strict example to the lower orders; but the likes of the Earl of Harrington, Earl Stanhope, and Sir Walter Trevelyan, the first president of the Alliance, were thought to be most eccentric in doing so. Such a renowned social and moral reformer as Lord Shaftesbury declined to support the Alliance and preferred to preach restraint. In general the upper classes were convinced that social life without alcohol was inconceivable; and even when Buckingham Palace renounced alcohol in 1916 as a gesture of wartime self-sacrifice, they notoriously failed to follow suit. The middle classes, in contrast, were seriously divided on the issue, but in the main their attitudes to drink reflected and magnified already existing religious differences far more than they contributed to any fresh divisions. Temperance and teetotalism received support from some evangelical Anglicans, a few Catholics, and some atheists, but its main base was in Dissent, the ardour of Congregationalists, Presbyterians, both Calvinistic and Primitive Methodists, and Quakers being particularly strong. This meant that support was strong in the lower middle class, the appeal of the pledge being as attractive as the appeal of the gospel religion itself in offering a road to purification, salvation, and the conquest of sin. It also meant the support of smaller numbers of the more substantial middle classes, including many manufacturers, the backbone of Dissent in wealth and position and crucial for the finances and organization of the cause. A large part of the middle class, however, either kept aloof from the movement or actively opposed its strident, sectarian extremism. This was mainly the Anglican middle class, although many outside the Church took a similar stance; they certainly did not condone intemperance, they were quite likely to denounce the beastly excesses of the working classes and advocate curbing them by moral and police discipline, but they drew the line at prohibition which was regarded variously as pious cant, political and social folly, or presumptuous illiberality. In some lights such differences were political, of the kind which exist within any class over policy issues; but the religious differences were themselves social, and the drink divide made them more marked. A moderate-drinking middle-class family did not mix comfortably with a teetotal middle-class family and had little in common with them. In the working classes, on the other hand, the differences were social first, political second, and religious only trailing in a poor third place.

The working classes were continuously berated by moral and social reformers for being the authors of their own miseries through the self-inflicted wounds of irrational and immoderate expenditure on drink, when with prudent budgeting they could afford adequate supplies of bare necessities. At the margin between poverty and destitution the argument had some force, which was statistically demonstrated by Seebohm Rowntree's survey of poverty in York at the end of the 1890s, *Poverty: a Study of Town Life* (1901). This showed that 15 per cent of the town's working-class population were in primary poverty where income was insufficient to buy the bare minimum of food and shelter, mainly because wages were simply too low but also because of illness, old age, death of the chief breadwinner, or presence of too many very young children. A further 28 per cent of the working classes were found to be in secondary poverty where family income was notionally quite adequate to keep body and soul together, but in practice was spent unwisely; expenditure on drink was the largest single cause of this secondary poverty – there were said to be others, like indulgence in unnecessarily expensive foods that were not good nutritional value for money – and the drink bill was largely for the husband's beer, supplemented by a little mother's ruin for the wives who were partial to gin. These precise percentages are open to question, and probably overstate the amount of both categories of poverty; while the moral overtones of the concept of secondary poverty, with its implication of individual responsibility and guilt, did not endear it to those who saw drinking as a response to the social environment, a result of poverty not a cause. Whether they were explained in terms of moral turpitude, incompetence, or sluttishness, or in terms of escape from intolerable conditions, the figures give a fair indication of the scale of the problem. No wonder, then, that many working-class leaders were on the side of restraint and abstemiousness, and that temperance was far from being an exclusively middle-class movement. On the other hand, drink remained of central social, cultural, and functional importance in working-class lives. Here was a dilemma, a cause of disunity that did not disappear until well into the present century.

The working class produced a long string of leaders who were strong temperance advocates, running from Henry Vincent and William Lovett, the teetotal Chartists, through 'new model' trade union leaders of the 1850s and 1860s like Robert Applegarth, and on to the 'new trade unionists' and early Labour leaders of the late Victorian years, men like Tom Mann, Will Thorne, John Burns, Keir Hardie, and George Lansbury. They had a large body of followers, working-class Methodists forming the core. Said by some to have embraced as much as one quarter of the English working class by mid-century, Methodism appealed most strongly to skilled workers, independent artisans, miners, and the Welsh; it did not make much headway with factory workers, in the large provincial towns, or in London. Whatever the sectarian basis of the rank and file, the leaders generally used secular and political arguments. Abstention, whether the result of persuasion or of the coercion of local option or prohibition, was expected to improve individual and family living conditions through better balanced household budgets, thrift, more regular work, and more rational and educative recreation. But besides opening the way to self-improvement and the achievement of self-respect, abstinence would establish a regime of working-class respectability that would be recognized as such by the middle classes; a sober working class would have the credentials and the capacity to occupy an independent place in the political process. The pledge, on this view, was the foundation document of an effective and coherent working-class identity that would secure for the class its rightful place in the community. Moreover, drink and its associated convivial rituals were regarded as a source of social as well as personal dissipation. They were distractions which impeded the development of class consciousness and diverted energies away from political action. For these reasons, some argued, drink was a device of capitalist employers for emasculating the workers, keeping them out of harm's way in a state of befuddled and mildly impoverished impotence and disarray. Thus the pledge became also an instrument for combating political apathy, for bringing union out of fragmentation, for liberating workers from false happiness and enabling them to see their true interests and to concentrate on their proper functions of clear-headed association, organization, and united political activity.

Not all working-class leaders, however, shared this kind of analysis. Everyone was against drunkenness and in favour of sober workingmen whose intelligence and energies were not drowned in drink. This did not prevent criticism of the temperance movement for attacking a symptom and diverting attention from the cause, which lay in housing conditions, overcrowding, work practices, or erratic movements in wages and employment, and could only be tackled by a general reform of the economic and social system. Moreover, the temperance cause itself enfeebled the working class by implying that the individual effort and personal decision of taking the pledge was a more important route to salvation and a better world than class solidarity and cooperative action; and it further denied the possibility and existence of class, by sucking working people into a pan-class movement and submerging them in a culture of sectarian religious bigotry that put a gulf between them and other more venial working people. Such were the views of the intellectual, proto-socialist Chartists, Ernest Jones and Julian Harney, shared without being finely articulated by the unthinking Feargus O'Connor, and echoed by the first working-man in Parliament, Alexander Macdonald, in 1874. Among early Labour leaders the personally abstemious Philip Snowden took a similar line in the 1890s in attacking the illusory panacea for all ills promised by the temperance message. In the twentieth century such reasoning triumphed by default, with the collapse of single-issue prohibitionist campaigning along with the decline of religious enthusiasms, and the public-spirited and politicized elements of the working classes emerged as more or less united behind the Labour party of the 1920s. For the Victorians, however, the split went deep; not merely a disagreement over policies, but a profound difference between lifestyles.

Very few leaders ever dared to appear in public as the champions of traditional popular inebriation, whether at festivals like Whitsun, or Hogmanay in Scotland, or as normal preludes to Saint Monday; nor did they often care to defend the central place of the pub in working-class culture. This, no doubt, was because the pub in itself was the great rival to organized politics, of much longer standing and with much stronger roots in local communities than any newly got-up movement for workers' rights. The local was an informal workingmen's club, not the mere shop retailing oblivion to solitary drunks and mindless morons which disapproving middle-class observers often pictured. Well-established traditional roles remained strong at the opening of the Victorian period. A regular clientele used the pub as the only available, and congenial, meeting place to transact their business. Friendly societies met there, subscriptions were paid in and benefits paid out at the pub. The trade societies, or craft unions, of skilled workers relied on pubs as their bases and as employment exchanges, 'houses of call' where tramping artisans could get information on local jobs in their particular trade. Similarly, special interest groups, the dog-fanciers or the pigeon-racers as it might be, often used pubs as the headquarters of their clubs. In the multitude of trades and industries in which subcontracting was prevalent the foremen, or butties, commonly held pay-day in a pub, a practice open to considerable abuse and a favourite target of reformers' attacks in the 1830s and 1840s. The publican might give credit, although usually no more than drinks on tick; he might hold the kitty for weekly savings clubs, which could be clothing clubs, Christmas clubs, annual outing clubs, Derby Day clubs, and so on; and he might well take bets, either as bookmaker himself or as agent.

If the functional roles were important, the social functions were even more so. The pub was an all-purpose meeting place, for friendship, sociability, conversation, gossip, debate (which in times of tension governments labelled conspiracy), and entertainment. More affluent classes had a range of meeting places at their command: homes large enough for private entertaining, gentlemen's clubs, masons' halls, rotary clubs, literary institutes, theatres, concert halls, and assembly rooms. The working classes had one, and used it intensively. The recreation and entertainments were self-provided, but out of the pub sing-songs grew first the singing saloons of the 1840s, and then, from the early 1850s, the more elaborate and commercialized music halls. Initially a music hall was simply an extension of a specially enterprising pub, both physically as a tacked-on structure and managerially as a publican's show. The concept was so popular that it very quickly became worthwhile to operate music halls as independent, self-standing, commercial concerns, often in costly buildings of considerable glitter and glamour. Particularly in the 1880s and 1890s, responding to the broadening of mass audiences with the general increase in real incomes, music halls spread throughout urban Britain and became firmly established as a central element in the public face of popular culture. An informed guess of the early 1890s put the average nightly audience at the thirty-five largest halls in London at 45,000; and it has been estimated that there may by then have been over five hundred halls in the capital, including large numbers of very small and often ephemeral halls of the original pub-adjunct style.

The performers were highly professional. A few became national figures, first of the high-earning popular stars. Audience participation, however, vigorous, lusty, and boisterous, remained an essential part of a successful performance. Above all, the sale of drink and its liberal consumption were vital to music-hall economics and to their popular appeal. Apart from one or two temperance halls, struggling optimistically to present expurgated versions of the genre, late Victorian music halls acknowledged their public-house origins with unconcealed swagger. Successful commercial exploitation of the working-class market, certainly; but also successful specialization and division of labour in providing for working-class tastes on working-class terms. It was not exclusively working-class entertainment. The 'naughtiness' of the nineties, insofar as it existed, exuded most loudly from the upmarket central West End music halls where aristocratic youth, guards officers, and colonial servants on leave mixed with a pert and perfumed version of low life. In the less central halls, particularly in suburban ones, lower middle-class clerks mingled with cloth caps in socially mixed audiences. The inspiration of the entertainment, however, was emphatically public-house, popular, and working-class. Its attraction of other classes was an early instance of cultural influences filtering upwards, a process of cultural permeation from below which became pervasive when backed by twentieth-century mass communications.

The character of the entertainments themselves, which had a definite populist and anti-aristocratic edge in the 1850s and 1860s, had become largely apolitical by the late Victorian period. They did indeed contain a vein of popular patriotism, imperialism, and xenophobia, appealing to the racialist fears and prejudices that were never far below the surface and which were fanned by the influx of East European and Russian immigrants, mainly Jewish, in the 1880s and 1890s, whose unfamiliarity and clannishness were resented and the competition of whose cheap labour was felt as a particular threat in London's East End and in the West Riding clothing trades. The flag-waving and the drum-beating, and to a considerable extent the anti-Semitic jokes, were essentially conservative in inspiration: it was to be a Conservative government which first imposed restrictions on immigration, in the Aliens Act of 1905. Music halls may thus have catered for the Tory workingman. If so it was a minor part of the appeal. Most of the entertainment dealt in romance, fantasy, and escapism, or in poking fun at the pretences and pitfalls of ordinary domestic and marital life; if the rich and the toffs were satirized it was not done to stir up class feeling but to show that they too had feet of clay. This was a programme for popular audiences who were indifferent to politics. Labour leaders and early socialists thought it was a puerile and mindless pap designed to lure the drinking workingman away from doing his class duty. This was unduly disparaging. The thinking workingman quite rationally preferred enjoyment in music-hall comfort to the discomfort of attending political meetings about remote and pointless causes.

Just as the growth in the size of the market and in popular purchasing power led the music hall to hive off from the pub, so also in different ways they detached many of its other roles from the multi-purpose early Victorian pub, and helped it develop into the specialized late Victorian recreational drinking place. On the business side as friendly societies and trade unions became larger, more permanent, more national, and more bureaucratic they needed their own offices and they found other places to hold their meetings. The move out of the pub was neither rapid nor complete. The smaller, local, friendly societies, whose members joined for the companionship and fun more than for the best actuarially sound benefits, were still meeting in public houses in the 1900s, and similarly the local lodges of the smaller craft unions could not easily be weaned from their customary pubs. Nevertheless, from the 1850s the move was perceptible. It was helped on its way by temperance rhetoric and agitation, as was the decline of wage-payment in public houses. But the impact of moral reformation through such actions as the formation in 1835 of a tectotal friendly society, the Rechabites, in the one case, or Shaftesbury's inclusion of an unenforceable clause prohibiting the payment of wages to mineworkers in public houses in his 1842 Mines Act, in the second case, was of much less importance than the growth in the scale of activities and managerial efficiency, which brought improved, professional, administration and the gradual elimination of petty subcontractors.

Reformist endeavours may have been of greater account in eroding some of the more educational and self-improving sides of the leisure role of the public house. Thus municipal museums, art galleries, public libraries, and indeed public lavatories, in all of which moral reformers had a hand, can be seen in part as non-alcoholic substitutes for early Victorian public-house facilities: these commonly included newspapers and broadsheets as well as lavatories, and the pub noted for its special museum-like collection of stuffed animals, fossils, or sporting prints was not unusual. Moves to provide specialized buildings, and specialized space in the shape of public parks, for specific functions were part of the drive to civilize the masses by making knowledge, culture, and healthy exercise accessible; but general motives of philanthropy, civic pride, and urban improvement were more responsible than efforts narrowly aimed at undermining the hold of the public house. In any case the major effort explicitly aimed at providing non-alcoholic alternative meeting places for the working classes, the movement for workingmen's clubs, boomeranged. The concept of such clubs, where the social, recreational, business, and political life of working people could be carried on away from the temptations of the public house, was canvassed by self-helping working-class leaders in the 1830s, and was taken up enthusiastically by temperance reformers. The support of individual clergymen, who spotted new vehicles for spreading moral and religious discipline, and the patronage of employers, who perceived a possible connection with work discipline as well, launched a few score clubs in the 1850s.

In 1862 the movement went national with the formation of the Workingmen's Club and Institute Union, under predominantly temperance leadership, with the objects of encouraging the establishment of local clubs, providing guidelines on their management and sets of model rules, and offering an association to which respectably managed clubs could affiliate. The expectation was that non-party teetotal clubs guided by middle-class benefactors would provide an apprenticeship in good manners and the proper conduct of committees, at the conclusion of which they would become self-governing outposts of class harmony. The reality was that dry clubs were neither popular nor viable, and the CIU quickly altered its rules to allow the sale of beer. Bar profits, in turn, quickly made the clubs financially independent, middle-class patronage was thrust aside, and they became thriving self-governing working-class institutions with a reputation for good company, good fun, good management, and orderly behaviour which undermined many temperance assumptions. There were waves of club formation in the later 1860s and in the 1880s. The CIUs were non-party, with a curious belief that 'politics should be discussed without reference to politics'. Spurred by the franchise extension of the second Reform Act and the urge to mobilize the new working-class voters, local political parties took advantage of the taste for workingmen's clubs by setting up their own examples, which were necessarily outside the CIU. These were specially numerous in the Lancashire and Yorkshire towns, and amongst them the Conservative clubs were the most successful, realistically putting the social and convivial functions first and recognizing that the political pay-off was a matter of generalized contented loyalty, not a question of incessant lecturing, discussing, and debating. By the mid-1880s CIUs had a membership of more than half a million, and the non-affiliated clubs may have had as many again. Here was a large group which had broken away from the pub, at least on club nights. But it had broken away in order to run a sort of cooperative pub substitute, a substitute which was a close enough clone to generate its own form of music-hall substitute or revival in the twentieth century.

Thus in the course of the nineteenth century the public house was reduced to a more purely social and recreational role, and its other attributes and functions were largely eliminated. This, however, represented a locational redistribution and refinement of the drinking habits of the working classes, not a triumph for the temperance cause and not an abandonment of the cultural importance of drink. Moreover, the pub retained its innovative vitality, pioneering new attractions as older ones attained independence and separated off. Billiards and darts, quoits and bowls, were given popularity by public-house patronage; while boxing, growing out of the earlier prizefighting, was by the 1890s in its equivalent of the early music-hall stage, largely an adjunct of selected pubs in the East End and south London and in a few provincial cities. Much well-intentioned effort had gone into providing alternative, teetotal, meeting places for the working classes; but while the church and chapel halls, and the later East End missions of the 1880s, moved beyond tea and buns for the poor and began to offer innocent games and sports as attractions, this showed that they found it wise to disguise their religious and social disciplinary motives, not that they were succeeding in making many permanent converts outside the ranks of the already convinced. A minority of the working class, composed principally of elements of the skilled workers and mining communities but also including fair numbers of agricultural labourers, was chapel-going, as dedicated to providence as to religion, and either teetotal or highly abstemious. The majority, which also included elements of the skilled and the miners, and most of the agricultural labourers, were at best reluctant and unconvinced church-goers, driven by fear of a landlord or desire to please an employer, and more likely never went near a church. For them the public house, and its offshoots like the music hall and workingmen's clubs, was the centre of social life, and Victorian efforts to popularize or impose counter-attractions or alternative community centres served to confirm and more clearly define the pub culture, not to erode it.

Erosion, when it came in the twentieth century, was due to material developments, not to social discipline: the result of bottled and canned beers, canned music, cinemas, and entertainments in the home, not the effect of preaching, education, or moral policing. It was as well that some of these developments were already in train by 1916, augmenting the persuasive power of the wartime spirit in inducing public acceptance of draconian restrictions; for Victorian governments, at the level of Home Secretaries and Cabinets, had been rightly chary of drastic interference, for fear of rendering the people ungovernable. Authority at lower levels, and outside the structure of civil government, in the churches, did not share such inhibitions. The efforts of town councils, magistrates, clergy, nonconformist ministers, and lay preachers to regulate, supervise, or repress popular drinking were insistent rather than effective. They were one factor among several, which included the self-discipline of working-class notions of self-respect, that made pub behaviour rather less rowdy and more decorous by 1900 than it had been early in the century; but the larger objectives, of sanitizing drinking places so that they were no longer spontaneous and uncontrolled social centres, or of drying out the population altogether, remained as remote and unattainable as ever. Lack of success, however, did not prevent either the shrill campaigns or the more measured deployment of the forces of authority being seen as menacing attacks on popular institutions. They served to alienate a large section of the working classes from the radical nonconformist middle class, who on many grounds of opposition to privilege and pursuit of equality seemed to be 'natural' friends and allies, but who were also the core of the temperance army. For similar reasons they contributed to the alienation of the majority of the working classes from organized religion in general, and to driving a wedge between the drinking and non-drinking fractions; above all they fostered an attitude to the authority of the state and its representatives which was at best wary and suspicious if it was not outright hostile.

Ordinary people encountered the state most frequently in the nineteenth century when in their cups. Drunkenness had long been an offence, but before there were regular police forces the means of enforcing the law were rudimentary. Village constables were unlikely to pay any attention to it, and watchmen in towns were concerned with the protection of property. Drunkenness was only likely to be noticed when associated with seriously disorderly behaviour or assault. The penalties for being drunk in public were raised, reflecting the growing gravity with which the authorities regarded such lower-class behaviour: for London a fine of 40s. (more than double a labourer's weekly wage), with the alternative of imprisonment, was introduced for the Metropolitan Police district in 1839, as against the ruling national fine of 5s., and in 1872 the national fines were put on a sliding scale from 10s. for the first offence to 40s. for the third. Heavy penalties did not deter; but the appearance of uniformed police on the streets certainly led to dramatic growth in the number of arrests and charges. It took time for a network of effective police forces covering town and countryside to become established, following the establishment of the Metropolitan Police in 1829 which is conventionally taken as the modern starting point: after 1835 many boroughs and some counties began to set up police forces, but it was not until 1856 that it became obligatory for counties, and only from the mid-1860s or early 1870s could it be said that the whole country was being policed in a recognizably modern fashion. Likewise, it took time for the number of offences known to the police to grow. The single largest category of these comprised the drunks and the drunk and disorderly cases, which soared from 75,000 in 1857 to over 200,000 in 1876, moving from a quarter to over 40 per cent of the annual totals of all lesser offences – common assaults, petty thefts, game law, vagrancy law, highway law, and local bye-law cases making up most of the rest – that were non-indictable and were dealt with by summary proceedings. Zeal against drunks moderated somewhat in the last quarter of the century, and police arrests and proceedings settled down at around 30 per cent of their annual hauls of non-indictable offences.

It was overwhelmingly a matter of police zeal, not of growth and fluctuation in the actual extent of drunken behaviour, which could not be objectively defined let alone measured. All that the statistics of offences show is that the more policemen there were, the more cases were brought. The police in some areas were probably urged by their superiors and their borough authorities to pounce more severely than in others, which would account for otherwise strange variations in drunkenness that made Manchester five times and Liverpool ten times as drunken places as Birmingham in numbers of drink offences per head. The police certainly had wide discretion in deciding whether to take no notice, to caution, or to arrest and charge. It was universally understood that gentlemanly drunks were not to be molested, although they might be helped home or into a cab; and many police forces had instructions not to harass respectable workingmen and to ignore any signs that they might be drunk and incapable. The great majority of those who were prosecuted clearly came from the lower levels of society, the unskilled, the labourers, and those who did not look respectable in their dress. They may, or may not, have drunk more and more intemperately than other classes. The figures for offences offer no clues. They do, however, provide an essential clue to the high proportion of police energies employed on harassing ordinary people over a matter of behaviour which was held to be socially reprehensible rather than any particular danger to persons or property; and they suggest that the common perception of the policeman, formed by the area of most frequent contact, was likely to be of an agent of middle-class morality intent on stamping out popular pleasures. Laws, and the expansion of organized forces for law enforcement, produced growing crops of offenders rather than profound changes in social habits. Marginal in curbing drunkenness, they may have had greater success in inducing more orderly behaviour inside pubs; but their main thrust was to give a clear and widely visible impression that the authorities had no friendly or protective intentions when patrolling the lower orders.

Such a perception of policemen, among those who most frequently felt their presence, could only be strengthened by the nature of the second most numerous class of offences, after the drunks, which concerned the street life of the working classes. These were a mixed bag of offences: many were in effect created by the police themselves in exercising their virtually untrammelled discretion in applying ancient common-law provisions against obstruction, nuisance, soliciting, loitering with intent to do a mischief, or suspicion of causing a breach of the peace; many more were created by municipal bye-laws against such things as street trading, street performers, street games, and street betting; a few derived from general legislation, as the last did from the 1853 Lotteries and Betting Act. In all, by the late nineteenth century, such street offences produced between 15 and 20 per cent of total annual arrests and summary proceedings. Hence, measured by results on the charge-sheets, half or more of ordinary police work was concerned with street life and drunks, aspects of popular life which happened to be considered unruly, immoral, or unattractive. The prevention or punishment of crime involving injury to persons or property was a minor part of their work.

Boroughs used their bye-law powers, and their police forces, to chase the people off the streets, or more likely to threaten to chase them off if their conduct was unacceptable. Hawkers, pedlars, and all manner of street-sellers could be controlled by licensing regulations, chivvied under the obstruction rules, and harried by bye-laws prohibiting their bell-ringing and trade-shouting; in many seaside resorts there were special bye-laws expressly to keep them off the beaches. In practice this meant that they were excluded from the select beaches and allowed elsewhere on sufferance, knowing that they could be moved on or charged if a constable thought they were causing a nuisance. Likewise in towns the laws were used to buttress the orderly respectability of main thoroughfares and quiet residential districts where householders fixed 'no hawkers' signs to their gates, rather than to attempt the aggressively provocative task of eliminating street-selling altogether. More aggression was shown against street games, where street races could fall foul of obscenity as well as obstruction rules, on the grounds that runners in shorts were naked, and where by the 1890s there were frequently bye-laws prohibiting the playing of football or cricket in the streets. The effect of such policing was marked. It made the streets, or at least the principal streets, more and more into sterile territory on which the public had the right of passage but nothing else, not to meet, assemble, loiter, sit, gossip, trade, or play. Other activities were swept away. Some were hastened into obsolescence in large-town conditions; some were given a helping push into the domestic sphere of private homes; and some were simply swept out of sight into backstreets and alleys where the police tacitly agreed not to tread. As with prostitution, which the police did not attack directly both because it was not in itself illegal and because it would have been futile, but which they did cajole and shepherd into informally recognized red-light districts, so with many other social activities the net effect of policing was more to move people on and change the location of behaviour than to change or suppress the behaviour itself.

Many, perhaps most, of the people who experienced the sharp end of this street policing were from the poorest levels of the working classes. They were members of marginal economies, like prostitutes, barrow-boys, or hawkers – although muffin-men or knife-grinders who serviced middle-class households are not known to have been much persecuted – they were children or youths, or they were sufficiently ragged and disreputable in appearance to convince magistrates that they were unreliable or dishonest characters, perhaps suitable for treatment under the vagrancy laws even if they were not literally sleeping rough and without visible means of support. Some, however, were undoubtedly respectable, decent, and law-abiding in their own estimation and in the eyes of their neighbourhood community, and felt that they were being victimized for doing what they and their parents before them had always done. Moreover, when it comes to street betting, any notion that the police were mainly performing a civilizing mission among the roughs wears very thin.

Gambling was prevalent in all social classes, with a strong and vocal anti-gambling group broadly corresponding to the temperance elements – in the forefront among nonconformists, and strongly represented in the professional and administrative middle classes. Betting on local events, prizefights, foot races, and private games had always been popular and common. It was the completion of the electric telegraph network, initially attached to the railways, in the 1850s which made news of racing results nationally and instantly available, and thus made possible the rise of organized, mass betting and the eclipse of other forms of wagering by the superior glamour, and apparent calls on skill and knowledge, of betting on horses. The general rise in working-class disposable incomes in the last quarter of the century made it possible to finance regular, and generally small, weekly bets; and the new, cheap, mass circulation newspapers of the 1880s with their pages of racing news and gossip and their special editions with racing results, serviced what every observer agreed was a very general and widespread increase in late Victorian popular gambling. Politicians and social reformers were alarmed, disturbed by the immorality and the unsubstantiated view that gambling was a royal road to self-inflicted destitution, and official enquiries were held in 1902, and again in 1923 and 1932. A guesstimate that before 1914 around 80 per cent of the working class were in the habit of betting more or less regularly was not thought to be implausible. There are, not surprisingly, no records of the numbers of gamblers; but a different and more cautious guess, which in effect said that in the early 1920s one third of the working class bet regularly and another third had an occasional flutter, may have been closer to the truth. Proportions of this magnitude, however imprecise, are large enough to make it clear that all levels of the working classes were involved in betting, skilled workers, respectable workingmen, factory workers, highly paid workers, and not merely the unskilled, the casual labourers, or the slum-dwellers who indeed could ill afford the outlays; such an impression of the composition of the betting classes is well supported by circumstantial and anecdotal evidence of shopfloor betting in factories and workshops.

To be sure, the police did not try to catch the punters themselves, any more than they tried to catch the prostitutes' customers. The law and its officers were targeted at the providers of services and their intermediaries, not at their consumers, at brothel-keepers, touts, and pimps, at bookies, tipsters, and street-runners. These could easily be dismissed as fringe elements of society, undesirables of irregular habits and indeterminate status inhabiting a twilight zone beyond the limits of normal life where the concepts and labels of an orderly, structured society did not apply and had no meaning. Such an attitude might evade the question whether such people were part of the working class, but could not disguise the fact that in the case of street betting at least the law was not directed at the eradication of a disreputable subclass but at the disruption of an everyday pursuit so common among the working classes that the attempt to convince them of its criminality was bound to be in vain.

The evangelical campaign against gambling secured the banning of lotteries in 1826, which had been used by governments throughout the eighteenth century as one means of raising revenue, the banning of public gaming houses in 1846, which banished casinos and confined gentlemen's gambling at cards to private clubs, and reached its Victorian climax with the Lotteries and Betting Act in 1853. This Act suppressed betting shops, which had been common in the major towns, and made off-course cash betting illegal. Credit betting, essentially possible only for the wealthy, and cash betting in the enclosures at the racecourses, remained permissible, because the anti-gambling lobby was not strong enough to challenge the great horse-racing majority in Parliament. In effect, therefore, if not in intent, this was class legislation. The Act merely drove the betting shops on to the streets, where an elusive but effective structure of mobile bookies, runners bringing betting slips and cash from home and shopfloor, and dogger-outs keeping watch for the police, quickly developed. Thus enforcement of the law came to depend chiefly on municipal bye-laws regulating the streets, and it was under them that the police conducted a continuous running battle against street betting. It was rarely an aggressively hostile fight, since the police appreciated that betting was so prevalent and popular that any attempt to suppress it entirely would make the police so cordially detested that they could not function on more serious matters where the tolerance of the community was a condition of successful policing. On the other hand, professional pride and commitment to law enforcement in general would not allow open acknowledgement that these particular laws were unenforceable. The result was a situation rife with opportunities for corruption, collusion, and favouritism. Many bookies claimed that they paid protection money to policemen in order to be left in peace; many dogger-outs claimed that, by agreement, they allowed themselves to be arrested and fined periodically so that they were left alone most of the time; and many policemen were diverted from matters like assault or house-breaking by the excitement of playing hide-and-seek with cunning and impudent bookies.

Several factors combined to produce mounting public concern about gambling in the 1890s. The enquiries of Booth and Rowntree appeared to confirm that gambling was second only to drink as a cause of secondary poverty, where unnecessary and frivolous spending forced families to go short of food and clothing. This attitude purported to make its suppression a matter of social policy designed to oblige people to spend wages sensibly, rather than a question of morality. At the same time the dramatic growth of the racing press, and the introduction from 1890 of uniform starting prices for every race, which were instantly telegraphed all over the country, were not unreasonably taken as evidence of a disturbing increase in popular gambling. Finally, the unsatisfactory and uncertain state of the law, which left the application of the 1853 Act to the varying interpretations and rules of municipal bye-laws, was made considerably more unsatisfactory by a decision of the House of Lords in 1897 that on-course cash betting outside the special enclosures which had been specified in 1853 was not illegal. This made the legality of proceedings against street betting which used starting prices determined on the course somewhat questionable. The result was a House of Lords enquiry into betting in 1901–2, and the Street Betting Act of 1906 which made all off-course betting illegal, instituting the regime which lasted until 1960. The 1906 Act should be seen, perhaps, as a tidying-up operation and as an instalment of a rational social policy for the containment of poverty, rather than as a final fling of the nonconformist conscience. Although it gave the police a uniform, national, basis for action, it was no more effective and no more consistently enforced than the previous patchwork of local regulations. Periodic police drives against the street betting, undertaken to impress local police committees by a show of vigour, did nothing to reduce the amount of gambling or convince ordinary people that it was a form of wrongdoing.

The attack on betting may have been largely ineffective, and in some respects half-hearted, but what counted was its simple existence and the vehemence with which anti-gambling sentiments were voiced from pulpit, council chamber, and magistrates' bench. These signalled not only the unfriendly attitudes of the authorities, especially the nonconformist authorities, to normal working-class behaviour, but also the division within the working classes between the nonconformists and the rest. The police were perhaps more tolerant and understanding than their masters, but their erratic application of the double standard which proclaimed that it was all right to go to the races but all wrong to bet off the course did nothing to earn respect or persuade working people that authority was anything but unsympathetic and baleful. Ironically, many of the early Labour leaders, whose overall aim was to promote the welfare and happiness of the people by gaining control of the instruments of authority, were as strongly opposed to gambling as they were to drink. In this they were prisoners of their nonconformist backgrounds and ran true to the high-minded self-discipline and austerity of the narrowly defined respectable working class from which most of them came; but they were ludicrously out of touch with the habits and values of the majority of the class they aspired to lead.

What street offences, including betting, were to the towns poaching offences were to the countryside: the sphere in which the law and the law enforcers were most visible, most frequently encountered, and least understood. Here at least Labour leaders did not display political innocence, for none are on record as staunch defenders of the game laws or scourges of poachers. This was more a matter of good luck than good judgement. There was no special feeling for the agricultural labourers' position, since most of the leaders were townsmen and most of the labourers, although voters after 1885, were not voters likely to strike the ILP or the Labour Representation Committee as the most promising and worthwhile supporters to try to cultivate. The lucky feature, which however yielded no known electoral dividends, was that denunciation of the game laws had been part of the stock in trade of radical nonconformity at least since the 1840s, and Labour leaders simply inherited the attitude. The attitude of rural labourers was never in any doubt. 'We labourers', as the organizer of the first agricultural labourers' union, Joseph Arch, often declared, 'do not believe hares and rabbits belong to any individual, not any more than thrushes and blackbirds do.' Hence it was regarded as natural to catch hares and rabbits, and possibly game birds too, as opportunity and necessity offered, and no amount of law-making, preaching, or lecturing could convince people that any sense of shame or guilt should attach to it. The majority of villagers may well have been honest, law-abiding, and not themselves given to poaching; but few thought of it as a crime, and many treated the local poachers with indulgent affection as champions of natural rights pitting their cunning against the illegitimate power of the landowners' agents.

The traditional popular view that game was there for the taking and that everyone had a right to hunt it was apparently well grounded in the basic rule of law that wild animals were incapable of having legal owners and hence could not be the object of theft. Abolition of the hunting monopoly of the privileged few, and assertion of the individual right to chase, kill, and eat wild animals, were objects alike of rebellious American colonists and rebellious French peasants in the late eighteenth century; vestigial indiscriminate shooting forays, to be seen in twentieth-century America and western Europe, bear witness to success in gaining these freedoms. In Britain the hunting privilege, confined by an Act of 1671 to persons with a landed property qualification, lasted until the Game Reform Act of 1831 which permitted anyone who took out an annual game certificate to pursue game, subject to the law of trespass. The same Act legalized the retail selling of game, by licensed game dealers. These were concessions to the luxury trade in venison and game birds for the urban wealthy, and to the smaller rural freeholders and the non-landed friends of the gentry whose pre-1831 shooting had been technically illegal, not to the labouring classes. For the snag about the legal doctrine of wild animals was that some animals were deemed to be a great deal less wild than others. When animals were confined to particular areas, like deer parks or rabbit warrens, and were bred and fed, whether for sport or for sale, they ceased to be ownerless in the eyes of the law and became the property of the person on whose land they were found, so that taking them without permission was theft, theft which the sporting gentry regarded as particularly wicked. Deer and rabbits were protected by law in this way throughout the eighteenth century as forms of private property; the growth in the habit of preserving pheasants and partridges, breeding and feeding them, was increasingly giving them the same kind of protection by the early nineteenth century. After 1831 all wild animals which a labourer might regard as food were legally regarded as the property of the person on whose land they were found; and if a poacher could not be caught in the act of theft, trespassing on private land in pursuit of game was an equally serious offence, carrying two months in prison, or a £2 fine, equivalent to about a month's wages for an agricultural labourer. Taking deer from deer parks at any time, and night poaching of other animals, carried far more severe penalties, of up to seven years' transportation (technically, although not frequently in practice, until its abolition in 1857) or two years' hard labour.

The means of enforcing these laws were every bit as savage as the penalties, until the use of man-traps and spring-guns to deter, and maim, poachers was prohibited in 1827. Countrymen might hold the game laws in contempt, as unjust, but they were obliged to respect the force behind them. The force was the private army of gamekeepers employed by game-preserving landowners, with the uniformed rural police forces arriving on the scene, between 1837 and 1860, in the role of powerful auxiliaries. A gamekeeper was a kind of specialized policeman in private employ: until 1831 he had power to search suspect persons and their homes without warrant, for poaching equipment and weaponry, and after 1831 he retained power to seize on sight any equipment, weapons, or dead game from anyone he thought to be poaching on his master's land, using reasonable force to do so. The gamekeeper's task was to look after the welfare of the game which his master chose to preserve, protect it from its predators, and deliver it in good order for lawful pursuit and killing for his master's sport. Much of his time was spent in looking after coverts, hatcheries, and breeding grounds, and in dealing with stoats, weasels, and foxes: this could cause bitter intra-class friction with the foxhunters, and one consequence was a growing geographical differentiation and separation of the best shooting districts and the best hunting districts as the Victorian pursuit of country sports became more organized, more time-consuming, and more heavily patronized. This in turn meant that gamekeepers were thicker on the ground and more likely to be encountered by ordinary countryfolk in the most-favoured shooting counties like Norfolk, Suffolk, Berkshire, or Sussex, than in the most fashionable hunting country of the Midland shires, Leicestershire and Northamptonshire. Over the country as a whole, indeed, friction and animosity between gamekeepers and the local population was by definition confined to the vicinity of game-preserving estates, while rabbits, main target for the poor man's pot, were also to be found almost anywhere on the other half (or more) of the countryside which was not preserved.

In the districts where they did patrol, gamekeepers were generally much disliked and feared, unloved by farmers as much as by labourers. Thus a Scottish tenant-farmer from Caithness told a Select Committee on the Game Laws in 1873 that 'gamekeeping is an idle trade and an idle class of men go into it', and asserted that 'I have never yet found any man that became a gamekeeper or a ghillie that was ever fit for one good day's work afterwards at any other business.' A Norfolk farmer told the same Committee that gamekeepers 'are generally men of bad character'. These were the agents of landlord authority, armed with statutory powers as well as shotguns, and they did not give it a good name. Farmers themselves seldom went poaching or confronted gamekeepers as armed adversaries; but they resented the preservation of game which damaged their crops, they resented not being allowed to touch birds or rabbits on their own farms unless they chanced to have an eccentrically enlightened landlord who gave them express leave, and they resented the habitually rude and inconsiderate manner of gamekeepers who could roam about their farms at pleasure in the course of their duties. Gamekeepers' vigilance was directed at human as much as at four-legged predators, and they treated them with similar roughness. Poachers sometimes worked in groups, and there were some organized gangs of commercial poachers supplying the urban game market with game birds or venison. These were equally ruthless and ugly customers, who could make a gamekeeper's job most unpleasant and dangerous, making the gamekeeper's roughness quite understandable. Pitched battles with poaching gangs, sometimes ending in shooting but less often in deaths because they necessarily took place in the confusion of darkness, inevitably attracted publicity and were used as excuses for maintaining or increasing the severity of the law. They were, however, infrequent. By far the greater part of the volume of poaching – in 1873 it was estimated at about three quarters of the annual poaching offences that were prosecuted, and no one knew how much more poaching there was which was not prosecuted – was of rabbits, which were of too little cash value to be of interest to the gangs. Labourers went rabbiting, with snares, ferrets, or terriers, not with shotguns for they had none; and the routine business of gamekeepers was with rabbiters.

Rabbits were big business for the working classes. They were sometimes referred to, perhaps with some exaggeration, as 'the workingman's Sunday dinner' and as the only form of meat eaten by the poor. In the 1870s it was thought that about 30 million hares and rabbits were produced annually in Britain and sold in the urban markets, with an import of several million more, mainly from Ostend and mainly for the London trade. They sold, in London, for 2s. to 2s. 6d. a brace. The untraded wild rabbits which the poacher took for his own consumption were worth about 6d. each; the reward for catching them was a meal, the risk was to be caught by a gamekeeper. That risk grew greater and greater as the generality of landowners grew fonder of sport and devoted more time, effort, and money to it. In 1836 there were 3500 licensed gamekeepers in Britain and perhaps a thousand or two more who did not take out a licence; by 1901 there were over 17,000 giving gamekeeping as their occupation, more than double the number of rural policemen. They were looking after a population of birds which had undoubtedly increased in at least the same ratio, but protecting them from a rural population which had declined by at least one fifth. Anyway, the popular notion was that the rural police provided gamekeeping reinforcements at the ratepayers' expense, an impression confirmed by the 1862 Night Poaching Act. That Act gave the police powers to search people on the highway on suspicion of poaching or intending to poach, and was passed at the request of chief constables who were concerned at a growing number of bloody affrays between poachers and keepers and wished to have clearer legal authority for intervening to keep the peace. It was much resented as blatant class legislation, for only labourers were ever stopped and searched: countrymen 'object very much to being subjected at any time to be assailed by a police officer and searched', as Joseph Arch put it. Agricultural labourers were simply strengthened in their conviction that the law, its officers, and the landowners' servants were allied against them, united in treating them with contempt and in thwarting them of their natural rights. Unsurprisingly, the number of poaching offences brought before the magistrates increased in sympathy with the number of gamekeepers and policemen, just as happened with drunkenness cases: there were about 4000 game law convictions a year in the 1840s and over 12,000 a year in the 1870s.

These figures did not signify a trebling in the amount of poaching, but simply a trebling in its detection. There was an increase in the efficiency of apprehension, but this in itself suggested that the increase in the law enforcement army had done little or nothing to increase respect for the game laws or to convince countrymen that poaching was morally wrong. In the triangular social relationships of the countryside, involving landlords, tenant farmers – the occupiers of around 80 per cent of the agricultural land and rising to nearly 90 per cent by the late nineteenth century – and labourers, the game laws were seen as the instrument of landlord privilege and self-interest. Hence the farmers generally lined up with the labourers on this issue, resenting the laws even if they did not care or dare to flout them openly. The farmers' grievance was eased, but by no means wholly removed, by the Gladstonian Ground Game Act of 1880 which gave them the right, without any permission from their landlord, to catch hares and rabbits on their own holdings, so that thereafter the labourers were more isolated and exposed. It would be a mistake, however, to overemphasize the power of the game laws to engender anti-landlord sentiments among the labourers; their resentment and fear was beamed more directly at gamekeepers and officious policemen, and more generally at the unfairness of the law. In most everyday matters their tensions and conflicts were with their direct employers, the farmers, who were directly and visibly responsible for low wages, harsh treatment, unreasonable work demands, arbitrary dismissal, seasonal laying-off, or eviction if they lived in tied cottages – all those conditions which made Joseph Chamberlain claim that 'the agricultural labourer is the most pathetic figure in our whole social system' in 1885, just as he had been in the 1830s. Landowners, by contrast, frequently appeared to be well-disposed and benevolent, caring about the sick and elderly, looking after local friendly societies or clothing clubs, visiting cottagers, and inventing make-work jobs on the estate when times were bad. A significant pointer was that during the 'revolt of the field' between 1872 and 1874, when agricultural labourers in many parts of midland and eastern England dared to combine and confront farmers with a union demand for a shilling a week wage-increase, and when selective strikes were countered by concerted lock-outs and evictions by East Anglian farmers, it was to local landowners that labourers turned for sympathy and support.

The 'revolt' and the union collapsed as swiftly as they had appeared; and from the mid-1870s, with labour-employing arable farmers anyway anxious to shed labour in response to falling agricultural prices and profits, agricultural workers were in a weak bargaining position and ex-union men were weeded out and obliged to move to the towns or emigrate. The episode had, however, brought to the surface the persistent paternalist affinity between landowners and labourers which formed a continuing strand in the normal relationships of the countryside. It was manifest not only in the gentry's voluntary welfare activities but also in the efforts of some landowners to protect labourers by denying control of tied cottages to tenant-farmers, and more generally in the assumption that agricultural labourers, newly enfranchised by the third Reform Act, would habitually vote for gentry, predominantly Tory, candidates. It was an assumption which, after an initial flurry of defiantly independent Liberal-radical voting in the 1885 election, was largely borne out by the shire results in the elections of the next twenty years at least; arguably a streak of this deferential or common-interest voting behaviour persists in some rural pockets a full century later. In important areas, therefore, the rural triangle found labourers and landowners together, with farmers on the other side of the hedge. The asymmetry of three-sided relationships was completed by a third set of alignments in which landowners and farmers were the allies and the labourers were isolated. This alignment might appear over perceived common interests, as in the fight over the Corn Laws in the 1840s when the majority of landowners and farmers fought for protection and high prices, while the labourers were interested in jobs and cheap bread; in less strident and more localized vein this act was repeated in the demands for agricultural protection in the 1880s and 1890s. The partnership appeared at its most active when property and public order in the countryside were under violent threat, as in the Swing riots in the autumn of 1830. It was at its most enduring in the framing, and subsequent administration, of the 1834 new Poor Law, the manifestation of political, legal, and local authority which arguably made the deepest, most bitter, and widespread impression upon the labouring classes, rural and urban, of all the acts of nineteenth-century officialdom.

The Swing riots which swept through many of the southern and eastern counties were about wages and jobs. Bands of labourers smashed threshing machines, which were depriving them of work, and intimidated farmers, parsons, and landowners with rick-burning and physical violence, to force them to promise to increase wages, or to reduce tithes and rents so that farmers would be able to pay higher wages. It has sometimes been argued, indeed, that the parsons and landowners were the objects of the labourers' most vituperative hatred, even though farmers bore the brunt of the damage to property. Crushing the revolt and re-establishing order was a matter of local landowner initiatives in recruiting special constables, many of them farmers, the yeomanry with muskets, and heavy work at quarter sessions and the assizes: an impressively ruthless demonstration of the mobilization of the full machinery of county society and the law to put the labourer back in his place.

The new Poor Law has been portrayed as a response to Swing, an attempt to reassert the authority of property-owners, especially landowners, over rural society by making their control of the apparatus of poor relief effective, and by using it to impose a rigid social discipline that would end the labourers' insubordination.

Less problematically, the new Poor Law was clearly designed in the eyes of the policy-makers to provide a long-term solution to Swing-like situations, for the principal object was to provide a mechanism which would cure rural overpopulation and under-employment, and hence remove low wages, so that in theory the reduced number of fully employed and reasonably paid labourers who survived on the land would have nothing left to complain about. It did not work, any more than have other policies at other times for ending underemployment or unemployment by getting tough with the unemployed. But the spectacle of an aristocratic and gentry Parliament providing a measure for the farmers, who were the main employers and ratepayers in the country districts, which they were to cooperate in administering at the expense of the labourers' comfort and dignity, was a successful demonstration of the operation of the rule of three in rural society. The three major elements in rural society – landowners, farmers, and labourers – paired off two against one in all three possible combinations, not in any chronological sequence but according to differing facets of their relationships, producing shifting patterns of attitudes and loyalties among individuals. Of the three partnerships the landowner–farmer axis was the one with most muscle; and whichever pairing held the stage, the labourer was always the toad under the harrow.

The new Poor Law was designed for rural conditions, albeit on a misreading and misunderstanding of the evidence on what those conditions actually were. It was applied to the whole country, and since it outlasted Victoria's reign as the basic framework for the treatment of destitution – legally until 1929 and practically through its buildings and institutional attitudes in many respects for much longer – it became almost incidentally the foundation of the state's social policy for an urban and industrial society. The instruments and symbols of the new regime were the workhouses, intended to be imposing, dominating, and frightening buildings whose pres-ence, and internal conditions, would deter the poor, not from being simply poor because poverty in the sense of not having enough was an unavoidable and not intrinsically dishonourable condition, but from degrading or pauperizing themselves by accepting poor relief. The main object of the prisons for the poor, or bastilles as they were quickly dubbed, was to end outdoor relief for the able-bodied. The theory was that the virtuous, honest, and determined able-bodied could always find work if they tried. If this involved moving to where the work was, so much the better: it would remove rural overpopulation. If it involved taking work at wages too low to support marriage or children, better still: this would end what were thought to be feckless marriages and unrestrained breeding supported and encouraged by indiscriminate outdoor relief and the payment of relief in aid of low wages under the old Poor Law. After 1834 the able-bodied could, in theory, only obtain relief if they agreed to become workhouse inmates. This workhouse test was designed to sort the sheep from the goats, and force most of the work-shy and idle to join the sheep because of the unpleasantness of the workhouse, leaving only the incorrigible and shameless to become workhouse goats.

The idea that the rural destitute were voluntarily unemployed was fanciful enough, for instance in face of the regular pattern of winter unemployment. The notion that industrial workers thrown out of work by cyclical depressions were individually responsible for their lot was patently absurd, as was the prospect of building workhouses large enough to accommodate the thousands who might need relieving in hard times. Employers, as ratepayers, were acutely aware not only of the unsuitability of the new regime for industrial areas, but also of the large capital cost of implementing it and the strong likelihood that it would turn out to be more expensive to operate than the old Poor Law. Its unpopularity among the workers, stoked with lurid and possibly exaggerated tales of what the workhouse regime would do to them and their families, was intense. There followed considerable resistance in the northern manufacturing districts, from within the employing and ratepaying classes, to the introduction of the new Poor Law, and widespread, often violent, popular protest. The anti-Poor Law movement was widely supported in the late 1830s, especially in Lancashire and the West Riding, and it led straight on into Chartism. It could be mistaken for a vehement expression of working-class feeling, were it not for the Tory gentry and employer leadership it enjoyed, and were it not for the fact that its temporary successes in delaying the introduction of workhouses, in Rochdale,

Oldham, Ashton, Todmorden, Huddersfield, or Merthyr Tydfil for example, were successes for recalcitrant local, middle-class guardians.

Resistance to the introduction of the new Poor Law in rural districts was less publicized than its urban counterpart, and it did not grow to the dimensions of an organized movement. It could, however, be presented as a more purely single-class outbreak, albeit in localized and disconnected incidents, for the labourers were out on their own in attacking meetings of guardians and smashing up workhouses in a scattering of village riots in Norfolk, Suffolk, and Essex in 1835 and 1836, with no support or sympathy from farmers or landowners. They rioted, however, to defend their 'traditional rights' to be given relief in cash not in kind, to be given it in their own homes not in a workhouse, and to go to a familiar village almshouse when sick or old, not to a strange and distant workhouse in some other parish of the new Poor Law Union: a defence of custom, not a call for a new social order. Disturbances and conflicts over the introduction of the new Poor Law lasted anything from a few months to several years; by the end of the 1840s they were over and the Victorian Poor Law was firmly in place. What was in place was not a pure version of the 'principles of 1834' but a fudged compromise which varied from place to place because the aspirations of the Act and the central administration for uniformity never crushed the autonomy of local boards of guardians, and in the compromise many traces of pre-1834 customs survived.

The most important fudge placated the industrial Unions and damped down their smouldering resentment. The General Outdoor Relief Order promulgated by the Poor Law Commissioners in 1841 to inaugurate the general enforcement of the 1834 law prohibiting outdoor relief for the able-bodied, was deliberately not applied to the industrial districts until 1852. Even then the Poor Law Board, the Commissioners' successor, permitted outdoor relief to continue to those able-bodied who took a labour test; that is, those who accepted such hard work, normally stone-breaking, as the guardians chose to offer, could receive relief in cash without having to enter the workhouse. Other expedients, such as granting outdoor relief to an able-bodied worker by pretending he was sick, were available to humane guardians or to economical guardians who knew that short-period outdoor relief was much cheaper than indoor relief. By such devices, but above all by a massive flow of private charity, major crises like the Lancashire Cotton Famine of the 1860s were handled without the Poor Law authorities having to open the workhouses to the thousands of cotton operatives who were thrown out of work. By 1886, when Joseph Chamberlain, as President of the Local Government Board which had replaced the Poor Law Board from 1871, issued his instruction to local authorities urging them to run public works schemes for the unemployed, which would be completely outside the Poor Law net, it was apparent that progressive official thinking was moving away from the 'principles of 1834' and seeking ways of protecting the respectable unemployed from the degrading workhouse test. In a similar spirit, guardians who were anxious not to identify Poor Law administration with the employers' interests, or to appear to use its machinery for strike-breaking, were developing in the 1890s the doctrine that it was legitimate to provide relief for the distressed wives and families of strikers, although not for strikers themselves since they were able-bodied who voluntarily chose not to work.

The administration and interpretation of the new Poor Law, therefore, were not rigid, uniform, or unrelievedly harsh throughout the nineteenth century, but varied according to political will, both central and local, and on balance became more liberal, although that trend was interrupted by periodic flurries of renewed severity when civil servants or guardians became alarmed that outdoor relief – always permitted for the non-able-bodied in distress – was getting out of hand and being abused by loafers and the work-shy. Parallel developments took place in the workhouse as an institution intended not merely to deter the able-bodied poor but also to care for the various categories of the unfit and handicapped who were too destitute to be able to help themselves. The original intention in 1834 had been to separate the aged, the infirm, the sick, the children and orphans, and the lunatics, from the able-bodied, by providing separate workhouses for each class, each of which would have a regime and discipline appropriate to the condition. This had foundered on the meanness of guardians when faced with the expense of building so many different workhouses, the administrative difficulty of looking after the small numbers generated by many Union communities, and the priority given to deterring the able-bodied: the policy was quietly dropped in favour of building large multi-purpose 'general mixed workhouses'. Once these were in place, however, there was a movement from the 1860s towards a piecemeal revival of the concept of separate and specialized provision. District schools for workhouse children were set up, by combinations of Unions, to which no stigma of social disgrace attached, and which were held by HM Inspectors in the 1880s to provide a better, and more practical, education than either voluntary or Board schools. Lunatic asylums were established, mainly by special county boards, although workhouses typically retained insane wards. Most striking of all was the development of infirmaries out of the sick wards which all mixed workhouses possessed. In London from 1867, and thereafter in most of the larger towns, separate Poor Law infirmaries were established, physically and administratively distinct from the workhouses. These had become by the 1890s one of the three main elements in the country's patchwork of hospital services, the other two being the great charity hospitals and the civic hospitals of the largest boroughs; the private hospitals for the middle classes formed a poor fourth, in contribution to total bed numbers and in quality of medical service. Non-pauper patients were being treated alongside paupers with no disgrace and no penalties, such as the disfranchisement that attached to the receipt of poor relief; and by 1900 infirmary building, and the payment of nurses and doctors, were the largest items of Poor Law expenditure.

These developments were possible only in the large centres of population, where Unions served big populations and had a large base of rateable values to tax, or where some cooperation and division of labour between Unions was practicable. Even then, exceedingly few ventured to specialize so far as to have a workhouse reserved exclusively for deterring the able-bodied, or went in for purpose-built or single-function old people's homes. In middling and small towns, and in country areas, the workhouses of 1900 remained much as they had been when first erected, and few professional, trained, or specialist staff were employed, although the attitude of the administrators may have softened somewhat. In favourable city locations the Poor Law framework had shown itself capable of supporting, grudgingly, the development of the rudiments of a network of health and social services. Some middle-class opinion was alarmed by the increasing indulgence in the treatment of the poor, and called for a return to the 'principles of 1834'. Much middle-class opinion, however, critical of the way in which relief was managed, and increasingly reluctant to ascribe poverty to moral delinquency, was ready for the grand inquest of the 1905–9 Royal Commission on the Poor Law; and ready also for the two great measures, old age pensions in 1908 and national insurance in 1911, which were to begin the break-up of the Poor Law by removing large parts of the problems of old age, sickness, and unemployment from its clutches.

How far the poor themselves appreciated these developments is another matter. They lay in the shadow of the workhouse, and the workhouse had an awesome reputation throughout the working classes which an infirmary and a school here and there, or a bit of concessionary outdoor relief, did little to dissipate. It is true that the post-1834 workhouses were not so bleak, harsh, and cruel as images drawn from *Oliver Twist* (which was in a pre-1834 setting) or the real-life 1845 Andover scandal, where starving workhouse inmates were reduced to gnawing the putrid bones they had been set to crush as task work, suggest. Workhouses were certainly meant to be unpleasant; on the Benthamite principle of 'less eligibility' they were designed to provide a disagreeable safety net which would prevent people dying of destitution, but only in living conditions which were 'less eligible' than those which the poorest independent labourer could provide for himself and his family. It was on the proper calculation of this equation that their deterrent power was deemed to depend. Nevertheless, the result of these sums generally did not mean that workhouse conditions were inferior to those of independent labourers, in material things: they did not provide less food, less clothing, less warmth, or less shelter. This was partly because some guardians found it unthinkable that, as a matter of cold calculation and measurement, they should provide less than the pitifully inadequate amounts which were all that labourers could afford in many districts. It was mainly, however, because the institutional discipline was itself the deterrent: 'less eligibility' was not a question of gruel, but of prison-like regimentation.

Workhouses did not endear themselves to the poor because on the whole they ate better inside them than out. The aspect of the regime most feared and dreaded was the rigid separation of the sexes and age groups. On entering the house, families were automatically broken up, wives were separated from husbands, and mothers from children; this happened to the aged as well as the able-bodied, and in some houses members of a family literally might not even see each other again until they discharged themselves and resumed an independent life. Alongside this misery – which could of course be a welcome relief for a battered wife or a quarrelsome couple – the other features of workhouse life seem much less repulsive. The drab workhouse clothing, deliberately intended to destroy individuality, and the standard workhouse haircut, which made paupers instantly recognizable if they went out in public; the strict hours, compulsory chapel, silent periods, exercise periods, and the largely pointless labour for the fit and not so fit in stone-breaking or oakum-picking: all these were regular features of institutional life. To the authorities they added up to conditions which sustained life in physically adequate and morally satisfactorily rigorous fashion, while discouraging all but the genuinely destitute from applying. To the poor they added up to punitive conditions, punishing them for their poverty.

In a somewhat self-fulfilling way the system worked, even though the policies outlined in 1834 were never implemented in their full rigour. As a proportion of the total population the number of paupers, receiving either outdoor or indoor relief, remained at around 7 per cent until the end of the 1840s and then fell steadily to less than 3 per cent from 1890 onwards. Plainly, by far the greater part of the 30 per cent of the town population of the United Kingdom which Seebohm Rowntree reckoned, on the basis of his 1899 study of York, might be living in poverty were doing so without resort to poor relief. The majority of the deserving poor were indeed, it could be argued, shamed, bullied, and intimidated by the gaunt spectre of the Poor Law and its workhouse test into shifting for themselves, just as the authors of the 1834 Act had intended. This kind of success was even more strikingly evident in the workhouses themselves. Right through the second half of the century the number of indoor paupers remained relatively constant at between 0.6 and 0.8 per cent of total population. The able-bodied were but a tiny fraction within this tiny fraction: already by the 1860s only 5 per cent of workhouse inmates were able-bodied unemployed. There is no means of estimating the actual amount of unemployment in the 1860s, but if it is assumed to have been at the probably low level of 5 per cent of the labour force, that would have implied a total of the out-of-work at least fifty times larger than the total of able-bodied workhouse inmates. Admittedly there was another group of the able-bodied obtaining outdoor relief even though that was contrary to the spirit of the Poor Law; but after counting them it was still the case that at least 90 per cent of the unemployed, at the assumed 5 per cent unemployment rate, never touched poor relief. The workhouses, in fact, had settled down into being institutions for the aged, the sick, the orphaned, and other casualties and victims. It may seem ironic that institutions built round the concept of deterring the able-bodied poor should have had so few of them to deal with, but their scarcity in the workhouses could be hailed as proof of success: the able-bodied may not all have been scared into finding work, but they had been scared away from living on poor relief.

Indeed, it was the very insignificance of able-bodied inmates which enabled, and even obliged, guardians to soften some of the forbidding harshness of the workhouse regime, a process widely observable from the end of the 1870s. Elderly married couples were often allowed to stay together, diets were improved, and by the 1890s the well-behaved elderly were allowed newspapers, tobacco or snuff, and personal teapots for making brews. These relaxations, and the concomitant development of Poor Law schools and infirmaries, were making workhouse conditions somewhat more caring and comfortable, somewhat less punitive. Regardless of any gradually softening reality, however, it was the initial brutal shock of 1834, which appeared to make poverty itself into a crime, that made the lasting impression on popular consciousness.

There was a small minority, to be sure, a kind of subclass of the more crafty members of the residuum, which learned to live with, or off, the Poor Law, and to play its rules for the meagre benefits of eking out a marginal existence. There were vagrants, tramps, and seasonal workers – hop-pickers and harvest gangs stand out – who used the bleak 'casual wards' of the workhouses as free overnight stopping places. There were individuals, and sometimes whole families, who were in and out of the workhouse as part of their way of life, using it perhaps for more than one spell in the year to plug the gaps in irregular employment. It would not have been surprising if such people disliked the workhouse, because of its discomforts and regimentation; but they certainly were not afraid of it, and did not feel any sense of shame or disgrace in exploiting the system. Moreover, they did not lose face or standing in the eyes of their fellows because of their reliance on poor relief. To this minority the workhouse was merely part of the landscape in which they lived, even if it was not notably benign. The majority, however, took a very different view, and Charles Booth was close to the truth in observing, in the 1890s, that 'the aversion to the "House" is absolutely universal, and almost any amount of suffering and privation will be endured by the people rather than go into it.'

Initially the workhouse had been avoided out of terror of the unknown fed by tales of the horrors and cruelties of the new bastilles. By the later nineteenth century the resolve to keep out of the workhouse at all costs, and not to touch poor relief at all except in sickness, had become a matter of avoiding social disgrace: avoiding not merely the moral disapproval and criticism of the middle classes, but avoiding above all disparagement and humiliation in front of friends and neighbours. The enormous importance attached to providing for a proper funeral, and skrimping and saving the pennies in order to insure against the shame of a pauper burial, was the most widespread and well-attested manifestation of this feeling. This was not done to curry favour with the middle classes, who as often as not strongly disapproved of what they saw as senseless and irrational sacrifices, sometimes causing severe hardship, hunger, and deprivation, which poor families habitually made in order to keep up their payments into a burial club or insurance policy. Neither was it done solely because pauperism in death was an ultimate and indelible stigma; there were cultural, religious, and customary imperatives impelling the desire to make provision for suitable rites and feasts that would do credit to the dead before relatives, friends, neighbours, or workmates, which were more positive motives than the mere negative avoidance of pauperism. Yet protecting the surviving family, and the reputation of the deceased, from the shame which a pauper grave would bring was a powerful ingredient in this behaviour. There were, no doubt, more multiple strands of motivation in the business of living than in the business of preparing for death; but the drive towards self-help, thrift, savings, friendly society membership, and the thriving extended family and neighbourhood mutual-help networks in illness, unemployment, or old age, can all be seen as evidence of the urge to keep clear of poor relief and the workhouse. Independence, self-reliance, and self-respect, pursued through companionship, co-operation, and voluntary collectivism, were hallmarks of the Victorian working classes: much of their fibre came from suspicion and abhorrence of the Poor Law, and to a lesser extent of charity, attitudes that were born of 1834.

Resort to poor relief, in other words, came to be equated with the loss of respectability, a concept nourished and enforced by local communities and peer groups whose sanctions of disparagement, ridicule, or ostracism were far sharper and more potent than the disapproval of middle-class moralizers or administrators. On this reckoning the respectable poor amounted, at any one time, to the 95 per cent or more of the total population which was not in receipt of poor relief. Even when allowance is made for the fact that many people encountered the Poor Law at some stage in their lifecycle, a very large fraction of the population clung to their respectability throughout their lives, albeit not uncommonly only by the skin of their teeth. Admittedly there is a superficial contradiction between this view, which sees the overwhelming majority of the working classes as 'respectable', and the normal Victorian – but largely middle-class – view which saw the 'respectable workingmen' and their families as an elite minority readily distinguishable by appearance and manner from the mass of the great unwashed.

There were indeed real and visible distinctions between the superior working-class world of lace curtains, front parlours, and best Sunday suits, and the much more unkempt world of the homes, dress, and language of the majority. But to apply the term 'respectable' to both is not so much a contradiction as an illustration of the variable and relative nature of the concept itself.

The poor who contrived to keep out of the 'house', though it might be at the price of living in squalid and penurious conditions, certainly succeeded in clinging to their respectability according to their own lights. The importance of recognizing and respecting this feeling was clearly shown when means were found for relieving the distress caused by unemployment during the Lancashire Cotton Famine of the 1860s without throwing open the workhouses, and without forcing the cotton workers to accept the humiliation of going on to poor relief. It was shown in a more sustained way from the 1880s onwards in the growing body of opinion critical of the justice or expediency of making the honest unemployed suffer the indignity of resort to poor relief. This line of thought was to lead to the Unemployed Workmen Act of 1905, intended to create local distress committees which would run public works schemes for the unemployed quite outside the Poor Law and its stigma; and thence to the Royal Commission on the Poor Laws, and to unemployment insurance. The originators of 'the principles of 1834' had deliberately set out to make poor relief not merely unpleasant and forbidding, but also degrading, aiming to harness moral and physical sanctions to deter all but the utterly destitute from applying. The irony of the Victorian Poor Law in practice was that the moral message became so effectively ingested into social canons of respectability, even while the physical sanctions grew less harsh, that it became more and more necessary to devise ways round or outside the Poor Law for supporting the respectable poor without damaging the respectability which derived, antithetically, from 'the principles of 1834' themselves. Any twentieth-century success in rendering relief, or in other words social security, morally neutral and free from the taint of social disgrace, has therefore in the eyes of some in the propertied and educated classes weakened or removed the restraints on scrounging, and has fuelled a persistent cry for more and more checks and domiciliary searches and work-availability tests, which is a thinly disguised yearning for a return to the good old days of 'the principles of 1834'.

Ordinary working people had not always associated poor relief with degradation, although many may well have been deterred from applying for relief through fear of being uprooted and forcibly removed to their possibly remote parish of birth or last legal 'settlement' under the laws that defined what parish had the obligation to support each individual, and which remained in force virtually unchanged since the seventeenth century, until the 1865 Union Chargeability Act. Indeed, the pre-1834 critics of the old Poor Law blamed the feckless and unrestrained behaviour of applicants who allegedly supported improvident marriages and swarms of children by battening on the poor rates as a matter of course, more than they blamed the laxity of the administration and the irrationality of the relief practices, for the evils and extravagances of the unreformed system. If popular attitudes turned within a generation of 1834 from affectionate attachment to the Poor Law, widely regarded in the 1820s and early 1830s in Cobbett's view as part of the Englishman's birthright, to general abhorrence of the Poor Law and all its works, this was a signal triumph for the power of legislation and government officials to change popular standards and values. Working-class respectability, in all its different levels, admittedly had no single taproot. Its origins were diverse, and it is best seen as a bundle of self-generated habits and values derived from past customs and present responses to living and working conditions, rather than as being either imitative or imposed from outside or above. Nevertheless, the internalization of the shamefulness of poor relief, so that the great bulk of the Victorian working classes accepted this attitude as their own, was a prodigious success, perhaps the one big success of the century, for the transmission of middle-class standards, through tough laws and institutions, to the working classes.

Society as a whole paid a high price for this success. Most obviously, large numbers of working-class families suffered unnecessary and avoidable deprivations, often self-imposed, in order to preserve their dignity, independence, and respectability. The stern unbending school of middle-class opinion, which came to be embodied officially in the Local Government Board and unofficially in the Charity Organization Society, accepted this as salutary and unavoidable, the necessary cost of keeping idleness and shirking in check. What ought to have been alarming to all shades of middle-class opinion, and to the propertied classes at large, was that working-class self-respect built on this kind of anti-Poor Law foundation inevitably contained attitudes of deep suspicion and distrust of governments and the authorities which administered the Poor Law. Since these were the authorities, along with the police, with which ordinary people most frequently came into contact, the alienation was not merely widespread but amounted to nearly total alienation from the state and all its officials.

Total alienation was, on the whole, not made any less likely by most of the authorities which were set up ostensibly to promote the health and welfare of ordinary people. The regulation of hours and conditions of work of women and children, at first for textile mills, then for most factory industries, and from 1867 for workshop industries as well, was intended to protect these weaker groups of workers from exploitation. Many male workers, indeed, welcomed the Factory Acts because they could be used, indirectly, to restrict their own hours of work as well. But the enforced loss of children's earnings, which was seriously damaging for many family budgets, was widely resented, so that the automatic popularity of the Factory Acts among the working classes cannot be taken for granted. The factory inspectors who enforced the laws were in any case so few in number that their contacts were with employers, not with the workers; their visits to the workplace came to be associated with unaccustomed strictness in the observance of rules, safety regulations, and attendance at school for half-timer children, interruptions in the work routine that were not necessarily welcome.

Similarly, sanitary, public health, and housing regulations were intended to improve the health of the whole community and to eliminate the worst, most squalid, and most overcrowded housing conditions. Sanitary inspectors and inspectors of nuisances were much thicker on the ground than factory inspectors, and were visible to members of the general public as well as to the slum landlords or lodging-house keepers on whom they acted directly.

But although the long-term results of their work were immensely beneficial to the health, cleanliness, and well-being of urban communities in particular, it would be a mistake to assume that their presence was invariably a welcome sight. Their appearance on the scene might well portend uprooting and eviction from buildings condemned as insanitary and unfit for human habitation, or at best an increase in rent if a bad landlord was chivvied into making improvements and passed on the cost to the occupier. Just as slum clearance schemes under the Cross Act of 1878, though resulting in some striking civic improvements on the model of Birmingham's Corporation Street, meant compulsory, and resented, displacement, and almost inevitable increases in overcrowding and homelessness in adjoining districts in the absence of adequate provision of new alternative housing, so the well-meant actions of inspectors of nuisances could result in homelessness, a condition not unnaturally felt to be worse than the meanest and most insanitary shelter which had been taken away by officialdom. Health visitors also, making domiciliary visits which could easily seem to be patronizing and uninvited intrusions on the privacy of the home, and offering high-minded advice on nutrition and personal hygiene which was absurdly irrelevant tc the poverty of its recipients, were not necessarily welcomed in working-class households. The appearance of women visitors, working for several voluntary agencies from the 1860s and increasingly employed by local authorities from the 1890s, eased some of the problems of the forbidding face of officialdom but left the income and culture gap between well-meaning middle-class women health visitors and the bewildered working-class women they visited imperfectly bridged.

In educational administration also the 'truant officers' who appeared to enforce school attendance after it became compulsory in the 1870s were no more welcomed by the parents than by the children they were sent to chase. The educated and self-educated levels of the working classes, essentially the skilled workers, the trade union members, and the better paid miners and factory workers, were already strongly in favour of schooling for their children and, in the main, already had the school habit before 1870: they had no occasion to tangle with the school attendance officers. The 1870 Act was largely designed to bring elementary education to the classes – the lower paid, the roughs, or the residuum – which had not previously sent their children to school, either because they could not afford it or because they thought it pointless. The parents with whom truant officers had dealings came from this stratum, and they strongly resented their presence and the basis and justification of their authority, a resentment which, in the early years at least, not infrequently gave truant officers a physically rough reception. To this section of the working classes the desire of the state to educate their children was unintelligible, and the attendance officers who were the arm of the law in this matter were simply a new confirmation that officialdom was meddlesome, interfering, and oppressive.

It would not be far wrong, indeed, to argue that the postman was the only representative of authority encountered in ordinary daily experience who was generally regarded as benign and helpful. His appearance in this role was an entirely Victorian development. Before the introduction of the penny post and the accompanying postal reforms in 1840 the postal service was a concern of politicians, businessmen, the well-to-do, and the privileged: it scarcely touched the mass of the people at all, except possibly as the carrier of newspapers that they read in public houses. The penny post brought letter writing within the reach of the literate working classes, but it was the development of door-to-door delivery, and the liberal provision of pillar boxes, which made large-scale individual communication possible. These things did not happen all at once. By the late 1860s deliveries to every house were offered in most large towns, but in rural districts letters were only delivered by messengers walking along a few prescribed routes, and the majority of farmers and labourers had to collect letters from sub post offices or receiving offices if they had any mail at all. It was not until the 1890s that bicycling postmen, in sufficient number, achieved 100 per cent house delivery throughout the land. At the same time the halfpenny rate for postcards, and the long-delayed acceptance by the Post Office of commercially produced postcards, launched picture postcards of varying tastefulness on their career of instant popularity, and mass communication by the masses had arrived. It therefore took half a century for the postman to become a universally familiar figure, but while on the way to that status he was never regarded as in any way a hostile or threatening kind of official. In the meantime the usefulness of the post office to the thrifty portion of the working classes, already apparent in the correspondence of trade unions and friendly societies, had been significantly increased by the establishment of the Post Office Savings Bank in 1861, a service much valued by the small savers who opened accounts in their millions over the next forty years. It was fortunate indeed that the nationwide network of post offices, unambiguously associated with non-discriminatory, non-charitable, and non-patronizing public service, lay ready to hand to supply the machinery for paying out old age pensions when the first major breach was made in the Poor Law in 1908.

The postman was a friendly, unassuming, unobtrusive official, a member of the working class himself. He was a small figure, however, to set against the policeman, the Poor Law guardian, the relieving officer, the workhouse master, the school attendance officer, the inspector of nuisances, or the gamekeeper who embodied the main weight of the authority of the state and the law in everyday experience. Alienation from authority did not breed any strong and united dislike of the system of government and desire to overthrow it, so much as a conviction that little good could be expected from authority. Working-class leaders who tried to mobilize support for winning power over the state, by parliamentary means, in order to use the power of the state for improving the lot of the masses encountered the obstacle of widespread working-class indifference. Many of the working classes perceived the state as simply a source of mischief, or at best as an irrelevance, in their lives, and saw little point or attraction in political activity. Among those in the upper and middle classes who actually wielded authority in the Victorian state there were many who attempted reforms, whether from political expediency or moral purpose, in health, housing, education, and working conditions: but their motives were suspect, their efforts were not greatly appreciated, and the idea of benevolent government did not carry popular conviction. The better-off workers provided for themselves and took pride in not needing or accepting assistance. The poorly paid, the casually employed, and the residuum, for whom most of these measures were designed, resented the interference; this was not unnatural, since the ideal solution which progressive opinion had in mind for them was to remove them from society and pack them off to purdah in isolated labour colonies, which happily were too costly ever to get off the drawing board. Each group and subgroup in society was thrown back on its own resources, material, moral, and cultural, and obliged by the alien image of authority to devise its own code of conduct, its own strategies for survival, and its own sanctions for enforcing them.

This made the structure of society more orderly and well-defined in 1900 than it had been in the 1830s and 1840s. Its weakness was a fragmentation into a multiplicity of sections or classes with differing standards and notions of respectability, as well as differing living standards. Its strength was in the opacity of the lines of division and distinction between the different layers of a multi-layered society, which meant that stark polarization into the battle lines of class conflict had not happened. Every group operated its own social controls, often devised in reaction to behaviour patterns which law and authority sought to impose, which worked through notions of what was acceptable and what was unacceptable conduct within the group, enforced by common opinion which could be expressed effectively by anything from raised eyebrows to smashing the tools of offenders against a code. This was respectability: but internalized and diversified; it had not turned out to be the cohesive force which its middle-class and evangelical proponents had imagined. The weakest group, because the most purely imitative in its standards, the least capable of generating its own culture, and the most despised by those from whom its moral clothes were borrowed, was the lower middle class; but weakness in the world of clerks and small traders was tempered by the grittiness of its nonconformist sections. The strongest was still, in 1900, the traditional ruling class of the landed aristocracy and gentry, with its equally traditional allies in the law and the Church, and its friends, allies, and in-laws from the wealthiest parts of business; but the ruling class was no longer quite clear about its own identity, or certain of its grip on power. The middle classes who were not preoccupied with getting accepted into the upper class were divided between the professional and the commercial wings, which had very different standards and life-styles. Whilst among the working classes differences of religion, within religion, and irreligion, and differences of unionization, and non-unionization, political and apolitical feeling, produced as many divisions and groupings as did differences in skill, earnings, and regularity of employment, so that the unity and coherence of the class was little more than a rhetorical device. It was an orderly and well-defined society, but it was not an inherently stable one. The Victorian experience bequeathed structural problems, identity problems, and authority problems to the twentieth century.

Further Reading

1. Economy and Society

Asa Briggs, 'The Language of "Class" in Early Nineteenth-Century England', in Asa Briggs and J. Saville, eds, *Essays in Labour History* (1960).

M. Brock, *The Great Reform Act* (1973).

D. Bythell, *The Handloom Weavers* (Cambridge, 1969).

S.G. Checkland, *The Rise of Industrial Society in England, 1815–85* (1964).

J.H. Clapham, *An Economic History of Modern Britain*, 3 vols (Cambridge, 1926–38).

Phyllis Deane and W.A. Cole, *British Economic Growth, 1688–1959* (Cambridge, 1967).

R. Floud and D. McCloskey, eds, *The Economic History of Britain since 1700*, 2 vols (Cambridge, 1981).

N. Gash, *Aristocracy and People: Britain, 1815–65* (1979).

E.J. Hobsbawm, *The Age of Revolution* (1962).

E.J. Hobsbawm, *The Age of Capital* (1975).

C.H. Lee, *British Regional Employment Statistics* (Cambridge, 1979).

Peter Mathias, *The First Industrial Nation* (1969).

B.R. Mitchell and Phyllis Deane, *Abstract of British Historical Statistics* (Cambridge, 1962).

Harold Perkin, *The Origins of Modern English Society, 1780–1880* (1969).

E.P. Thompson, *The Making of the English Working Class* (1963).

G.N. von Tunzelman, *Steam Power and British Industrialization to 1860* (Oxford, 1978).

2. The Family

G.L. Anderson, 'The Social Economy of Late Victorian Clerks', in Geoffrey Crossick, ed., *The Lower Middle Class in Britain, 1870–1914* (1977).

Michael Anderson, *Approaches to the History of the Western Family, 1500–1914* (1980).

W.A. Armstrong, 'The Interpretation of the Census Enumerators'

Books for Victorian Towns', in H.J. Dyos, ed., *The Study of Urban History* (1968).

J.A. Banks, *Prosperity and Parenthood* (1954).

J.A. Banks, *Victorian Values: Secularism and the Size of Families* (1981).

J.A. Banks and Olive Banks, *Feminism and Family Planning in Victorian England* (Liverpool, 1964).

Leonore Davidoff, 'Mastered for Life: Servant and Wife in Victorian and Edwardian England', *Journal of Social History*, VII (1974).

'Fertility in Marriage', *Census of England and Wales*, 1911, Vol. XIII, Part II, especially Table XXXV.

'Fertility of Marriage', *Census of Scotland*, 1911, Vol. III, especially Table XLVIII.

Margaret Hewitt, *Wives and Mothers in Victorian Industry* (1958).

E.H. Hunt, *British Labour History, 1815–1914* (1981).

J.W. Innes, *Class Fertility Trends in England and Wales, 1876–1934* (Princeton, 1938).

Theresa M. McBride, *The Domestic Revolution* (1976).

Angus McLaren, *Birth Control in Nineteenth-Century England* (1978).

Standish Meacham, *A Life Apart: the English Working Class, 1890–1914* (1977).

R. M. Titmuss, 'The Position of Women', in *Essays on the Welfare State* (2nd edition, 1963).

E.A. Wrigley and R.S. Schofield, *The Population History of England, 1541–1871* (1981).

3. Marriage

Geoffrey Crossick, *An Artisan Elite in Victorian Society* (1978).

Leonore Davidoff, *The Best Circles* (1973).

Leonore Davidoff and Catherine Hall, *Family Fortunes: Men and Women of the English Middle Class, 1780–1850* (1987).

F. Engels, *The Condition of the Working Class in England in 1844* (1st English edition, 1892).

L. Faucher, *Manchester in 1844* (1844).

John Foster, *Class Struggle and the Industrial Revolution* (1974).

P. Gaskell, *The Manufacturing Population of England* (1833).

P. Gaskell, *Artisans and Machinery* (1836).

Robert Q. Gray, *The Labour Aristocracy in Victorian Edinburgh* (1976).

T.H. Hollingsworth, *The Demography of the British Peerage*.

Supplement to *Population Studies*, XVIII (1964).

Derek Hudson, *Munby, Man of Two Worlds* (1972).

Elizabeth Isichei, *Victorian Quakers* (1970).

Jean Robin, *Elmdon: Continuity and Change in a North-west Essex Village, 1861–1964* (1980).

Lawrence Stone, *The Family, Sex and Marriage in England, 1500–1800* (1977).

I am also indebted to two unpublished theses:

Phillida Ballard, 'A Commercial and Industrial Elite: a Study of Birmingham's Upper Middle Class, 1780–1914' (PhD thesis, University of Reading, 1984).

Maureen Elizabeth Montgomery, 'Transatlantic Marriages and the British Peerage, 1870–1914' (PhD thesis, University of East Anglia, 1983).

4. *Childhood*

Michael Anderson, *Family Structure in Nineteenth-Century Lancashire* (Cambridge, 1971).

Virginia Berridge and Griffith Edwards, *Opium and the People: Opiate Use in Nineteenth-Century England* (1981).

John Burnett, ed., *Destiny Obscure: Autobiographies of Childhood, Education and Family from the 1820s to the 1920s* (1982).

Carol Dyhouse, *Girls Growing Up in Late Victorian and Edwardian England* (1981).

Margaret Hewitt, *Wives and Mothers in Victorian Industry* (1958).

Pamela Horn, *The Victorian Country Child* (Kineton, 1974).

John Hurt, *Education in Evolution: Church, State, Society and Popular Education, 1800–70* (1971).

J.S. Hurt, *Elementary Schooling and the Working Classes, 1860–1918* (1979).

Phillip McCann, ed., *Popular Education and Socialization in the Nineteenth Century* (1977).

Standish Meacham, *A Life Apart: the English Working Class, 1890–1914* (1977).

Linda A. Pollock, *Forgotten Children: Parent–Child Relations from 1500 to 1900* (Cambridge, 1983).

Robert Roberts, *The Classic Slum* (Manchester, 1971).

James Walvin, *A Child's World: a Social History of English Childhood, 1800–1914* (1982).

E.G. West, *Education and the Industrial Revolution* (1975).

Anthony S. Wohl, *Endangered Lives: Public Health in Victorian Britain* (1983).

5. Homes and Houses

Clive Aslet, *The Last Country Houses* (New Haven and London, 1982).

M.W. Beresford, 'The back-to-back house in Leeds, 1787–1937', in S.D. Chapman, ed., *The History of Working-class Housing. A Symposium* (1971).

John Burnett, *A Social History of Housing, 1815 1970* (Newton Abbot, 1978).

David Cannadine, *Lords and Landlords: the Aristocracy and the Towns, 1774–1967* (Leicester, 1980).

C.W. Chalklin, *The Provincial Towns of Georgian England* (1974).

Geoffrey Crossick, *An Artisan Elite in Victorian Society* (1978).

M.J. Daunton, *House and Home in the Victorian City: Working-class Housing, 1850–1914* (1983).

H.J. Dyos, *Victorian Suburb: a Study of the Growth of Camberwell* (Leicester, 1961).

David Englander, *Landlord and Tenant in Urban Britain, 1838–1918* (Oxford, 1983).

S.M. Gaskell, 'Housing the Lower Middle Class, 1870–1914', in Geoffrey Crossick, ed., *The Lower Middle Class in Britain, 1870–1914* (1977).

Mark Girouard, *The Victorian Country House* (New Haven and London, 1979).

Robert Q. Gray, *The Labour Aristocracy in Victorian Edinburgh* (Oxford, 1976).

Anthony Howe, *The Cotton Masters* (Oxford, 1984).

Stefan Muthesius, *The English Terraced House* (New Haven and London, 1982).

Donald J. Olsen, *The Growth of Victorian London* (1976).

Robert Roberts, *The Classic Slum* (Manchester, 1971).

W.D. Rubinstein, *Men of Property* (1981).

M.A. Simpson and T.H. Lloyd, eds, *Middle Class Housing in Britain* (Newton Abbot, 1977).

Lawrence Stone and Jeanne C. Fawtier Stone, *An Open Elite? England, 1540–1880* (Oxford, 1984).

Anthony Sutcliffe, ed., *Multi-Storey Living: the British Working Class Experience* (1974).

Mark Swenarton, *Homes Fit For Heroes* (1981).

F.M.L. Thompson, ed., *The Rise of Suburbia* (Leicester, 1982).

P.J. Waller, *Town, City, and Nation: England, 1850–1914* (Oxford, 1983).

Anthony S. Wohl, *Endangered Lives: Public Health in Victorian Britain* (1983).

6. Work

Michael Anderson, *Family Structure in Nineteenth-Century Lancashire* (Cambridge, 1971).

Michael Anderson, 'Sociological History and the Working Class Family: Smelser Revisited', *Social History*, 3 (1976).

Lady Bell, *At the Works* (1907; reprint 1985).

Maxine Berg, ed., *Technology and Toil in Nineteenth Century Britain* (1979).

Maxine Berg, *The Machinery Question and the Making of Political Economy, 1815–1848* (Cambridge, 1980).

Geoffrey Crossick, *An Artisan Elite in Victorian Society* (1978).

M.J. Daunton, 'Down the Pit: Work in the Great Northern and South Wales Coalfields, 1870–1914', *Economic History Review*, 2nd ser. XXXIV (1981).

Robert Gray, *The Aristocracy of Labour in Nineteenth-Century Britain, c. 1850–1900* (1981).

Royden Harrison, ed., *Independent Collier: the Coal Miner as Archetypal Proletarian Reconsidered* (Hassocks, Sussex, 1978).

E.J. Hobsbawm, 'Artisan or Labour Aristocrat?', *Economic History Review*, 2nd ser. XXXVII (1984).

E.H. Hunt, *Regional Wage Variations in Britain, 1850–1914* (Oxford, 1973).

E.H. Hunt, *British Labour History, 1815–1914* (1981).

Paul Johnson, 'Credit and Thrift and the British Working Class, 1870–1939', in Jay Winter, ed., *The Working Class in Modern British History* (Cambridge, 1983).

Gareth Stedman Jones, *Outcast London* (Oxford, 1971).

Patrick Joyce, *Work, Society and Politics: the Culture of the Factory in Later Victorian England* (Hassocks, Sussex, 1980).

David S. Landes, *The Unbound Prometheus* (Cambridge, 1969).

A.E. Musson, *British Trade Unions, 1780–1875* (1972).

A.E. Musson, 'Class Struggle and the Labour Aristocracy, 1830–60', *Social History*, 3 (1976).

Henry Pelling, *Popular Politics and Society in Late Victorian Britain* (1968).

Richard Price, *Masters, Unions and Men: Work Control in Building and the Rise of Labour, 1830–1914* (Cambridge, 1980).

Alastair Reid, 'Intelligent Artisans and Aristocrats of Labour: the Essays of Thomas Wright', in Jay Winter, ed., *The Working Class in Modern British History* (Cambridge, 1983).

Neil J. Smelser, *Social Change in the Industrial Revolution* (1959).

7. Play

Peter Bailey, *Leisure and Class in Victorian England* (1978).

David Cannadine, *Lords and Landlords: the Aristocracy and the Towns, 1774–1967* (Leicester, 1980).

Raymond Carr, *English Fox Hunting: a History* (1976).

Hugh Cunningham, 'The Metropolitan Fairs: a Case Study in the Social Control of Leisure', in A.P. Donajgrodzki, ed., *Social Control in Nineteenth-Century Britain* (1977).

Hugh Cunningham, *Leisure in the Industrial Revolution, 1780–1880* (1980).

Leonore Davidoff, *The Best Circles: Society, Etiquette and The Season* (1973).

Frances Finnegan, *Poverty and Prostitution: a Study of Victorian Prostitutes in York* (Cambridge, 1979).

Brian Harrison, *Peaceable Kingdom: Stability and Change in Modern Britain* (Oxford, 1982).

Eric Hobsbawm, 'Mass-Producing Traditions: Europe, 1870–1914', in Eric Hobsbawm and Terence Ranger, eds, *The Invention of Tradition* (Cambridge, 1983).

G. Stedman Jones, *Languages of Class: Studies in English Working-Class History* (Cambridge, 1983).

David C. Itzkowitz, *Peculiar Privilege: a Social History of English Foxhunting, 1753–1885* (Hassocks, Sussex, 1977).

Theresa M. McBride, *The Domestic Revolution* (1976).

Ross McKibbin, 'Work and Hobbies in Britain, 1880–1950', in Jay Winter, ed., *The Working Class in Modern British History* (Cambridge, 1983).

Robert W. Malcolmson, *Popular Recreations in English Society, 1700–1850* (Cambridge, 1973).

Tony Mason, *Association Football and English Society, 1863–1915* (Brighton, 1980).

H.E. Meller, *Leisure and the Changing City, 1870–1914* (1976).

Willie Orr, *Deer Forests, Landlords and Crofters: the Western Highlands in Victorian and Edwardian Times* (Edinburgh, 1982).

J.A.R. Pimlott, *The Englishman's Holiday* (1947).

Frank Prochaska, *Women and Philanthropy in Nineteenth-Century England* (Oxford, 1980).

Richard Roberts, 'The Corporation as Impresario: the Municipal Provision of Entertainment in Victorian and Edwardian Bournemouth', in John K. Walton and James Walvin, eds, *Leisure in Britain, 1780–1939* (Manchester, 1983).

Doreen M. Rosman, *Evangelicals and Culture* (1984).

Dave Russell, 'Popular Musical Culture and Popular Politics in the Yorkshire Textile Districts, 1880–1914', in Walton and Walvin, eds, *Leisure in Britain*.

Wray Vamplew, *The Turf: a Social and Economic History of Horse Racing* (1976).

Judith R. Walkowitz, *Prostitution and Victorian Society* (Cambridge, 1980).

John K. Walton, *The English Seaside Resort: a Social History, 1750–1914* (Leicester, 1983).

James Walvin, *The People's Game: a Social History of British Football* (1975).

8. *Authority and Society*

Sydney Checkland, *British Public Policy, 1776–1939* (Cambridge, 1983).

M.A. Crowther, *The Workhouse System, 1834–1929* (1981).

A.E. Dingle, 'Drink and Working-Class Living Standards in Britain, 1870–1914', *Economic History Review*, 2nd ser. XXV (1972).

J.R.D. Dunbabin, *Rural Discontent in Nineteenth-Century Britain* (1974).

A.D. Gilbert, *Religion and Society in Industrial England: Church, Chapel, and Social Change, 1740–1914* (1976).

Brian Harrison, *Drink and the Victorians* (1971).

Brian Harrison, 'Pubs', in H.J. Dyos and M. Wolff, eds, *The Victorian City: Images and Realities*, I (1973).

Ross McKibbin, 'Working-Class Gambling in Britain, 1880–1939', *Past and Present*, 82 (1979).

Hugh McLeod, *Class and Religion in the Late Victorian City* (1974).

Hugh McLeod, *Religion and the Working Class in Nineteenth-Century Britain* (1984).

P.B. Munsche, *Gentlemen and Poachers* (Cambridge, 1981).

James Obelkevich, *Religion and Rural Society* (Oxford, 1976).

Roland Quinault and John Stevenson, eds, *Popular Protest and Public Order* (1974).

David Roberts, *Paternalism in Early Victorian England* (1979).

M.E. Rose, *The Relief of Poverty, 1834–1914* (1972).

R.D. Storch, 'A Plague of Blue Locusts: Police Reform and Popular Resistance in Northern England, 1840–57', *International Review of Social History*, XX (1975).

R.D. Storch, 'The Policeman as Domestic Missionary: Urban Discipline and Popular Culture in Northern England, 1850–80', *Journal of Social History*, IX (1976).

Pat Thane, *The Foundations of the Welfare State* (1982).

F.M.L. Thompson, 'Landowners and the Rural Community', in G.E. Mingay, ed., *The Victorian Countryside*, II (1981).

Index